THE BA...
CO...

VIETNAM FIRE SUPPORT BASES
CORAL AND BALMORAL, MAY 1968

Lex McAulay

By the author of THE BATTLE OF LONG TAN

ARROW

'The courage of your enemy does you honour'
Arab saying

Arrow Books Limited
62-65 Chandos Place, London WC2N 4NW

An imprint of Century Hutchinson Limited

London Melbourne Sydney Auckland
Johannesburg and agencies throughout
the world

First published in Great Britain 1990

Printed and bound in Australia by Griffin Press, Adelaide

ISBN 0 09 169091 9

Contents

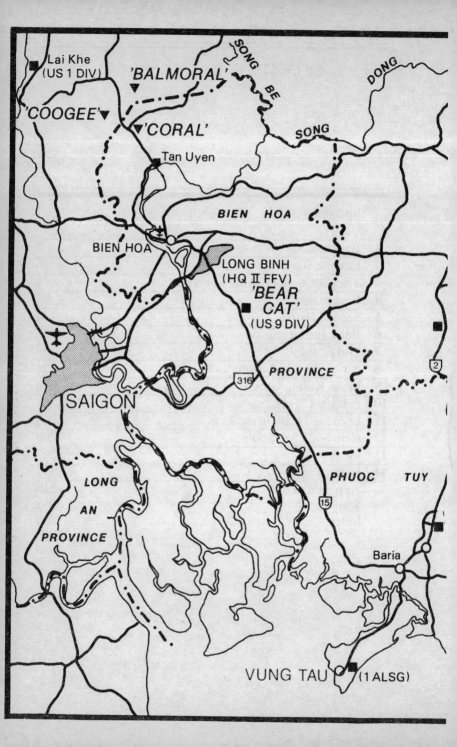

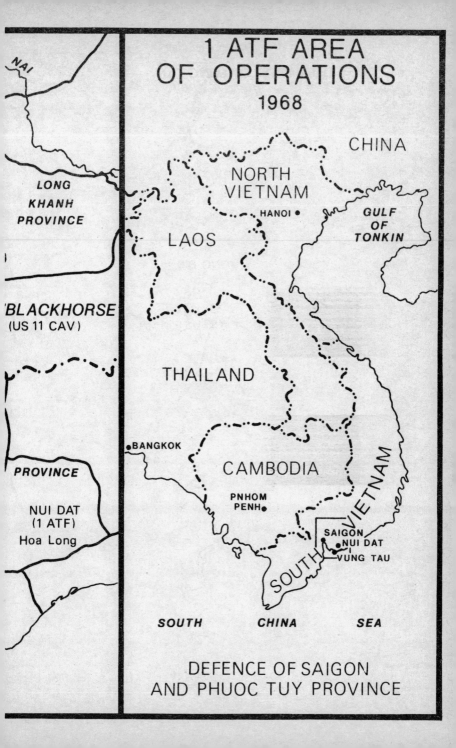

Also in Arrow by Lex McAulay

THE BATTLE OF LONG TAN

Introduction

Battles are won in the hearts of men
Montgomery of El Alamein

Though little known outside the Australian Army of the time, the actions north-east of Saigon, around Fire Support Bases Coral and Balmoral, in May 1968 were important. The 1st Australian Task Force (1ATF) units involved played a large role in disrupting the plans of the North Vietnamese to continue their attacks on Saigon; the numerically inferior Australians moved into an area the North Vietnamese and Viet Cong had almost made their own, and severely mauled the 'home team'; the Australians had to adapt, literally overnight, from a war of patrolling, ambushing and dispersal to limited war in which the enemy came looking for a fight, which required defensive positions, concentration of force and different tactics; Australian tanks proved their worth, after twenty years in the military wilderness; Australian gunners fought close-combat actions in defence of their guns, at the same time responding to requests for artillery support; at the end of the operation, 1ATF dominated their area.

While individual articles about particular events or phases of the operation were printed in newspapers and magazines, the importance of the operations was not really brought to the attention of the Australian public, nor to the Australian Defence Forces.

The Battle of Long Tan has for many years been described incorrectly as the largest battle fought by Australians in Vietnam, or indeed as the only battle fought in Vietnam. The significance of Long Tan is that it decisively averted an attack on the ill-prepared 1ATF base. It was really only a two-company action, expertly supported by artillery, fought in one afternoon.

North-east of Saigon, in May and June 1968, elements of the entire 1ATF were involved to a lesser or greater degree in the operations for some twenty-six days, during which they repulsed several regimental and battalion attacks, plus endured bombardments by missiles and bombs of varying size, as well as initiating fierce close-quarter actions in well-prepared and defended enemy bunker systems.

The operations north-east of Saigon are noteworthy because of their duration, the numbers of Australians involved, and enemy reaction. The lessons learned in adapting to the 'big league' were mastered swiftly, and 1ATF improved as a fighting machine.

Two battalions of Australian infantry, with artillery and armoured support, helped break up North Vietnamese attacks on the capital city of Saigon, at a time when losses of men meant nothing to Hanoi in its attempt to dominate the 'peace talks' in Paris.

I hope that this book provides an interesting and accurate account of the actions as seen by the participants. It is respectfully dedicated to the memory of the late Major General Jack Kelly, at the time of the battles CO 12 Field Regiment RAA; Major George Constable, OC 161 Reconnaissance Flight AAvn; Warrant Officers Jack Cramp, Ron Pincott and Brian Tobin, all three having been characters and soldiers in First Battalion, The Royal Australian Regiment.

It is also dedicated to the wives, mothers and families of the men who fought and served in Vietnam. Few, if any, of the soldiers understood the daily worry and nagging fear of those who remained in Australia, the worry and fear intensified at each announcement of casualties, and subsiding a little when it was declared 'all next-of-kin have been informed'. Families bore a special burden, and it is my secondary hope that this book will help explain what it is that the soldier 'does not talk about at home'.

1 Background

Well then, to work! Our cannon shall be bent
Against the brows of this resisting town;

                                            King John *(ll. i.)*

THE CAUSES OF THE WARS in Indochina have been written of extensively. This background to the Australian battles northeast of Saigon in 1968 is necessarily general and is not intended to supplant longer and more detailed works.

It should also be remembered that the war in Vietnam must be kept in perspective. From 1945 to 1975, and beyond, the major concerns of the US, and its allies, were the implacably hostile USSR and the PRC. Vietnam was only one of a host of smaller problems which either grew or lessened as the years passed. US (and allied) actions and reactions evolved against the backdrop of possible Soviet and Chinese moves, not only in Vietnam, but elsewhere.

Vietnam never really held absolute and unchallenged centre stage in Washington, though its importance increased. Writings on Vietnam rarely admit that anything else held the attention of the US administrations. In the 1940s and 1950s there were Communist-led insurrections in Greece, Malaya, the Philippines and Indochina; there was the defeat of the Chiang Kai-shek regime on the Chinese mainland, the war in Korea; bombardments and aerial combat over the straits of Formosa; tensions raised over Berlin and other places around the world. When dissatisfaction with Communist rule in central Europe was crushed by the Soviet Army and various secret police organisations, most notably the brutal invasion of Hungary in November 1956, there were fears that a general war could ensue. These and many other events competed for attention.

To meet the perceived threats, exemplified by the massive

Soviet tank armies, the US and its major allies created armed forces which were organised, equipped and trained to fight large battles similar to those of World War II. Long-term career prospects before, during and after the Vietnam campaigns were shaped and assessed against the European theatre, not in the counter-revolutionary warfare fields. Apart from battlefield incompetence, careers were ruined by failure to conform to the conventional wisdom.

Almost all the equipment used by the forces of the Republic of Vietnam (RVN), the US and their allies in South Vietnam was conceived and developed for use in Europe, as were organisations, staff and communications procedures. Some modifications were made to suit the locale, but basically it was a case of 'making it fit'.

One of the central figures in the administration of John F. Kennedy was the Secretary of Defense, Robert S. McNamara. With his young team of 'whiz kids', McNamara was going to produce a lean, cost-effective Defense Department, to conform with the young, vigorous, forward-looking image of the Kennedy era. Vietnam was just another of the many problems facing the US, all of which could be solved by correct analysis, followed by remedial action.

In Vietnam, the weak link in all this was the personal factor, the need to report optimistically, to 'get on the team'. Consequently, reporting exaggerated success and ignored failure or shortcomings. Correct analysis was often impossible, or much, much too late. Possibly the two greatest farces in the spectrum of Vietnam reporting were the famous (or infamous) body-count, and the Hamlet Evaluation System (HES). In an increasingly desperate attempt to find that magical charm which would give an accurate evaluation of the qualities of the RVN forces, it was decided that the number of enemy counted killed in action was the touchstone. It was false, particularly in a counter-revolutionary war. HES was an attempt to quantify the influence and authority of the RVN throughout the hamlets and villages in South Vietnam, and which required regular involved reports on the security situation at hamlet level. As with body-count, exaggeration soon rendered the programme useless as a yardstick of real progress. An apocryphal tale relates how the computer in Saigon was given all the HES data, and asked when the war would be won; the reply was that it had been won two years ago.

Organisations very rarely change their structure, procedures and methods of operation as a result of internal pressures. It is outside forces which compel change. The US organisations involved in the war in Vietnam were not intended to concern themselves with Vietnam, and it alone, so while many intelligent people at all levels could see what needed to be done, none were powerful enough to bring about the necessary change.

The US and allied involvement in the fighting in Vietnam could be likened to an accomplished pianist being handed a violin and required to perform before an audience, on the premise that 'It's all music, isn't it?'.

Australia's involvement was basically that of the small ally who is anxious to show that he too will assist in the dirty jobs now, in the hope that the bigger ally will recall this in some time of future need by the smaller. In the late 1950s and early 1960s, Australia's senior politicians and public servants included many who easily could recall the dark days of 1942, when London had to admit it was unable to help repel the onrushing Japanese, and US victories in the Coral Sea and at Midway were won more by good luck than good management—despite code-breaking. It was in Australia's best interests to keep the Americans involved in our part of the world, and to show them that we'd be in there with them. As well as Vietnam and the spectre of an expansionist Communist China, Canberra was worried by an aggressive Indonesia, under President Sukarno, who had announced his intention to destroy the confederation of Malaysia, and in 1964 had begun military operations against it. Australia needed the USA in the south-west Pacific.

Having joined the US and its allies in South Vietnam, Canberra could get on with more pressing matters, and the military involvement could run on until another decision was needed. The massive structure for intelligence-gathering and reporting in Vietnam produced a flood of paper which

5

poured across the desks of the relevant desk officers in both Vietnam and Australia. One of them had to reduce that mass to a single sheet of paper which was delivered to the offices of the Prime Minister and Cabinet. There it was reduced further, to one paragraph.

Australia's military involvement in Vietnam began with the despatch of a small group of thirty advisers in August 1962, and from there grew to the deployment of an Army Task Force with infantry, armour, artillery and logistics units, plus RAAF squadrons of transport, helicopter and bomber aircraft, and RAN destroyers, helicopter crews and HMAS *Sydney*, the aircraft carrier converted to a troop- and supply-ship.

The Australian Army had prided itself for years on its ability to engage in jungle warfare, but in Vietnam, despite a large measure of independence, it had to conform to operational requirements of the host government in Saigon and the US operational command. Much of the Australian force's equipment was of US manufacture, from small arms in the infantry section through the armoured personnel carriers, artillery pieces, helicopters, transport aircraft and destroyers of the RAAF and RAN. It is worth remembering that all this equipment was paid for, as was every ration consumed, helicopter support flight, round of artillery fired and bomb dropped at the request of the Australian (and New Zealand) force in Vietnam. Everything provided by Vietnam and the United States was paid for by Canberra and Wellington; other allies had a different arrangement.

Protest against the involvement in Vietnam had been increasingly vociferous, but was seen by most Australians to be from the left, particularly the Communist-dominated organisations. The 1966 Federal election was fought almost solely on the subject of Vietnam, and the Liberal–Country Party Coalition Government was returned to power with eighty-two of the 124 seats in the House of Representatives, Labor gaining only forty-one. This was the greatest majority enjoyed by any Australian government to that time, and was only surpassed in 1975, in the elections held after the dismissal of the Whitlam Government, when the Australian voters gave Labor only thirty-six of the 127 seats.

In Vietnam, by 1968, the Australian forces had begun to see the effect of their policies and tactics in the area allotted to them, in Phuoc Tuy Province. The resident VC military units and organisations had been severely mauled, and some progress had been made in disrupting the VC political structure. The Australians could deploy some of their force, at the request of the US command, out of Phuoc Tuy, into areas closer to Saigon.

The tapestry of Vietnamese history is well woven with wars, rebellions, revolts, dynastic struggles and militant expansion at the cost of their neighbours. From ethnic beginnings in the south of China and in the valley of the Red River, some forty centuries ago, and gradually moving south along the lowlands of the eastern seaboard of Indochina, they were pushing back the Khmers from the Mekong delta area in the mid eighteenth century. Only the arrival of the French empire builders halted this phase of Vietnamese expansion.

After ninety years of French colonialism, the Vietnamese eventually regained independence after a bloody nine-year war. The French learned little in those nine years, but the Vietnamese did, and finally the French were decisively defeated at Dien Bien Phu in 1954. Ho Chi Minh, the leader of the independence movement, was Communist, and in the mid 1950s leaders and people in the western democracies, with vivid memories of World War II, were alarmed at the spectacle of militant expansionist Communism. It was feared that the hordes of the Chinese People's Army would flood across South-east Asia and the Pacific, and it was with this horror in mind that the South East Asia Treaty Organisation (SEATO) was formed. It also was one of the root causes of western involvement in Indochina after 1950.

Germany and Korea had been divided between Communist and democratic governments since 1945, and at the 1954 peace talks in Geneva, held to decide the ending of the French colonial regime in Indochina, it was decided that Vietnam also should be divided. Elections were to be held in two years to allow the population to decide which form of government it preferred.

This part of the Geneva agreements was vague, and South

7

Vietnam, not being a signatory, later rejected it. The North decided to destroy the government in the South, and reactivated the anti-French resistance movement, which had ostensibly been dissolved.

The French had left the region with little in the way of personnel and organisations necessary for a nation to function. The North, with government in Hanoi, was supported by the Communist bloc, particularly China and the USSR, while the South was assisted by Free World nations, mainly by the USA.

Ho Chi Minh, a long-time Communist revolutionary, was portrayed by astute propaganda into a loving grandfather figure, far removed from the ruthless leader of a group who determined to seize power by any means, but particularly followed the quote from Mao Ze-dong (Mao Tse-tung): 'Political power comes from the barrel of a gun'.

In the South, the government in Saigon was led by a Catholic bachelor-mandarin, Ngo Dinh Diem. Early success in the struggle to bring order from the chaos of the post-French era caused Diem to believe he was infallible. In addition, he was increasingly isolated from reality by the evil influence of his brother, Nhu, and Nhu's wife. Dissent and disagreement was repressed, and turned into active resistance.

Skilfully manipulating the anti-Diem feeling, the long-simmering xenophobia of the Vietnamese, the taste for newly won but barely enjoyed nationalism, and the deep desire of peasants to own the land they worked, the Communists gathered to themselves the disaffected from all walks of life, and armed resistance developed to the stage where by mid 1964 the Saigon regime was being destroyed politically, militarily and economically.

Despite denials from Hanoi, there were more than enough captured documents, weapons and equipment, as well as prisoners, to show conclusively that the military and political struggle in the South was controlled by the (Communist) Lao Dong Party in the North. The southern headquarters was called Central Office for South Vietnam (COSVN), and operated from the jungles of the South Vietnamese–Cambodian border area, or inside Cambodia.

The US and its allies gradually increased support for the Saigon regimes which replaced Diem, who was overthrown and murdered in a military coup. This support grew from small beginnings to despatch of military units in early 1965. The twelve months from June 1965 saw American, Korean, Australian and New Zealand combat units battling Viet Cong and North Vietnamese Army forces (NVA) in a successful effort to prevent the overthrow by force of the Saigon government.

The élan, numbers and material might of the Free World Military Assistance Forces (FWMAF; hereafter, simply, allies) inflicted tremendous damage on the enemy. In addition, the US Air Force was mounting ever-heavier bombing raids on the North, as US President Lyndon Johnson endeavoured to bring home to Hanoi the realisation that they would not be allowed to execute what amounted to an invasion of the South without cost to themselves.

By July 1967 Hanoi was aware that the US military operations in South Vietnam, accompanied by air strikes in the North, had almost defeated North Vietnam's war effort. It was decided to launch a nation-wide offensive in the South, co-ordinated with peace talks in Paris. The strategy of talking while fighting was an old Asian way of wearing down enemies, and had been used successfully by the Communists since the 1920s.

Assessments by their own organisations had led the Hanoi leadership to believe that the population in the South would take part in a 'general uprising', so that the Saigon regime of President Thieu would collapse under a battering from the Vietcong–North Vietnamese Army forces (VC/NVA) assisted by a popular revolt.

It was decided to launch the attacks during the traditional holiday period of the Lunar New Year (Tet) of 1968. The Tet period is far more significant than the western equivalent. Along with the fireworks and festivals, it is the occasion for serious family worship of revered ancestors, and preparing to enter the New Year in a correct manner. Both Hanoi and Saigon observed Tet, and both the VC/NVA and Saigon forces usually declared a truce for its duration, despite claims by both, each year, of transgressions against each other.

An historical precedent had been set for an attack during the actual holiday period: the Tay Son revolt of 1789, against Chinese forces in Hanoi, had achieved surprise and success by attacking during the celebrations.

US Presidential elections were to be held in 1968, and the efforts of the anti-war movement were well known in Hanoi. The effect in the US itself of the large-scale attacks planned for South Vietnam would possibly be of benefit to Hanoi.

The Tet Offensive, as it became known, was a military and political defeat for the VC/NVA in South Vietnam. The 'general uprising' was ignored by the population, and the Army of the Republic of Vietnam (ARVN) fought well in defence of the towns and cities of the South.

But as reports of the debacle were received in Hanoi, the gloom was swept away by news of the effect of the offensive on the US media and politicians.

Overwhelmed by the sheer scale of the attacks, and without waiting to see a definite outcome to the fighting, the media presented the Tet Offensive as a VC/NVA victory. The US began looking for a way out of the war.

A minor attack, with significance far beyond its actual effect, was the assault on the US Embassy in Saigon. Nineteen VC fought their way into its grounds and were killed or captured there, in and around the ornamental garden beds. Hasty, ill-informed reports by media persons ever-conscious of their byline and the need to beat their competitors with news, any news, led to tales that the VC were inside the embassy, firing out at US soldiers, that the paratroopers landed by helicopter on the roof had to fight their way down, floor by floor, with orders to take no prisoners, et cetera, et cetera.

The fact was, and is, that the US Embassy had an outer wall a short distance from the actual building, to lessen the effect of missiles and explosives. This wall was constructed of perforated ornamental brick, similar to Besser blocks, and allowed some light and breeze to pass, but severely restricted vision outwards or inwards. The alleged VC occupants of various floors of the building would have been confronted with a view of these ornamental bricks, and no arc of fire.

No VC entered the building, because as soon as the sound of the explosion which blew a hole in the fence was heard, the US Marines on duty in the foyer shut and barred the large doors. The VC were all killed or captured in the grounds, or minor buildings nearby.

The erroneous impressions and half-baked opinions of untrained observers braving quick peeps at the attack on the US Embassy, delivered in haste, without checking and presented as 'news', epitomise the reporting of the war in Vietnam, and of the Tet Offensive in particular.

None of the representatives of the media, despite their claims that only they understood the war, were astute enough to predict the opening of the attacks in the holiday period. But the ARVN had had enough foresight to allow only half of their troops to go on leave, instead of the normal 80 or 90 per cent, and the allied formations were also in a state of alertness. It was these precautions which allowed the ARVN/allied units to react swiftly once the VC/NVA struck.

During January movement of enemy forces had been detected, and a threat to Saigon was seen developing. By 29 January, half the US and allied forces in the region were positioned within helicopter range of the vital areas there. ARVN and National Police units moved to defend various headquarters and locations.

Utilising the advantage of surprise and time before the opposing forces could react, the VC/NVA launched their attacks, gaining entry into towns and cities. No important military objective was held, and only a few were taken. The 'general uprising' failed to materialise.

By 19 February the first series of battles were over, and from then to 10 March the ARVN and their allies set about clearing the enemy away from the populated areas. On 11 March a combined Vietnamese–allied operation, Quyet Thang (Determined to Win), was launched, targeted against VC/NVA in the regions around Saigon. By 7 April 2650 enemy were claimed killed. On 8 April Operation Toan Thang (Complete Victory) succeeded Quyet Thang. On 19 April Colonel Dac, an assistant political officer in VC Sub-region 1, which was near Saigon, surrendered. He had had enough of the unrealistic missions imposed on the fighting troops by COSVN.

Dac said that another offensive, using 10 000 reinforcements who had been poured down the Ho Chi Minh Trail, was to begin in about a week. Actually the attacks came in early May.

In the Korean War, the Communist Chinese had launched fierce attacks, regardless of the cost in lives, attempting to influence the peace talks at Panmunjom; the Viet Minh had done the same at the opening of the Geneva talks to end the war against the French in 1954. Now in 1968 the same regime in Hanoi demanded further attacks in an attempt to dominate the peace talks being convened in Paris.

In the vernacular of the times, the May attacks became known as 'mini-Tet'. VC/NVA casualties were again heavy.

In particular, VC casualties were such that they never really recovered, and ironically eased the way for the total domination of the South by the Hanoi regime after the collapse of 1975.

Since the beginning of Operation Quyet Thang on 11 March 1968, the tempo of VC/NVA attacks had slowed down, from 260 reported incidents in the time 3–9 March, to sixty-nine during 13–20 April. An analysis of VC/NVA activities showed emphasis on resupply and replacement of personnel, despite urging by COSVN to make new attacks. The units were just unable to do so. Even without the information from Dac, intelligence staff were able to deduce the May attacks, that they would be mounted along the same avenues of approach used in February, and the objectives would be Saigon–Bien Hoa–Long Binh, with possible diversions against other targets.

'Mini-Tet' began on 4 May, with ground assaults and rocket attacks against the expected targets. 7 NVA Division and 9 VC Division, plus other formations, totalling eleven regiments, were operating in the Saigon–Bien Hoa area. For the period 4–9 May, their casualties were 4135 counted dead.

As part of the ARVN–Free World (allied) operations, which defeated the VC/NVA Tet Offensive, 1st Australian

Task Force (1ATF), commanded by Brigadier R.L. Hughes, deployed two of its three battalions to the east of the huge US logistics complex at Long Binh. There they broke up VC/NVA attempts to attack it and Bien Hoa city.

1ATF was under operational control of Second Field Force Vietnam (IIFFV), the intelligence staff of which had identified a major NVA infiltration and approach route or corridor to Saigon passing through the area where the Australians were to be committed. The corridor ran north-east to south-west, with the bank of the Dong Nai River as its left boundary and the town of Tan Uyen as an important point on the left edge of the route. In the area were exchange points in the VC/NVA system, for reinforcements, PW, logistics, information, etc.

At the time, the US forces were operating intensively, defending the Bien Hoa–Long Binh complex, and the north and west of Saigon, as far west as Ben Cat and Cu Chi. In addition, fighting was going on further to the north in South Vietnam.

At HQ IIFFV, the Australian liaison officer was Major A.B. 'Alf' Garland, most recently second-in-command of 7RAR, which had returned to Australia. In the US system, a liaison officer is a message carrier, but in the Australian he represents his commander, is (or should be) up-to-date with the current situation, and can have useful discussions with the relevant formations. In addition to his liaison duties, the Australian officer at HQ IIFFV was also employed in a section of the plans office of Operations Branch, involved with planning for operations of the US 25th Division, 199th Light Infantry Brigade and 1ATF.

The Australian commander in Vietnam, Major General A.L. McDonald, had directed that as 1ATF was operating outside its normal area, and near the important Saigon–Long Binh zone, it should be employed in an active role. Accordingly, Alf Garland, at HQ IIFFV, had studied the region and selected three likely areas where 1ATF could be committed against the enemy, with the prospect of success against them. One of these was the much-used corridor north of Tan Uyen, on the banks of the Dong Nai River. Later it

13

was titled Area of Operations (AO) Surfers.

The area was gently undulating, with no prominent mountains or hill masses, and sloped gently away to north and south, to the rivers Song Be and Song Dong Nai respectively. It was covered with a patchwork of open grassy land which became swamp in the wet season, bamboo clusters, scrub, rubber plantation and rice paddies. One creek, the Suoi Ba Pho, ran through the area, roughly from north-east to south-west. Route 16 ran approximately north-south, bisecting the AO. There were no major population centres or terrain features in the AO.

Garland quickly travelled between Saigon, Long Binh and Nui Dat, having discussions with, and briefing, the relevant commanders and their staffs. The Australian nicknames were selected so that Garland and 1ATF operations staff could discuss them without too much worry that the enemy would identify the actual locations. So it was decided to commit 1ATF to the location later known as AO Surfers. Within it were two sites for battalion patrol bases, to be called 'Coral' and 'Coogee'. The name 'Coral' was decided on by the 1ATF operations officers, as it was the name of a female friend.

On 10 May 1968 IIFFV officially requested that 1ATF be deployed into Area of Operations (AO) Surfers.

Apart from its earlier operations east of Long Binh, the Task Force had mainly operated in Phuoc Tuy Province, and its techniques and tactics had already been successful against the VC formations and units there.

The effects of patrolling, ambushing, food denial and operations against the Viet Cong Infrastructure (VCI) were felt in those VC units by illness, poor food and lessening quantities of medical supplies, plus the steady drain of casualties. Geoff Cameron, GSO2 Intelligence at 1ATF, immediately noted the difference in the quality of the enemy. 'The VC were sick, half-starved. These men were totally different, very fit and well equipped.'

Cameron's Intelligence staff compiled a Special Intelligence Summary (Intsum), No. 1/68, issued on 7 May, in which it was stated that IIFFV believed the three enemy divisions

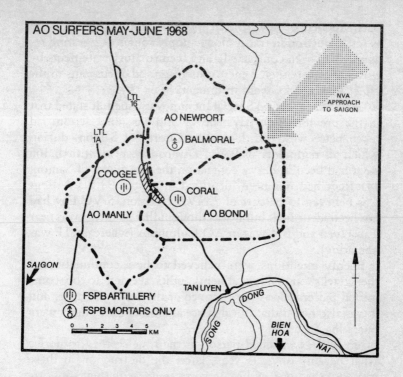

AO SURFERS MAY-JUNE 1968

NVA APPROACH TO SAIGON

LTL 16

AO NEWPORT

LTL 1A

BALMORAL

COOGEE

CORAL

AO MANLY

AO BONDI

SAIGON

FSPB ARTILLERY

FSPB MORTARS ONLY

TAN UYEN

SONG DONG

BIEN HOA

NAI

0 1 2 3 4 5 KM

had built up their personnel strength since the heavy losses around the time of Tet, and were now assembling for a resumption of the offensive. Of 7 NVA Div, neither 141 nor 165 Regt had been identified in contact for thirteen days, and they were thought to be north of Tan Uyen. Five VC Division formations were also thought to be nearby, with 275 Regt, 274 Regt and 88 NVA Regt. The three regiments of 9 VC Div were thought to be north and west of Saigon, out of the intended Australian AO. The VC Dong Nai Regt had been severely mauled on 4 May, and was scattered in the area of Di An. Other enemy regiments were mentioned as being south of Saigon.

The Intsum stated that the belief that a renewal of the offensive was imminent was based on information of movement forward by enemy units, contact with reconnaissance elements near Saigon, attempts to bring weapons into the city

15

itself, reports of new rocket positions around the cities and bases, reduction in traffic along supply routes (suggesting re-supply had been completed), and confirmatory statements by prisoners, surrendered enemy and captured documents to the effect that attacks were imminent.

On 9 May a second Special Intsum was issued. It stated that in the previous two days, heavy and sustained action had taken place west, north-west and north of Saigon, during which all regiments of 9 VC Div had been identified; 165 Regt had been in heavy contact on the 8th, north of Saigon; 141 Regt had not been identified in action; 88 NVA Regt was believed to be part of 7 NVA Division; 5 VC Div had not been identified, but it was thought that 275 Regt was near Tan Uyen and 274 was in AO Columbus (where 1ATF was operating).

Enemy intentions were believed to be a continuation of the attacks on Saigon. Enemy units seemed to be com-mitted piecemeal, as they arrived at the scene of battle, and it was also noted that Local Force and Main Force units were operating together.

No ARVN or allied person at the time seemed to notice what became obvious years later: the destruction in these battles of the Local and Main Force units, with their support-ing Viet Cong Infrastructure elements, would lead to the easy assumption of total power by the political cadres and military forces of the North. The VC/NLF were defeated both by their military and political enemies in Saigon, and by their fellows in Hanoi.

By 10 May, two days before the Australians actually arrived, US units in the area of AO Surfers had contacted five enemy Main Force regiments: 141 and 165 NVA Regiments, and the VC Dong Nai, 274 and 275 Regiments, plus six VC Local Force units ranging from battalion to platoon, includ-ing a Rear Services (logistics) Group. In addition, the village of Binh My, which would be in AO Surfers, was known to be an important staging area and resupply point for enemy moving either north or south.

At this time, the forward echelon of HQ 1ATF was located at the US base at Bearcat, with the main headquarters back at Nui Dat, in Phuoc Tuy Province. On 10 May it produced the operation order for the move to and operations in AO Surfers.

1ATF's mission was to 'occupy blocking positions within AO Surfers to interdict enemy withdrawal routes from the South and SW'. To the west of the Australians would be the 3rd Brigade, US 1 Division; to the east, 2nd Battalion 506th Airborne Regiment of 3rd Brigade 101 Airborne Division; to the south, HQ and 1st Battalion ARVN 48 Regiment, ARVN 5 Division.

The enemy were described in Annex A to the operation order:

Since the start of the third enemy offensive on 4 May 68 it has become apparent that substantial enemy Main Force and Local Force units have either passed through AO SURFERS, or can be expected to do so in the near future. Enemy units moving South or SW through the area can be expected to be tactically deployed moving as units or sub-units under a co-ordinated command structure and to possess high morale. Conversely, it can also be expected that enemy elements moving North or NW, away from heavy fighting near Saigon, will be moving in small groups, may be disorganised or even lost, and their morale will be low. One point worth remembering is that large enemy groups will be moving fast, probably on trails, and may often extend beyond our normal killing zones in ambushes.

Paragraphs 3 and 4 listed the enemy units identified by prisoners and captured documents as 'contacted in or near AO SURFERS': 141 Regt (strength 975), 165 Regt (694), 274 Regt (720), 275 Regt (strength unknown), Dong Nai Regt (800–900); 'operating in or near' AO Surfers were 3 VC Local Force Bn, C300 Dong Nai Company, C302 Tan Uyen Platoon, C303 Company, Di An Platoon, totalling about 500 members, and 83 Rear Services Group (a logistics unit, of 900 people).

The logistics units would naturally be used for that purpose, and the smaller elements such as the Tan Uyen Platoon and Dong Nai Company could be expected to serve as guides, escorts, reconnaissance teams and similar. Allowing for the normal uncertainties of determining enemy strengths, the enemy main force 'in or near' Surfers could be expected to be between 3000 and 4000. It would be unlikely that all these would be employed against the Australians.

Paragraph 6 stated that the village of Binh My was known to be an important troop staging area and supply depot, going on to say that:

This village is a logical choice for a staging area, since it is located at the edge of forest and rubber plantations. To the south is a relatively open area with little cover from visual and photo reconnaissance which would have to be travelled by night by VC/NVA forces. The village is the last place where troops can rest before a long night's march South; it is in close proximity to several suitable routes for swift travel South; and it has VC guides who can lead troops who are unfamiliar with the area.

The operation was to be conducted in three phases: the fly-in of two infantry battalions (1RAR and 3RAR) on 12 May; the establishment of Fire Support and Patrol Base (FSPB) Coral and move by the infantry into their blocking positions 12–13 May; the move to Coral on 13 May of the 1ATF Forward HQ, the US self-propelled artillery (A Battery 2 Battalion 35 Artillery Regiment), and the rear echelons of the 1ATF elements for Coral.

AO Surfers was to be divided into smaller AO for each infantry battalion, with 1RAR receiving the eastern portion, called 'Bondi', and 3RAR in the west with 'Manly'.

3RAR was to fly in first, and secure the landing zone for the helicopter-borne artillery and 1RAR, establish 161 Field Battery RNZA in FSPB Coral, leave a rifle company and a section of mortars to protect Coral, then move to Manly and 'interdict enemy withdrawal routes from the South and SW'. 1RAR was to establish 102 Field Battery RAA at Coral, clear Route 16 from Coral to Tan Uyen for next day's road convoy, then begin operating in Bondi 'to interdict enemy withdrawal routes from the South and SW'.

There is no reference to enemy moving in the opposite

18

direction 'under a co-ordinated command structure and [expected] to possess high morale' as described in the Enemy Annex.

Annex B to the order, the Air Planning Table, visualised the fly-in commencing at 0700 hours 12 May and ending at about 1300 hours, depending on the shuttle flights required for some units. The direction of fly-in was to be from the east, with the units deposited on four separate landing zones: 3RAR to the north, 102 Battery to the east, 1RAR to the south and 161 Battery to the west. Reality was to be somewhat different.

The senior officers of 1ATF, on a helicopter reconnaissance of the new area, were flown at 1500 metres, below which the pilots would not descend because of the possibility of ground fire. All they could gain was a general impression of the surrounds and, as Lieutenant Colonel Bennett, commanding 1RAR, later put it, 'it was very hard even to get a feel for the ground, except one could see that it was an old plantation area, and it looked fairly wild'.

When he asked the American pilot why he would not go lower, Lieutenant Colonel Jim Shelton, CO 3RAR, was informed that they would be shot down by machinegun fire. So the unit commanders circled at high level, trying to see the ground and select landing zones for the fly-in next day.

Staring down from that height, probable sites were selected. The problems of the 1ATF fly-in next day stemmed from the refusal to fly lower on this reconnaissance.

Captain Noel Sproles was a member of A Section, 1 Topographical Survey Troop, who had become one of the two permanent duty officers in the Task Force HQ in the field. He flew with Geoff Cameron to Bien Hoa to collect the necessary maps for the operation, then accompanied Cameron to a briefing given by the ARVN at Tan Uyen. The briefing was well done, with maps, trained presenters, and so on. They said plainly that the area was strongly held by enemy, and each time they had entered it they had suffered heavy casualties. Sproles thought Cameron was impressed and duly noted this information.

On 11 May a briefing was held to inform relevant officers of the move to and operations in AO Surfers. Some of the audience were a little sceptical of what they were told.

Tony Hammett, OC D/1RAR, was struck by the casual way in which Geoff Cameron referred to NVA formations of divisional size, to regiments and so on, being active in the area into which the Australian battalions were to move. After the briefing, Hammett discussed it with a fellow company commander, Bob Hennessy, who agreed and observed that they 'could be in for an interesting operation'. Reinforcing Hammett's sense of foreboding was the attitude of an RAAF pilot he knew, Don Porter, who flew in to attend the briefing. Hammett believed that pilots in general developed a feel for the level of enemy activity and presence in the areas over which they flew. He formed the opinion that Porter 'did not like the feel of this particular operation, because there were a hell of a lot of enemy about'.

An Army pilot, Lieutenant Peter Spoor, 161 Reconnaissance Flight, had been in Vietnam since September, and now had some eight months experience flying over it. He, and he believed the other pilots, 'had a lot more concern there would be action' in the new area.

Lieutenant David Brook, 102 Battery, attended the 1RAR briefing, noted in his field message book the estimated locations of HQ 7 NVA Div and HQ 69 VC Artillery Command and 'TF to interdict movement north and south; company size ambushes at night, platoon patrols by day. Mission. Occupy blocking positions in AO Bondi to interdict enemy withdrawal routes from south and south-west.'

At a lower level, Second Lieutenant Garry 'Pepe' Prendergast, commanding 6 Platoon, B Company 1RAR, was disturbed by the briefing he received, and queried the bland assumption that B/1RAR, with less than ninety men in the field, was to move beyond mortar range of Coral and patrol an area said to be inhabited by an estimated twenty times that number of enemy. He cannot recall receiving an adequate answer, but went ahead with his men.

However, 'outsiders' often do not realise that intelligence staff deal throughout the day and night with information about enemy units of all sizes, and quickly tend to develop a more personal relationship with the opposing side. A casual style of speaking about them is one of the first results of this relationship.

In addition, many reports of enemy movements, strengths, locations and intentions were often shown to be greatly exaggerated, or sheer fiction. When the rocket attacks on the Saigon–Long Binh area began, and the Allied Forces desired to know the units, launching places, et cetera, suddenly agents produced a flood of information, little of it of value. The author recalls reading a report in early 1968 to the effect that the VC 10th Atomic Division was moving to attack Saigon 'next Wednesday'.

At Nui Dat, on one occasion, the Intelligence Officer told Brigadier Hughes that 1ATF was in trouble: there were two VC regiments to the north, one to the east, and two to the south. Hughes asked what the IO recommended be done, and the reply was, 'Do nothing, sir. I think it is all from the one reporter.' The regiments were figments of the imagination of the same agent, who travelled the province reporting to the various organisations and being paid by each.

'If we believed every report,' said Brigadier Hughes, 'we would have packed up and gone home, because we would have been over run at a moment's notice.'

Lieutenant Colonel Jim Shelton, CO 3RAR, recalls that they were 'always being warned that intelligence was locating large numbers of enemy. We'd go into an area, and there'd be nothing there, not even a cigarette butt'.

Through experience, 1ATF had learned to be sceptical of reports of large numbers of enemy at their doorstep.

In addition, the two battalions of 1ATF which would go into AO Surfers had been operating for the previous three weeks east of Long Binh–Bien Hoa with little contact, despite reports of large numbers of enemy in their AO. They had moved, searched, moved, searched and now were faced with another move ...

Another important factor to be kept in mind when considering the opening moves into and around FSPB Coral is the state of mind of the Australians. The personnel and units comprising 1ATF in early 1968 had never been attacked by large numbers of enemy; on the contrary, they had always been the hunters, seeking the hunted. They did not consider themselves prey.

Despite the many units of regimental size and divisional level reported as contacted in or near the AO by the Americans, and full information provided to the Australians, 1ATF believed that they would be searching for enemy suffering from heavy casualties, some disorganisation and probably with low morale, trying to move away from the battles closer to Saigon.

The members of 1ATF had been on the current operation for three weeks, and moving from one AO to another, constantly patrolling and changing location within these areas. They assumed that they would be able to continue to operate as they had done, as they had been trained to do: arrive in an area and dominate it by continuous and aggressive patrolling, using superior junglecraft to confuse the enemy, keep him off balance and whittle him away.

The 1ATF plan for operations in AO Surfers, for dispersed artillery batteries and rifle companies spreading out through the surrounds to their own hunting grounds, does not indicate belief in any strong enemy reaction.

Lieutenant Colonel Jack Kelly, commanding the artillery, 'felt quite frankly because we had been on the move so much, I didn't feel that we were going to encounter them'.

One of his officers, Second Lieutenant Matt Cleland, 102 Battery, could not recall being told anything about the enemy in the new area, and in any case was fully occupied with his duties in charge of the left-hand section of three guns.

Captain Mick Bindley, with service in Borneo against the Indonesians during Confrontation, was commanding Support Company 1RAR, and also was the Regimental Signals Officer. He attended the briefing, and believed that 'we were going on what could best be described as a mopping-up operation, to intervene with the enemy who were fleeing from Saigon. I had no recollection of any indication that we were going into the middle of a nest of two NVA Regular Divisions.'

1RAR had arrived about two months previously, in March 1968, and had experienced light contact in the operations since then. The CO was Lieutenant Colonel Phil Bennett, a Korean War veteran. The battalion had trained hard for this tour of duty and was generally confident of being able to perform well. It contained a good leavening of members with at least one previous tour in Vietnam, such as WO2 Ron Pincott, on his third tour in Vietnam, and in his third war. Another unit character was Sgt Frank 'Dinky' Dean, the longest serving member in the unit, who had been with it since it was formed originally from volunteers for the occupation of Japan.

Lieutenant Colonel Jim Shelton commanded 3RAR, which was well experienced, having been involved in the heavy fighting in Baria, capital of Phuoc Tuy Province, in the Tet Offensive and in operations since then.

The artillery deployed to Coral comprised two batteries of 12 Field Regiment RAA: 102 Battery RAA and 161 Battery RNZA. Whereas the Australians rotated units through a tour of duty, the New Zealanders rotated individuals through the same unit. 161 Bty had contributed significantly to the Australian victory at Long Tan in August 1966, but the personnel had changed several times since then.

12 Field Regiment, commanded by Lieutenant Colonel J.D. Kelly, had been unable to train to the standard desired by Kelly and many of his officers and NCOs, due to requirements in Australia, which included raising and sending a battery to Malaysia. Kelly had to decide who would go to which place, and sent the best footballers to Malaysia.

The battery of Australians deployed to Coral was perhaps well prepared for what was to come, even though it was not foreseen. One gun Sergeant, Ray Dial, was a physical training instructor, and he helped bring the gunners to a high pitch of fitness, plus emphasised infantry training, to the stage where Lieutenant Colonel Kelly thought they would make a good infantry company.

Major Gavin Andrews commanded 102 Battery, and was a competent gunner, having topped his course at the School of Artillery, Larkhill, UK. He makes the point that batteries at

23

that time of the involvement in the war in Vietnam were fully occupied with training themselves and in working with an infantry battalion, but rarely with their parent regiment. 'I know for months I pleaded, tried to get the battery up to strength, tried to get into the battery National Servicemen who would stay there [for most of their time of service], then off we went and trained. Of course, I exercised with 3RAR because their battery in Vietnam was going to be the New Zealand 161 Battery. It wasn't until we were in Vietnam that we met 1RAR.

'So the regiments were always a little bit unco-ordinated, and perhaps 12 Field Regiment, as a regiment, did lack some training on a regimental basis. That was a fault of the system, rather than individuals. As a battery, we were lucky; we had a good build-up to go to Vietnam.

'One of the very important things about that battery, to me, was that they were very efficient technically. They were very confident in their guns, and their ability to place fire very close to the infantry. It was a thing with me to have the confidence of the infantry, and it was instilled into the battery, from top to bottom, that their job was to support the infantry, and support them well.'

One thing which helped 102 Battery achieve its high level of proficiency was that it had calibrated thirty 105mm howitzers, which were intended to replace the light Italian pack howitzer which the first units took to Vietnam. The lighter guns could not accept the sustained firing, and were replaced with the older, heavier, US M2A2 105mm pieces.

Captain David Brook, a qualified surveyor, was Battery Captain (BK) in 102 Battery. He also thought that the battery was technically very competent, but weak in tactics, in appreciations of the ground and in defence. As an umpire on a recent exercise in Australia, he had noted, and spoken of, the lack of attention paid to local defence both by the artillery and by the infantry commanders. He believed that 'for too long the artillery had trained alone, not with the infantry, and we had only paid lip service to it'.

Brook also noted that there was nothing in writing concerning the local defence of gun positions. After the actions at

24

FSPB Coral, the Directorate of Artillery produced something for units to read and consider.

Lieutenant Ian Ahearn, Gun Position Officer (GPO) in 102 Battery, who graduated from Duntroon in December 1966, also believed that it was true the regiment 'lacked training and experience in operating as a regiment', but that within the batteries the men were fit and well trained, the technical level of expertise was high, 'the real lack of training was in the level of experience and knowledge of the regimental officers'. There had been no practice in defence of a fire support and patrol base, nor did it appear to him that people 'understood what was required for fire support base defence'.

102 Battery, like everyone else in the Army, went through the toughening course at Canungra, but were fit enough, and self-confident enough, to find it easy. This grated on the staff at Canungra, who gave 102 a poor report. However, the HQ Battery of the regiment was less well-prepared, allowing the Canungra people to assert their superiority, so the HQ gunners received a magnanimous report praising their effort. Lieutenant Colonel Kelly knew his sub-units well enough to read between the lines.

A final word on 102 Battery from David Brook: 'There was a certain arrogance about us; we thought we were good, but perhaps were not as good as all that.'

Major 'Blue' Keldie commanded A Squadron, 3 Cavalry Regiment, the M113 APC unit in 1ATF. Keldie's initial commitment to the move into Coral was to provide convoy escort for the rear echelons who would arrive by road on the 13th, after the fly-in the previous day. His M113s would also be quite busy with other escorts in the area.

His M113 commanders were provided with vehicles fitted either with a turret or an exposed position with the vehicle commander standing in the open hatch behind a .50cal machinegun, protected partially by a shield. Keldie and other Armoured Corps people had long requested turrets for all vehicles, but this had not been achieved. Soon, in the night actions at FSPB Coral, his turretless APCs would be unused due to the very high chance of the exposed commanders being hit while trying to navigate through the base.

A smaller, but important, unit was the recently arrived tank squadron, C Squadron 1 Armoured Regiment. Commanded by Major Peter Badman, it was below normal strength of four troops each of four tanks, plus specialist vehicles, and consisted of two troops and a small HQ.

Many people, including some in armour, simply did not believe, or had strong doubts, that the 50-ton Centurion tank could operate in South Vietnam, particularly in the wet season. The Centurion was British, intended for the battlefields of Europe, and went some way to restoring the prestige of British design and production teams, who throughout World War II had failed to produce a tank capable of taking the field with a performance equal to the opposing German vehicles.

Students of the Vietnamese resistance to the French were quick to note the successful ambushes executed against columns of French armour and mobile troops. However, for the type of operations in which 1ATF was engaged since its arrival in 1966, tanks could have been useful. The Australians were not pushing columns into mountain territory along narrow roads through passes, but asserting control over an agricultural province.

The first the Armoured Corps knew that tanks were to go to Vietnam was when it was announced in parliament in October 1967. Whereas the infantry units were able to train with the knowledge that they were due to go to Vietnam or Malaysia at a certain date, Badman's tank squadron was hurriedly thrown together and sent away with little training or experience in working with one another. What with equipping the unit, deciding on the specialist component necessary, individual training, which included the battle efficiency course at Canungra, from which no one was exempt, Badman could arrange only one two-week period of train as a squadron before departure in late January 1968.

Since then, his Centurions had participated in several infantry–tank exercises and a few minor clashes with the enemy, none of which did much to improve understanding between the 'tankies' and 'crunchies' (the infantry). Crunchies were accustomed to working with their own kind, where silence and stealth in the jungle paid dividends. APCs were acknowledged as necessary but, significantly, APC commanders repeatedly remarked that they were expected by some infantry to operate as tanks—that is, exploit the advantages of mobility, armour protection and firepower.

The infantry in general regarded the tanks as noisy, clumsy monsters which delighted in bumping into trees so that water, red ants, snakes, branches or even the entire tree fell on to the foot soldiers. Worse, the tankies were able to carry items regarded as luxuries by the crunchies, who had to live from the packs on their backs.

These were the main fighting units which would participate in the combats in AO Surfers. In support were headquarters and supply units, RAAF and RAN helicopter crews.

1968 became the year of decision in the US involvement in the Vietnam War. Hanoi had gambled and lost, but been presented with the opportunity to continue the game. Saigon, the capital of the South, could still be attacked, and perhaps partially occupied. Even the ability to attack was a victory of sorts, so the young men from North Vietnam were led unsuspecting to the edge of the giant cauldron.

2 Into the Big League

Prepare you, generals;
The enemy comes on in gallant show;
Their bloody sign of battle is hung out,
And something to be done immediately.
                                    Julius Caesar (V. i.)

It will be recalled that Lieutenant Colonel Jim Shelton's 3RAR was to fly in first and secure the landing zone for the arrival of the guns and 1RAR, then move out to the west, to AO Manly, leaving one rifle company (D/3RAR) and a platoon to protect the guns.

Major Geoff Cohen, Shelton's second-in-command, was to go to the HQ of the Big Red One—the US 1st Infantry Division—to assist with co-ordinating the 3RAR helicopter lift with activities of the flanking American units. While at HQ 1ATF in connection with administrative matters, he was told of his new role.

So, on the afternoon of 11 May, he was briefed by Ian MacLean and Geoff Cameron, then flew by Sioux helicopter of the US HQ.

This was easier said than done, as Cohen and the pilot had some difficulty locating the Divisional HQ, the weather was bad, and there was a great amount of military activity around and below them. At one stage the Sioux provided a ringside seat as they watched jets, helicopter gunships and artillery fire fall on NVA attacking the 3rd Brigade of the US Division.

Finally, at dusk, Cohen was delivered to Divisional HQ, and found, not to his surprise, that the Americans were fully occupied with the high level of activity in their own area. What was of immediate concern to him was that the duty staff in the US headquarters seemed unaware of the impending 1ATF operation, and had not received prior warning of his mission. Cohen had not been provided with a radio by HQ 1ATF, so was out of contact with his unit and formation.

He had also come straight from the field, dirty, with no rank badges, carrying all his field equipment such as large pack, webbing, et cetera. At one stage, the Americans became suspicious of his identity, and put him into a room under guard, while his bona fides were checked, as well as the operation and formation which he claimed to represent. After two hours of frustration, direct talking and demands, Cohen was put on a radio to 1ATF. Having both identified himself and made contact with 1ATF, finally it was agreed that US infantry would escort him to secure the 3RAR LZ.

During all this, the HQ was rocketed and mortared—which was a frequent event.

The American caution in accepting Geoff Cohen at face value may have been caused by two incidents which happened about that time: an Australian soldier, on a motorbike, was arrested a couple of hundred kilometres to the east, on Highway 1; he was absent without leave from his unit, and had been passing himself off as a colonel at the various US units and camps he encountered, but someone realised he was much too young for the claimed rank; and, while at a US unit seeking information about enemy in the Surfers AO, Geoff Cameron himself had been called to listen to a tape of a radio message, purporting to come from Australian parachute troops in difficulty and calling for help; Cameron was able to inform the Americans, who were ready to go to the rescue, that it was a fake, probably a VC ploy.

From the 1ATF Commander's Diary (the Operations Log):

2205 TF to 1RAR and 3RAR: Due to delay in securing the LZ, all timings for the move tomorrow have been put back 15 minutes. When helicopters arrive they are to be held to comply with this.
2345 US 1 Div to 1ATF: There is a heavy contact now going on at XT898275. Estimated a company-plus of VC in a dug-in base camp.
0015 IIFFVto 1ATF: 1 Div are still in contact. Although they will still be able to clear the LZ, request Route 16 be used as a boundary until contact broken. Estimate this will be at approximately 1000H or 1200H.

1ATF to IIFFV: Request denied.

The location of the heavy contact was only some 3000 metres west of the intended location of Coral.

After the confusion and frustration, Geoff Cohen was finally flown to a US battalion FSPB west of the intended Australian LZ and, with an under-strength company, walked in the last hours of the night to the location. Given the continuing heavy scale of contact in the area, the US 'grunts' (infantry-men) understandably were not enthusiastic about the fast march through the dark to some unknown patch of scrub.

They arrived in the LZ area just on first light, and deployed, well spread out in case of mortar or rocket attack, with a weather eye on the tree line to the west and south-west. The uncertainty of enemy reaction loomed large. Cohen then waited. His only contact with 3RAR was through the radio of the US company commander.

At dawn Lieutenant Colonel Shelton, with his small HQ party and the commander of the New Zealand guns, Major Hitchings, took off in a Huey flown by the commander of the US helicopter unit. Flying ten minutes ahead of Major Bert Irwin's B/3RAR, they approached the LZ—K Pad at grid reference XT925284—selected from several thousand metres above on the previous day.

The intention was to do a last-minute check of the LZ, but as the lone helicopter approached, the passengers saw the battle between the Americans and dug-in VC still going on in their intended AO, west of Route 16. Lieutenant Colonel Shelton radioed 1ATF and asked if they knew of this, receiving the reply that he was to contact the US commander at the nearest Fire Support Base, go on with the landing at Coral, but not to go into the intended 3RAR area of operations until the Americans had moved out.

Later, querying the presence of a battle about which he knew nothing, Shelton found that a message had been sent to him, but because of transmission difficulties did not arrive in a clear form before he arrived at the scene of the fighting.

Prudently waiting for a gap between artillery missions,

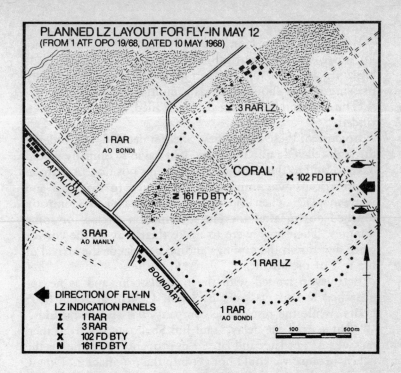

PLANNED LZ LAYOUT FOR FLY-IN MAY 12
(FROM 1 ATF OPO 19/68, DATED 10 MAY 1968)

3 RAR LZ

1 RAR
AO BONDI

'CORAL'

102 FD BTY

161 FD BTY

BATTALION

3 RAR
AO MANLY

1 RAR LZ

BOUNDARY

DIRECTION OF FLY-IN
LZ INDICATION PANELS
I   1 RAR
K   3 RAR
X   102 FD BTY
N   161 FD BTY

1 RAR
AO BONDI

0   100   500m

Shelton's Huey landed at the US fire support base, and he spoke to the US colonel, who told him that 'a guy with a funny hat' had taken some infantry to secure a landing zone, but had departed some hours before. After quickly arranging that the intended operations of their respective commands would not interfere with each other, Jim Shelton took off again, as he put it, 'to look for Geoff Cohen's hat'.

By this time, Irwin's B Company was approaching, in the terminology of the times, 'in-bound' to the landing zone.

Cohen and Shelton established contact, but only by the messages being relayed through helicopter radios.

Shelton's helicopter descended, then lifted again, as the pilots saw what had not been visible on the high-level reconnaissance: the LZ, and rest of the 'cleared' area, was covered with saplings and scrub, up to three metres tall, making it impossible for Huey operations. The helicopter commander vetoed the landing at that location.

B Company was moments away, and the rest of the air-lift was gathering momentum, off to the east, but the landing zone was unusable. Behind Jim Shelton, metaphorically pressing on his shoulders, was a multi-battalion airlift.

'The situation had changed,' he recalled, 'before we'd even landed.'

Because of these difficulties, Shelton decided, and ordered through relayed radio messages, that Irwin's company would have to land to the south-east of Cohen's position. A platoon of Americans was immediately deployed to that area and were in place when the leading elements of B Company touched down, after the Huey formation circled for some minutes. Then they were to make their way to the correct place, cut down the saplings and prepare it for the arrival of the rest of the air lift.

Bert Irwin landed with the first platoon, and as he approached K Pad was met by Geoff Cohen, at about 0805 hours, while the rest of the company was still flying in.

'That started the delay,' said Jim Shelton, 'and from then on, we just got later and later. I'm probably to blame for the delay, because we could not get into the original LZ. I knew the whole layout of the TF depended on us getting into the LZ (K Pad) as planned, so that's why I had to say to B Company, "You've got to cut that LZ, because the whole build-up depends on that LZ being used."'

3RAR Operations log:
0754 B Company to HQ: Callsign 2 [B Company] landed at Zone.

The results of the previous day's imperfect reconnaissance now began to be felt, as valuable time passed, and the rifle companies waited. At time of writing, 1987, it is not clear whether this setback to the planned sequence of lifts was compounded by US requirements for nearby elements of the 1st Division, who were in action in their own AO, requiring helicopter lifts, gunships and jet fighter ground attack missions, which all would interfere with the 1ATF move in some way.

Thirty minutes later, helicopters were lifting troops to K Pad, and at 0930, 3RAR informed 1ATF that B and C Companies were complete there. Ten minutes after that, D Company 3RAR began to fly out of its old position.

As the Australians began to flow into the LZ, and there seemed to be no problems, the US company, which had done a good job in securing the LZ area, started to move back to their own unit. Geoff Cohen recalls that they thought the locale 'somewhat unhealthy'.

A young 3RAR officer who found himself temporarily unemployed was Second Lieutenant Bill Studley, 2ic of the battalion mortars. A second intake National Service officer, he had extended his period of service so as to go to Vietnam. He subsequently continued his Army career, and in 1987 was CO 6RAR. After previous actions, particularly at FSPB Anderson, during Operation Coburg, the mortar platoon was battle-hardened.

Like many others, Bill Studley had come to take 'little notice of Intsums and Intreps, as they always over-estimated enemy strengths. To believe them would have led to ulcers'.

Having flown in with the battalion reconnaissance party, he was told to find a tree and wait until the mortar platoon arrived. He also had been an interested spectator of the military activity below the helicopter, particularly the air-strike watched from the circling Huey. While sitting under his tree, he watched a group of Australians going past, taking compass bearings and marking trees, and assumed they were from 1RAR or 1ATF. He recognised Major Brian Murtagh leading the party, having met Murtagh when Army units deployed to Tasmania to fight bushfires. Major Murtagh was 2ic of 12 Field Regiment.

Meanwhile, the Australian and New Zealand artillery parties were having their own share of the day's frustrations, which merely began with the delay.

Major Murtagh took in the regimental reconnaissance party, which included Captain Mick Ekman, Captain David

Brook, BK of 102 Battery, RSM Les Partridge, Sergeant Arthur Penn and necessary radio operators. As the Chinook arrived in the area, it was not able to land, because jet fighters attacking enemy positions were active in that piece of air space. The Chinook circled and eventually landed, the gunners walked out and found the American troops there.

Arthur Penn, Regimental Survey Sergeant, was standing next to Major Murtagh when a US brigadier general described the area in general terms, said he was handing over to the Australians, climbed into his helicopter and left.

The recce party checked the location, and found that they were some 1000 metres away from the desired location, so set off in that direction. Behind them other elements of the artillery units began to arrive over the landing zone.

Captain David Brook had watched the falling bombs and napalm while the helicopter circled then, after landing among the US infantry, he noticed they were all lying on the ground, watching for enemy, with little of the usual casual US manner about them. As he was leaving the US perimeter, he recalls a big Negro sergeant saying, 'You don't wanna go out there, man, that's tiger country.'

However, off they went.

Soon after this, Lieutenant Ian Ahearn, Gun Position Officer of 102 Battery, flew in with his own recce party and that of 161 Battery, which was under Lieutenant Rod Baldwin. Expecting to find both US soldiers of the Big Red One and 3RAR, they did find Americans who were prepared for them. Ahearn noted airstrikes to the south-west, and in conversation with the Americans learned they had been in action for the past two or three days. Ahearn had no idea where Major Brian Murtagh was, as he was in a separate helicopter and on a separate radio net.

The New Zealanders and Ahearn spent some time trying to determine where Murtagh could be. To complicate matters, the Chinooks carrying 161's guns called on the radio, saying they were en route, and had to deposit the guns on arrival or the entire fly-in would be disrupted again.

Then Murtagh was contacted, and it was decided the New Zealanders would accept their guns now, where they were.

Ian Ahearn thought that 102 Battery would be only some 100 metres away, and that the entire position would be about 400 metres square, or perhaps 1000 metres, depending on who else arrived. However, he had still not actually seen Murtagh, and when Ahearn asked for Murtagh's location, was told he was just 'along the track'. He went to look, but failed to find him or his party, returned to ask some US troops if they had seen anything of Murtagh, and was told they had seen some Australians moving north-west, into what was believed to be 'Indian country'.

Second Lieutenant Bob Lowry, with Ahearn, noticed (as had David Brook) that the American troops were all down on the ground, there was no one standing up, and they were alert and watching for enemy movement.

Again contacting Murtagh by radio, Ahearn was given a position some 1500 metres away, asked for coloured smoke to be thrown, and took a compass bearing on it, was told to join Murtagh, and began to march in that direction. Behind him the Chinooks began to deliver the New Zealand guns.

Meanwhile, Captain David Brook, with Murtagh, had spent an uncomfortable time, which he estimated to be an hour, or even an hour and a half, alone in the middle of the grassy area selected for the battery, Murtagh had told him to remain there, while the rest of the recce party went off. He had all his worldly possessions on his back, an F1 sub-machinegun and a complete copy of the operation order. He wondered what would have happened if he was 'jumped' by enemy during that time. It seemed evident that no one believed the enemy were around, or capable of significant action.

After walking some 1500 metres, into what had been a rubber plantation, Ian Ahearn found the regimental HQ party. He asked if Murtagh realised 161 Battery was so far away, expressing concern at the 'enormous gap', but was told that as the TF was deploying to the location, this amount of space was needed. Ahearn was 'sceptical, and we had a discussion, but as a Lieutenant I had no prerogative to advise'.

The map showed a set of ruins nearby, and Ahearn decided to go there to do an accurate survey of the present position, pin-pointing it. With a signaller and Lieutenant Bob Lowry, who commanded a section of three of 102 Battery guns, Ahearn moved off into the rubber trees. There they found over a hundred freshly dug weapon pits, an AK47 round and a 'hard lolly with a Ho Chi Minh wrapping', all of which was reported to Murtagh. This information apparently went no further.

Brian Murtagh's party had begun erecting a 292-aerial, to provide better communications with the units coming along behind, or still waiting at the distant assembly points. Communication was made with the New Zealand guns. Only two Chinooks were allocated for the artillery unit, so the big helicopters made a series of flights, bringing one gun at a time, then cargo comprising the rest of the battery and regimental HQ. Work began on digging-in the command post.

The combined strength of Murtagh's and Ahearn's parties was no more than fifteen people, and these were the security force for what became the landing zone for both 102 Battery and 1RAR. The infantry companies began to arrive, like the guns, in what Ahearn describes as 'fits and starts'.

Major Peter Phillips, commanding D/3RAR, arrived and was surprised to find the waist-high grass, having studied the air photos and expected much more open terrain. Having been detached from his parent battalion and placed under command of Major Brian Murtagh for defence of the embyronic base, he found Murtagh 'fairly soon after we had dropped in, and then we had a confused afternoon, because I was never too sure exactly where we were; we seemed to have been landed at the wrong point.

'Because we had lost so much of the day, we came to some arrangement. There was a gap between the rubber trees; we'd move our company up and sit there, where we could get good views over the open ground on either side of the rubber [plantation section]. Now whether that was where we were intended to go or not, I'm not sure, but that was agreed with Brian Murtagh on the ground, and we duly went off and dug in there.'

So Phillips' company moved north-west, away from the hustle and bustle around the gun position, into the square of rubber trees, from where they could observe and bring fire to bear on the open areas north of the main road running diagonally through the AO, and west of the gun position.

One of the patrols sent out by Phillips was 4 Section, 11 Platoon, commanded by Corporal Dave Mancer. When they reached the road, they saw along the sides the abandoned charred wrecks from an ambush, wondered about the action which caused the destruction, and began watching for enemy. Later, Mancer wondered also if the enemy had already seen them, because he had a distinct feeling that 'something was going to happen'.

In Geoff Cohen's opinion, the confusion, disruptions and less-than-satisfactory airlift were caused by a failure to understand that 1ATF was moving into an area which was much more active than those where it had been recently; that the US formations there were heavily engaged and had different organisations and procedures, et cetera; there was insufficient planning; and no command and control at 1ATF level of the actual lifts (flights or formations) of helicopters when they eventually were in the air delivering the Australian and New Zealand units to Coral.

Back at the Australian base camp at Nui Dat, the Deputy Task Force Commander was looking at the map in the command post. He was Colonel Donald B. Dunstan, later CGS and then Governor of South Australia. He said to the Duty Officer, 'They're in the big league now!'

At 1200 hours 1ATF Forward reported to Nui Dat that 3RAR was complete at Coral, and 1RAR would begin to arrive shortly.

The man responsible for organising the fly-in of 1RAR was Captain Mick Bindley, commanding both Support Company and the Signals Platoon of that company. Despite the shortage of maps of the relevant area, he obviously needed one, and had it marked with the proposed company locations. He had no idea that the battalion was 'going into the middle of a nest of NVA', but believed it was to be mopping-up NVA retreating from Saigon.

Bindley commanded the battalion reconnaissance party, and his duties included the landing zone layout for the arriving companies and headquarters, dispatching the companies to their proper areas, and taking the HQ to its area. The map he was given had marked on it the intended position of Coral, and the smaller areas into which the AO had been divided, in preparation for the patrolling which everyone thought would take place. 102 Battery were delivered to a position 1000 metres to the east of the one marked on the map.

The first fly-in was aborted, and the flights of helicopters wheeled in the sky, going back to FSPB Harrison, where the soldiers waited for several hours. Valuable time was passing.

The 1RAR War Diary records the delays:
0722   to TF   Recce party airborne.
0725   from TF   There has been a delay of 20 mins—recce party to
*   return and wait at your location.*
0930   to all   Appears to be at least one hours delay.

The second flight delivered the advance party at about midday, and Bindley noticed the New Zealand 161 Battery of 105mm howitzers already on the ground.

Then came what he recalled as his first surprise of the day: there was an American infantry company in the area, a large battle was raging some distance away to the west and north, and the commander of the US company said he was to remain until the Australians were ready to take over. The US officer told Bindley that the gunfight in progress involved a battalion of the Big Red One—which had made a midnight insertion into the area and been in battle ever since.

Some nine kilometres away to the north, the NVA 141 Regiment was watching with interest the easily visible shapes of the artillery fly-in. Whatever was going on there would have to be investigated.

Bindley was to report to Major Brian Murtagh, of 12 Field Regiment, and saw him in the distance, with his own small group of artillery men, striking off to the east through the shrubbery, towards what Bindley realised later was the landing of the Australian 102 Battery of 105mm howitzers. He could have chased after Murtagh, but decided to remain and lay out the LZ for the arrival of the following companies of the battalion. He began the distribution and display of the coloured panels which denoted the assembly areas for the respective rifle companies.

In an interlude, two big Maoris came past, carrying a New Zealander suffering from heat exhaustion. The US officer could not understand why a Dustoff was not called at once to evacuate the man, and Bindley said, 'I can't explain New Zealanders to you, but I'm sure he'll be all right.' The American seemed to accept this.

Then, Bindley recalls, 'What I can best describe as a spit-polished helicopter arrived, with horns painted on the front of it, and out of it appeared a very spit-polished Brigadier General Assistant Division Commander of the Big Red One. I was very conscious of my appearance, having been on operations for three weeks, and we were completely red from the soil we'd been in and I felt extremely scruffy at the time.'

However, the Brigadier General was quite friendly, and explained the battle was likely to continue for some time, then showed Bindley on a map the locations in the area where the US Division had engaged the enemy in heavy contact over the recent weeks, suffering casualties in the hundreds at some locations. Bindley began to understand that the Australians were in for an interesting time. The American's final words were, 'Tell your CO that you won't need to go looking for them. They'll come looking for you.'

By this time it had become clear to Bindley that the insertion of the Australians was not going according to plan, and that, in the distance to the east, what he was watching was the arrival of 102 Battery. As 1RAR was to land next to the guns, he put the Assistant Quartermaster in charge of the advance party, took off his webbing, and with only his rifle set off along the paths of the former rubber-tree plantation through the scrub towards the noise and dust of the fly-in of 102 Battery.

However, halfway there, despite the presence in the neighbourhood of several allied units, he began to feel a trifle lonely, and rebuked himself for going alone through enemy country, albeit for a short distance. He arrived at 102's position, to find that they were going to remain there despite the separation between them and 161, and the concern felt that one of the batteries had been delivered to the wrong place. It was a little after 1400 hours. Unknown to him, rifle companies had been arriving at the place where he was going, while he had been waiting.

While Mick Bindley was walking north-east wondering if the patch of scrub was really as deserted of enemy as it seemed, in the opposite direction, trotting south-west, was the reconnaissance party of the NVA 2 Battalion, 141 Regiment.

Bindley decided to move the 1RAR LZ to the 102 Battery position, and called his party to come across and join him. His heavy pack and webbing was carried by the already burdened members of his small group. Precious time for 1RAR's intended operations that day was trickling away.

The reason for the delay has been recounted above, and the machines made available were not necessarily the same type for which the move had been organised. Instead of the small Huey, some of the larger Chinook had been allocated, which meant a revision of the size of the groups into which the companies had been divided.

Tony Hammett's D Company 1RAR was reorganised into Chinook-loads, climbed in and flew away from FSPB Harrison. No information was given Hammett, who sat in the seats with the rest of his men. The Chinooks began to circle. Hammett looked out and could see 'about half a dozen smoke grenades going, all different colours. I had no idea what was going on. The crewmen were looking out, the Chinook circled, and we came in to land in a large cleared area which had been a rubber plantation.

'We got out and looked around. I was looking for the red D Company air marker panel carried by Brian Altham, the company 2ic. We would then go to rendezvous on him. There was nothing, there was nobody. The only sign of movement was some 200 metres away, some guns. There was no sign of Mick Bindley or anybody.

'I knew coming behind me was the rest of the battalion; they were right up our hammer. I grabbed someone and told him, "When C Company comes in, grab them, tell them what's going on and where we think we are. Do the same with B Company and battalion headquarters, to make the best of the confused situation, until we find Mick Bindley and the rest of the battalion recce party."

'I then said to my Forward Observer, Gordon Alexander, "Go over and see the guns, they'll know where they are." So off went Gordon.'

At the gun position, Alexander spoke to Ian Ahearn, the Gun Position Officer (GPO), and one of the Section Commanders, Bob Lowry. They told him of the newly dug positions in the rubber trees just north of the guns, and that they thought that there was 'something funny going on'.

Lieutenant John Salter, commanding 10 Platoon in Hammett's company, had as his Platoon Sergeant, Ray Curtis, who also had completed the Battalion's first tour in the theatre. Like the others, they reacted to the order to get to an LZ. Curtis recalls that 'away we went, with no information as to where we were going and what we would be doing when we arrived'. There was little information to give the soldiers—merely that this was another move to another area, and this time the whole battalion was going. From the LZ, they were flown to 'a large grassy area which had once been a rubber plantation'.

On arrival at what they came to know as Coral, Salter noticed 'people seeming to mill around, the Mortar Platoon setting up and the guns beginning to arrive. 10 Platoon eventually got together. Then, in the area of the LZ, before we moved away, someone found a skeleton, the decayed remains

41

of an NVA, fully equipped, sitting under a tree. Not a VC in black, but the NVA grey.'

Ray Curtis and the others saw and commented on the discovery, which 'started us thinking. Though the area was quiet, there was a sort of feeling that everything wasn't right. There was some confusion as to our exact location, and apparently conflict about where the guns were or should have been.'

The irrepressible Corporal Paul 'Richo' Richardson, on his second tour, said to the skeleton. 'You shouldn't have waited so long for us, mate,' as he led his Section past.

Despite his wisecracks, Richo was well aware that his men were still new to the business, this was probably the first time they had seen an actual dead enemy, and thought the whole affair so far was becoming a little nerve-wracking, that there was a feeling in 'the atmosphere, you knew there was something wrong, it was not the right place to be in'.

Richo's second-in-command, Slug Lewis, walked up and asked, 'What the hell is going on?' to which Richo replied, 'Be patient. Go and talk to the old Charlie there, he'll tell you more than I can at this stage.' They waited for John Salter to return from Company HQ, where Tony Hammett was passing on their orders for the night.

Hammett's 12 Platoon was commanded by Geoff Bowcock, and after arrival at the LZ, without bothering about anyone else, they struck off on the task they had been allotted back at FSPB Harrison: move 1000 metres west and ambush the road there. Bowcock didn't have a map, but reasoned the road was obviously there. He had time to notice that no one but D Company seemed to be at the landing area, but got his platoon together and struck off into the scrub.

Lack of a map did not make things easier, and after walking the estimated distance to the road, they simply kept on going until they did arrive there. Bowcock reported this on the radio, and it seemed to him company HQ was surprised to be informed of his location, and ordered him back to the LZ for new tasks. The disgruntled platoon retraced their steps. There at Coral Bowcock was given a map and told of the new role for the company.

Another NVA corpse, also fully dressed and equipped, was found by members of 6 Platoon B Company as they left the helicopters. The remains were in metre-high grass, and puzzled Brian 'Jazza' Smith, the sergeant, as there was no immediate sign of cause of death. But as soon as he saw them, 'the hairs rose up on the back of my head, and I just knew that they were nearby'.

As 6 Platoon arrived, a disagreement between two of the Diggers reached flashpoint, in the middle of their deplaning activity. One of the men was so angry that he fully intended to shoot the other. 'It was a serious thing,' recalls Jazza Smith. 'He was going to kill the bloke, no two ways about it. He had his rifle pointed, he was going to shoot Jock with it. The platoon commander, Garry Prendergast, had other things to do, and said, "Sergeant, fix that up", so I kept Maurie with me and sent Jock off. So my action, apart from being tail-end Charlie, was to keep those two apart.'

'Just after that, in the long grass, was this fellow lying, with his clothing, webbing and everything, as if someone had laid him out there like a picture in a museum.'

Information about the combats involving the Big Red One had not filtered down to the arriving platoons, but the old soldiers' sixth sense was niggling at the minds of some of the Diggers.

Second Lieutenant Gordon Alexander, the Forward Observer with D/1RAR, who had been sent to ask the artillery where this place was, came back with the information, while Hammett scanned the area for D Company of 3RAR, who were to have secured the landing zone, but could see nothing of them.

Mick Bindley did arrive, as Hammett recalls, 'sweat-drenched, very angry', demanding to know 'Where the bloody hell have you fellows been? What are you doing over here?'

Hammett countered with the same question, and was told the reconnaissance party had been deposited some 1000 to 1200 metres away, and the message from the US Brigadier General.

Tony Hammett mentally reviewed the indicators that 'this

was a different sort of war': the disquiet about the area felt by Don Porter, the RAAF pilot; the briefing references to NVA regiments and divisional headquarters; the dead NVA on the landing zone; the American Brigadier General's comments about the present scale of battle in the neighbourhood.

A platoon which was to play a small but crucial role in the coming night had also arrived. The Anti-tank Platoon of Mick Bindley's Support Company flew in, and was given a patch of ground to occupy on the edge of the area. Anti-tank Platoon was commanded by Lieutenant Les Tranter, a CMF officer on full-time duty, who had been commissioned just over three years, and had joined 1RAR the previous October. The platoon was equipped with both 90mm and 106mm RCLs, as well as the normal M60 machineguns. The 106mm weapons had been left behind, but the two 90mm were carried, with eight rounds for each: two HE, two HEAT and four flechette. The 90mm crews carried 9mm pistols for personal weapons.

The platoon also included the tracker teams of a dog and handler. In all, Les Tranter had sixteen men with him. Their firepower made them a formidable group, and he always was ready to move the platoon to another part of any position to reinforce or counter-attack if necessary.

Among the artillery contingent was the detachment from 131 Divisional Locating Battery, who had been packed and waiting for most of the day. One of a four-man listening post team was John Dellaca, who saw their Chinooks also waiting, parked outside the perimeter of FSPB Anderson.

Finally, they flew into Coral, and Dellaca's team was told to go to the distant 161 Battery. Like many others, after the three weeks' constant moving and operating with little contact, they accepted the information that 'the area is completely secure', swapped their M60 machinegun for some full-sized picks and shovels (to make digging easier) and walked casually through the long grass to the New Zealanders, laden with water in jerrycans, boxes of rations, their radios, weapons and personal gear. Dellaca and one of the others had their rifles converted to fire on fully automatic if needed, and acquired the large thirty-round magazines, so did not worry about leaving the machinegun behind.

It was after 1600 when they arrived, and set to digging a set of interconnecting pits so they could operate where they lived and slept. They were told that one of the gun batteries was not in the correct position, that they were too close for correct mutual fire support, but did not find out which battery it was.

They placed some Claymore mines to their front, and were glad to see some 3RAR infantry come up nearby with a tripod-mounted M60.

Second Lieutenant Bill Studley had been waiting for the 3RAR mortars to arrive and, when they did, led them to their position near the New Zealand guns. They immediately began digging pits for the mortars and themselves, and arranging all the necessary matters: communications, machinegun positions, night-time rosters, preparing ammunition, and so on. This continued beyond dusk.

Meanwhile, in the 102 Battery position, a great deal of physical work had been in progress. One of the tasks was digging-in the CP, for which the bulldozer could give limited assistance. A hole five metres long, 2.5 metres wide and two metres deep was needed, and the sweating gunners set to work. A sandbag roof had to be constructed over the original hole, and communications strung to the gun pits. It was dusk before the 102 Battery CP was finished.

Stan Carbines, one of the battery survey party, assisted in the heavy work. To give the HQ gunners a break from the routine, and broaden their experience, some of them were detached to the gun crews. Another battery surveyor, Neil Lloyd-Jones, was with No. 2 gun, and despite the physical work involved, enjoyed the relief from the heavy digging for the CP.

When the gunners began working in the area, they found, scattered in the long grass, the pottery bowls which had formerly collected the dripping latex from the rubber trees. Ken Walker said, in jest, 'Gee, I don't like the look of this. The nogs will come back tonight to pick up their bowls.' Many a true word said in jest ...

While the artillery and rifle companies were arriving at and moving around the position, away to the south was the road convoy en route from Nui Dat. Comprising the vehicles and other members of the units, the convoy was to stay overnight at the camp of the HQ of the US 9th Division, at Bearcat. They would drive on next morning to FSPB Coral.

It was after midday when the 1RAR rifle companies began to arrive. There was little time to brief the commanders, and when Lieutenant Colonel Bennett and the battalion HQ were delivered, it was so late that he decided they would remain where they were, just east of 102 Battery, for the night, and move away to continue the original plan in the morning of 13 May.

Travelling with Phil Bennett was his direct support artillery battery commander, Gavin Andrews. As the helicopter circled before landing, Andrews also had noticed the intense helicopter activity and could see smoke from distant artillery batteries, as well as hear on the artillery radio nets the numerous calls and messages which made him realise that they were 'coming into a very active area'.

Bill Raggatt, second-in-command of A/1RAR, noted in his field message book: '1620 Coy arrived FSPB Coral. 1640 Depart for night location.'

Major Col Adamson, commanding A Company, was met by Kim Patterson, who agreed that this was not the intended location, showed him where they were, and told him to get along to the original ambush position. Then Adamson was presented with three Starlite scopes, for night vision, which he was to learn to use 'on the job'. The company moved off, endeavouring to fulfil the original plan.

They arrived in place shortly before last light, and moved into what Adamson described as 'more a company harbour with an intention to ambush' than an ambush position. To the south-east they could hear firing from the B Company area.

C Company was commanded by Major Ian 'Digger' Campbell, who had seen service in Korea, Malaya, Papua New Guinea and with US forces in peacetime on Okinawa, as well as having instructed at RMC Duntroon. His task was to clear the road south to Tan Uyen, for the north-bound convoy next morning. Originally, he was to have commanded the defence, with his company, of the gun position, but his orders had been changed. Thorough checking of the roadsides only allowed slow progress, and at the end of an hour about 1000 metres had been done, so he put two platoons abreast and 'marched at best speed' until dark.

The rifle companies were dispersing to their given distant positions, to begin the normal Australian tactics of patrolling, ambushing, searching, moving, hunting down the enemy, keeping him off balance. Few, if any, realised that the enemy here were fresh from the north, well armed with automatic weapons, rockets, mortars and heavy machineguns, eager for a fight, and outnumbered the Aussies several times over.

So, to defend HQ 1RAR, Mick Bindley deployed the platoons of Support Company, placing the Anti-tank and Pioneers in a semicircle north and east of the HQ, with the signals and other attachments on the opposite side.

Digging to below ground level was begun. Bindley felt worried that the two artillery units were so separated, but had to assume that a link of some sort had been made.

The intention was to remain for the night only so there was no co-ordination of the defences with the neighbouring units. Anti-tank Platoon being closest to the artillery, contact between them was made, and it was agreed the gap over the open ground in the intervening space would be covered by the 90mm RCLs of the infantry.

Les Tranter, commanding the Anti-tank Platoon, showed his men where he wanted the 90mm RCLs and M60 machine guns emplaced, left his section commanders to fill in the spaces with the other pits, and walked over to the artillery. There he co-ordinated the positioning of the right-hand machinegun with his own left-hand M60, and did the same on his right flank, with Les Myers' Pioneers. Tranter then checked the arcs of fire of his platoon weapons, and all began, or continued digging.

As he turned away from talking to Lance Corporal Phil Pascoe, the commander of the right-hand section, and faced the north-west, Tranter experienced a flash of foresight. He said, 'Phil, tonight we are going to be attacked, be hit heavily, and tomorrow morning, over there, we'll pick up a bloke, laying on his back, hands crossed on his chest, and babbling in his tongue.'

Pascoe replied with the mandatory down-to-earth reply, to the effect that Tranter had been reading too much of the wrong thing, or smoking too much of the wrong weed, to which Tranter agreed, and walked away to his own position.

Marching off to the east was Bob Hennessy's B Company, with Garry Prendergast's 6 Platoon in the rear, and the last man his sergeant, 'Jazza' Smith. In the hot and dusty conditions, laden with extra water in jerrycans and waterbottles on web belts carried over all their other gear, the move was anything but enjoyable. 'It was quite boring,' remembers Prendergast, 'hot, and just wandering in and out of this thin, sparse bloody scrub, trees about three metres high.'

Accurate navigation in the area was difficult, and the company tended to weave a little as the pathfinders tried to find their way to the allocated night position.

In all the previous patrolling, B Company had not been involved in any sort of action, and was beginning to feel left out of things, so Bob Hennessy had asked Lieutenant Colonel Bennett for 'something to do'. The result was their mission to move 3000 metres to the east, to ambush the track junction, with the comment, 'I hope that satisfies you.'

Hennessy began to be annoyed by radio messages from the battalion headquarters, first that they seemed to be going in the wrong direction, then that they were going too slowly, and if they could not make it to the crossroads in time, they could stop earlier. Hennessy stubbornly insisted that the company would go to the assigned location, and pressed on through the evening.

Among the men of 1RAR on their second tour was John Kearns, from South Australia, posted as an Interpreter to the Battalion Intelligence Section—despite having only a few words of the Vietnamese language at his command. With the experience of the 1965–6 tour behind him, John noticed nothing unusual in the preparations of the battalion for the move to Coral except for one thing: arrival into the position seemed a little late in the day.

However, he did not know of any enemy in the immediate area and was not unduly worried. He noticed 'a small bull-dozer going flat out making bunds around the artillery gun positions'.

1RAR's mortars arrived by Chinook helicopter, and the platoon commander, Captain Hugh McInally, showed his second-in-command, Lieutenant Tony Jensen, the general area they were to occupy. Jensen then picked the exact location, placed the four mortars in position, and work began on digging pits for the weapons, plus scrapes for the men, the command post, and preparing the ammunition. One section of mortars had been left at the Nui Dat base.

In general, the entire Mortar Platoon was experienced, as it included men from 7RAR who had remained after that battalion returned to Australia, and men who had already done a previous tour of duty in 1965–6.

One of these was Corporal Bob Hickey, who had been in B Company during that tour. A professional soldier, he did not query that he would accompany the battalion this time. However, his wife had recurring nightmares of his death if he did so, and so disturbing were they that she approached the chaplain. It was obvious that the Army would melt away if members were to be removed from battle because of the dreams of relatives, so a compromise was reached and it was arranged that Hickey would go to the Mortar Platoon. They had suffered no fatalities from enemy action in 1965–6.

At 1610, the 1RAR War Diary recorded 'last sortie on the ground at Coral'.

At 1637, 1ATF was informed that 1RAR was clear of FSPB Harrison.

A double slit trench for the battalion CP was dug as soon as Lieutenant Colonel Bennett decided to remain at the place, and later it was enlarged to form a better position. Individuals had shallow pits, called shell scrapes, to give them personal protection. The deepest of these in the HQ area was probably little deeper than 60cm.

Col Adamson's A Company moved away through the

scrub, into an ambush position some 2000 metres to the north-east of the guns. Battalion HQ would catch up with him tomorrow.

Bob Hennessy's B/1RAR had pushed on to the east, through the low scrub, burdened by extra water and rations, finding navigation difficult in the featureless terrain, thus making slow progress. The heat squeezed its toll from everyone.

C Company, commanded by Ian 'Digger' Campbell, had begun its journey to the south, to secure the road for the convoy on the morrow.

As the afternoon slipped away, Tony Hammett 'kept pressing battalion headquarters that we wanted to get out, because the last thing I wanted was to have to occupy an ambush position in the dark, and the feeling, the omens, were not good. At four o'clock I got permission to move to our ambush position.'

Hammett decided to move as fast as possible, by the most direct route, through the busy mortar position, north through a patch of standing rubber trees where he expected to find D Company 3RAR, across the road and into the rubber trees on the other side, thence to their intended location for the ambush.

'I put Salter's platoon out first, because they were the greyhound platoon of D Company. If I ever wanted the company to move fast, I put him out in front, and he'd put his own greyhound out: Paul Richardson.'

Having been chatting with the RAN pilot and gunner in a US Huey—part of the RAN Flight of the 135 Assault Helicopter Company—and handing over a stag's head complete with antlers which had been found, Salter's 10 Platoon began leading Hammett's D/1RAR out to the north. They moved through the Mortar Platoon, with comments between the groups, to the effect that 'You blokes are shooting through again?'

Richardson's section was leading, and the unease he felt earlier was continued, as he 'had this feeling, the same feeling I had in the operation in the Ho Bo Woods, where I knew somebody was watching me, and the hairs on the back of my neck were sort of standing up, and it was that unnerving feeling that this wasn't quite right.' (The Ho Bo Woods was a successful operation in January 1966, on the first tour, when a VC HQ was overrun west of Saigon.)

As Hammett himself came through the mortars, he greeted Jensen, busy digging. The Mortar Platoon had been under Hammett's command at FSPB Anderson recently, and he'd had to 'keep on their hammer to dig, dig, dig'.

Now Hammett said, 'G'day Alf, I see you're the Outpost of Empire here, and I'm pleased to see you've learned your lesson about digging.'

Jensen replied with a grin that 'Evergreen Four is said to be out there', pointing to the rubber trees where Hammett expected to meet D/3RAR. Evergreen was 3RAR's name on the telephone switchboard, 'Four' being for D Company, the fourth.

Jensen's radio operator, Jack Parr, and others, saw the rifle platoons filing past, heading towards the distant rubber trees, and assumed they would not be going far, and would be relatively close by.

Joe Griffin, a 1967 National Service intake soldier and one of the 11 Platoon scouts, saw a mate sitting in the mortar position. John O'Brien had transferred to mortars, and called out, 'Hey, Griff, if you need any help, just call and I'll drop a round over for you.' Griffin never saw him again.

Gordon Alexander, D Company's Forward Observer, began talking to his counterpart with D/3RAR, to warn them that D/1RAR was approaching, and was assured that a watch was being kept for them. However, the 1RAR soldiers moved on and on, into the block of rubber trees, and found no one. Alexander reported this to Gavin Andrews, commanding the guns behind him.

The leading soldiers of Hammett's D Company came to the road running north-east to south-west. Paul Richardson looked along it, and saw 'all these APCs that were burned out, it was quite a sight, right down the road, left and right sides. God knows whether they were American or ARVN.'

Richardson called his platoon commander, John Salter, forward. He and the others took in the scene, and again

51

had something to 'start us thinking'. Ray Curtis and Paul Richardson had been in the area some three years previously, with no enemy contact, and it seemed to be the same, except for the quiet charred hulks.

Tony Hammett came forward to join Salter, and together they looked around, wondering why they had not come across D/3RAR. Hammett reported this to 1RAR.

The feeling that all was not well was nagging at Gordon Alexander's radio operator, Blue Ericson, who remarked several times that 'there is something funny going on here', and Alexander himself also felt 'an atmosphere in the air'.

Crossing the road by tactically manoeuvring the platoons, D/1RAR moved on through cleared rubber plantation and past old fire support positions similar to that they had left, and at about 1800 hours were approaching a north–south track, when Richardson's forward scout, John 'Squizzy' Taylor, 'suddenly flew to the ground'.

Richardson walked up behind him, and asked what was wrong, to which Taylor replied, 'There's somebody standing over there watching us.' Richo 'looked up, and about fifty metres down the track, on the left, was this guy in sort of a khaki uniform.'

There he was, a man in khaki uniform, with full webbing equipment and weapon, watching them. Then, as Salter was walking forward, the man 'shot through'. The man would have seen people dressed similarly to himself, with floppy hats, webbing and packs, weapons, moving quietly. There were no distinctive domed US steel helmets, brightly coloured patches of unit insignia or scarves usually sported by some US and ARVN units. Not sure of the location of allied troops, and as the man had done nothing hostile, the Australians cautiously moved forward, Hammett moving Geoff Bowcock's 12 Platoon into the lead. Richo Richardson and his men were now at the tail-end of the company.

About 100 metres short of the intended ambush position, Hammett halted the company, and gathered his platoon commanders and signallers to do a reconnaissance of the location and indicate where the platoons were to go. It was about 1820 hours.

Hammett noticed Bowcock's platoon sergeant, Trevor Warburton, 'very much the relaxed platoon sergeant, rifle under arm and a roll-your-own hanging out of the corner of his mouth', and then the forward scout nearby giving 'thumbs down and thumbs up and a shrug of the shoulders'.

The scout, nicknamed 'Roo-dog', because of his physical build, was unsure of the identity of a couple of faces peering through the scrub and grass ahead. Warburton, cigarette in mouth, said, 'That's a nog', snapped his rifle up, aimed and fired, hitting one of the Vietnamese.

RPG rockets flashed overhead and the Australians began manoeuvring. Hammett found himself member of a fire support group, near one of the corporals, and said, 'Right, all yours, Corporal Cunningham', thinking that 'this is a bit unusual: here's a company commander, in his group of platoon commanders, in the fire support role, giving orders to a section commander, saying "Right, it's all yours."'

Gordon Alexander saw the tracers flying, realised he was in a cleared area, and jumped 'into my fire position, which happened to be a little shrub, half a metre tall, with three leaves on it'.

As the firing was away up at the head of the company, and there was no activity in his immediate area, Richo 'was still standing there, sort of watching all the bullets go up through the whole length of the rubber plantation, and I turned around to look where my section was, and they had done the perfect contact drill. It took me about five minutes to go and find them.' Richo pointed out to the section that the firing was not at them, but going overhead, so it was a good opportunity to become accustomed to being under fire.

The Vietnamese, probably part of a reconnaissance element, fled before the quick assault could reach them, leaving one dead behind. Hammett saw him to be 'very big North Vietnamese, well built, well dressed, well equipped, well fed. Nothing lean or gaunt about him, and on him was Cambodian money.'

One of the enemy had been dressed in black, probably the local VC soldier acting as guide, and the others wore green, the NVA uniform.

53

Gordon Alexander, the artillery Forward Observer, called for gunfire on to the enemy position, and was gratified to see it arrive some 250 metres ahead, within thirty seconds, into the suspected enemy position on the far side of a cleared area.

Perry Neil, a National Serviceman and volunteer for infantry, as well as Vietnam, was normally a forward scout, but at this time was bringing up the rear of 4 Section 11 Platoon, 'having a rest', as he termed it. He had just noticed some diggings nearby when the firing began. The rest of 11 Platoon began running forward, but the last few of 4 Section found bullets flying around them, and advanced ducking, dodging and going to ground.

Perry thought that the section commander did not believe they were under fire, and kept yelling at them to keep up. Then an M79 from somewhere exploded behind Perry, he looked back at the cloud of dust and decided he was not staying there, so galloped forward, passing some of the other fellows.

One Australian was wounded, and at first this was thought (and is still by some today) to be a freak result of the artillery—the piece of metal had flown parallel with the soldier's back, through his pack, and clipped his cerebus, blinding him. Alexander was deeply affected, and discussed it with Gavin Andrews. Together they went over the incident, deducing that the wound was caused by NVA small arms fire from the north-east, as a piece of artillery shrapnel would not have such a trajectory.

Bringing up the rear, through the rapidly darkening plantation, Richo took the opportunity to show his men what a recently killed enemy looked like, so diverted from his route and filed them past 'this guy lying there on the side of the track with a neat V in his forehead'. He said. 'This is the guy you are fighting; that's his dress and gear; you get a good idea of it.' They moved on, behind the company, some of the stomachs heaving.

Captain Altham, Hammett's second-in-command, organised the Dustoff and the company then moved on to its night position, a triangular ambush placed on the inner sides of a track junction. 10 and 11 Platoons were placed to fire along the tracks to the apex of the triangle, with Geoff Bowcock's 12 Platoon forming the base, facing roughly back towards Coral.

By this time it was dark, and though Hammett gave the order to dig, it is unlikely that all obeyed, or that the pits which were dug were very deep. It had become obvious to all that there were enemy around, as other companies had reported sightings.

At 1810 hours, 1ATF was informed of the results of the fighting by the US 1 Div on 11 and 12 May: thirty-six NVA killed, and the unit identified as 141 Regiment.

All the information was available to indicate an enemy interest in the area, and that the enemy were not fleeing remnants of units decimated in the Saigon battles: the heavy contact by the US Big Red One, visible to many of the Australians; the warning from US officers; the US requirement for helicopters which radically altered the fly-in of the Australians; the unease of the helicopter pilots during the aerial reconnaissance and at the briefing; the contact by D Company with clean, fit, well-equipped members of (probably) a reconnaissance group; all the signs of previous heavy fighting in the area. But the pattern, the collection of all these, as pieces of a puzzle, was disrupted by the disorder of the fly-in, and overwhelmed by the need to move from Harrison to Coral and deploy. There was no one able to stand back a pace, observe the signs, and present their deduction to anyone in command.

So the four rifle companies had marched off to their respective tasks, away from their headquarters and the guns. Later, many people of various ranks would ponder the events of the day and night, wondering why there was not more actual belief in the information of strong enemy nearby. A similarity might reasonably be drawn to the much larger and more famous Allied operation to seize the bridge at Arnhem in September 1944. The Allies had recently been successful in France and Belgium; the enemy had been shattered; attention of the planners and executors of the operation had been almost entirely taken by the enormous effort involved in the airborne landings of three divisions; information of German armour at Arnhem had been received but not really believed —everyone had seen the debris of the Wehrmacht littering the roadsides and fields.

Similarly for the smaller operations intended for AO Surfers, the enemy obviously had been beaten, and the problems of the disrupted fly-in to Coral may have tended to outweigh the information about the enemy there.

Meanwhile, at Coral itself, as the afternoon slipped away into dusk and evening, Lieutenant Tony Jensen, 1RAR Mortar Platoon, turned his attention to co-ordinating the defence of the mortar area with the units around him. With Lieutenant Ian Ahearn, Gun Position Officer of 102 Battery and a Duntroon classmate, he went looking for the infantry who would normally be forward of the support weapons such as mortars and artillery. They were able to locate and coordinate with the 1RAR Anti-armour Platoon, and with the artillery, deciding on the position of each other's machine-guns, but could not find any infantry of D/3RAR.

Jensen was told that D Company 3RAR 'was in front', and assumed they had linked with the anti-armour positions. It was getting late, there were other things to be done, and Jensen had to turn his attention to them, feeling that things were 'not particularly satisfactory, but nevertheless that was it'.

It was decided that 102 Battery would man two M60 machineguns forward of its Nos. 4 and 5 guns; RHQ and Jensen's mortars would man two more; telephone lines were laid linking Brian Murtagh's HQ, 102 Battery, Jensen's mortars and HQ 1RAR. No arcs of fire were co-ordinated officially, except on a personal level, as when Jensen went across and spoke to Bombardier Andy Forsdike, who was in charge of the artillery HQ machinegun group.

Captain Mick Ekman conducted the O group for the regimental headquarters people. One of the minor dispositions made was that of Sergeant Arthur Penn, and three Gunners, Robinson, Major and Gow, to man an all-night listening post behind the position, at the edge of a small track. The three young gunners had arrived at Coral in the mid-afternoon, and this was their first taste of operations in Vietnam—they had arrived in-country four days earlier.

Other young gunners were part of the outer perimeter near the HQ battery CP. Bombardier Andy Forsdike had with him Gunners Mal Hundt, Vic Page, Kershaw, Sawtell and Soper, who manned a series of scrapes on the north and west of the position. Further forward were two more, manned as listening posts. However, these soldiers were required to perform several duties during the night, manning the radio, the machinegun and the listening post in rotation. This meant a great amount of constant movement backwards and forwards from one pit or scrape to another. Sawtell and Soper, radio-operators, replaced each other on the radio. Vic Page at one time was sharing the listening post with Rod 'Ginger' Orford, but at another was manning the M60 machinegun.

When given the M60, Andy Forsdike asked if it had been test-fired, and was assured by a sergeant that it had. With their personal weapons, Forsdike's group had the machinegun with 200 rounds, an M79 with three, and a field telephone. Some of the soldiers, such as Mal Hundt, had been in Vietnam for five days. Like everyone else, they were tired after the move-in and digging, and realised they had not dug deep enough. Ginger Orford and Vic Page, in fact, were reprimanded for digging during stand-to; they had not realised it was so late.

They were shown the left and right of arcs of fire of the machinegun, told of the presence of the 1RAR mortar people to their front, but nothing was said of any enemy in the immediate area.

At the position of 102 Battery, Gavin Andrews had walked over from the 1RAR HQ, and discussed with Captain David Brook the defence problems facing the battery. The choice was between putting up wire defences or digging trenches, and Andrews opted for fire trenches.

In the gun position, Second Lieutenant Matt Cleland realised that, as darkness closed down, 102 Battery was 'very much underprepared, by no means complete', as his Left Section of Nos. 4, 5 and 6 guns prepared for the night.

Bob Lowry, commanding the Right Section of Nos. 1, 2

and 3 guns, had helped to marshal the arriving guns, done a share of the digging for the CP—'no one was exempt'—and dug his own shell scrape, next to that of Ian Ahearn. He was the Duty Officer in the battery CP.

While the officers had their own problems, some of the soldiers had worries of a different nature. Stan Carbines and others who had dug the 102 Battery CP were allocated a perimeter position on the south-western edge of the gun area, near the road running through the old plantation. Having just dug the CP, they were tired.

'As night began to fall,' Stan recalled, 'our BK [Captain David Brook] noticed that three others and myself did not have a pit to sleep in, so he ordered us to dig a hole. We were exhausted, but reluctantly picked up the shovels and mattock and dug a hole for the four of us. Thank Christ he did that.'

Another tired artilleryman was Bob Carbury ('Carbs'), the Quartermaster storeman for 102 Battery. Like the others, he had waited, then flown by Chinook with all his Q-store items, which he was still unpacking by moonlight at the end of the day. He threw a tarpaulin over the stores, and went to the Orders Group, where he was told there were infantry in the distant trees, and that the area was safe, having been checked by the Americans. Carbury was one of a machine-gun team consisting of himself, the air despatcher, the medical orderly, the hygiene dutyman (the 'blowfly'), and two armourers. The M60 would be placed pointing down and across the road, to the south-west.

Carbs was sprawled under a tarpaulin, beginning to go to sleep, enjoying the thought that he would not be called for any sort of duty that night, when David Brook came by, and told them all to dig, as he believed something was going on, and they could get mortared. Dig they did, but only shallow scrapes; proper digging could be done tomorrow. Nevertheless Carbury admits that Brook 'saved my life, and a couple of other blokes' lives as well'.

David Brook himself prepared his bedding at the base of one of the spindly trees, cleaned his F1, which had become very dirty as a result of the numerous dust-raising helicopter landings, and waited for the night.

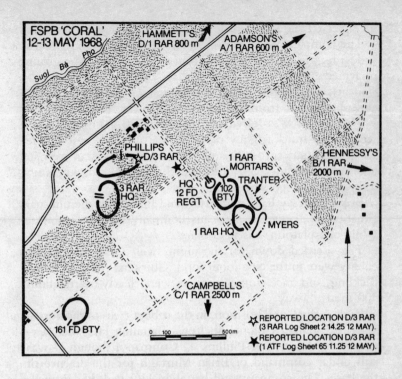

At the top of the map:

FSPB 'CORAL'
12-13 MAY 1968

HAMMETT'S
D/1 RAR 800 m

ADAMSON'S
A/1 RAR 600 m

Suoi Ba Pho

PHILLIPS
A/D/3 RAR

3 RAR HQ

HQ 12 FD REGT

1 RAR MORTARS

102 BTY

TRANTER

HENNESSY'S
B/1 RAR 2000 m

MYERS

1 RAR HQ

CAMPBELL'S
C/1 RAR 2500 m

161 FD BTY

0   100   500m

☆ REPORTED LOCATION D/3 RAR
(3 RAR Log Sheet 2 14.25 12 MAY).

★ REPORTED LOCATION D/3 RAR
(1 ATF Log Sheet 65 11.25 12 MAY).

At last light, John Kearns, Intelligence Section of HQ
1RAR, looked around the Coral position. To the north were
the guns of 102 Field Battery; in the east, in shell scrapes
were the Anti-tank Platoon. North and east of the guns, in
the 'dirty rubber', he presumed was D/3RAR. He knew that
the other rifle companies of 1RAR were away, out of his
sight. He realised, but did not feel alarm, that the position
was incomplete, and that while the guns were dug-in, the
infantry were mainly in shell-scrapes.

Off to the east, Bob Hennessy's B Company was at last
nearing its ambush site—a track junction. It was very nearly
dark when he halted the platoons, told the soldiers to eat
what they could in the way of biscuits or similar, and took his
platoon commanders forward to reconnoitre the actual layout
of the ambush.

So many signs of recent movement had been found that

59

he expected the cross-roads to 'look like Piccadilly Circus'.

The company began to file forward, in the gloom, when suddenly 4 Platoon found itself on a parallel axis to a group of armed enemy, about thirty metres away. The second section instantly swung into an immediate ambush formation, and opened fire from the kneeling or prone position.

The enemy was 'obviously experienced, as his reactions were super-quick'. They dived to the ground, among the waist-high undergrowth, and were gone. It was all over in less than a minute, and in the nearly complete darkness no follow-up was possible.

Bob Hennessy had suddenly found himself in the unusual situation of trying to place his company into an ambush, while one platoon was in contact.

They settled down for the night, well aware that many enemy were in the neighbourhood. Chickens could be heard cackling, and once women's voices were clearly heard, about 300 metres away.

Back at the Coral position, in the rubber trees to the north-west, Lieutenant Colonel Shelton's Battalion HQ was merged with Major Peter Phillips' D Company, though D was still under command of Brian Murtagh for the defence of the base. The company and battalion HQ had dug in well, as both Shelton and his Operations Officer, David Candow, were Korea veterans as well as having experience in Vietnam; they expected enemy reaction during the night.

'David Candow and I said we were going to get hit. We were pretty certain something was going to happen, and kept pressing on people to dig in.

'It wasn't a nice neat battalion perimeter. We had a company-plus over with the New Zealand guns, other companies out in their own little perimeters, ready to go [to AO Manly] when we got the green light, and then we had battalion headquarters tucked in with D Company, who were not under my command. We were just going to fight it out. We just waited.'

Night of 12 May 1968 began.

3 They'll Come Looking For You

for I have dreamt
Of bloody turbulence, and this whole night
Hath nothing been but shapes and forms of slaughter.
Troilus and Cressida *(III. iii.)*

SO THE DISPERSED AUSTRALIANS and New Zealanders settled down for the night. The heat of the day gradually lifted, and the tired infantry and artillerymen, in their sweat-damp greens, tried to sleep or waited until the end of their turn of duty in the forward machinegun positions or headquarters.

Away in the distance were the normal sights and sounds of the deep tropical Vietnamese night: far-away twinkling diamonds as flares ignited over some post or patch of jungle, low rumble of artillery, thin whistle of passing jets high and unseen in the trackless sky, lower down the blinking bright red ruby of helicopters drumming along on some busy-bee task.

To the south, the road convoy from Nui Dat to Coral was spending the night at the US 9th Division camp at Bearcat, and the Aussies were enjoying it. John Goodwin, National Serviceman and radio mechanic in 1RAR, was pleasantly surprised to find that 'when we arrived, it was like driving into a major city. The Yanks had all the mod cons; swimming pools, putt-putt golf, tennis courts, clubs with poker machines and draught beer—whatever you wanted. We enjoyed their hospitality, plenty of beer.

'As a little sideline, I met a Yank sergeant who worked in the morgue of the 9th Division, and he shouted us to pizzas which he kept on trays on a slab in the morgue. A little morbid, but just a thing that happened.'

Away from the lights, poker machines, beer and other amusements, in the darkness around Coral, people watched and waited through the hours.

61

Then reports began to come in to the various headquarters of noises, movement and other signs of enemy nearby. But as there was no defence command post for the position as such, because most of those present were moving away in the morning, there was no central reception point for all these reports.

On an early shift of duty on the M60 machinegun forward of No. 6 gun of 102 Battery, Gunner Greg Ayson heard noises, and reported them to his Gun Sergeant, Max Franklin.

At 1925 Bob Hennessy's B Company reported a contact with an estimated ten enemy, who withdrew to the south; no other results were known.

At 1941 Col Adamson, A Company, reported seeing two red flares which appeared to be answered by others to the north. Adamson had radioed a bantering message to Hammett, informing him of the basic principles of aiming, a light-hearted dig because D Company only had one enemy KIA in the previous contact. It did not please Hammett, but neither did it please battalion headquarters, and Kim Patterson sent a 'terse rocket' about misuse of the radio.

It began to rain, the big drops splattering and then streaming down the dark sky, and some of the Diggers took the opportunity to collect it in their tent shelters.

In the blackness of the D Company ambush position, along the paths through the rubber plantation, Richo Richardson was not enjoying it. 'I was lying there next to this big mound of dirt that was obviously cleared out for making the road. I wasn't actually in the jungle itself. I remember all the mud sliding down off this bloody mound and I was cold and wet.'

Off to the south-west, in the 3RAR mortar position near the New Zealand guns, the rain filled the pits. Some missions had been fired at the request of the rifle companies, and the mortars had to be kept ready for action. Bill Studley, the platoon 2ic, assured himself that this was done, then baled out his pit by using his steel helmet, settled down and went to sleep.

The rain cleared. It was midnight.

At the M60 machinegun position between the artillery HQ

and the mortars, Bombardier Andy Forsdike and his partner, Kershaw, decided they needed a leak, so got up and moved forward several paces, to be greeted by a burst of green tracer flashing from the darkness. They rolled back into the pit, wondering who it could be, and their HQ blamed it on Jensen's mortars. Major Brian Murtagh radioed Jensen, and accused him of firing towards the gunners, but Jensen replied that the Australians used red tracer, and what had streaked towards Murtagh had been green.

A two-man group of enemy had been fired on by the machinegun of 1RAR Mortar Platoon, and some fire was returned, passing over Murtagh's position. In hindsight, this was obviously a reconnaissance. At the time, it was not known if the shooting had killed or wounded the two. Jensen reported by radio to battalion HQ.

Hugh McInally, commanding the mortars, was at the 1RAR CP, but not told until some time later of the event, and was more worried by it than the remainder of the HQ. As a former warrant officer, with Korean War service, he probably realised the implications more readily than the others.

Hammett's earlier feelings of misgiving were reinforced by the sight, in the distance, of 'tracer going off to the north. Greeny sort of tracer going up in the air, and again I had the feeling that all wasn't well'.

Back at Coral, the duty people had also noticed this. John Kearns, Battalion Intelligence Section, was on duty in the CP. At 'about midnight, reports came in from the guns of green and red tracer fired into the air'. Later it was realised that these were markers for the advancing NVA, showing the direction to the Australians.

At about 0145, Forsdike's M60 machinegun crew, out in front of the artillery position, saw a group of shadowy figures crossing the dirt track before them. Still uncertain about what was going on, the young gunners spoke to their artillery CP by field telephone, asking if it was known who was moving.

The CP radioed Tony Jensen, who denied it was any of his men moving about. The dark figures moved to where the burst of fire had come from over an hour before, and stopped. Quiet returned for a few minutes, then loud rustling in the grass again had Forsdike telephoning for permission to fire. All his crew were 'laying dead still'.

Again, caution guided the reply, as the location of friendly troops was not known for certain, and the soldiers on the forward machineguns were known to be young and inexperienced: hold fire.

The night crawled on. There were frequent intermittent contacts with small groups of enemy passing the positions of A and D Companies. These were generally moving to the south-west or south.

Suddenly, at about 0200, in the HQ of D/1RAR, in their triangular ambush position, Hammett heard a burst of fire from the machinegun in 10 Platoon which was facing northeast, up the track, then several simultaneous explosions in 11 Platoon, at once followed by more firing.

But the enemy were gone into the blackness. Artillery and flares were called, but the short conflict was over.

Corporal Boyd had seen movement, fired, and at once several RPG7 rockets had been fired back with devastating effect. 11 Platoon had eleven casualties requiring evacuation. The rockets, seeming to be aimed at machinegun positions, had burst in the trees above them, adding splintered wood to the jagged metal fragments slashing among the prone Diggers.

The platoon was awake, because of the previous movement and activity around them. It was so dark that little could be seen, but as the man next to him began firing after the machinegun opened up, Joe Griffin 'kneeled up, ready to fire, when there was a flash in front of me. I was hit by shrapnel in most of my body. I know I was conscious through most of my ordeal, moaning a lot, and asking when will the medevac be coming.'

In 11 Platoon, Perry Neil had done his turn on watch, and was asleep when the firing began. He began firing, and expended two magazines in a series of short bursts, and rolled slightly to his left to insert the third, when he noticed figures moving out in the darkness, called to warn 'Hobs' on the machinegun that there were enemy to the left, and was about to give a more exact direction, when he saw the flash of 'an RPG, and it scored a tree burst just above Larry Sheppard, hitting all but one of our section'.

Recovering from the blast of the exploding RPG above him, Perry Neil heard the platoon commander, Dick Utting, calling to keep firing, and then someone saying they were all hit over that way. Perry heard himself yelling with the pain of the wounds, then said to himself, 'What are you yelling about?', stopped it, and checked himself for wounds. Both legs and right arm were numb and immovable.

At one blow, the platoon had been reduced by 40 per cent. 4 Section had one KIA and seven WIA, with only Private Thomas being unhurt; 5 Section had one KIA; 6 Section had four WIA.

Richardson, off to the flank, could 'hear this horrific screaming, that went on, and obviously it wasn't the enemy screaming, it was somebody from our platoon, or 11 Platoon, that was making this horrific noise. It went on for about five or six minutes, and I thought, "This is going to put the fear of Christ up my blokes."'

Boyd had tried to fire the Claymore mines, but the wires had been cut. Whether Boyd's firing had upset the enemy preparations for an attack will probably never be known. One enemy was killed, one AK47 captured.

The two fatalities, McNab and Sheppard, were the first suffered by 1RAR on its second tour of duty. Robert McNab had been in the Army only since April 1967, and departed Australia for Vietnam on 27 March.

There was some disagreement among the members of the company as to what caused the explosions, and opinions ranged from RPGs, to 122mm rockets, the Claymores being turned around, to 57mm or 75mm RCLs. However, following their normal tactical arrangement, the NVA would have had RPGs at the head of any group moving to contact, or deploying for assault.

Col Minner told Perry Neil that Bob McNab was dead, hit in the chest, and died almost at once. Perry was given a cigarette, the light shielded by a hutchi, and the extent of his wounds determined: both legs, right arm, side and stomach, plus the base of his penis. He said to 'Hobs', 'Look, that bastard's made me into a hermaphrodite!'

In the shambles, in the darkness, the splintered trees, the dead and dying all around, Joe Griffin was impressed by 'the medic, Private Ted Wardle, who did a great job with our section. I remember him asking me to hold a pad on Sheppard's head wound, while he worked on other wounds from which he later died. Ted Wardle told me later that he killed a death adder about a foot away from me.'

Thinking about it later, Griffin felt that the NVA had not been far away throughout the night, and obviously knew where the Aussies were. Quite possibly, the small party in the previous contact had not gone far, and over the hours may have built up a picture of the platoon and company positions, or even gone to bring back to the scene a couple of RPG gunners, who were simply to aim at the centre of the estimated Australian position. Movement had been heard, and figures seen moving around the ambush.

Perry Neil also was impressed by the calmness of all concerned, after the initial short period of confusion following the impact of the volley of RPGs. He remembered that his M16 was still loaded and cocked, and asked someone to unload it, as he could not do so himself.

Back at Coral, 102 Battery had been called to action, firing in support of Hammett's men. Nos. 4, 5 and 6 guns had been swung around from the east to the north for this fire mission, a move which was to have drastic consequences on the night's events. During the daylight hours, when they had been observed by the NVA reconnaissance teams, the guns had been pointing east, and an attack from the north would have been perfectly aimed to hit them in the flank. But up to now, for most of the Australians, the firing and explosions were just an interruption to the night's sleep.

In the artillery regimental HQ, Arthur Penn and his newly arrived group of gunners were taking turns, with the other staff, on the CP radio and out at the listening post, a position along a drain behind the CP. By this time, he and Gunner Major were resting between shifts in their shell scrapes some twenty metres from the CP.

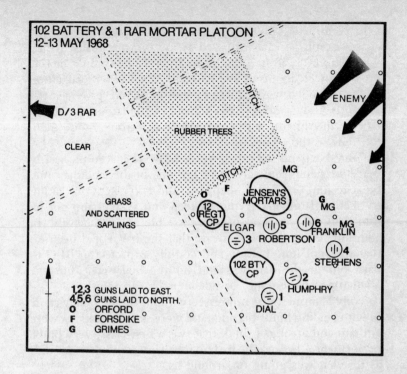

102 BATTERY & 1 RAR MORTAR PLATOON
12-13 MAY 1968

ENEMY

D/3 RAR

RUBBER TREES

CLEAR

DITCH

DITCH

MG

GRASS
AND SCATTERED
SAPLINGS

O   F

JENSEN'S
MORTARS

G
MG

12
REGT
CP

ELGAR

5

6
FRANKLIN

MG

3
ROBERTSON

4
STEPHENS

102 BTY
CP

2
HUMPHRY

1,2,3 GUNS LAID TO EAST.
4,5,6 GUNS LAID TO NORTH.
O   ORFORD
F   FORSDIKE
G   GRIMES

1
DIAL

Battery Captain David Brook was in bed, under his mosquito net, at the base of a spindly tree. Ian Ahearn, Gun Position Officer, also was in bed, in his shell scrape, under his hutchi.

Matt Cleland, commanding the 102 Battery Section comprising Nos. 4, 5 and 6 guns, was talking to Sergeant Max Franklin, commander of No. 6 gun. Around them, the work of cleaning up after a fire mission and preparing for the next went on: removing the packing and expended cases, opening and preparing new shells.

Bombardier Larry Darcy, No. 5 gun, was recording the expenditure and type of rounds fired.

In his four-man sleeping pit near the 102 Battery CP, Stan Carbines, tired from the work of building the CP and the pit, tried to go back to sleep, knowing that he was not required for CP duty that night.

In Hammett's ambush position, quiet returned, and the enemy seemed to have moved away. No one realised they were detouring around the location, en route to their target, the unprotected guns of 102 Battery. A helicopter evacuation of the wounded was requested, and the RAAF provided the Dustoff. An LZ was selected in front of 10 Platoon, and Captain Brian Altham, with Corporal Mick Strong, stood there to guide in the Hueys.

Perry Neil and the other wounded were placed on hastily made stretchers and carried to the side of the landing zone. Next to him was Larry Sheppard, and Perry kept on talking to Sheppard, quietly trying to keep him awake, and not let him drift off into unconsciousness. He got no answer. In addition, Perry was well aware that the NVA had been on that spot not long before, and he fully expected an RPG to flash out of the darkness and hit the helicopter, but the Vietnamese were gone, or not intending to interfere.

Tony Hammett was impressed with the flying. 'They came in with landing lights blazing, and were sitting ducks, as were Altham and Strong. I think that was a first-class, very brave performance, because he had no idea, any more than we did, as to what was going on around us.'

At 0308, Hammett sent details of the action; at 0310, he reported the Dustoff helicopter on the ground in his location; at 0312, that it had departed. Only the living were taken; the dead remained for a later flight.

As the Dustoff was completed without major problems, the gunships were circling prior to departing, talking by radio to the 1RAR CP, who thanked them for the assistance, and the helicopters turned away to their base, still talking to the Australians. The sound of their rotors faded away in the heavy soft tropical night.

Quiet returned to Coral.

For Perry Neil and the others, there was the rapid flight to the US 24th Evacuation Hospital, initial treatment and then operations, from which they awoke next day in hospital wards. 'We were treated like kings, because we were Australians. They thought we were great; couldn't get over our accent. All they wanted to do was talk all the time.'

At 0340, Hennessy's B Company reported a contact, with no detail. The NVA were by-passing them, en route to Coral.

In the gun positions of 102 Battery, Neil Lloyd-Jones, normally a battery surveyor, but 'having a break on the guns', began to prepare to take his turn on the M60 machine-gun, out to the front of the guns. He had about fifteen minutes before he was due to go, so lit up a cigarette, 'to enjoy the delights of a Marlboro in the tropics'. Later he was told the M60 crew was also enjoying a smoke at the same time, with a blanket draped over their heads.

However, Mick Grimes did not smoke. He and Schwarze were carefully deepening the machinegun pit. Like everyone else, they had spent a hectic day, closing down one position, moving and setting up another, with fire missions included, and the machinegun position had not had much work done on it by darkness.

Captain Mick Bindley, both Signals Officer and commander Support Company 1RAR, did a final check of the communications between the comms centre and the Anti-armour, Pioneer and Mortar Platoons, satisfied himself that the sentries there were alert, and went to his shell-scrape, which was not very deep because of the small amount of time he had been able to spare from his many duties. Sleep came easily; it had been a tiring day and he had just done a tour of duty in the battalion CP.

Captain Phil Davies, Adjutant and Assistant Operations Officer, began to think of going to his scrape to try and get some sleep. He got up out of the 1RAR CP and walked over to the shallow pit, next to where his batman was already asleep.

Lieutenant Colonel Bennett had been receiving the reports of movement and activity outside the position, but in the darkness it was impossible to do anything. He recalled that 'the frequency with which they were being reported started to concern me. It was a matter of trying to determine whether it was simply a sense of foreboding which was occurring amongst the platoons, and therefore perhaps imagining or thinking they were hearing things, or whether there was something about. There had been no reports at all from 3RAR Group, who were sitting astride an alley which one would have thought the enemy might use.'

3RAR were deployed in a roughly north-south line of company positions to the west, closer to Saigon, the direction from which it was thought and expected that the withdrawing enemy would appear.

If, since beginning this current tour of duty in Vietnam, 1RAR had undergone more serious enemy probing, harassment or reconnaissance, the reports from the forward positions would probably have been received with less scepticism. But the battalion had not had that experience.

In Jensen's mortar position, Corporal Bob Hickey, whose first tour in Vietnam had been with a rifle company of 1RAR in 1965–6, came back to Jensen and told him that he could hear 'about 400 noggies gibbering fifty metres away'.

Jensen went to the shallow scrapes of the mortar CP, and the soldier on duty there at the radio went around the position waking everyone. Jensen collapsed the small tent over the CP, and tried to convince Kim Patterson, at the battalion CP, of the large number of enemy nearby. Patterson was sceptical. It was 0405 hours.

Andy Forsdike and his M60 team from HQ 12 Field Regiment, out to the left of the artillery position, were still trying to see into the darkness, to identify who or what was out there in the night.

Then, in young Forsdike's words, 'everyone froze as a green flare followed by a red flare went high into the sky and all hell broke loose. The enemy who had crawled in stood up, not realising they were so close to us. Then everyone, including the NVA, went to ground as a heavy barrage of mortars and rockets came into the gun position.'

Bob Lowry, Duty Officer in the 102 Battery CP, heard the rockets whishing overhead, and his first thought was, 'Aw hell, rockets!' Then he ordered stand-to.

Further left of Forsdike, in the pit on the edge of the irrigation ditch, Ginger Orford woke to find himself alone; Vic Page had gone to do a turn on the machinegun. Orford could hear people coming quickly down the ditch, and decided it was time the shallow listening post was left, and he would be better off back in the main position. He walked rapidly—'I didn't run'—back to the pits, and told a warrant officer that there were many enemy coming, and was ordered in tones of disbelief to 'settle down'. Ginger thought, 'You'll settle down when you see what's coming!'

Around to the right, in their own machinegun position, Mick Grimes and Schwarze ducked as the bright tails of the rockets flashed overhead; the bright explosions dazzled them; then sixty to 100 metres away, in front, Grimes saw 'a couple of lines of figures moving forward, they seemed to just appear, to stand up from nowhere. I could hear them talking, being rallied by officers, I heard a bugle ... it reminded me of a US Marine movie of the war in Korea, with hordes of Chinese attacking with bugles blowing. There were lots of green tracer.'

Woken in his shell scrape, Ian Ahearn, 102 Battery Gun Position Officer, saw what he thought were green flares, then realised they were green tracer rounds, heard the noise of rockets and explosions, leaped up and ran to the CP. There he found 'bedlam', with RPGs striking the gun position, communications to the guns disrupted, but a message was received from Sergeant John Stephens, No. 4 Gun, that an assault wave was to his front; he requested permission to fire small arms; it was given.

Ahearn thought Bob Lowry was coping well, asked if he was OK and was assured he was, then said he was going out to the guns. Lowry was 'illogically concerned' because Ahearn was not wearing a shirt, so took off his own and gave it to him.

Being inside the CP severely restricted vision, and it was hard to know what was really happening outside. Bob Lowry posted one of the CP staff with a pistol to watch the door, but gave a stern explicit warning what would be done with the pistol and a part of the gunner's anatomy if he shot any of their own people.

At No. 6 gun, Matt Cleland heard a yell from Grimes and Schwarze, with the M60 out in the darkness, looked over the earth bund in that direction, and 'saw them, lined up across the battery, some fifty metres out. At this stage, all I had was my pistol, so I emptied it over the side of the bund.'

Mick Grimes opened fire, sweeping along the line of figures, seeing some fall, but the gaps instantly filled by others, then the links in the machinegun belt jammed it, and he completed 'the fastest IA [Immediate Action] ever done. By now they were close, fifteen metres away, and we were under small arms fire. How we were not peppered is beyond me.'

Then Max Franklin called the two men in. With RPGs roaring overhead, among the green tracer, yelling NVA at their heels, Grimes and Schwarze began the race back to the dirt bund around the gun. Carrying the gun and what ammunition remained, 'moving by instinct, as they seemed to be all around us', Grimes was hit in the hand. 'There was a sharp pain, and I did not realise what had happened until I did not have the use of my hand, the index finger was shot off. In the half-light, my hand looked like uncooked hamburger.' The machinegun had fallen to the ground.

In the gun position, Neil Lloyd-Jones' enjoyment of his Marlboro was disrupted, his 'first reaction being that someone was firing sort of crackers at us, one of them hit the ammo area of the gun next to us, there was a fire there, the biggest pressure was to get it out. But you could hear this noise, and suddenly these things, these RPGs, were flying everywhere. We were still sort of in a state of shock.

'Everything seemed to happen at once, and next thing we knew people were running around like chooks with no heads.'

At No. 6 gun, Matt Cleland had emptied his pistol at the NVA, turned to Sergeant Max Franklin and told him he was going to get his F1 submachinegun, then ran the thirty or so metres to his scrape, picked up the weapon, ran to tell Ian Ahearn, in the CP, what was happening, and ran on back to No. 6 gun.

But as he was passing No. 5, Franklin grabbed him, saying, 'There's no one there any more.' The NVA had forced the gun crew out, and all were along the back edge of No. 5

gun. Between them and the enemy was that gun and a dirt wall.

Franklin had taken the time to remove the firing mechanism from the gun, rendering it useless to the NVA.

As the NVA reached the bund around No. 6 gun, they would crouch or lay on the outer face, reach up with an AK47, and spray a magazine blindly around the interior, then shower the other side with grenades, many of which did not go off, and remained next morning. The 102 Battery supply of grenades was held centrally, to regimental orders, and not on issue to individuals; the gunners could not reply with their own grenades.

Some NVA ran around the bund, into the living area of the crew, and ransacked the belongings. From further back, some of them were seen, but not fired on, as it was not known for sure they were enemy or Australians. Later it was found that grenade booby-traps had been set among the sleeping areas, and also that one NVA had thoughtfully collected all the ration-pack chocolate he could find.

One of the items stolen was Mick Grimes' pack. Some days later, patrolling to the east, Bob Hennessy's B/1RAR would find it again. Later still, a dead NVA would be found wearing some of Grimes' jungle-greens.

Grimes and Schwarze had safely made their way behind the bund, Grimes somehow making his way to his personal pit, where he picked up his own rifle, as the machinegun was now back there somewhere, with the yelling NVA. He was sent back to the CP, blood streaming from his hand.

Greg Ayson had carried the M60 on the move-in to Coral, and it was now outside the bund, so he was unarmed, and he was 'crawling around the pit armed with a machete'. Later he took Mick Grimes' rifle.

David Brook, 102's Battery Captain, was woken by the mortars, then an RPG detonated in the tree above him, but without harming him. He picked up his F1 and tried to cock it, but 'it made a funny sound'. When cleaning it thoroughly the previous evening, he had not rescrewed the barrel correctly and the barrel now also obeyed Murphy's Law and fell out!

He ran to the battery CP just as Mick Grimes was brought in. The wound was dressed, and Grimes was given medication, then a pistol, and told to 'shoot anyone he didn't know' who tried to get into the CP. The medication affected his eyes, and later people found a pistol waving in their face as he tried to carry out his duty.

Arthur Penn, Surveyor Sergeant, with the three young gunners in shell scrapes behind the regimental CP, could feel the ground shaking as the mortars exploded close by, and 'couldn't guess the number of rockets that went over our heads. We kept fairly low, Gunner Major and I, initially'.

Then they could hear clearly 'the chatter, the talking, the yelling of the North Vietnamese. I had done a three-week Vietnamese course before I went to Vietnam, and that night I wished I had my instructor with me, because I didn't know what they were saying, but did know they were coming in great numbers and were close!'

Bob Carbury, who had slept soundly through the normal noise of the guns firing in support of Tony Hammett, was wakened by 'a funny sound roaring overhead, like somebody letting off skyrockets, and I stuck my head up for a look. Ed, the air despatcher next to me, said to get down, that they were rockets.'

One went through the Q-store tent, and a shower of mortars followed. His stores were riddled with shrapnel. Under the noise of weapons and explosions, Carbs and those with him could hear the Vietnamese shouting as they attacked.

At the adjacent 1RAR mortar position, RPGs had splattered around the pits, and small arms fire was aimed at the sound of Tony Jensen's voice whenever he raised it to call to the mortar crews. Looking to the east, he could see many shadowy figures assaulting.

His radio operator, Jack Parr, could see the enemy 'silhouetted as they came up the rise towards us, very close together, almost shoulder to shoulder. They were making lots of noise, and were very close, about fifty metres away. They must have crept in very close, until they could see the perimeter position. The probing patrol must have indicated where we were.'

Parr manned the battalion mortar radio net, and began reporting on it, leaving the shooting to the mortar crewmen.

The assaulting waves of NVA were so close that the mortars could not easily fire on them, and then they were so close that only small arms could be used. Corporal Jock Whitton had asked permission to fire the mortars almost straight up, but the NVA came on too fast. Jensen told his men to hold their ground, as there was nowhere else to go except back to the artillery positions of 102 Battery, and in addition there were the mortars and a large amount of ammunition which was not going to be abandoned to the Vietnamese.

South of Jensen, in the 1RAR HQ, John Kearns saw the first salvoes of RPG rockets burst in the air, but then they dropped and reports came in of rockets bursting in the areas of neighbouring units.

Phil Davies, at his scrape near the 1RAR CP, had just taken off his webbing equipment, but not even sat down. He heard the mortar primaries, waited and heard the bombs explode near the artillery position, turned and ran back to the battalion CP.

Too late. In the few seconds since the primaries sounded, everyone else who had a duty reason to be there was already inside, and he stood looking down at a 'seething mass of bodies'. Lieutenant Colonel Bennett looked up and asked him what he was 'doing up there', to which Davies replied that his duty position was manning the rear link radio to 1ATF.

Bennett stated the obvious—'there's no room for you here', and Davies returned to his pit, waiting to be called if needed. There he sat with his batman, spending a 'useless night', taking in the sights and sounds, entirely uninformed of events, passing the time by discussing a wide range of subjects, their only visitor the CSM Support Company, Warrant Officer Don Watts, who periodically walked over 'to check if you're all right, sir'.

In a pit about five metres from the CP was Graham Dawes, a National Serviceman, who acted as batman for Lieutenant Colonel Bennett and Major Kim Patterson. Unable to see the enemy, but watching for them, Dawes also spent the night observing the flashes and explosions, listening to the conversations in the CP and the radio voices.

Mick Bindley, sleeping after his long day arranging the fly-in and siting the battalion HQ position, awakened to the sound of mortars, and his first fleeting thought was that it was his own, then realised it was the enemy. As he had in Borneo when mortared by the Indonesians during Confrontation, he asked himself if he was afraid, knew he was not, then rolled over to look out of his shell scrape, leaned on his right arm, and realised that while he might not be scared, his trembling right arm was the 'scaredest in Vietnam at that particular time'.

Bindley leaped up and quickly ran to the comms centre, from where he would control the defensive battle for the battalion HQ.

Quickly, Kim Patterson, in the 1RAR CP, called the gunships which had recently left the area, hoping they had not changed frequency, or were now engaged on another task. To his delight, they answered, and he told them of the attack. The pilots banked back to the north, preparing for action.

Andy Forsdike's small group of young artillerymen from regimental HQ was overwhelmed by a mass of Vietnamese, who seemed to be talking and shouting, with one voice in particular noticeable to the Aussies, who assumed it was someone giving orders. Then, as Vic Page called out that the M60 was jammed, Andy said they would swap pits, and they did so. Forsdike and Mal Hundt found they could not clear the gun, could not even cock it to begin the procedures.

But the NVA had got in behind them, and Forsdike heard a grenade explode to his rear, and a grunt from Page. Andy called to him, Page said he had been hit in the back but was OK, and they continued with the stubborn M60. Mal Hundt fired the M79, but his on-the-job training ended when the three rounds were expended, just as he had figured out how to use it.

He said to Andy that he was shaking, and Forsdike replied, 'Bloody oath, I've never been so scared.'

The NVA were swarming past, shooting at the mortars and gun position. One fired pointblank into a pit, instantly killing Gunner Sawtell. Forsdike thought two men behind them would take care of the enemy going past his small group, but unknown to him, one of the two men had been hit and the other was helping the wounded man back to the aid post. He was there in the midst of chaos, with two men, one of them wounded, and one other dead, with no communication, as the phone had been hit. All around were NVA, exploding RPGs, flying tracer, shouts and cries in a foreign language ...

The gun crews of 102 Battery were responding to a situation they had never encountered before. Sergeant John Stephen's, No. 4 gun, called for small arms ammunition, then for permission to fire his anti-personnel splintex rounds. Each gun had a normal complement of six of these rounds, which contained a mass of 7200 arrow-shaped darts. Permission was given, and the rounds were slammed into the cannon breeches, the gun muzzles horizontal.

The battery had not fired this type of round often. The fuse was set at .05 second, and the first rounds seemed not to function, so the setting was changed to muzzle-burst, and then the attacking waves were seen to be devastated. Later it was found the shells on .05 in fact had flown past the assault waves, exploding in the faces of the next wave of enemy who were forming-up to attack, some 400 metres away.

Ian Ahearn, in the battery position, recalls 'all was now bedlam', and he got the Battery Guide, Warrant Officer Les Wheeler, to organise ammunition resupply to Stephens' gun.

A rocket hit had flattened the tyres and damaged the trail of No. 2 gun, and its ammunition was being taken to Stephens' position. Geoff Grimish was carrying a round to the gun from his own position, and distinctly saw an NVA jump up on to the bund and aim an RPG, but ignored him, buoyed up with 'a feeling of invincibility', and a split second later the NVA was gone: he had been standing directly in front of the cannon muzzle as it fired.

The Vietnamese probably also was carried along on a wave of 'invincibility', having come down the jungle trails from the north, constantly lectured by the political officers, been told that he was at last in the South, that he was at last going into the attack, and he may have been one of those who had publicly vowed at the final morale-raising meeting to penetrate into the heart of the enemy position. He probably felt triumphant as he climbed the dirt bund, aimed his RPG . . .

One mortar crew-member had fired his magazine at the on-rushing enemy, then ran back to the nearby artillery position, was hit and dropped his empty rifle while crossing the bund. Later 1RAR recovered it.

Two of the mortar platoon members made it back to No. 5 gun position, remaining there until morning.

Comfortably asleep in the four-man pit dug near the 102 Battery CP, Stan Carbines had woken to 'rockets and mortars going overhead and small arms firing. It was like a fireworks display. We sat up and tried to find our rifles in the dark. The machinegun was quickly placed in position pointing across the road. Our hole was about five metres from the ammunition bay of No. 1 gun.'

An RPG rocket arced over the position, exploding on the ammunition bay of No. 1 gun. The tarpaulin and contents flashed into flames, and the ammunition itself began to burn. Only metres away were young Carbines and his three mates in the pit they had reluctantly dug. Now they valued its depth, realising that they would have taken some of the blast if they had been sleeping above ground.

But the fire gave Carbines and his friends 'a big decision. Should we stay and protect the rear of the CP, or get away from the burning ammunition? We stayed.

'We did not know at the time, but the Gun Sergeant [Ray Dial] had taken his crew further down the road away from us. Fortunately none of the high-explosive rounds went off, but we heard an occasional fizz as they burned.'

So there they stayed, among the tracer, rockets, flares and noise, four young Aussies, in danger of exploding ammunition, with the guns under attack, conscious of their importance to the CP if assaults should come from across the road, and despite no further orders, determined to hold their position and fight. They received no acclaim, and expected none, but give a tiny example of young soldiers, down through the ages, holding their position among confusion and uncertainty.

Many people ran to try to put out the fire, and when that was soon seen to be impossible, to carry away the ammunition. David Brook burned his hands doing it, and in the firelight saw the ground flicking and spraying as bullets hit around them. Later, he found that his shirt had been pierced by a bullet which slightly grazed him, unnoticed in the hectic activity. Brook was experiencing a feeling of 'fearlessness and exhilaration', the first time he had known it, and only later realised how dangerous the night had been.

The brilliant fire provided an obvious reference point for the circling helicopters, who could be directed on to targets in the darkness at a distance and direction from the flames.

The Light Fire Team (LFT) was trying to distinguish friendly and enemy forces in the confusing, ever-changing pattern of darkness and multitude of flashes and coloured light below them. In their circling they were passing close to the distant New Zealand guns, where John Dellaca and his Listening Post team were watching and listening. 'The gunships had not fired, but all of a sudden as they zoomed over us lines of tracer squirted up at them from the ground. I remember thinking how stupid that was. Just like provoking a pair of angry dogs. As the tracer would go up, they'd pounce. From that point, the helicopters went into action.'

Over on the far side of the grassy expanse from John, in his pit by the 102 Battery Q-store, tent riddled with shrapnel, Bob Carbury saw the gunships 'come in across the clearing, let rockets and guns rip, they had the place lit up, and you could see the Vietnamese caught in the middle. They were hammering them from all directions.'

To the right, or south-east of the guns, was Les Tranter's Anti-tank Platoon, with its 90mm RCLs. Tranter had been woken by the noise of the attack, and seconds later his radio operator, John Swan, arrived, so excited he lapsed into his native Gaelic, which Les could not understand. The Diggers were already standing-to, and Tranter reminded them to fire only at known targets. There was to be no blazing away into the night.

Some enemy came close and were fired on with the 9mm pistols. Tranter was mindful of his ammunition supply— only eight rounds for each of the two 90mm RCLs—and telephoned battalion HQ to suggest use of them if the CO, Lieutenant Colonel Bennett, agreed. Permission was given to engage opportunity targets.

Tranter went to the left-hand gun, manned by Corporal Doug Dupille and Private Terry Rich, and passed this on. Dupille said he could see enemy to the front of the artillery and mortars, then Tranter was impressed to hear Dupille and Rich going through their firing drill, reciting the orders aloud, down to 'Firing now', and the round crashed out.

Dupille had aimed at what he thought was an enemy mortar position.

Almost at once, RPGs and machineguns fired back, and while prone under this hail, Les asked if they had heard the round explode. No one had, and they despondently thought it had gone high, not realising that the range was so short that the detonation had followed so close on the thunder of the firing that they had not heard it.

Les was moving around his platoon, but was steadily fired at, with red and green tracer flicking past. Then the battalion CP rang to ask who was moving, as the bullets were going over the CP.

During the action, ignoring the flying bullets, rockets and assorted lumps of metal whizzing by, Sergeant Terry Schmidt calmly walked around the Anti-armour Platoon pits, with two jerrycans of water, asking if everyone was all right, if they needed water ... Years later this image of him would remain strong with many of the Diggers, and their normal respect for him as an NCO was greatly increased from that night onward.

More 90mm and some small arms was fired at enemy movement detected to the front, and at an attempt to push around to the right. Tranter was confident the firepower of his platoon could cope with any probe in his direction. They could see, now and again, in the distance against the sky and treeline, faint silhouettes, but no targets worth engaging.

It was obvious the main action was over on their left, and they continued to fire across the front of the guns and mortar position. In his after-action report, Tranter included the statement that the M16s worked well, with no stoppages.

In the 1RAR mortar position, after the first wave of NVA had passed, Tony Jensen saw 'a mass of enemy doing fire and movement across the position', and heard voices calling what he presumed to be orders, as often words would be followed by small arms or RPG fire. Many of the battalion had brought packs they preferred over the issued Army version, and Jensen was a little annoyed later to find that his pack, in his recently abandoned sleeping pit, had received a direct hit from an RPG. The NVA were systematically firing at each pit, tent or sign of occupation.

Some of the wounded mortar crews arrived at Jensen's position, and he told them to get into his own sleeping scrape, which had already been hit by an RPG. A short distance away, among the pits, Jock Whitton was hit, and Graham Stevens tried to drag him into a pit, but an RPG impacted next to them, killing Whitton and wounding Stevens.

The NVA swept through the 1RAR mortar position, across the open ground to 102 Battery, then some returned to the mortars.

It seemed to Jensen that the NVA appeared surprised to find the mortars. There was a lot of what he thought was excited talk when the NVA realised what they had come upon, and clanking noises as they tried unsuccessfully to dismantle them, then again unsuccessfully to fire them on the 102 Battery position. No one seemed to know what to do. There was no one in charge of either dismantling them, carrying them and the ammunition away, or of using them correctly. Any attack planned from a good reconnaissance would presumably have included attention to the prize of the available mortars.

Jensen was looking around the side of the dirt spoil, when he sensed another human presence, and looked up, to see, calmly gazing at him over the mound, 'a face, there, looking down at me. I just froze—my M16 was pointing in the wrong direction—he was a big bareheaded man in khaki, wearing a Vietnamese belt and a holstered pistol, hands behind his back, peering down at me. He just strolled away, but did not get far. I shot him. We found his body next day.

'I thought at the time, from his manner, that he was a Political Commissar. He had papers and a note-book, and also a brand-new Russian pistol, still wrapped in its greasy paper.'

Almost immediately after, dirt sprayed over Jensen as a burst of machinegun fire hit near him, then a grenade thumped on to the outer face of the spoil, rolled to the edge of the pit and exploded as Jensen squashed himself against the dirt wall of the pit, below it. Quickly he swung his M16 in that direction and fired. Sand and grit had affected his M16, and he had to cock it between shots.

Simultaneously, Jack Parr, manning the mortar command net, had noticed the same NVA light machinegun team with an RPD. They seemed to be coming towards him and Jensen, so firing across Jensen's body, Parr too shot at the three-man team. His M16 also would only fire single shots. In retrospect, Parr thought this was good, as it stopped him wasting ammunition with bursts of automatic fire.

Nothing else came from that way, and next morning three bodies were found there.

Other enemy were passing so close that Parr regretted the lack of handgrenades, as he could have used at least a box of them, despite the problem of not being sure exactly who everyone out there was.

All through this, the guns of 102 Battery nearby were firing, the enemy were firing, and flares were popping to life in the sky. The gunships were making their dives, rockets flaring and zipping ahead, glowing red tracer streaming down, the chopping sound of rotors mixing with the noise of battle on the ground: the threnody of Vietnam.

As the 1RAR mortars could not operate, Parr contacted 3RAR, who came on to the 1RAR mortar net, and gave 'guesstimates' of range and bearing to the enemy mortar baseplate positions, checked them with Tony Jensen, then corrected the resulting 3RAR fire as best he could. When he could hear the NVA mortars begin again in different locations, Jack was able to bring the 3RAR mortars on to them.

In his mortar position near the distant New Zealand guns, Bill Studley had been awakened by the sound of the NVA mortar primaries as they began the attack on Coral, and before he was fully awake had realised what was happening. As the battle progressed, he was relieved that the enemy attacked from the direction they had, and not through the location held by the New Zealanders and his men, as they would have been able to flood them with weight of numbers.

Another weapon called in to support the Australians was the venerable C47 transport, which had been armed with miniguns and flares, and called 'Snoopy', 'Spooky' or 'Puff the Magic Dragon' (shortened to 'Puff'). These produced one of the more memorable sights of the Vietnamese night sky. Armed with two or three miniguns, they poured a river of tracer fire on to their targets. One minigun alone, at a range of 1500 metres, in a four-second burst will place 400 bullets into a circle of ten metres diameter.

As well as the 3RAR mortars, Parr was also talking to the pilot of a Spooky circling above. The pilot was firing very close to the defenders, and Parr was 'looking up at it, coming straight at us, the tracer was just like rain, a rain of tracer from the plane, and it seemed to be coming into our position but at the last minute seemed to curve away, so he was laying down some close fire support there.

'The miniguns on the plane made a terrible tearing sound, rather awesome if you were enemy and you heard that. It was tremendous, just listening to that, and getting that fire support, it was so encouraging.'

But as the hail of fire from the miniguns swept across the ground and began to get closer to his position, Andy Forsdike realised that no one knew they were still there, with the M60 outside the artillery area. The only information he had since the beginning of the fighting was gained from listening to the loudspeakers in the gun position. He was very conscious of the shallowness of the scrapes as compared to the deeper pits behind him. When the edge of the bullet hail began to hit close by, he decided to move his small group back.

He later thought it the 'biggest mistake I could have made'. They got up to go back, and at once the tall Hundt was noticeable. NVA nearby fired, and hit him in the right wrist, spinning him around. He grabbed the wound and kept on moving, then bent over and was hit again in the stomach.

But this time his wounds came from Australians, who had called out, but heard no answer in the uproar, and fired. Mal fell, and crawled along to the right of the regimental artillery HQ CP, when a fellow gunner recognised him, said he would help, grabbed Hundt's webbing to pull him into the pit, and managed to shoot him in the right thigh with his M16. Mal felt no pain from this wound, but could feel the hot blood running down his leg. His troubles were not over.

Then Forsdike was fired at from three metres range by NVA, who hit and killed Gunner Ian Scott instantly. Forsdike and Gunner Hood—who had joined them—fired back, hitting two NVA, and the third got away in the darkness.

After checking Scott, Forsdike and Hood stayed where they were, not daring to move as the NVA began to move back past them. Forsdike estimated at least twenty passed over them, and Hood fired once, two rounds, drawing a burst of retaliatory fire which missed.

Then a mortar round burst nearby, stunning both men. When near dawn, Forsdike came back to consciousness, and crawled back to the gun position, calling out as he came close. His arrival surprised everyone, as all survivors were thought to be back in the position.

This was probably fire called in by Jack Parr, 1RAR mortars, who had been adjusting fire across the open area between his position and the guns, on to the enemy who were gathering and reorganising in that space.

Meanwhile, Mal Hundt had been laying on the ground, waiting for the ammunition bay to explode, with the index finger of his good hand pushed into his left ear, his right pressed into the dirt, waiting and wishing for a Dustoff. His troubles still were not over.

As the action intensified, activity in the 1RAR CP became more hectic. Present were the CO, the Ops Officer, the IO, two radio operators and two members of the Intelligence Section. The radio operators were continually passing the handsets to the officers, while trying to record the messages; the Intelligence Dutymen were marking the positions of the enemy on the map, and, with the IO, trying to determine the VC/NVA locations by marking the reported crossbearings—compass bearings from the Australian positions to the enemy —and time of flight of the RPG rockets.

When it had become obvious that a large enemy ground force was to the front of the mortars, artillery and antitank positions, the Intelligence Dutymen in the 1RAR CP were told to take their weapons to the entrance, use it as a weapon pit, and protect the CP. John Kearns did so, looking out at the hail of small arms and rockets flying overhead. He could see the initial flare as the rocket was launched, then the flame as the motor ignited ahead of the launcher, and finally the explosion as it impacted.

At the 102 Battery CP, Ian Ahearn organised a ready reaction force to be used to counter-attack any penetration of the gun position made by the NVA, and tried to work out a plan for retaking No. 6 gun, believed held by the enemy.

Ahearn received no orders over the defence net—mortar hits early in the attack damaged the regimental HQ radio antennas—so 'as far as I could see, we were on our own'. His own regimental-net radio was destroyed, but on the battery-net radio he was able to maintain contact with the battery commander (Gavin Andrews, with 1RAR HQ) and the 1RAR rifle companies.

John Stephen's No. 4 gun was firing over open sights, and when the splintex rounds were gone, they used high-explosive. Sergeant Robertson's No. 5 gun was ordered to cover No. 6 gun, and if the enemy tried to take it away, to destroy it.

At one stage, David Brook was acting as No. 3 on the gun, and as a round hit a tree out there among the enemy, distinctly saw, in the flash of detonation, arms and legs flying.

No. 5 gun was raked by machinegun fire, later found to be from the M60 dropped by the wounded Mick Grimes. Grenades and M79 rounds silenced the NVA crew. Sergeant Skeeter Humphry's No. 2 gun was hit by an RPG, which damaged the trails and flattened the tyres. When the gun had to be man-handled around, this caused some difficulty, but the crew succeeded.

All orders to the guns were relayed by voice. Matt Cleland took up position half-way and shouted to Nos. 4 and 5 guns. Nos 1, 2 and 3 guns were used to answer calls from the rifle companies; 4 gun was firing at the enemy, 5 was ready to engage the enemy in 6, which was left to them until the situation improved.

Ammunition to the gun positions was taken by members of the battery, including Bombardier Riley, the Transport NCO, who drove his Land Rover back and forth, despite enemy fire, in what Ian Ahearn described as 'a cool, calm manner'.

At one time, Matt Cleland looked across and saw, in the flare light, some thirty enemy about 200 metres away. He called for the machinegun, but when it was brought up it failed to fire. Later it was found that cleaning had been done to a greater degree than required, and a gas plug not normally touched had been replaced the wrong way, rendering the weapon useless.

Ian Ahearn's problems with radio communications were only part of those afflicting the battle. Because of damage to radios and characteristics of types of aerials, Captain Peter Desmond, GSO3 (Operations) at Nui Dat, far away in Phuoc Tuy Province, found himself relaying fire orders and co-ordinating artillery support for Coral from the neighbouring allied artillery units. Every gun in range was firing. At one time an estimated forty-four batteries of artillery was on call.

Meanwhile, in his shell scrape behind the artillery regimental CP, Arthur Penn decided to go and check on two of his Gunners, Robinson and Gow, who had been in position at the listening post, further along the drain. He stepped down into the drain and began to walk along it, a flare went off, and

'I recall seeing flashes in front of me, feeling the weapon kick in my hands, and a smacking or hitting sensation around my mouth, the lip and nose area.

'Realising I'd been shot at, I rolled back, over the lip of the drain, into the weapon pit where Gunner Major was. Just at that time, somebody yelled "Grenade". I looked up and saw a stick grenade coming towards us. I was just at the side of the weapon pit. The grenade appeared to land on Gunner Major—whether it did or not, I don't really know—and I made a feeble attempt to reach him, but he had got out of the pit, did a push-up, so to speak, from the pit into the drain.

'Unfortunately, I must have been half over the pit (reaching for Major) when the grenade went off, because I got concussed, my right hand immediately started to ache, and I felt I had been hit in the chest. I took stock of things, heard a few more shots and waited for the worst to happen.'

Penn later found out what had happened: Gunners Robinson and Gow had seen the two North Vietnamese, begun to shoot at them, saw them throw the grenade and yelled a warning, then Robinson had shot both. He and Gow went back to see what had happened to Penn and Major.

Arthur Penn's own weapon had been damaged, taking the force of the bullets which were aimed at him, and Major's was damaged by the grenade. Penn went to his pit and got the M79 grenade launcher there, and the four of them huddled in position, looking and listening, hearing the voices of their own friends behind and the NVA further out on the sides.

Penn took the three Gunners back a little way to what he considered a better position, 'to form a small, ever so small, defensive line with the four of us. I reported to our Adjutant, Captain Mick Ekman, and busy as he was, he had time for me to tell him what was happening outside.'

From the CP staff, two more rifles were given to the four-man defence post. Penn took them to a small hole dug by the bulldozer, and they placed sandbags along the side closest to the enemy, resupplied themselves with ammunition, and waited for what might happen. The four of them comprised a separate little world in the galaxy of light and noise all around them: 105mm howitzers firing in the gun position; tracer, machineguns, rockets; radios squawking in the CP, loudspeakers blaring in the gun positions; voices of Australians and Vietnamese; and sounds of digging out near the uncollected stores still by the LZ.

'But through all this', recalls Arthur Penn, 'poor old Gunner Robinson wanted to have a cigarette, and I refused him, because we were the last line of defence for the CP, and as soon as he lit up it would expose our position. He asked me on several occasions if I'd give him a cigarette, and I said no.

'The rest of the night, from our point of view, was watching and waiting. Without our small group being there, things may have been different. If we hadn't been there to stop the small group of infiltraters who came around the back, we don't know what might have happened. The CP may have been jeopardised, but it wasn't the case; we were able to hold out. It seemed, and it will be, the longest night of my life.'

David Brook ran across to Bob Carbury's Q-store and together they ferreted around in the piles of items for the never-used boxes of handgrenades.

With Ian Ahearn, Brook went to the inner wall of No. 5 gun, and they grenaded the neighbouring pit containing No. 6 gun. Brook did not see any sign of the NVA next to them, and has since wondered if the damage to the gun was caused more by the grenades rather than the satchel charge the enemy were said to have used on it. Indeed, he wonders if No. 6 gun was overrun in the true sense of the word.

Ian Ahearn, though, is in no doubt that damage to the gun was caused by a satchel charge, not grenades, and that NVA were actually in the gun position.

The roar of battle was clearly audible to the distant companies, and it was obvious to all what was happening.

North-east was Col Adamson's A Company, who had been bypassed by enemy groups earlier. Adamson realised that the enemy were not retreating from Saigon, but in fact heading that way. Neil Weekes, commanding Adamson's 3 Platoon, 'stood up on the paddy bund nearby, and observed the rockets, flares, tracer, indicating Coral was under attack'.

Information passed on the company radio-net was sketchy, but it was known that the mortars had been overrun.

To the east, among the winding tracks and low scrubby trees, in the B Company position, with Bob Hennessy, the noise was also heard. What information there was available was passed to the platoons, and all lay around the triangular ambush position, either trying to read some meaning into the noise to their west, or ignoring it. The first indication Hennessy had that Coral was actually in peril was when his Mortar Fire Controller, Rowdy MacLeod, told him not to call for mortars, 'as there aren't any'.

Digger Campbell's C Company had gone south, to secure the road to Tan Uyen for convoy movement next day. The company medic, Lorne Clarke, could 'quite distinctly hear in the distance an incredible battle. We didn't know what was happening. There was artillery, mortars, a lot of automatic fire.'

But through it all, Digger Campbell was sleeping soundly, unaware of the distant drama.

To the north, in the D Company ambush position, the tracer flying up was easily visible, and Richo Richardson thought, 'well, I'm not going to lay here and be miserable, so I broke the rules of the ambush, and sort of sauntered up to platoon headquarters, who weren't far away, and asked what was going on.'

John Salter stated the obvious. 'At the moment, I think the Fire Support Base is being attacked.'

'Oh, jolly good. Who is up there protecting them?'

'No one.'

This was a rifle company joke, because Richo recalls that 'we didn't put a great deal of faith in Support Company protecting anybody, and all the other rifle companies were out, obviously doing the same thing we were doing.'

He went back to his section, where they divided their attention between the ambush and the uproar to the south, while he tried to think of something useful to say, telling the Diggers that obviously the HQ was all right.

Geoff Bowcock, commanding the adjacent 12 Platoon, recalls it: 'Crystal clear in my mind is, sitting back in that clearing, and firstly seeing the lights, then hearing the noise, emanating from Coral. It was a bit like sitting back at a firework display. We felt sort of distant from it, divorced from it all. We've got *our* little war and we're not doing *too* badly; we're not too sure of what's going on down *there*.'

Nearby, at the company HQ, Tony Hammett was listening to the radios. On the artillery net, 'we could hear 102 Battery was firing a number of three-gun missions, and judging by the terse communications, the situation around the base was horrific. There wasn't that much on the battalion net, except we gained the impression that the mortars and guns were under attack.'

He could see the Spooky 'flying square circuits, turning over and then letting loose this tremendous volume of fire downwards, and I thought how vulnerable we were if that DC3 mistimed one of its turning points.'

On the far side of Coral, the south-west, was the New Zealand 161 Battery, the 3RAR companies, and with 161, the four-man team from 131 Div Loc Battery. John Dellaca and the other three had lowered their hutchis, and watched 'the massive RPG attack, we could see the RPGs quite clearly, where they were fired from, but they then began to airburst near us, and we all got into our pits. The air was full of tracer. We could hear the splintex fired by 102 Battery, the whoosh of the little arrows, and it alarmed us to know they were using it.'

There was so much noise that the listening post was unable to really locate enemy positions, but they could tell that the mortars and RPGs were fired from different locations. They were not attacked all night, though other elements of 3RAR had minor contact. They sat or lay, listening to the battle and identifying the different types of weapons.

Nearby, in the 3RAR mortar position, Bill Studley was also watching the action, and having been on the receiving end of air power at FSPB Anderson, was a little worried, like Tony Hammett, that the gunships might accidentally hose the area of the New Zealand guns.

From his battalion HQ in the rubber trees north-west of the embattled guns and mortars, Lieutenant Colonel Jim Shelton clicked radio frequencies over to that of 1RAR command net, and told Phil Bennett that he 'would be keeping a watching brief' on the net. Throughout the battle, he was impressed by the calmness of Bennett's voice coming through the radio, and felt that Bennett obviously 'had a grip on it'.

Shelton's battalion doctor, Lippett, was very conscious that there were wounded men over in the battle area, and asked if he could be given a patrol to go over and give what assistance possible. Shelton had to explain that anyone moving in that direction would probably be killed, and Lippett would have to wait.

Possibly the youngest of Shelton's soldiers was Private Wayne Meech, 19½-year-old member of the Assault Pioneer Platoon. Before the action started, he had no idea that friendly troops were so close, but once it began, thought they were close enough to reach out and touch them. He could clearly hear the chattering voices of NVA passing close by, and wondered if 3RAR would be attacked next. From his viewpoint, the battle was almost directly in front of him, slightly to the right. At one stage, he heard a large number of NVA talking slightly to his left, then a very loud explosion, and was told afterwards that it had been the destruction by explosive charge of one of the 102 Battery guns, which had been hauled off into the scrub by the Vietnamese. (No guns were hauled away, the dirt bunds would have prevented it, let alone fire from 102 Battery and Les Tranter's weapons on the flank.)

This chattering probably was the same heard at one stage by Bill Studley, in the 3RAR mortar position, giving him his 'next big fright'. They could see shadowy figures moving past and clearly hear the voices. Presuming the enemy were approaching to attack, and having all weapons and Claymore mines at the ready, Studley prepared to 'beat them to the draw' and open fire first. He telephoned Major Tom Martin, at 161 Battery, and informed him of this intention, but was quickly told to 'sit tight'. The NVA moved away into the night.

After the battle began, John Kearns' replacement for duty arrived at the 1RAR CP, and he moved out on to the battalion HQ perimeter. John's pit was on one side of the track running up to the mortar position, and in another on the other side of the path was Corporal Graham Jones, another second-tour veteran. Together they looked down the track which went through the position, east to the anti-tank gun location. Now and again they could see figures moving in the area of the mortars and artillery positions.

In the chaos around the battalion mortar pits, Tony Jensen and the survivors of his platoon fought on. At the very beginning of the attack, he had called for artillery and mortar fire—from 3RAR, on the far side of the perimeter—to be placed on his own position, but it was not necessary, as he and Parr were able to adjust the falling rounds to within twenty metres of his pits. This, with the deadly splintex rounds from Les Tranter's Anti-armour Platoon and 102 Battery, combined to cause many casualties to the nearby enemy.

Laying back to back with Jack Parr in their respective scrapes, they maintained communication with the outside world with their bullet-damaged but working radios perched behind the dirt removed from the holes.

In the 102 Battery CP, a wounded Gunner, Steve Nichols, had been laid on the bench at the rear. He had been given morphia, so was not fully conscious. When it seemed likely that the nearby ammunition bay might explode, Bob Lowry, the Duty Officer, told the staff to sit down, below the level of the ground and earth wall, in case of blast from it. Then Lowry looked around, and saw the wounded Nichols. He was reluctant to move Nichols, for fear of damaging his injured eye, but could not crouch in safety while the wounded man lay there, so stood up, to reassure Nichols, who was not fully awake anyway.

For a long time, there had been no contact between the mortars and the guns, but at last Tony Jensen acknowledged the calls from Ian Ahearn, who had gone to No. 5 gun pit in an effort to determine what had happened to the infantry mortar platoon, and it was arranged that splintex would be fired across the mortar position. He called to his men to get down, and the lethal hail from five rounds slashed overhead. Later it was found that the mortars which the NVA had tried to carry away had been damaged by the metal arrows. In fact, some of the steel projectiles were still lodged in the barrels, and the weapons were replaced.

Brigadier Hughes and the remainder of Task Force HQ at Bearcat were kept informed of the situation through an Australian Liaison Officer with the adjoining US brigade, who relayed the messages from the Signals detachment at Coral, whose aerial had been hit, and had its range reduced.

Perhaps because of the distance and delay in communications to him, Brigadier Hughes was not unduly worried at the prospect of the guns or battalion being overrun, but also wisely allowed the commanders on the spot to fight their battle undisturbed.

Outside the main arena, each in their own little world in the darkness, the rifle companies watched the distant battle: tiny bright tracers fleeting skyward, sudden flash of rockets, glow of explosions, beautiful scarlet rain of circling miniguns, hard white glow of flares, relentless regular blinking from anti-collision lights of aircraft circling in the blackness like sharks waiting to dart in; and always the noise: blam of RPGs detonating, slam of 105mm shells, harsh burble of minigun, distinctive woka-woka of Huey rotor blades, placid drone of C47, rattle of automatic small arms; all beyond the black trees around the company position.

Col Adamson's A Company, to the north-east, knowing the enemy had flowed past them; Bob Hennessy's B Company, with enemy still around them; Digger Campbell's C Company, away south along the Tan Uyen road; Tony Hammett's D Company, in the aftermath of their own bloodletting; all watching, listening to the battle and the radio traffic, trying to visualise the action, wondering how it would evolve, how it would affect them, how their friends were faring at Coral.

In the 1RAR communications centre, Mick Bindley realised that listening to the battalion radio net was providing him with information, but not the full story of what was happening in the area. He could hear, and see, Lieutenant Colonel Bennett, standing above ground, talking by radio to the gunships in the dark sky above, and was struck by the CO's skill and coolness as he directed their attacks.

Kim Patterson also was impressed by Bennett's action, particularly in standing erect despite the amount of firing, in order to see and control better than was possible in a pit.

John Kearns noted that the CP 'appeared calm and controlled, but hectic. The sigs [radio operators] were trying to recall everything, but it was coming in so fast that unless you were a shorthand typist it was impossible to do so. The info was marked on the map, but the time and other detail was in the mind of the CP staff. The actual logging was very sparse, what with every position reporting. Comms were good, but the landlines to the mortars and anti-tank were broken by rockets, so radio was used.'

Standing-to in their pits, the men of Les Myers' Assault-Pioneer Platoon were spectators to the battle, dividing their attention between it, behind and to the left of them, and to the darkness to their front, from where more enemy could very likely appear.

Like Tony Jensen on the far side of the position, Myers saw, in the flare light, the mass of NVA swarming forward to attack the artillery. There seemed to be no distinct tactical formation, just a mass of figures in the harsh brightness. The sight remained his most vivid memory of the entire operation.

Frightened by the horrendous night, Tiber, one of the dogs from Les Tranter's tracker teams, broke loose from its handler and fled across the battlefield, heading for Mick Bindley's comms centre. Tranter radioed an urgent message, Bindley looked out, saw the dog, leaped out, chased it and made 'one of my less successful rugby tackles at it and missed, then asked myself the very reasonable question: what the hell was I doing chasing a dog around at this time of night? and very smartly returned to the pit.'

The dog later returned, but was found to be useless for its military purpose and was given to the Australian Embassy staff in Saigon.

For the first time, John Kearns saw a Hueycobra helicopter

gunship in action. 'Charlie had a 12.7mm heavy machinegun mounted on a trailer towed by a tractor. They turned the gun on the ground troops, but then he fired on the choppers. He happened to pick on a Hueycobra ... the pilot just turned on his tail, went back down the line of tracer coming up at him and wiped him out with a snap of the fingers. It appeared so pathetic ... the thud-thud-thud-thud of the 12.7, and then the almighty roar of the minigun and rockets from the Huey-cobra. They hit the trailer and it disintegrated. I saw the parts left the next day. The tractor, trailer and 12.7 left much to be desired [as working machinery].'

Captain Mick Bindley also saw this, and it seemed as if the upward stream of tracer wavered as the gunship began its firing dive. Many others noticed the air-to-ground duels.

The colours—green and red—struck Geoff Grimish of 102 Battery as those of South Sydney, in the Sydney Rugby League, so later he 'had a good bet on South Sydney, who went on to win the premiership that year'.

At about dawn, the gunships noticed NVA fire coming from the drainage ditch lining the rubber plantation, and made runs hosing machinegun bullets and rockets along its length. But the enemy had realised they had not much time to be well away from the base before full daylight exposed them, and they were already filtering eastwards.

Jet fighter-bombers also struck, creating for Geoff Grimish 'the one everlasting memory of the first night. The smell of cordite and the smoke from the battle completely engulfed the battery position and surrounding area. The fighters had been strafing, and were invisible through the smoke until they were only metres away, when they made their vertical climbs. The visual effect was that the jets appeared to be leaping out of the ground itself.'

Gradually the defenders realised that the enemy tide had ebbed and was flowing out, into the sea of trees to the east and north. Hammett and Adamson reported contact, with what was obviously enemy withdrawing from the battle area.

They called for artillery, to bring it on to the retreating enemy, and so created for Gavin Andrews, commander of

102 Battery, his most vivid memory of the entire operation, 'the one I feel privileged to have. The answer from the guns for this battery target was, first, two guns fired, then three, then five, then lastly the badly damaged gun fired a couple of rounds, and all guns were firing.

'The gunners had shrugged off the events of the night, and begun to function in their primary role, that is, give close support to the infantry. I felt extremely proud of them, as I did on many occasions, but that time is very special to me.'

(Actually the sixth gun did not fire, as its return mechanism had been damaged.)

At about the same time, Ian Ahearn and Tony Jensen established radio contact, and Jensen was asked if his survivors would remain there while a clearing patrol swept out from the gun position; this was agreed. Ahearn then led a group of gunners sweeping across to the mortars, finding the Australian and NVA dead, plus a wounded NVA, who was searched and given treatment.

Thirty-eight enemy dead were counted, many in the mortar position. One of the vivid memories of the time for Ian Ahearn is his first sight of a dead Australian soldier, made more poignant by the fact that 'I didn't even know his name'.

Thinking back on the night battle, when he had time later, Ahearn acknowledged that it 'taught me the resilience of the Australian soldier, and confirmed that he does operate with a lot of initiative'.

Dawn and the new day became evident to Mick Bindley and the crew of the battalion communications centre when they noticed many thin beams of light entering through the holes in the tent roof, which had been in good condition at sunset.

At 0720 the 1RAR companies reported their own and enemy casualties from the night's activities. At 0738 Lieutenant Colonel Bennett informed 1ATF of his intention to relocate his companies in defence of 102 Battery.

1ATF began to adapt to the requirements of the big league.

4 Reappraisal

No plan survives the first contact of war.
Clausewitz

THE EARLY MORNING LIGHT flooded the scene at Coral, glistening on the dry silvery-topped grass. Dead and wounded of both sides littered the area—olive-khaki and grey of the NVA, jungle green of the Australians; scattered weapons and equipment; craters from mortar, artillery shell and rocket among the emplacements and pits; shattered trees and fallen branches in the rubber plantation; patches of blood-stained earth from where the fallen had been carried away; crushed grass and bushes where they had been dragged off; ripped and torn tents; gleaming empty cartridge cases, smoke from the artillery position ...

Mal Hundt, with his numerous wounds from friend and foe, was cautiously puffing on a cigarette, not daring to 'drawback' the smoke 'in case the smoke came out the holes in my stomach', and waiting for the Dustoff.

Arthur Penn, wounded in the shooting in the drain behind the artillery regimental CP, took in the 'foggy, overcast, dusty morning. I looked around, and everyone was covered in grey mud. That's one thing I do remember. We were absolutely covered in it. There was a strong smell of cordite and gunpowder. I was starting to suffer a small amount of pain in my mouth, right hand and chest.'

Penn, with his three Gunners and other men he could gather from the regimental HQ party, began searching the bodies of NVA scattered nearby, making sure that all were dead, and there was no danger from them.

For Geoff Grimish, the morning was 'exhilarating, with the smell of cordite and the fresh morning air', like after a

97

good game of football.

Alan Floyd, gun number, lay behind the dirt bund, wondering what the day was going to bring. The night had been unlike anything in his experience.

Bob Lowry, who had been Duty Officer in the 102 Battery CP, came to Bombardier Larry Darcy and told him to take a clearing patrol from the battery position, sweep through to the mortars and around to the rear of the artillery HQ CP. So Larry collected Bombardier Burns and such gunners as he could find at the moment, and began clearing to the left, starting from No. 6 gun. Alan Floyd was with them.

Greg Ayson, member of Max Franklin's No. 6 gun, and member of the clearing patrol, was later surprised to realise that 'all the training at Canungra, all the rigmarole you go through, came out then. Out we went, no hesitation about it, and we did a fairly good job of clearing the area.'

They had only gone some fifty metres when Ayson shot a live NVA soldier lying in the grass with a grenade ready to throw. The rest of the sweeping force went to ground, Larry Darcy finding himself face to face with another NVA, looking down the muzzle of the AK47 and into the eyes of the Vietnamese, and fired several times at the man until Burns called out that he was already dead. From Larry's point of view he could not see that the top of the man's head was gone, killed instantly as he tried to crawl up to the guns during the night.

They swept on, killing another NVA, and arrived at the mortar position, where there were bodies and equipment littered everywhere. Larry saw one Australian with at least three dead NVA around him, then came on a couple more, easily identified by their boots sticking out of the grass. Then they were called back to their gun positions, as Les Tranter's Anti-armour Platoon was also clearing the position.

Tony Jensen was still in his pit among the 1RAR mortars, and was told to remain there while other units swept across to him. The platoon had suffered five killed and eight wounded, leaving five. Jensen and Parr would remain at Coral, while the other three returned to Nui Dat.

The platoon was later brought up to strength temporarily

98

by attaching two sections of 3RAR Mortar Platoon. Later the section which had remained at Nui Dat was brought up, and the normal strength attained with reinforcements. The efficiency of the platoon remained unaffected, as these were experienced men from 7RAR.

The artillery position was, in Ian Ahearn's words, 'a mess. No. 6 gun was useless, having been hit by heavy machinegun fire and a satchel charge. No. 6 position had been showered with handgrenades, many duds littered the pit.'

As well as No. 6 gun, Skeeter Humphry's No. 2 gun had to be replaced, and the bulldozer was riddled with small arms fire and another one had to be flown in. Debris, shell containers and packing had to be removed. Stephens' No. 4 gun had fired eighty-four rounds over open sights, and Robertson's No. 5 gun had fired another five or six over open sights.

The battery position had to be secured, cleaned up and the defences improved, but all the while the unit had to be prepared to function in its primary role, its reason for being: provide artillery support for those in need. Despite the close-quarter attack, and hail of fire during the night, the battery still was able to fire three missions during the action. While clearing the area and cleaning up, it was found that the aiming posts, which had small lights on them, and which were placed to be visible from the gun position, had been turned around to act as markers for the NVA.

Regimental HQ had lost two killed—Gunners Sawtell and Scott—and three wounded: Page, Hundt and Larment. 102 Battery had two wounded: Gunners Mick Grimes and Steve Nichols.

When he went back to his listening post on the edge of the irrigation ditch, Ginger Orford found a dead NVA in it, killed by a hit in the side of the head. Orford was taken by the youth of the enemy, who was only about 17, not much younger than himself.

Bombardier Andy Forsdike knew Scott had been killed, and it was hard for him to accept, as they had been talking such a short time before, but 'you realise that's a mate there. I helped carry him to the helicopter, and I just didn't want to talk to anybody'. Then he saw people picking up Sawtell, and that hurt also, as they had gone through recruit training together. 'I had tears in my eyes, and I'm not ashamed to admit it.'

When the first Dustoff arrived, Mal Hundt was rushed out to it, but there was a burst of firing from one of the clearing patrols, the carriers went to ground, dropping Mal as they did so. He was picked up and slid into the top rack in the body of the helicopter, his last memory of Coral being himself leaning over the side of the stretcher and vomiting on the Aussie underneath. He woke again in an American hospital.

Also in the chopper was Mick Grimes, in blood-encrusted greens, nursing his injured hand. On arrival at Long Binh, he was able to assist with the stretchers, using his left hand.

While the Dustoff approached, Gavin Andrews was talking to the wounded, and was touched by the repeated apologies from Grimes, for losing the M60.

RSM Les Partridge walked over to Sergeant Arthur Penn, and told him he was being evacuated. Penn went over to the helicopter pad, where the casualties were being gathered. He was given the intravenous bottle connected to Gunner Vic Page to hold as they waited.

As they circled the battlefield, gaining height over safe ground, Arthur Penn looked down at the gun position, 'thinking back on what had happened during the night, and I couldn't help feeling a bit older, and had a feeling they'd be all right now, because they'd survived that night, things would return to normal and I'd see them all again in the near future.'

The helicopter thrummed away south to Long Binh, and he saw a convoy on the road below, and later realised it was probably the rest of the Task Force on the way to Coral.

Meanwhile, Les Tranter's Anti-armour Platoon had been tasked to sweep from their position on the south-east around to Jensen's mortars, and into the rubber trees. As they moved through, searching the bodies, checking them and the weapons and equipment for ammunition and booby-traps, Ken Crane, on the right, shot one NVA who was about to throw a grenade.

Then they came to the area of Doug Dupille's target, at which he had fired the first 90mm HEAT round. It had really been a 60mm mortar position, identified by the marks, large quantities of blood and many drag marks showing the round had exploded on target.

Then, in the mortar position, Tranter's vision of the night before was realised. There, just as he had seen, was a man, an NVA, on his back, hands on his chest, over a wound, babbling despite a wound to his tongue. They pressed on, past the mortars, into the rubber, while helicopters strafed the distant edge of the section of plantation.

Mick Bindley was able to notice the professional way in which the soldiers of Tranter's platoon methodically searched the area, examining the enemy bodies scattered about. The NVA were turned over using grapnels, a precaution against booby-traps. Without prompting, working smoothly together, the Diggers worked as they had been trained to do.

An unseen NVA fired a burst, which kicked up dust around the feet of Private Brett Charlton, who reacted with an impromptu dance, to the amusement of some. Les Tranter thought it was for all the world like a scene from a Western movie, in which the villain fires into the ground, making someone dance.

About 200 metres into the rubber plantation, Tranter called a halt, spoke to the CP by radio, and moved his men back to the mortar position to assist in the work there.

The bodies were being carried in to a central area, the Vietnamese in an open space near 102 Battery, the Australians closer to 1RAR HQ. For some of the Aussies it was a 'disturbing thing' to see Australian boots sticking out of the end of the groundsheets covering their own dead.

Les Tranter had sixteen men with him, enough for four stretchers, and he purposely had them carry four of the mortar platoon dead, to bring home the fact that Australians, and friends, could get killed in this business.

Bob Carbury, 102 Battery, 'realised I was in the middle of a war when they brought the bodies in. The NVA were piled in front of our gun pit. The dead Australians upset us a bit, and that was when we realised we were in the middle of a blue.'

In their sweep Tranter's men had found and checked six-teen bodies and recovered thirteen weapons, plus a large quantity of webbing and other equipment, documents and personal belongings. Later another body was found in the bush where they had fired M16s at a group of enemy during the night.

Flying up from Bearcat, Brigadier Hughes and Lieutenant Colonel Jack Kelly, CO 12 Field Regiment, could see the position of the night battle from some distance away, marked by the smoke from the fire in 102 Battery's position. On landing, Kelly went straight to the battery, and walked around the gun positions with the Battery Commander, Gavin Andrews. Brigadier Hughes went to 1RAR HQ.

Kelly saw 'a mass of enemy bodies, basically where they had fallen. It was a graphic demonstration of how close they had got, in fact, to the gun pits themselves, and a graphic illustration of how they were killed.

'We proceeded to No. 6 gun position. When I got there, they were still recovering, and were getting rid of dead and wounded. But they were calm, the gunners, and quite in charge of their job. There was no panic at all.'

A reorganisation of the defences was obviously necessary, and Kelly had to consider a possible move of 102, to a better defensive position. However, a large amount of work had already been expended on the present site, and a move would mean starting again from the beginning. The enemy's inten-tions for the night were not known. It was decided to leave 102 where it was. Work began, and continued for the next few days, on improving the existing position.

Meanwhile, the remainder of TF HQ Forward had moved to Coral. Captain Noel Sproles, a Survey Corps officer, was one of the original two permanent TF CP Duty Officers, the other being New Zealander John Collinson; they were classmates from OCS Portsea. Noel Sproles had woken early, to begin packing the CP for the move to Coral, and when he arrived was told of the night battle there, which had not ended yet. One of the additional Duty Officers, Alan Vickers, from the tank squadron, had been on duty through-out the hours of battle.

The radios were turned off, packing done, and they piled all the equipment and themselves into a Chinook, which took off for Coral. The sun was not quite up. When the helicopter arrived, it was unable to land as the area was not cleared yet, so they circled in the early morning, then sank on to the LZ.

Sproles got out and looked around. 'There was a reasonable amount of confusion, and people walking about everywhere, dazed. I met a long-time friend, Mick Ekman, 12 Field Regiment, and he would hardly say a word to me.'

Ekman told Sproles of his encounter with an NVA, emptying his magazine at the Vietnamese who was standing on top of the bunker, while the NVA fired his AK47 magazine at Ekman ... neither hit the other. While this was related, Sproles could hear firing in the distance.

He walked over to the TF CP, 'which was a hole in the ground with a rubber tree log over it and radios on the log. There was John Collinson with TF HQ in the hole.'

One of the tales told to Sproles was that the occupants of the hole had watched a group of NVA running past, and a soldier asked the sergeant-major what they should do, getting the reply, 'Do bloody nothing!' There was no way the TF HQ delegation could have defended their position against the NVA, if they had attacked. Collinson, for one, had only a pistol with one magazine.

Another arrival very early was Dr Neville O'Connor, who had been RMO 7RAR, then gone to 8 Field Ambulance at Nui Dat. With two medical assistants, he flew in to Coral, to allow the 1RAR doctor to get back to the battalion matters, while O'Connor and his team took over the evacuation classification of the casualties. O'Connor had time for a quick look around the area, noticing the damaged guns, the litter, the enemy in the ditch, and the general activity in the position, then set to work. Later he established a holding area for future casualties, and eventually had a permanent location, with a phone, tent and some equipment. The idea was that casualties from the different parts of the base would be sent to him and evacuated. The Engineers would also dig his aid post, and one of O'Connor's memories of the time is their attempts to make it waterproof, learning from experience as they did so.

In company with Lieutenant Colonel Bennett, Brigadier Hughes walked around the position, noting 'a general air of calm, but in one or two places a slight shock at having fought a pretty heavy battle through the night. There was an air of competence. Even the gunners were sort of patting themselves on the back. They had fought the typical gunners' defensive battle, with open sights and flechette, all their drills that they had gone through and probably believed would never come to fruition; it had happened, they were fighting on open sights.

'There were many young men wanting to tell their stories, but I then had to get off and on to the other jobs.'

David Brook, BK of 102 Battery, had occasion to remember the Brigadier's visit: he berated Brook for walking about with his shirt out, and for not having shaved yet. Hughes had also spoken sharply to other officers for the same reason.

This was not simply a case of a senior officer berating juniors; there was a good military reason for speaking to them in this way. The euphoria and excitement after the event had to be channelled into re-establishing normal routines, so that everyone was ready and able to resume operations.

Lieutenant Colonel Jim Shelton, CO 3RAR, had gone across to the battle area, and reported to the Brigadier, who asked when his battalion could move off into AO Manly, as planned. Shelton replied that he could move by 1000, and this was agreed on. The 3RAR companies would begin to move on foot out to the previously planned areas and begin ambushing and patrolling. Later, 161 Battery would be lifted by air to FSPB Coogee.

Brigadier Hughes, and, he believed, everyone else as well, immediately understood that the night before had shown the Task Force was in a different type of warfare. 'We were no longer in jungle warfare, where small patrols could wander through and meet small enemy patrols. We tended to keep the battalions concentrated in defensive positions and patrol in strength.

'We still had to clear the area, we still had to patrol, we still had to find the enemy, and this was done by company patrols. The company could look after itself. A platoon may not be able to, but a company could. This was much more open country and they could operate as company patrols.'

Brigadier Hughes decided to concentrate 1RAR on Coral, and maintain it there, while moving 3RAR to the west, to Coogee. From Coogee the north-west part of the TF AO could be more easily covered. Absorbing the situation, he began to plan the defence of Coral. Around him, the post-action activity went on.

Lieutenant Colonel Bennett had the following message sent to the units involved in the night battle:

Today this callsign with G10 and G98 ably upheld the honour and traditions of those before us. I now believe that an enemy battalion has been severely mauled and our own losses more than accounted for. I congratulate you all on a job well done with steadiness and bravery second to none. We will all remember this day with pride in our achievements. Let us all thank God for the courage which has added to the honour of our country.

(G10 and G98 were 102 Battery and 12 Field Regiment HQ Battery.)

The small bulldozer had been wrecked by RPG and machine-gun fire, so was to be flown away by Chinook. However, the slings intended to carry the 'dozer under the belly of the helicopter became slightly tangled, and the pilot decided to bounce the 'dozer to straighten them. Unfortunately, the 'dozer caught in the barbed wire which was up, and flew away with it trailing, uncoiling and stretching out behind. Sooner rather than later, it would recoil like a giant spring . . . David Brook and others saw it, and called a warning to get under cover. 'Back it came with a vengeance' and all had to be relaid.

Crossing his small Signals Platoon area, Bindley was surprised, then infuriated, to find two of his sigs peacefully asleep in their shallow pits. He roughly woke them, and set them to work carrying the casualties. It was only later that the pair had a chance to explain that they had slept on simply because no one had woken them for any duty; like many soldiers they were able to sleep through loud noise, waking to the sound of their names spoken or whispered. Bindley realised the truth of what they said, and apologised.

Later, Bindley looked up from his labours to see 'a vast convoy, all stopped along the tracks leading into the position; and the startled faces of the individuals in the leading vehicles. Close to them were the Australian bodies, alongside the track, and further away the crowded NVA corpses.'

It was the convoy from Nui Dat and Bearcat, and the people in it suddenly understood that Coral had been the scene of intense action.

Stan Carbines, surveyor with 102 Battery, saw them arrive, feeling that 'it was a great sight. I felt like cheering, but we just gazed at them as they approached up the road. They spread out over the position.'

One of the observers in the convoy was John Goodwin, radio mechanic with 1RAR, now manning an M60 machine-gun on top of an M113. After the night before, enjoying the recreation facilities at the US base at Bearcat, John noticed the bodies lined up, covered by groundsheets, with the boots poking out, and to him 'the effect was devastating. The silence was deafening, and I think that was when I realised I was in a war.' The realisation was emphasised when he found that three of the dead were good friends, one he had known since childhood.

Another of the new arrivals was Lieutenant George Hulse, commanding 1 Troop, 1 Field Squadron, Royal Australian Engineers. (The Squadron Commander was Major John Kemp.) After four years service as an infantryman, Hulse had gone to OCS, and on graduation been allocated to Engineers. He also saw the boots poking from the end of the covers, and was struck by the thought that the name for the operation Toan Thang (Complete Victory) fell a little flat.

The section of mortars which had remained at Nui Dat were called together by Sergeant Ken Phipps and told of the fighting at Coral, together with the list of casualties. Many of the National Servicemen who had come into the platoon had trained together as infantrymen, and had accompanied each other through their military careers. Leigh Boneham felt 'extremely hurt' when told Errol Bailey was dead, thinking of Bailey's wife and family.

They packed and prepared to move to Coral.

Major Col Adamson, with A Company 1RAR to the north-east, had his men clear their immediate area, then prepare to move back to Coral.

The main elements of B Company, in the field to the east of Coral, had called in a Dustoff helicopter to remove the body of Private Trimble, killed in a brief exchange of fire at dawn. Once again the pilot earned the admiration of the soldiers. 'The ambush site,' said Garry Prendergast, commanding 6 Platoon, 'was a triangle thing, and left to right would have been thirty metres. All right for night, but not for day. And apart from the shape of the trees, there wasn't much room to land.

'I remember Bob Hennessy saying over the radio that there was a helicopter coming, then he appeared over the tree-tops, and literally turned on his tail and sat it down. He was incredible.'

Hennessy was also impressed. The American pilot had been told that the enemy were in contact, to the south-east, and he flew in fast, low and direct, and to Hennessy 'pulled it around, turned it as a motorcyclist corners, put the Huey on the ground, and Trimble and a soldier with an ankle injury were flown out in seconds.'

Some of the soldiers realised that the long night, with their feelings insecure and vulnerable, was their introduction to war; and, like Private Tim Foster, understood 'that people were going to die in this country. It sent shivers up my spine.'

After the events of the night before, as soon as they stood-down in the dawn, B Company had set to digging deeper as fast as they could. There was no need to urge the soldiers to greater efforts. They realised they might have had to stay there. Then they were told to move back to Coral.

The orders were passed by radio, with the company commanders listening to Lieutenant Colonel Bennett, and acknowledging as appropriate. B Company were to continue to the east and as Hennessy was about to acknowledge this, he had to dive into his pit while a flurry of mortar bombs sailed into the position. He informed Bennett of the mortars, as a matter of course, and was surprised to find that the orders continued, but he was now to return at once to Coral.

To the south of the battle, Digger Campbell's C Company was to secure the road from Tan Uyen, for the convoy. Campbell had slept through the noise of the distant fighting. 'Much to my annoyance and professional shame—I could have done little to assist—I woke next morning to learn the Fire Support Base had been fighting for its life. My radio operator had decided not to call me, as the company received no direct radio calls!'

They had watched the vehicles roll past. They were also out of water, and had to watch some Americans driving past, but drinking cold cans of beer. Two cans were thrown to a group of the infantry; one burst and the other was shared by about twelve men.

The water problem became acute. Finally, as Lorne 'Doc' Clarke, the medic, recalled, they 'found a well in a funny little old Vietnamese building in the middle of a field. The water was quite far down, and we tied toggle-ropes together, put a helmet liner on the end, and kept on dropping it down. The water was absolutely putrid, full of dead frogs and lizards. It was all we had.' Clarke told the soldiers to use their water purification tablets, and let the water stand for an hour, but realised that 'naturally the minute my back was turned the order was disregarded'.

Meanwhile, in their ambush position to the north of Coral, from which they had evacuated their casualties of the night before, and watched the distant battle, Tony Hammett's D/1RAR began the activities of the new day in normal infantry fashion, by moving out to check that their immediate front was clear of enemy.

Hammett sensed that 'the feeling in the company at that stage was one of low morale and shock, because this was the first time that we'd experienced the horrors and reality of war, in that people do get killed, and it came as a bit of a shock to the company that we'd suffered casualties and were

108

in for an interesting time, to say the least.

'I remembered RMC days, and Warrant Officer George Chinn in particular, making the point that when you'd had casualties, the best thing you can do, to help soldiers get over the shock, is to get into normal routine as quickly as you can.'

In John Salter's 10 Platoon, Paul Richardson 'didn't know if he had any other name in his brain or not, but Richardson was next on the list, and I took my section out to do a clearing patrol out across the track into the jungle on the other side. Anyway, I found this long big ditch, and in it were all these little pits dug into the wall, and fresh footprints everywhere. Obviously it had been used yesterday or during the night. I could smell that Asian smell, very, very fresh.' They returned to the ambush position.

Tony Hammett then went round the platoons, making sure that the usual morning procedures were in operation: some cleaning weapons, some shaving, some cooking or eating breakfast, putting polish on boots, and that the anti-malarial Paludrine tablets were being taken.

Only the living casualties had been flown out in the night; the two dead were still in the position.

Back at Nui Dat, Second Lieutenant Phil Busby, 12 Field Regiment, had just completed a turn of duty, from 0300 to 0800. All that was known was the bare essentials of the action at Coral, that there had been 'some sort of attack; little known'.

It was not until the morning briefing for the rear echelons of the units at Nui Dat, at 0800, that members of the battalion were told 'there had been a pretty severe contact, and the Intelligence reports were spot-on'. Only later did information start to arrive with detail, and notification of killed and wounded.

Staff Sergeant Terry Loftus, Company Quarter-Master Sergeant (CQMS) for Bob Hennessy's B/1RAR, later began to receive information about casualties. Loftus knew that his duties concerning them would entail collecting, cleaning and crating for dispatch the personal effects of both dead and the wounded who were evacuated to Australia. The belongings of the dead were sent to the next-of-kin; those of the wounded sent on to the unit assuming responsibility for them.

In addition, he would be responsible for ensuring that the demands for resupply items from the company in the field were met. Mostly these were normal pieces of military equipment, but on occasion something very different would be requested, as when 6 Platoon asked for thirty Cherry Ripe chocolate bars. To the amazement of the then-platoon sergeant, the chocolates arrived. It took him a long time to live it down. Even today, somehow, mysteriously, an empty wrapper sometimes appears on his desk.

Meanwhile, in the artillery position of the New Zealand 161 Battery, some 1500 metres west of Coral, the listening post team of John Dellaca and the other three Diggers, Pablo Briggs, John Basford and Bluey Piesley, had been told to return to Coral. Far differently from the casual way they had strolled across the previous afternoon, now they adopted a tactical formation and crossed the intervening grassland as alert soldiers. In the grassy area they came across dozens of mortar craters which had been made during the night, 'overs' from the enemy bombardment.

To the north of Coral, Tony Hammett's soldiers saw a number of enemy moving past, obviously leaving the area of the battle. They fired on them, with unknown results. Later, from due east, about 300 metres away, fire began cracking through the D Company position. Hammett thought there were one or two enemy there, in a cleared area of what had been a rubber plantation.

Corporal Boyd was sent to deal with them, but no sooner had he begun to move than the fire swelled to include at least three automatic weapons. Hammett 'then made up my mind very quickly that the answer to this was a company attack. I also had the feeling that this was the best thing that could happen to the company that had some casualties during the night. The best thing we could do would be to get out, hook in, and have a go . . .

'I gave some very quick orders, and fortuitously the plan

allowed us to do what really amounted to a classic company attack. We had the right Forming-Up Place close behind a big bund, a big drain, which was at right angles to the axis of attack; we had a covered approach from where the enemy fire was coming; the ground couldn't have been better suited.'

Geoff Bowcock's 12 Platoon was to provide fire support, while Salter's 10 Platoon actually assaulted, with the weakened 11 Platoon in depth, behind 10. Artillery and helicopter gunship support were called for by radio. At this time, personally hustling 10 Platoon at the double down to the FUP, Hammett realised he needed his experienced CSM, Ron Pincott, who was absent in Long Binh.

As Hammett was urging the soldiers along, he heard Corporal 'Greasy' (so named for prowess on the football field) Jones saying, 'The ★★★★'s mad, the ★★★★'s mad, you only do this in training or in "Combat" [the TV series], you don't do this here!'

'Come on, Corporal Jones,' called Hammett, 'we're gonna do one!'

The platoon spread out, about six or seven metres apart, along the drain at the base of the bund. Paul Richardson was left assault section, 'Greasy' Jones the right, and the third section provided depth.

The helicopter Light Fire Team arrived and began to circle.

Gordon Alexander was already calling in an artillery fire mission, but as battalion headquarters wanted to give all the assistance possible, which meant gunships, he now had to halt the guns, until the helicopters had finished.

Not far away to the south-east, most of Col Adamson's A Company, moving back to Coral, had been forced to ground by the heavy volume of fire coming from Hammett's little battle. Unable to go forward or back, Adamson and two of his platoons hugged the dirt in an open paddy, while his other platoon, under Mal Meadows, who were in the lead, pushed on to Coral. Adamson told Meadows to find Kim Patterson, be informed of the company task and position, go there and reconnoitre it, and be prepared to brief Adamson when he finally did arrive.

Neil Weekes, commanding Adamson's 3 Platoon, saw

Corporal 'Shorty' Thirkell sheltering behind a 250lb un-exploded bomb as the intermittent hail of bullets cracked around the prone Diggers. The hot sun and inquisitive red ants added to the discomfort.

Meanwhile, to the north where all the shooting was going on, in his portion of the ditch, Paul Richardson was looking across the open ground to the jungle on the far side, saw the gunships approach and felt alarm rise as they began firing towards the Diggers, then thought that somebody should tell them to reverse the procedure, but no one did so.

They swept in, firing with explosive M79 40mm rounds at the reported enemy position, and kept on doing so as they passed over the assembling D/1RAR, who could see 'these pops coming closer and closer, straight through the platoon, out the back, down past CHQ'. Ray Curtis, standing slightly behind Salter, saw the explosions coming and it 'scared nine lives out of me. One round landed between me and the signaller; luckily they were coming almost straight down, and the blast went right into the ground. If it had spread . . .'

Richo watched 'the 40mm grenades, coming straight through the platoon, and there were guys ducking for cover everywhere, even before the bloody assault got started.'

The line of explosions raced among the scattering Diggers, puffing dust beyond the line of soldiers. Luckily, the rounds were fired at too sharp on angle, and were impacting into the sandy soil, which absorbed the force of the detonation.

There were some rapid directions flashed by radio, and the LFT turned their attention to the correct target. They fired their rockets and machineguns, then swung away.

As the gunships flew off, Richo Richardson watched them, noting, 'I couldn't see that they were doing much damage to anybody because the fire was still coming out of the holes in the paddock.'

Gordon Alexander was a bit peeved, as 'I had to take the artillery off, then readjust it back in again after the strike. It caused a messed-up fire plan, and a fat lot of good the gunships were anyway. We could assume the enemy were unscathed, mainly because we copped it along with them.'

To Tony Hammett, the misdirected attack was yet another bad omen. Nothing seemed to be going right for D Company.

He observed that this incident had done nothing to lift the spirits, 'and I could see the company was less than enthusiastic. I then said, "Fix bayonets" and it was probably the rabbit out of the hat, the thing that did the trick. The very act of putting the bayonets on the weapons seemed to have a (pun) steeling effect on them, as though they realised "all right, we mean business" and the bayonets were going on the weapons.'

Richo heard the call, looked to his left, and 'to my amazement everybody was fixing bayonets. I passed it on to my section, and we just got them on, and the word came to go and up we got.'

Salter looked over the ground he was to cross, and saw it to be 'as bare as a badger's bum, with grass about 8cm high, and in the middle a partly demolished old FSB, where the NVA were'. He became aware that everyone was looking at him, in the manner familar to him from officer training establishments: 'OK, platoon commander—what do you do now?'

'Artillery was falling ahead, a really magnificent sight, on the distant treeline, but not on the enemy, who were too close.'

Hammett hurried his HQ over behind Salter's, calling, 'Come on, come on, get going, we're off.' The line of green-clad figures surged forward, up the three-metre-high dirt wall of the bund and drain side.

Then he saw 'big George King, carrying Paul Richardson's M60, clamber up over the bund, and as he got to the top, suddenly fell over backwards. This was a great how-do-you-do, no sooner get up and someone goes neck-over-turkey. He'd been hit by an AK47 ricochet, on the basic pouch, only gave him a hell of a scare.

'We then started to advance over some 200 metres of sandy soil, grass and shrubs about knee high.'

10 Platoon climbed out of the ditch and advanced, initially in a posture described by Salter and Curtis as a cross between a crouch and a squat, then quickly all were upright, moving forward, firing as they did so.

113

Paul Richardson: 'There was none of this business like you train for, with fire and movement: gun group ... go; rifle group ... go; you know, one leg on the ground. It was all up and at it, this great line of Diggers, all trying to walk only as high as the grass.'

The enemy saw the assault line appear out of the trees, and turned their attention to it. The volume of fire poured out by the AK47s snapped around the Diggers, around and above Richardson's right-hand section.

Hammett had insisted that the company never fire from the hip, only using aimed shots, and now called this out to the soldiers of Salter's platoon as they walked in line, at first trying to keep low, then gradually straightening as they fired more aimed rounds at the enemy position.

Off to the flank, Bowcock's platoon opened fire in support, to at least distract the enemy, and if possible to force them to cease their firing. Again, excitement overrode training and they all fired rapidly and simultaneously—and all suddenly had empty magazines, causing an embarrassing lull in the neutralising fire. Hammett radioed a definition of fire support to Bowcock: irregular rate, from a variety of positions, at the rate necessary to keep enemy fire down.

While doing this, he recalled that it was only a year previous that he was saying the same thing to Bowcock and the others on the ranges at Holsworthy and Singleton, and thought, in the middle of the attack, that one never stops training. Bowcock asserted control of the firing, and it continued more effectively.

Looking around, trying to see everything and maintain control, Tony Hammett noticed his radio operator, a National Serviceman, Ross Coulter, 'a very refined fellow, whose instincts were against war, but came and soldiered on to the best of his ability. I remember seeing him, radio on his back, eyes all lit up, with 10 Platoon, firing his M16 in the direction of the enemy, saying words to the effect of "You know, I never thought I'd feel like this," and I replied, "Right, great, but make sure you're putting those rounds to good effect."'

Moving and firing, Richardson's section reached an old

American position, still with US helmets and items of clothing littered about. The AK47 fire increased and drove the upright soldiers to ground. Salter yelled to ask what was wrong on the flank and Richo replied that he was under heavy fire, but as they came down off the top of the diggings the rounds began to go by overhead. The NVA did not bring their fire lower.

One soldier was slightly wounded when a grenade he threw into a seemingly deep bunker bounced out again, a splinter drawing some blood. Greg Hansen, carrying the medical satchel, thought that at last he had a real casualty, and was a little annoyed to find the injury hardly worth attention.

Three NVA in a shell crater, who had been bypassed because they had been very quiet and immobile in its depths, had suddenly popped up and begun firing. Hammett turned to look for 11 Platoon, who should have been close behind, to deal with such matters, and saw they were too far back.

The NVA had decided to make their presence felt, but their intentions outstripped their ability—their shooting hit no one, and drew upon themselves the attention of the attacking Diggers. Ray Curtis said: 'They decided to stick their heads up and take a few shots at us, why I'll never know, because if they'd kept down we'd have walked right past them and left them alone. They took a couple of shots, and we wondered what we were going to do, because they weren't in the direction we were going in the attack, and after a while Hammett suggested using M79 to keep their heads down.

'Donnelly and Richo took their M79s and rifles with bayonets attached, and using fire and movement, went up and took these fellas out—killed all three.'

Tony Hammett, meanwhile, watched Jock McDonald aim his M79 and 'popped a beautifully aimed HE round into the crater' where the other enemy were, then Greasy Jones 'immediately jumped up and shot one NVA, then had a double feed in his M16, and without missing a beat, bayonetted the second, then butt-stroked and bayonetted the third. It was all over in seconds. I was about fifteen metres away, closest to Greasy, and doubt if I will ever forget it. We got on with the final stages of the attack.'

The assault swept on to the end of the cleared area without actually seeing any more enemy. Paul Richardson moved his machinegunner, Gill, to the right, and told him to rake an area where the road met the jungle, on that side. Gill put 500 rounds into the vicinity, and the enemy fire ceased. As the assault closed on a derelict M113, Richo could not be sure that it was not occupied by NVA waiting to engage them if they went past, so ordered Billy Stinton to fire an M72 66mm anti-tank rocket into it. By this time, spirits were so high that the explosion drew cheers from the platoons.

The NVA seemed to melt away in the face of the attack, and did not remain to meet the line of advancing Aussies.

The assault came to an end, with the troops on the ground reloading magazines and preparing fresh belts of machinegun ammunition for firing, but another need made itself felt.

It was now after eleven o'clock, and the company had not been issued water since it was at the previous AO the day before. Richardson 'gave poor old Ray [Curtis] a bit of a serve about the poor administration with no water resupply', but none was to be had. The company was to march back to the Fire Support Base.

Meanwhile, John Dellaca and the listening post team had arrived back into the artillery area at Coral, after walking back from the distant New Zealand guns. They were put to work with the burial parties, and saw 'many NVA killed in the ditch along the track running into Coral. We'd find a body in the long grass, hook a rope to it and pull it over, then put it into the big scoop on the front of the loader. They were in greens, with pith helmets or cloth hats, with civilian clothes in their packs. Many had been bandaged, but had died, and some were at the end of long drag marks.

'I took a hammock off a dead NVA, and unrolled it, and found it had all these splintex arrows in it.'

As the replacement mortar platoon soldiers arrived, Leigh Boneham, the platoon plotter, walked through, noticing 'the terrible smell of death ... things in disarray ... the look of the faces of Tony Jensen and Jack Parr, almost of disbelief ... We dug a couple of trenches side by side, and shaved the top off (the centre) to make a CP and place the plotting board.'

116

Digger Campbell's C Company, having secured the road for the convoy, was collected by APCs and driven up to Coral, when they moved into their part of the perimeter. Signs of the battle were still evident, and made an impression on the soldiers.

Campbell was 'met and briefed by a grave ops officer— Kim Patterson. It was not a time to go socialising or inspecting what had happened'. The row of dead enemy brought home to his soldiers that the foe were 'no longer targets, but people'.

Deploying across the axis of the NVA attack, C Company waited for A and D Companies to arrive so the positions could be decided upon, and digging begun.

At 1302, 1RAR received Hammett's radio report of the action he had fought across the open ground to the north of Coral.

When the firing stopped, Col Adamson's A Company was able to continue on their way to Coral, arriving in the early part of the afternoon. Their route took them through areas used by the NVA on the previous night, and they noted the many diggings, the square vertical shape of the NVA pits, many with overhead protection or cover, scattered bodies, weapons and equipment, and detected several booby traps left by the departing enemy.

En route to Coral, A Company encountered a wounded NVA from the night before. Col Adamson described him as 'badly wounded in the left shoulder, in pain, carrying his RPG and half-a-dozen rounds for it, and an AK47, but when we went to grab him, he took a swing at us.' The prisoner was disarmed and taken away for medical attention.

They re-entered the position through the mortar platoon, and the area stuck in Adamson's memory as 'a shambles'. They finally realised just how bad the previous night had been, and in Adamson's words, were 'sick at heart' as they passed on to their allocated part of the battalion perimeter.

Col Adamson found Second Lieutenant Mal Meadows, who had preceded him into Coral during the wait for Tony Hammett's action to end, and located the companies on the flanks of his sector of the battalion position. He soon realised he would be unable to cover all the ground in his allocated sector. Linking up with Bob Hennessy's B Company on the right, Adamson extended his three platoons to the left, in the order 1, 2, 3.

Meadows had 1 Platoon, Bob Sutton had 2, and the left-most 3 Platoon was commanded by Neil Weekes. Depth in the company was provided by Adamson's HQ and Support Section, plus the depth sections in the platoons.

Between Weekes' left and the next company, Digger Campbell's C Company, were some 450 metres of open grass and scrub. Adamson had decided to concentrate his force on the track which ran into the Coral position from the north-east, along which the enemy had advanced—in the drainage ditches—during the attack. He 'perceived the enemy to be a man of habit', and if he returned would do so along the track.

The platoon commanders and machinegunners of C Company were brought to the edge of their position, and shown the distant end of Weekes' platoon. Pegs were placed to mark the extremities of the safe directions of fire, so that weapons could be used to cover the front of A Company across the grassy expanse, and the reverse arrangements were made, for A to fire across C's front.

Col Adamson also went to 102 Battery, pointed out the gap in the infantry perimeter, and hoped the gunners would be able to fire flechette through there if the need arose. After their experiences of the previous night, the mortars and guns wanted infantry where they could see them, and know they were there, instead of relying on merely being told 'infantry are over there'.

Neil Weekes, on the exposed left of A Company, had twenty-two men in his platoon, and had to put all three sections forward, with depth provided only by his platoon headquarters, some fifty metres back. Standing erect, he had a view out to 400 metres over the grass in the clearing.

Weekes also noticed the track and irrigation ditches which led into the company position, and believed that if they came again, the enemy would approach through the same area to the north and east, using the rubber plantations and bush, and come along the tracks and irrigation ditches, which provided a convenient route.

Bob Hennessy's B Company had taken position to the right of Adamson's platoons, but in a much more compressed area, which he later estimated would have been suitable for about one and a half platoons. But this was hindsight. What his position did achieve was concentrated firepower, what he called 'wall-to-wall SLRs', south of Adamson. Behind Hennessy was battalion HQ, and the Pioneers and Anti-armour Platoons.

At Coral, the Australian dead and wounded had been flown out, a large communal grave dug for the NVA bodies, and after these had been searched by the Intelligence staff, were thrown into the hole.

The Dustoff had landed near Stan Carbines' four-man pit, from which he had watched the battle during the night, despite the burning ammunition close by. By this time, he was feeling hungry and opened a can of baked beans, just before a sergeant 'asked a few of us to bury the dead enemy. When I saw the bodies, I looked at the beans and just tipped them on the ground. Many of the NVA had been hit by high-explosive and splintex from No. 4 gun.'

Captain David Brook, BK of 102 Battery, had been told by Gavin Andrews, the battery commander, to write citations for awards for the battery members. Brook refused, saying that everyone had been doing their job and he did not believe decorations were warranted. Someone else wrote them, and some were awarded.

In the area of Coral occupied by TF HQ, Noel Sproles was less than pleased at what he called a 'day of confusion. There were three field [grade] officers who claimed to be responsible for the defence of the HQ, and there were some big conflicts. For the first time in my army career I said something rude and abrupt to an officer of field rank.'

Sproles had taken his own and John Collinson's gear and begun to dig their pit and living area, but had been moved twice by Majors, was digging the third pit, and the commander of the Signals unit came across and commented on how kind Sproles was to dig there, because someone else would be occupying it. Sproles flared up, told the Signals major what he thought of the situation, 'and told the world that I was not going to be moved. My total impression of the time is that no one knew who was responsible for what.'

Sproles later thought to himself how much expertise had been lost since World War II, when so many brigade-level moves and operations had been made. He did not have a high opinion of the senior officers, or some of the senior staff.

Another man with a less than happy attitude was George Hulse, of the Engineers. He had noted the adjacent ruins, and thought the rubble would be useful for the imminent engineering tasks, but was told that even though it was rubble, it still belonged to an absent Frenchman who had not given permission for its use. Wondering whether he was at war or not, he looked around the area, noting the basic nature of the diggings, the lack of defences, and knew he was going to be busy. From an infantryman's point of view, he was not pleased to see the rubber trees and bush which would give the enemy a covered approach up to the edge of the open area, but his disquiet lessened when he learned that rifle companies would occupy positions in those directions.

Meanwhile, off to the north, returning from their company attack, were Hammett's D Company 1RAR. The lack of water, the baking heat, the after-effect of the assault, all combined to bear down on the moving infantrymen, and Richo had two cases of heat exhaustion. He told his men to open their shirts, their trouser flies, roll up their sleeves, and let as much air as possible cool them. In this very unregimental manner they arrived back at Coral.

Despite the heat and general conditions, they had to clear the ground carefully, in case there were more enemy between them and Coral. As they moved through the patch of rubber plantation where they had thought to find D/3RAR, on the afternoon before, during their march out to the night ambush position, they found dozens of square pits dug by the NVA during the night, and a pale-blue communications cable lying there. It was obviously the Forming-Up Place for the attack on the mortars and guns.

'Now we started to realise something big was going on,' said Geoff Bowcock, commanding 12 Platoon. 'What are we going back to?' Some of his platoon, in time-honoured fashion, had been grumbling about the constant changing of plans: what they were told at FSPB Harrison was changed on arrival at Coral; what they were told then had been changed again this morning.

Then, as Richo recalls, 'the first people we struck were D and E Platoon. Well, you know, they said, "You should have been here last night, you buggers, out there doin' nothing." They had all this bloody barbed wire up, and I think they had about four machineguns pointing at us as we came in. Good old D and E Platoon. They said, "You shoulda been here" and all this garbage, and I said, "Listen, I'm too bloody tired to listen to you wankers. Just piss off and leave us alone." I moved the section away so they wouldn't get into any donnybrooks with them.'

Tony Hammett was met by Kim Patterson, the Ops Officer, who told him D Company was to occupy a position on the perimeter between Digger Campbell's C Company and the Engineers of John Kemp. Hammett remembered thinking that this informal way of allocating the company position contrasted sharply with 'those hours and hours we spent on bleak windswept hills at Singleton and Puckapunyal, planning the layout of a company defensive position'.

However, it was because of the experience gained in those 'hours and hours' that the companies could be so well positioned with such little fuss. During training, Lieutenant Colonel Bennett had emphasised the practising of occupying quick defensive positions, and now the benefits were reaped. Hammett placed his two strong platoons forward, almost at right angles to each other, linking with his flanking units, and the weaker platoon and HQ behind.

While Hammett gave his orders to the platoon commanders, the hot, tired and very dry men waited while the officers were at the O Group, which allowed time for water to be produced. In 10 Platoon, Richo thought Ray Curtis stole the jerrycans from D and E Platoon. Later, they moved back, past D and E, into the patchy shade of the old rubber plantation, and his section became the right forward section of the platoon share of the perimeter.

To the right, extending into the open ground, was Geoff

Bowcock's 12 Platoon, while behind was the depleted 11 and Hammett's small HQ. Behind D Company itself were D and E Platoon. Tony Hammett 'found to my horror that we had more wire, Claymores and machineguns behind us than we had in front of us. They were right behind us. Old "Buddha" MacDonald was their CSM. The Engineers, being Engineers, were pretty well organised and defended. We had nothing.'

John Salter looked back at the TF HQ area, seeing results of the night before, and noticed what 'seemed to be fence after fence, wondering aloud if it was to keep D Company out or the enemy out'.

Salter's 10 Platoon, like the others, received a single roll of barbed wire, which was duly strung out to their front, and the rest of the day was spent in a quiet way, trying to clear the long grass from before them.

Sergeant Ray Curtis recalled a well in the ruins nearby, but a search found it to be dry. Kemp's Engineers were busy trying to find a suitable location for a new well, but this took time to locate and dig. For the immediate future, water had to be flown in. In a few days time, nature provided more water than anyone wanted, but on the afternoon of the 13th, it was desperately needed at Coral.

Like the other companies, and indeed, like everyone else at Coral, they began digging. Getting below ground level was first priority. Luckily, the grey sandy soil was easy to move. However, some people, who should have known better, were reluctant to dig, even in those conditions. Their laxity was forcefully borne home a few nights later.

Digger Campbell, from his position in the rubber trees, got 'quite a shock to see, to my left rear, people building an impregnable wire barrier, which effectively wired them in and us out. We couldn't have run away if we'd wanted to!' After what he called 'some well-directed and rude remarks', his company was able to get more than the single strand of barbed wire for their front.

Many of the defenders of Coral had been able to go out into the front of the position, to look at the ground where the NVA had been able to assemble, attack and die. They noticed the numerous vertically dug holes in which the Vietnamese had waited, the white cable used to mark part of the area, possibly as a guide into the location, or as the start line for the attack (line of departure, in military terminology).

Ginger Orford, HQ battery, thought that he 'could have made a fortune selling Ho Chi Minh sandals'. Dozens, if not hundreds, littered the ground, dropped or lost by their owners. The NVA and VC often went into the attack barefoot, with their sandals tucked into their belts.

It was obvious to all who had thought about the events of the night of the 12th that a much greater disaster could have occurred during the night. As it was, the NVA had attacked from the direction which was probably least beneficial to them, even though it provided them cover all the way through the bush and rubber plantation, to the very edge of the clearing. The 'ifs' were clear: if the assault had come from the south or west; if the artillery had not had their guns pointing at the attack waves; if the attack had been made on 161 Battery; if the LFT supporting the Dustoff had not been so close and returned so quickly; if the battalion HQ had arrived earlier in the afternoon and moved away, taking with it the Anti-tank Platoon and its 90mm RCLs ...

'From a professional point of view' Ian Ahearn 'felt slightly sorry for the NVA commander. The attack was well laid out. The FUP was sixty to eighty metres out from the gun position. Although he'd been detected by the mortar platoon machinegun, no great action was taken against him. He selected his position well; the FUP protected him from direct fire, and an FUP that brought him in from the side the guns were not pointing when he did his reconnaissance.'

However, due to the requirement to realign the guns to support Tony Hammett's D Company 1RAR, the NVA had found themselves assaulting into the very muzzles of the 105mm guns. Ian Ahearn also points out that 'the fact we had chosen to bund the three guns to the north did a great deal to reduce casualties as these bunds were over a metre high and enemy fire was over a metre to a metre and a half high, enabling us to move around the gun position. In essence, it was a good plan gone wrong through a fluke. If we had not used those three guns, that is, used the three southern guns, or if not adjusted the final fire position for D Company, I have no doubt the enemy plan would have succeeded.'

Back at Nui Dat, Captain John Bullen, with the Survey Troop, which was fully occupied improving the maps of the area, noted the night's details as they came to hand, in a comprehensive record of the events of his time in Vietnam. John listed the names of Survey Corps people away with the force at Coral, and wondered how they had fared during the fighting. The remainder of his day was 'fairly busy with routine tasks and some heavy map demands. Heavy but brief storm late in the afternoon. Much lightning and thunder amidst the usual deafening firing of the artillery. To bed early—on the midnight-until-dawn shift in the CP.'

Sergeant Arthur Penn and the wounded were delivered to the casualty admittance section of an American hospital at Long Binh. Gunner Vic Page was taken straight in and work began on him, while the others, walking wounded, were sorted as to priority and 'were treated fairly well straight away. Just as I was about to be treated,' said Penn, 'it seemed all hell broke loose in the hospital, because when we were hit, the Big Red One was hit, and for two hours I was unfortunate enough to sit in the doorway to the casualty section, and I sat there and watched pre-surgery treatment for what seemed to be an endless number of American soldiers with all sorts of wounds.

'If anything stuck in my mind about Coral, about Vietnam, it was that two-odd hours I sat there and waited. It wasn't pleasant. The staff, particularly the black guys who were the nurses, and the lieutenants, or sisters as we called them, and the doctors, the work they did—there was no panic. It was a case of doing their job and they did it very well, and were very comforting. I believe a lot of credit should go to them for the way they treated and looked after those guys.'

An American lieutenant nurse took him away and attended to the wounds in his hand, and he was then taken to the dentist, because the bullets that struck his F1 had either ricochetted or knocked a piece of the gun into his front teeth, snapping them off. What rankled Arthur was that as he was going to the dentist, all muddy, dirty, with bandaged hand and thick lip, a couple of nearby Americans saw him, recognised him as being an Australian, and said aloud they guessed he had fallen off the back of a truck. Not even recognised as an honourable battle casualty!

After surgery on his jaw, gum and lip, he was returned to the ward, but, being the senior walking wounded from the action, had to identify the artillerymen who had been killed, and escort others who came to do the same for the infantry casualties.

Later in the day, the Australians were taken to a helicopter and flown to Nui Dat, where the senior medical officer decided they should go on to the Australian Hospital at Vung Tau. So on to another helicopter, and they flew further south, to the beachside camp of 1st Australian Field Hospital.

When they arrived 'fairly late in the afternoon, the reception we got was one of disbelief. We were the first to come through, and nothing was too much trouble. Everything they did, everything done that day, I think, was for us'.

The Coral casualties were placed in the same ward, operated on, cared for and received a stream of visitors. Soon there were too many casualties for the hospital to accommodate, so the Rest and Convalescent Centre was taken over as an annexe to the hospital, and the lightly wounded moved there. After a bout of diarrhoea, and a case of infection in his chest wound, Arthur was told he would be going back to Australia on the next plane. But there was a rush of more serious cases, and his departure was delayed. On the condition that his wounds healed cleanly, he was offered a choice of staying or going back to Australia, and he chose to return to 12 Field Regiment, arriving back not long after the end of the Coral operation.

Still with the Americans were the more seriously wounded, such as Mal Hundt, who had passed out on the helicopter. He woke in the airconditioned cold of the ward, with a young woman asking him his age, date of birth, et cetera, and then a priest approached. '"I don't want all this."' he

125

thought. '"I'm getting a sheila asking my life history in one ear, and a padre in the other." A few days later I woke up and saw all the tubes hanging out of me.' After nine days with the US hospital, he was moved to the Australian hospital at Vung Tau, where he had 'an enjoyable back rub from an Australian girl. They were great'.

He was later flown to the Australian hospital at Butterworth, and was again dropped going from the aircraft to the ambulance. His problems were not over. He badly needed to urinate, but was unable to do so. The hospital staff told him not to worry, a catheter had been inserted, and it would all happen automatically. After hours of suffering with a visibly distended bladder, and his repeated complaints, the catheter was withdrawn—and it was found that the closed end had not been snipped off. Mal recalled vibrating like a deflating balloon with the pressure of the escaping liquid.

At Coral, the war was still going on.

The chaplains reacted quickly to the events at Coral. The 1RAR Catholic Chaplain was Father John Tinkler, who had been an Army chaplain since 1965, had travelled to Vietnam on HMAS *Sydney* with many of the battalion, and alternated time in the bush with his colleagues. He did two weeks in the bush and two at Nui Dat, never carried a weapon, and was deeply conscious of his role in a military organisation. Hearing of the battle, he talked his way on to a helicopter going to Long Binh, and spent the next days there, meeting the casualties as they arrived, and doing what he could in the wards.

As usual, the Diggers could not resist joking with each other and the Americans around them. When Joe Griffin awakened after surgery, he was astounded to see a woman bending over him, looked at her closely and commented. 'You know, you're not bad, for a Yank.' This caused great amusement among the Americans.

Soon after, an American wardsman stopped Father Tinkler and asked him if he knew what a night-cart was, to which Tinkler replied it was a sanitary waste disposal system, and briefly explained it. The American had already been told of it by the Diggers, who added such detail as the people who operated the carts had to live at least two towns away because of the odour, but they had invited the Yanks to visit the big cities in Australia, as the new hotels had a new invention there, where one merely pressed a button to get rid of everything. They expressed disbelief when told that all American homes had similar equipment.

A strong believer in the effectiveness of correctly placed tripod-mounted machineguns, Tony Hammett requested tripods for D Company, and enlisted the aid of WO2 Buddha MacDonald, CSM HQ Company and 'an old machinegun man', to conduct a quick course on the tripod-mounted M60. The guns were then positioned to fire 'on beautiful fixed lines, literally six inches above the ground', across the fronts of both D and C Company. They were to prove very effective.

14 May was to see six patrol clashes, roughly in a circle around Coral, as the Australians and Vietnamese tried to find out what the other side was doing. Quite possibly, there were other times during the day when VC or NVA may have seen the Diggers patrolling and not fired, but in any case, the combats which did take place showed the NVA commander in the area that he could not send groups through the vicinity of Coral, or attempt to approach the base without being prepared to fight and to lose men.

On this afternoon, two actions fought within half an hour of each other, by two separate platoons, resulted in two Distinguished Conduct Medals being awarded to junior ranks. For soldiers, the DCM is second only to the Victoria Cross, and is only awarded for exploits in battle.

Early in the morning, Geoff Bowcock had taken two of his three sections out to the north-west, patrolling. They had passed the ruins, crossed the road, and the Suoi Ba Pho, going on to the edge of the rubber trees, without seeing anything except signs of the recent actions. He stopped at about 1200, put his sections down in a defensive position, and radioed for further orders, was told to return, and gave his orders to the corporals.

They would start back, but swing west for some 400 metres, and return on a parallel track to their outward route. Corporal John Pearce, a highly thought-of NCO, began leading the way back but had only gone some twenty-five metres when a volley of automatic fire cracked around them. In the next few seconds Pearce was killed, and three others wounded.

Three enemy, who had probably been following them, or coming along their trail, had opened fire from behind a large tree. If they had not fired then, they soon would have been seen and engaged, or engaged if they tried to move away, so opening fire first was their best choice.

Bowcock called the second section, and they ran to one side, to flank the enemy; crossing a gully, firing on the move, they swept through the enemy position, but no one remained. All that was left was bloodstains and empty cartridge cases.

Bowcock now had to organise the evacuation of his dead and wounded. There were too many for them to carry, and they were some 1500 metres away from Coral. He radioed for a Dustoff.

Back at HQ 1RAR, there was alarm when the grid reference of the contact was received. It had only been intended for the patrol to go 500 metres. Tony Hammett had queried the order, when it was decoded, and been assured what had been sent to him was correct. Fortunately, he had a witness in another company commander, who had been present when the decoding and subsequent query was made.

Out in the contact area, Bowcock was having a frustrating time trying to persuade the Australian helicopter pilot to come in and land for the casualties. The pilot insisted on a guarantee that the landing zone was secure but Bowcock could only say what he knew: that his immediate area was clear of enemy. Despite strong language and a description of the severity of the injuries, the pilot would not descend. Finally, a passing American pilot came up on the air, and asked what the problem was, then volunteered to land. He did so, while the Australian helpfully circled the area looking for enemy.

The incident still angers Bowcock many years after the event. The casualties were lifted into the sky, and in Bowcock's words, 'disappeared into the medical system, out of the platoon'.

The other rifle companies of 1RAR also had been patrolling. South-east, on the far side of Coral, at 1250 hours, Second Lieutenant Chris Forde's 5 Platoon B/1RAR had stopped, when the sentry fired on a party of enemy: six unarmed bearers and four armed escort. In a short gunfight, the VC escort tried to outflank the Australians but were turned away, and the enemy escaped after abandoning twelve kilos of rice, some cigarettes and sandals. Two VC were wounded.

Later, north of Forde's contact, at 1630, Bob Sutton's 2 Platoon was in an ambush position at a track junction, looking west, with visibility about twenty-five metres in clear ground, then broken for about fifty metres. Then thirteen enemy, well camouflaged, were counted moving along the far side of the clearing. The Aussies held fire to allow them to get closer, and to see what their intentions were. They seemed to be waiting for someone, while collecting more camouflage, and two actually moved into the ambush position while doing this, but were not fired on. Then they started to move away, and the left forward pit opened fire with SLR and M60.

The enemy split into two groups and escaped. The SLR and M60 could not cover the area with enough fire to damage the group, and it was suggested that M72 or other high-explosive rounds should have been used.

Thirty minutes later, 700 metres to the north, 7 Platoon contacted nine enemy, presumed to be from the earlier clash. Seven enemy were killed and the other two captured, with all nine weapons, for a loss of one Australian killed and one wounded.

Lance Corporal David Griffiths was the section 2ic, armed with an M79 grenade launcher. The tall grass in the contact area hindered his accurate use of the weapon, so he stood up, but was seen by the enemy and fired at, being wounded in both arms, and Corporal Dawson, the section commander, was hit and killed instantly. Griffiths ignored his wounds, picked up Dawson's weapon, and took command of the section. He personally killed three NVA and the two who surrendered were influenced to do so by Griffiths' actions. He suffered a third wound, in the chest, during the continued fighting. David Griffiths was later awarded the Distinguished Conduct Medal for this feat.

The machinegunner had long complained about carrying such a weapon, stating that he was a conscientious objector, and asking to be relieved of the duty. During the battle, he did what Digger Campbell regarded as 'the bravest, or perhaps stupidest, thing I've ever heard. At pointblank range, instead of shooting an NVA, he practically arrested him.'

Later, at 1730 hours, Forde's platoon again contacted a number of enemy. While sweeping through some open ground, Forde had two sections abreast, about 100 metres apart. His left-hand section moved into a copse to clear it and surprised a number of NVA in the trees, preparing to ambush the right-hand section and Forde's HQ.

At a range of five metres, Forde's men fired, and in the firefight killed four enemy for the loss of Private Chris Nesbit killed and Private Norden wounded. Four AK47s were captured, but one M16 was lost to the NVA.

The bare facts of the small battle fail to convey the reality of what occurred in that patch of bush. Private Richard 'Dick' Norden, of Gundagai, was awarded the Distinguished Conduct Medal for his actions. The citation for the award describes Norden's part in the fight.

In the initial contact both the forward scout and the section commander were wounded some twenty to thirty paces in front of the remainder of the leading section, which was isolated from the remainder of the platoon due to heavy and accurate enemy fire.

Private Norden, a member of the leading section, asked for covering fire and ran forward under heavy fire to the wounded section commander. He killed one Viet Cong whilst moving forward, and having expended his ammunition recovered the enemy's automatic weapon which he used against further Viet Cong while assisting the wounded section commander back to the section. Due to this initial action, the life of the section commander was saved under intense enemy fire.

Although wounded in his initial move forward, Private Norden again advanced to the forward scout. He was fired on by an enemy soldier, but pressed forward and reached the scout, killing the Viet Cong, who had been using the scout as a shield. Private Norden, having determined that the scout was dead, returned to the section, collected grenades, and cleared the area so that the body of the scout could be recovered. His three attacks into the enemy position, on his own, resulted in the enemy position being secured.

Private Norden showed a complete disregard for his own personal safety, and by his courage and devotion to duty ensured the evacuation of a wounded man and the recovery of the body of the forward scout. Private Norden personally killed at least three Viet Cong in this action.

(The medal was presented by the Governor of New South Wales, Sir Roden Cutler VC. Sir Roden is said to have remarked to 'Dick' Norden that he did not know what one had to do these days to win a VC, implying that Norden deserved one. Norden left the Army and joined the Commonwealth Police. Sadly, he was killed in a low-speed motorcycle accident in 1972.)

Captain Bob Hennessy, the company commander, believed that 'Norden's DCM was well won. I think of his coolness, his courage, his resolution. The way he went out and winkled those guys, the way he exacted immediate retribution for Cowboy Nesbit's death, will always remain in my mind.'

Even from the company position, Hennessy could hear the voice of Forde shouting orders 1000 metres away: 'Never a faint heart, Blue, a wonderful officer.'

During the contact, Forde had been operating under some difficulty, as the handset for his radio had been smashed in the earlier contact, and the noise of an Army reconnaissance helicopter which was overhead during the action made it almost impossible to relay information by voice.

However, both contacts were successful, particularly the latter. If the platoon had not been spread out to cover the area, the enemy would have been able to initiate the ambush, would have been difficult to locate and close with, and Australian casualties would have been heavier.

Meanwhile 3RAR had moved west to FSPB Coogee, to achieve the necessary separation for more efficient use of the available firepower, and to begin dominating their AO by intensive patrolling and ambushing. Three contacts were made, with one enemy killed.

The effect on the enemy of these clashes, in one of which an entire group, possibly a whole squad of nine, failed to return, can only be surmised. They must have realised that their former occupation was now challenged. A porcupine with deadly spikes protruding in all directions had taken up residence.

On that afternoon of 14 May, at Coral, Col Adamson was walking to battalion HQ when he met Lieutenant Colonel Bennett, who asked what Adamson thought the enemy would do next. Col was ready for just such a query, and 'reached into my basic pouch, and pulled out a copy of "The Enemy" pamphlet, and said, "Sir, he's following precisely what the textbook says. He's probing, he's trying to draw fire, he hasn't forgotten us. We're sitting right across his main supply route, and he's trying to determine the extent of our boundaries. Probing is the order of the day." I think he thought much the same thing.

'In fact, about half an hour after I left him, we caught a sniper sitting in a tree about 300 or 400 metres out. We knocked him off.'

(Instructional staff from Army schools of the era will doubtless be pleased to know that at least one member of the Army actually gained something from 'The Enemy'!)

So far, the actions at Coral had been almost exclusively fought by 1RAR and the elements of Jack Kelly's 12 Field Regiment there. But Australian armour was operating near-by, and was soon to make its presence felt.

Major J.D. 'Blue' Keldie was commanding A Squadron 3 Cavalry Regiment (A/3 Cav) at this time, operating in the Binh Duong–Bien Hoa area. Keldie and his squadron HQ, at Bearcat, were ordered to escort six 6000-gallon fuel tankers via Saigon and Tan Uyen to Binh Co. There they would be received by a US cavalry unit, 1 Squadron 4th Cavalry, known as the 'Quarterhorses' from their abbreviated unit designation, 1/4 Cav.

Keldie realised this escort operation was of great value, as it provided a reconnaissance of ground over which the Australian armoured vehicles were to pass and fight later. Despite two minor ambushes, the convoy fought its way to the delivery point, and A/3 Cav moved to Coral.

Keldie's vehicles spent the next two days rushing back and forth in the area, escorting convoys of Australian or US vehicles. Twice they traversed Route 15, allegedly closed to allied traffic by enemy pressure.

While returning from one handover, Keldie's men received an indication of just how many, and how confident, the enemy were in the area. Ahead of them, crossing the road, they saw a company of NVA, who passed so quickly that the APCs could not deploy fast enough to bring fire on to them.

The area was covered with grass about two metres in height, which made detection of people in it very difficult unless they passed close by, or crossed an open space such as a road. The best Keldie could do in these circumstances was call by radio for armed helicopters from Bien Hoa, who arrived and attacked the NVA, being able to see them from above.

In addition, the APC HQ and 1 Troop ran into an ambush, presumably laid by local force VC, who seemed to be confused by the rapidly moving armoured vehicles, which were travelling at about forty kilometres an hour. The APCs did not slow, but sped through the ambush just north of Long Binh.

Before moving to Coral, some of them were able to spend a night in the relative civilisation of the air-base at Bien Hoa, and as the M113s rolled past the airstrip, Geoff Murray, a driver in Bruce Richards' troop, recalls looking at two Boeing 707s filled with smiling, waving Americans on their way home.

Later in the afternoon, Lieutenant Richards lined up his men and gave a short talk about being on good behaviour in the US establishments they might visit. Geoff Murray does not have many memories of the night, but one of them is of being asked by 'a big crew-cut Yank duty sergeant what the idea was coming in here and patting our girls on the ass'. Another episode involved borrowing a jeep, speeding alongside the airstrip and rolling the jeep over, with none of the three Aussies aboard it suffering injury.

In another club—or it may have been the same one—Dave Brooks, who commanded Murray's APC, found himself on the stage, accompanying the girl singer, to the acclaim of the audience, though he cannot recall the song.

Next day, reality intruded, when Brooks' Section led all the way to Coral. Horror stories about the place abounded, and they were told they were sure to be heavily ambushed en route. Nothing happened.

In the artillery position at Coral, Bob Lowry, commanding the left section of three guns of 102 Battery, was standing by a pile of galvanised iron, calling in an approaching helicopter, but as it neared the ground, the rotor blast began to lift and hurl the sheets of iron. Lowry realised he was in danger, and started to run. Then, for some reason, he stopped, grabbed a water can, turned and lifted it chest high, just in time to take the force of a flying sheet of iron.

The heat and humidity were oppressive, in the last days before the wet season broke. Water remained a problem throughout the occupation of Coral. Tony Hammett noticed something which incensed him. After morning stand-down and before evening stand-to, he would go around the company position to check that normal procedures were being followed, and that the Claymores in the D and E Platoon defences were not armed. In his travels, he noticed that the supply of water was much more lavish in the rear positions, with a few people having a jerrycan each, and one actually had a portable shower erected. His soldiers were getting one jerrycan for eight men.

Hammett went back to his area, told the Diggers where the water was, adding 'go and help yourselves. So the soldiers used to quietly wander up and help themselves to any jerrycan of water that they found.'

Other people recalled the shortage of water, and the 'Administration' paragraph of the TF after-action report stated that water-supply at Coral was difficult, with air being the only means of replenishment, requiring five Chinook sorties daily, delivering about 3000 gallons each day in new rubber fuel bladders.

Second Lieutenant Glen Duus, an Army Sioux pilot, flew the Engineer commander, Major John Kemp, on a reconnaissance for a likely water-supply point. They saw water in the Suoi Ba Pho, but also noticed pits and other holes in the ground, and the strange behaviour of a number of local people, ostensibly farmers, who totally ignored the circling helicopter. This was very unusual, and the location did not appear to be secure enough for the many trips necessary to collect the amount of water needed.

At dusk, Neil Weekes' 3 Platoon suffered two wounded, in circumstances which he believes were never resolved. Corporal Shorty Thirkell was moving to the pit of Lance Corporal Cebria 'Frank' Matons when there was a burst of fire, wounding both men. Officially, they were hit by RPG fragments, but Weekes suspects it was machinegun rounds from the APCs in the position, who had not been informed of the location of the flanks of the infantry companies, and were to cover the gap between A and C Companies with their fire. As the APCs fired out, towards the enemy, after the wounding, it was never able to be determined exactly what did happen.

In the hospital, Matons told Father Tinkler that he had started to pray that night. Tinkler thought that at last the young fellows were turning to prayer, so he asked Matons what he had prayed for, to be told, 'I've been ★★★★ hit once, don't let 'em hit me again!'

In the hospital, Frank Matons was reunited with another mate, Joe Griffin, wounded in the volley of RPGs fired into the 11 Platoon position on the first night. After surgery, Griffin was held in the US hospital for a time, and almost sent away down the US medical evacuation system until it was realised at the last second that he was an Aussie. In this confusion, his medical records while with the Americans were lost and remain so to this day. Evacuated to Australia, he spent six months in Concord Repatriation Hospital, where he met and married his wife.

Other distractions for Australians in an American hospital followed, including the awarding of US Purple Heart medals to all the wounded, the Diggers just missing out at the last second. Mick Grimes has vivid memories of Mal Hundt in great pain, coughing as directed by the nursing staff to clear blood clots from the tubing in his stomach. Another feature was the trio nicknamed the 'Three Monkeys', 1RAR Diggers with bandaged eyes, ears and jaw.

Being able to walk about, and getting bored, one day Grimes went wandering, and found himself in the very end ward, to see all the patients in oxygen tents, all with 'horrendous injuries', quadruple amputations . . . He only saw the first four, and fled. It was where the hopeless cases were placed to die.

One American came to Perry Neil (wounded by the RPG volley into 11 Platoon before the attack on Coral), and asked him to teach him how to swear, adding, 'Goddam, you Aussies sure can swear great!' Perry told him to use 'bloody' every second word. A hospital orderly came around asking who wanted to drink from the extensive list of beverages, and Perry heard him say 'tea', so asked for it. It arrived in the American style, cold, with ice cubes, in a glass . . . the disappointed Digger could not drink it.

Later that night, Bob Lowry, in 102 Battery, was told that one of the Bombardiers was refusing to do his turn on guard. Lowry went across to see what was the problem, and found the man very disillusioned, having lost faith in his section mates. Lowry told the Bombardier that he would go with him on guard, and they went to the pit, sat on the edge, and Lowry asked what was going on.

During the attack on the gun position, with RPGs and mortars exploding all around, and the ammunition bay on fire, when the Bombardier had run to his own shell scrape, he had found it occupied by someone else who refused to vacate it, and had the rank to back his decision. This had thoroughly disillusioned the young soldier. He had had enough.

Lowry began explaining in a reasonable manner that things were not so bad, when there was a movement in front, and instantly his pistol was pointing that way, then he looked over to see the Bombardier laughing; it had been a rat. That laughter eased all the tension, the problem disappeared, the Bombardier regained his sense of belonging, took the wider view, and Lowry returned to the CP.

But the enemy were active. Pieces of rag were found tied to the barbed wire, and through the Starlite scope single figures could be seen crawling around in the gap between A and C Companies. The NVA and VC were busy adding to their information about the base.

It began to rain heavily, drenching the soldiers who sat waiting for the expected attack. Les Tranter's platoon reported that stones were being thrown into the position, presumably in an attempt to make them fire and reveal their positions. Tranter was discussing this with the RSM, who advised throwing grenades back, when lightning struck the telephone line, giving him a shock. Soon after, his hutchi collapsed with a sudden loud snap, frightening him and drenching him with the gallons of water which had been collected. Two of the weapon pits were flooded.

Fire Support Base Coral had little to recommend itself to its occupants, who were sitting in grey mud and water, after two days of baking heat, patrol clashes, a night battle, and now torrential rain.

During the day, in the outwardly more peaceful area of Phuoc Tuy Province, John Bullen was able to visit the refugee village of Ap Suoi Nghe, north-west of Nui Dat. Some of the building materials had been provided by the Australians, and Bullen's surveyors were busy subdividing blocks of land for agricultural use. He returned to Nui Dat and noted that there had been no rain, but 'the atmosphere is humid and dark'.

Later in the evening he read a newspaper account of the deaths in Saigon a week before of four Australian newspapermen. Bullen had often met them in the Mess, and thought only the day before that he had not seen Mike Birch for some time. Later he found that the four, and one survivor, had ignored direct warnings about going to the place where they were killed by the VC.

The Australian newspapers had reported the actions, along

137

with other events in the war. General Khang, commanding the ARVN III Corps Tactical Zone, and Lieutenant General Jonathan Seaman, commanding II Field Force Vietnam, had been quoted as saying that the enemy thrust on Saigon had been crushed. The Saigon Government stated that the nine-day offensive had destroyed 10 700 homes, creating 104 000 refugees. ARVN and allied deaths in the nine days were 416, while 5200 enemy were killed. (These figures were later agreed by the commander of the VC military forces.) In an editorial, the Sydney *Daily Telegraph* observed that 4000 VC and NVA had been killed in the offensive so that at the Paris Peace Talks Hanoi could attempt to bargain from a position of strength.

In fact, counted enemy dead came to 5757, with 418 PW, an average of 640 killed each day, higher than in the Tet fighting, when the average had been 600.

The rains which came at night flooded every pit, except those covered and drained properly. Noel Sproles, TF CP duty officer, came off duty confident that John Collinson had kept theirs dry, and was irate to find Collinson asleep in a pit full of water, only his head sticking out. This was the pit Sproles had dug for them; now he spent the day baling it out and working on it, then went back on duty.

He woke after falling asleep at the radio to find Brigadier Hughes sitting alongside him, reading the reports. Hughes had not been pleased to find the Duty Officer asleep, but presumably realised the burden on them. Sproles and Collinson were expected to man the radio twenty-four hours a day, seven days a week, plus dig their own pits, cook and so on for themselves, with no assistance. Extra officers, including Alan Vickers from the tank squadron, were brought in to ease the load, and later, when Armoured Command Vehicles (ACV) were used, matters eased somewhat, but on the first days they were, as Sproles recalls, 'consistently tired'.

The Engineers had dug a hole and were building the TF CP, which would contain the TF HQ elements, Artillery and air HQs. Supplies for this were available, but another of the omissions noted by Noel Sproles was that there seemed to be nothing in the way of similar supplies brought in for anyone else. Naturally, being in that line of business, the engineers themselves were well supplied, but Sproles resorted to 'midnight requisitioning' of steel pickets and corrugated iron for the pit he shared with Collinson. Being on duty at night, Sproles could go out of the CP and carry material such as the iron sheets to the pit, and cover it with sandbags. Collinson refused to indulge in such ways.

On the midnight shift at Nui Dat HQ, John Bullen noted that it was a 'quiet session with little action. Forward HQ is having difficulty maintaining communications due to the heavy rain falling there.' Reading preliminary reports of the previous day's fighting, he formed the opinion that most of the enemy casualties were inflicted by air power, and reflected that 'I hate to think how we could manage without the over-whelming air power we possess'.

Actually, sustained accurate artillery and mortar fire was responsible for inflicting most casualties, as it had been since 1914. Aircraft of all types were constrained by weather, ability to detect the target, and being able to stay in the location for only a limited time, among other shortcomings.

15 May was relatively quiet, and patrols from both battalions made only three contacts, with one enemy killed.

On the 15th the APCs escorted yet another convoy to Nui Dat, and returned again to Long Binh with one more, then moved on to Coral, arriving at 1500 hours.

Keldie had with him about thirty-five AFVs; HQ A Squadron, 1 Troop, plus one element and one section of his Support Troop. The Task Force commander, Brigadier Hughes, met him as he came into the base through the barbed wire. As Keldie recalls, Brigadier Hughes said to him. 'You are to lay-out a defence of this firebase; it will not be penetrated. You are to co-ordinate and command the local defence.'

Brigadier Hughes' intention was to have 'Keldie do the co-ordination of the defence of the various elements within the Task Force area. The battalion commander, Bennett, had the responsibility of fighting his own battalion, he had his own part of the perimeter, and he was responsible for that. Keldie, on my orders, tied up the co-ordination of Bennett's right flank with his own APCs, the guns, the engineers, the supply units, that were on the battalion's right flank, moving around to the other flank. Keldie, on my instigation, did the co-ordination, particularly with the minor units, but I commanded the defence of the whole area.'

Keldie realised that with only three hours of daylight remaining, he was faced by several obvious problems, not the least of which was simply reconnoitring the ground. So he set off with his four section commanders on a foot reconnaissance of the area, which measured about 700 metres by 400 metres.

Reconnaissance completed, Keldie decided that the major threat to Coral was posed from the north and north-east. In that direction, in the distance, was thick forest, which gradually became lighter as one neared the FSPB, and then became the cleared but old rubber plantation in which Coral was located. An enemy's approach from this direction would be much easier than from the other sides of the base. In addition, north and north-east were the directions from which the NVA were approaching Saigon.

Keldie had to co-ordinate the following in defence of Coral:

the flanks of 1RAR, holding the most vulnerable north–north-east sector;

102 Battery, Royal Australian Artillery, the direct support battery for 1RAR;

A Battery, 2/35 Artillery, a self-propelled US unit, which had to be allocated a position on the perimeter through sheer necessity, though it was on the least vulnerable sector;

1 Troop 3 Cavalry Regiment, also on the perimeter; engineers from several Australian units, comprising about fifty men, also allocated a sector;

the Task Force signals squadron, who were also allocated a sector, and as Keldie recalls, 'did a fine job'; and

another group of about fifty men, 'a real mixture', whose main weapon was a 106mm recoilless launcher (106mm RCL), also allocated a perimeter sector to defend.

An Orders Group was assembled, and Keldie designated the defence sectors, largely based on the various units as they occupied a part of the perimeter. Commanders for each of these sectors were named, and allocated numbers on the separate radio net created for the defence co-ordination of the base. Work then began to get as much as possible done before darkness fell again. In Keldie's words, 'It was purely a case of bringing the strings together and creating a co-ordinated defence.'

Keldie located his CP in the centre. His counter-penetration force was to be 1 Troop. Routes to likely vulnerable points were chosen, marked and walked along by the vehicle commanders, to give them some idea of what they would encounter if they had to drive inside the base at night, in the midst of a battle.

Keldie recalls, 'The whole area looked like a mess of tapes at one stage.'

Gus Ballentine, Troop Sergeant in 1 Troop of Keldie's squadron, tried to memorise the gaps between the infantry positions, in case of a night move, from his position behind D and E Platoons—at whose defences Hammett's D/1RAR had remarked—and made what preparations he could, in light of his considerable experience.

There can have been few, if any, occasions since the early days of World War II when such a mixture of Australians has held a forward base so lightly, in the presence of large numbers of determined enemy.

The quality of both sides became evident, as their reconnaissance teams sighted and clashed with each other. Each must have realised the other was preparing for the coming night.

Keldie himself saw his opponents, while involved in siting the 106mm RCL. 'While debating where it should go, I was actually looking down a light track through the long grass. I was in the perimeter, the gun commander was wheeling it to where I wanted it, and the ammunition handler was standing outside, looking back at the alignment of the gun. I noticed standing behind him three people, all with short haircuts. They were a recce party from an NVA regiment, equally fascinated with what we were doing, because we hadn't fired on them. Little did they know we had no ammo for the 106.

'We went about our business; they went about theirs. It was indicative of how close the reconnaissance was, and how vulnerable we were in that tall grass.'

In the 1RAR sector, Tony Hammett had continually sent out patrols into the rubber trees to his front, dominating the area out to the road, along which he put observation and listening posts. He was under no illusions as to the ability of his opponents. 'You had to keep patrolling in front of your own area, otherwise you never knew who was creeping up, and the VC-NVA were adept at close reconnaissance. Their individual skills, fieldcraft, camouflage, observation skills were superb, and the only way to keep them out was to keep patrolling.'

Time was slipping away, and so much remained to be done. At 1730 more barbed wire was strung, and by great efforts, at last light, two-thirds of the perimeter—that held to be the most endangered—benefited by two double Dannert fences as an outer, with an inner single one-Dannert fence. All sectors had Claymore mines positioned.

At least, that was what was thought to be in position. The rifle platoons of 1RAR had little faith in the single strand of wire stretched along their fronts. Many were aware of, and commented on, the thicker barriers behind them, protecting the inner units. More than a few people resolved to 'acquire' the necessary steel pickets (posts) by the age-old army methods.

As well as the more obvious preparations by the infantry, armour and other groups on the ground at Coral, the equally important preparations by the artillery, to call down the devastating blows from distant guns, had been made.

Back at Nui Dat, John Bullen of the Survey Troop wrote in his journal that it had been a very quiet day and he had been able to catch up on a lot of minor tasks. His main item of note was the continuing lack of glasses for one of his draughtsmen, who had broken them in January—fourteen weeks ago —and would have to wait at least another five weeks, which

142

Bullen described as a 'disgraceful situation' for a medical system.

As darkness fell at Coral on 15 May, Keldie was 'reasonably confident we had a fighting chance' of keeping the enemy out of the base.

Gus Ballentine, 1 Troop sergeant, prepared to sleep, with his stretcher under his hatch in the APC, so that the radio and weapon were close by.

In the CP of 102 Battery, Stan Carbines was on duty, as battery surveyor, with Trevor Bryant. Having spent the previous night in the pouring rain, keeping their weapons and ammunition dry, waiting for an attack, he wondered if it would eventuate this time.

The rifle company infantry had also been assessing the likelihood of attack. Paul Richardson, in 10 Platoon D/1RAR, had estimated from his past experience that attack on the first night was unlikely, but expected an attack, if it was to be made, on the night of the 15th.

Sitting by John Salter's pit, he had remarked, 'If the buggers come, they'll come tonight.' However, Richo had not dug a pit for himself, and casually thought of using the section rubbish pit if necessary. But 'it was full of bloody tins at this stage'.

It was a beautiful night. At about 2100 the moon came up, and Richardson, lying under his hutchi, smoking, thought 'Yeah, bloody perfect night for them,' before he dozed off.

5 Second Battle

An enemy will usually have three courses open to him. Of these, he will select the fourth.

von Moltke

SILENCE SETTLED around the mass of Fire Support Base Coral. The infantrymen, the gunners, the armoured, the engineers, the signallers ... smelling of sweat, tobacco, gun oil, Vietnamese dirt impregnated into the cloth of their uniforms ... some sleeping, some awake, listening to hissing radio or watching along the mass of a machinegun, wondering when Charlie will make his move, thinking of Australia, or leave to Vung Tau, or Hong Kong, Taipei, Bangkok ...

At 1907 the companies of 1RAR reported, in turn, that they were standing-to.

There had been little during the day to indicate an impending attack, apart from the relatively small clashes and sightings of single enemy. The activity was what could be expected from an area known to be used by the enemy.

Eleven kilometres away to the north and east, the NVA units began their approach march through the night. Battalions, companies and platoons were led away from their afternoon positions, along the paths and trails reconnoitred and known by the guides and local forces used for this purpose. Some of the young NVA had only entered South Vietnam one or two days before this night, and excitement must have surged at the thought of being about to take part in the destruction of some of the enemy, so close to Saigon.

At 2000 reports began to come in to the various CPs, filtering back to Keldie's Armoured Command Vehicle (ACV), a huge thing, as Geoff Cameron described it, 'as big as a two-storey block of flats'. A series of light signals, flares and rockets were being launched into the night sky.

144

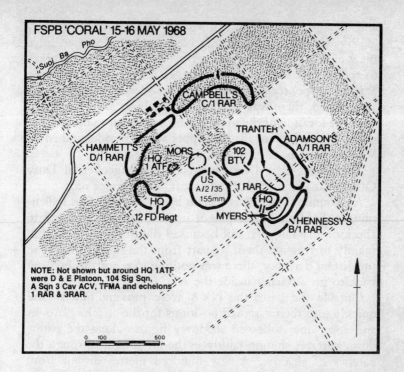

FSPB 'CORAL' 15-16 MAY 1968

CAMPBELL'S
C/1 RAR

TRANTER

ADAMSON'S
A/1 RAR

HAMMETT'S
D/1 RAR

HQ
1 ATF

MORS

102
BTY

US
A/2/35
155mm

1 RAR

HQ

HQ
12 FD Regt

MYERS

HENNESSY'S
B/1 RAR

NOTE: Not shown but around HQ 1ATF
were D & E Platoon, 104 Sig Sqn,
A Sqn 3 Cav ACV, TFMA and echelons
1 RAR & 3RAR.

0   100   500
                       m

At first the Australians were unaware of the exact meaning
of these, but as the operation continued, and the signals were
repeated each time, they soon understood what each was intended to mean, and began to read them, to know what the
NVA were intending. They then recognised the signals
for mustering the troops and for indicating the direction of
attack.

Prisoners later confirmed that because of reliance on not
using radio, runners were employed. While these were adequate in daylight, they were inefficient at night, particularly
in battle, so the system of lights and flares was devised and
used even when it became obvious that their enemy understood them.

At 2100 the listening posts were brought in, and Tony
Hammett thought they 'certainly came back in pretty fast'.
The streams of green tracer in the sky had been seen by many

145

and the significance was not lost on everyone.

Private James, commanding Neil Weekes' 7 Section since the wounding of Corporal 'Shorty' Thirkell, came to Weekes to report that they could see an NVA sapper, through the Starlite 'scope, trying to cut the wire. Weekes went forward and looked, there was the quiet figure busy at the wire. To keep the location of the machinegun unknown to the enemy, it was decided to engage the sapper with grenades and M16. Weekes went back to his pit, and to sleep.

The 1RAR War Diary logged the changeover of Duty Officers at 2315: Mick Bindley off, Phil Davies on.

At around midnight, as was his habit, Sergeant Gus Ballentine, in Keldie's 1 Troop, got up and 'prowled around to check on my Diggers, not because I did not trust them, but mainly to reassure them.' Apart from the signs of tracer in the distant dark sky, there was nothing to report, so he went back to his stretcher inside the APC.

Outside the base, the NVA were moving quietly and quickly into their assigned positions for the attack. Platoons and companies followed shadowy figures along the paths, dusty surfaces shining faintly in the moonlight, through the patches of shadow. A few hundred metres distant from Coral, they were led to the end of the length of communications cable that ran to the line where the attack would begin. Each man took the cable in a circle formed by thumb and forefinger, and moved on more quietly.

Waiting along the cable were more guides who took the soldiers to their attack positions, along the drainage ditch noted by many Australians in past days. Also in the ditch were the medical teams, with their stretchers and supplies. To be close to the enemy was safe, for they would be reluctant to call in their artillery and air so near themselves.

Along the ditch crouched or lay the assault waves; some even had time to snatch a quick cigarette, glow and smoke carefully hidden. Then they waited; soldiers with Asian patience, leaders and cadre busy with the last-minute matters which inevitably arise. But there was reason for confidence, as they were now safely arraigned for the battle, undetected by the foreigners just over there, across that silvery sea of grass, over the field of moonlight.

Also waiting were people in the base, counting the minutes for their duty shift to end. In 1RAR HQ area was Ned Kelly, veteran of the first tour of duty in 1965–6, now a driver. Together with Morry Bedford (also known as 'Barney Rubble'), he watched his sector with an M60 machinegun. He looked at his watch, and remarked to Bedford that in another twenty minutes they would be able to wake Harry White and John Goodwin, and get some sleep.

It seemed to Ned that he had no sooner said it than they heard mortars firing out in the darkness.

At 0215 an accurate and moderately heavy mortar barrage suddenly fell on the artillery positions, TF HQ and Keldie's CP. All these would have been easily seen and marked for the bombardment by the active NVA reconnaissance teams earlier. Then salvoes of RPG rounds began streaking into the position, also seeming to be intended for the command area of Coral.

Keldie's ACV alone had six antennae, while TF HQ used the 'pancake antenna', which looked like 'a griddle sitting in the sky', and gave very good communications but was easily seen. Being so obvious, these attracted many of the hundreds of RPG rounds fired during the night.

Paul Richardson, who had dozed off thinking the night was right for an attack, was woken by the 'bloody horrific noise', and slid out of his shelter, but did not pull the cord to collapse it. His laxity in not digging meant that he had nowhere to go below ground away from the showering rockets, so he slid into the rubbish pit, and 'sat amongst all these bloody empty pork-and-bean and bloody ham-and-lima-bean tins, and thought, "This is no bloody good." I looked up, and right between me and platoon headquarters was this dead rubber tree, and I thought if one of those rockets hits the tree, I was gone. So I started to shovel out the section rubbish pit, and that eventually became my fighting pit. Mind you, I dug the thing fairly smartly, too. It was down to a reasonable scrape by the time the rockets finished.'

At TF HQ, Noel Sproles and John Collinson were still in a pit without overhead protection, and looked out at the beginnings of the attack. Leaves were fluttering down, like autumn, on to them as the rockets streaked through the rubber trees over their heads. Then they heard a familiar sound, a cracking thumping noise, and realised that rounds of small arms were passing overhead. A machinegun was firing at the HQ area also.

'Rudely awoken by a lot of noise, mortars and whatever else', Gus Ballentine, of Keldie's 1 Troop, jumped off his stretcher, and was 'quickly on top—and just as quickly down again! Looking through the periscope, it was like what one may see now on video clips: tracers, flares and general mayhem. Radios crackled, and our Troop was on standby. I remember that my Troop leader's APC would not start'.

The memory of that sight, 'the crazy nightmare of tracers covering Coral like a king-size spider web', remains with him to this day.

Not far away from him John Flood and Paul Moss leaped up in their APC, and collided trying to shut the back door, Flood nearly losing fingers in the hasty slamming of the heavy metal. To add to discomfort under fire, the vehicle was fitted with a turret, but the hatch would not close properly. John sat under it, looking up 'waiting for the bomb to come down. Bombs exploded in front and at the back, destroying the jerrycans, and I remembered what my instructor told me, that APCs are impervious to mortar attack, thinking this is the time we're going to find out if it's true.'

3 Troop of Keldie's APCs was lined up on the western side of the base, and mortars began exploding in a row along the line. Nearby Engineers thought safety lay inside the vehicles, and several scrambled into one. A very close near miss rocked the M113, and the visitors promptly clambered out again, into their pits. This was all watched with hilarity by Wally Fiedler and other members of the nearby Assault Pioneer Platoon of 1RAR, whose amusement was increased next morning, at the sight of all the engineer heads poking out of water-filled pits.

Lieutenant Colonel Bennett, 1RAR, had not thought an attack was intended, but as the reports came in he realised that the enemy were preparing to do so. He soon noted two things of interest: 'Firstly, that they virtually used the same line of attack to the base, which was pretty stupid of them, and secondly, there was very little evidence of diversionary activity on the flanks of that main axis of attack. The whole thing was fairly unprofessional, I thought at the time.'

Reports from all the companies poured into 1RAR HQ, with details of compass bearings to the enemy positions.

Along the irrigation ditch, and in the trees to the north and east, the assault troops and second wave began to move forward, in their little clusters of three men, under their own flaring RPG trails. Ahead were the intermittent flashes of exploding mortars and rockets. All depended on getting across that field of grass, into the enemy position.

Task Force Commander's Diary:

0240 1RAR to TF: A Company 1RAR under attack. Continued mortar and small arms fire.

It will be recalled that there was a large gap between Col Adamson's A Company and Digger Campbell's C Company. An intense barrage of mortars and RPGs fell on the left of Adamson's position, causing casualties to almost an entire section in Weekes' platoon. Even in the darkness, the NVA seemed to know where to direct their fire.

Neil Weekes, sound asleep, had to be woken by his batman, Schultz. The infantry had become so accustomed to the sound of artillery nearby that the enemy mortars did not wake them. He tried to report that they were being mortared and hit by RPG rockets, and soon realised how the NVA were able to place accurate fire on him.

A prominent tree grew out of the platoon position, and it became obvious the enemy were using it as an aiming mark and reference point. The rockets and bombs hailed down around Weekes' men, who were head and shoulders above ground, trying to see the foe.

Young and Wallis were killed by mortars, and others were wounded. Private James went back and reported to Weekes, and together they crawled forward, where Weekes checked the casualties. The machinegunners, Anderson and Monty, were unhurt, so Weekes decided to move them back near platoon headquarters.

149

The NVA assault waves began to advance, and from his vantage point in the middle, Keldie had 'a very good view of what they looked like coming in. The first attack came in due east. I was looking across the back of the artillery position, which could not do much—fire support had to come from Coogee and Corps and IIFFV artillery. It was an interesting sight to see the initial assault wave moving at night. Their AK47s and support weapons looked like a firework display at first, as they were moving in what I regard as one of the most near-perfect formations I have seen.'

But, facing those formations and assessing the situation around his platoon, Neil Weekes gave 'an order I thought I would not ever give: "Fix bayonets!" There were a few queries, so I called again, "3 Platoon, fix bayonets!" Someone said aloud, "Hell."'

Having lost a third of his position, Weekes prepared to defend the area remaining, all too aware that the gap to C Company was now wider. He noticed the attackers were led by small groups armed with RPGs and AKs, who did not seem to be paying too much attention to him, but pushing on towards the guns of 102 Battery.

On the other extremity of A Company, Mal Meadows' 1 Platoon was bordering the B Company area, with Gary Prendergast's 6 Platoon as his right-hand neighbours. Meadows was dozing in his shell scrape, when his batman, Rod Quarrell, woke him with, 'Skip, they're out there.' They had watched the flares and tracer, and waited.

Then as the attack began, they could see shadowy figures some forty to fifty metres away, to the front. As well as pushing hard past Neil Weekes' platoon, the NVA put pressure on Bob Sutton's position, in the centre, and also tried to move Meadows' group, and get in between him and B Company, but to Meadows it seemed 'fairly desultory on their part. I had the impression of probing, rather than assault in force. They got to within about thirty metres—the ones we were shooting at were rather more than a cricket pitch away.'

Lieutenant Colonel Kelly, CO 12 Field Regiment, had never had faith in the ability of the mortar-locating radar, and had recommended against its purchase. It could track a single bomb in the air, but became confused if there were more in flight. Kelly, determined to get some use from them, placed them in a visible position so the enemy would fire at them. Then, in the old way, compass bearings were taken to the origin of the enemy fire; these were reported to HQ; and where they intersected was the probable position of the enemy, so was shelled.

(Major General Kelly described this use of the radars in an interview with the author in July 1986. Div Loc Battery members may now realise why their equipment was under fire in 1968.)

Counter-battery fire was placed on the locations from which the NVA were reported to be firing.

At the 102 Battery CP, Trevor Bryant was outside, sitting on the sandbags, and did not need the yell of 'Trevor! Mortars!' from Stan Carbines; he was already moving back inside. The bombs exploded around the CP, some less than a metre away.

Almost at once, a fire mission came over the radio, and Bryant and Carbines jumped to their plotters, writing out the co-ordinates, calculating the distance and bearing. But the accurate mortaring had damaged the wire communications with the guns; no information was going either to the guns or to the CP from them; the canvas cover over the CP was torn by the explosions, allowing light to flood out.

Ian Ahearn came in and took command, ordering Stan Carbines to cock his rifle and watch the door for enemy. Ahearn had been asleep, awakened by the mortar barrage, and run through it to the CP, 'closely followed by a mortar which hit the corner of the CP. Communications were knocked out, and the mortars walked through to the American A Battery, 2/35 Artillery.'

Bob Lowry, in the shell scrape next to Ahearn, also woke to the sound of mortars, and heard the series of clangs as the hatches slammed shut on the big US self-propelled 155mm machines. He and Ahearn had checked the other was awake and OK, then counted '1—2—3—GO!', jumped up and run to their respective posts. Lowry took position behind his section of guns, shouting the fire orders, as again the loudspeakers were out of action.

Bombs had hit around Humphry's No. 2 Gun, flattening the tyres again; Sergeant Robertson, who had played an active role around No. 5 gun position on the previous attack, was hit by shrapnel, and lost an eye.

Again, throughout the attack, orders had to be relayed by voice. Again, despite the bombardment, three-gun fire missions were shot in support of the rifle companies of 1RAR, defending their part of the base. The CP was 'constantly hit by small arms fire, as a sniper in the tree line to the west gave us his undivided attention.'

Ian Ahearn had been disliked by many of the younger soldiers, particularly the National Servicemen, but that night, as on the first attack two nights previously, he won their admiration by the way he conducted himself, ignoring the danger, and performing the duties of GPO.

The accurate bombardment had driven everyone into their trenches. John Goodwin, radio mechanic in 1RAR, realised that the collection of 11 × 11 tents, radio antennas and what he described as 'a very dominant tree in our area' had made it easy for the NVA observers to locate them, and deduce the position as a HQ.

The forward troops, on the perimeter of defence, were taking some pleasure from the fact that the missiles were going past them and hitting among the rear echelons. Events like this have been a source of amusement in armies since the beginning. The front-line soldier tends to forget that some of his own friends are, for one reason or another, in the rear echelons, and this night was no exception.

Goodwin was part of an M60 machinegun crew. The gun had been set up on the dirt between two shell scrapes. Not far away was Eddie Knight, from A Company, who had been sent to the battalion HQ for treatment to slight burns suffered when he rolled on to his small field cooker. He was to return to A Company next morning, and had not dug any sort of a hole for protection. When the mortaring began, Knight ran from the 11 × 11 tent, and to John Goodwin's discomfort, 'did a big swallow dive and landed on top of me in my shell scrape'.

It was Goodwin's first time under fire, and 'at first I didn't know what the hell was going on, but I was lucky, because the guy with me, Harry White, was on his second trip. He spent the first tour, in 1965, as a forward scout, and was very experienced. Harry was telling me what was going on, what was mortars and what was rockets, and as they got closer they got louder. They got that loud, they were right on us, and Harry wore a mortar bomb in the middle of his back.

'Harry was killed. It could have been worse. There could have been three of us killed. Anyway, after the mortars and rockets ceased, but there was plenty of small arms fire, I called to Captain French, in charge of the echelon area, and reported Harry was hit. No one believed me at the time, because it had cleaned his shell scrape out as clean as a whistle.

'After some argument I finally convinced him, and we searched for Harry and found him about twenty metres away.'

Brigadier Hughes had a commander's caravan, a US item mounted on the back of a 6 × 6 truck. When the mortaring began, he decided that initially the best place for him would be underneath this, between the rear wheels.

Many of the people at Coral had noticed the caravan, and thought it was an obvious target. Major John Taylor, commanding the TF HQ Company, wondered if any other actions in modern warfare had been fought around a caravan.

About twenty metres away was Ian MacLean, Operations Officer, who began a dash for the TF HQ CP, but as he was passing the tent of Lieutenant Colonel Kelly, another salvo of bombs began to fall, so MacLean swiftly diverted and dived into a trench he could see inside Kelly's tent. But Jack Kelly was in it, in bed, as MacLean arrived at speed.

When the lull came, MacLean gathered himself and made another dash for the CP, only to run full tilt into one of the stay wires for a radio mast, giving himself a wire burn across his chest. Eventually he made it to the below-ground CP.

Captain Alan Vickers, from the tank squadron but employed as a TF CP Duty Officer, had gone to bed looking forward to a night's sleep, as he was not rostered that night. The bombardment woke him, and he spent the night 'lying in a shallow hole—I am not a great digger—holding a pistol and wondering what the hell was going on.'

At 0250, 1RAR had asked TF to request Light Fire Teams and Spooky, but this had already been done. Two gunship teams and Spooky were on the way.

TF Commander's Diary:
0315 1RAR to TF: We are now in contact with Spooky. Flares from Spooky now lighting the area. C Company also under attack, but not as heavy as that of A and B Companies.

Despite repeating themselves by putting their main attack in against the same part of the base as they had on the previous assault, the NVA were making their presence felt against Col Adamson's A Company. The left-hand section of the left-hand platoon, Neil Weekes' 3 Platoon, had been heavily hit. Adamson ordered Weekes to abandon the battered section area, and consolidate within a smaller platoon position. Adamson 'could not see any sense in hanging on to that widening gap [across to C Company]'.

He then radioed Digger Campbell to inform him, and asked for M60s to fire across it. On the C Company front, under the canopy of rubber trees, five enemy had been killed only fifteen metres from the pits. There was no wire barrier at this spot, and it was believed the enemy did not really know where the Aussies were. One Bangalore torpedo, one RPG, an RPD light machinegun and three AK47s were captured next day.

In the midst of all this, A Company noticed enemy sappers using Bangalore torpedoes to blow the feeble strands of wire stretched across the company front—an indication of where the enemy were likely to attack.

Soon after, what Adamson believed to be the main enemy thrust came down the track leading into the position—as expected. When the attack was halted, the enemy flowed left and right, trying to force an opening. Now the artillery Forward Observer and Mortar Fire Controller were able to bring in fire across the front of the company, and into the gap to the left.

'Strangely enough,' noted Col Adamson, 'they didn't really try to exploit the gap between the companies, which leads me to believe that their reconnaissance perhaps wasn't as good as we gave them credit for. They really had a day and a half to take a look and see where our defences were. From my point of view, their main attack was centred down the track.

'They tried to circle around to the right, and around to the left, but they didn't exploit it. B Company, to my south, had very little action that night. We had the guns and mortars firing right on the wire and in the gap. Maybe that's why they didn't exploit it.

'If they'd realised before the attack that gap existed, there would have been no holding them back.'

Despite Col Adamson's comments. Neil Weekes believes the enemy were trying to get through the gap, but were prevented from doing so.

For the young NVA coming on across the grass, the night had suddenly turned hideous. Friends and comrades alongside were suddenly slammed away, back and down or sideways, by invisible hammers ... all around, from knee height to overhead, vicious crack-crack-crack of bullets ... from in front and the right, frighteningly swift slivers of fire as tracer bullets flicked by ... then among them, behind them, all around, massive inhuman explosions as the artillery and mortars crashed down.

But they had come to fight, and the enemy lay ahead there where the rockets flew, so ignore everything else, go on ... Already the teams were busy carrying away the casualties, the weapons and equipment, grabbing the fallen by hands, feet, legs, belt, hauling them back through the grass to the ditch ... then beyond it to the distant trees.

TF Commander's Diary:
0325 1RAR to TF: Have contacted Light Fire Team, and they are now being directed by 1RAR for use by A, B and C Companies, to their front.

Mal Meadows was holding the right flank of A Company position, and realised that there seemed to be no real attempt to exploit the gap between him and Gary Prendergast in B Company, so moved across to be closer to his own left section, where he thought most enemy pressure was applied.

By what can be catalogued as 'fortunes of war', an eight-inch artillery shell from distant US guns fell short, landing some thirty metres in front of the company positions. A group of NVA were obliterated, exactly as wished fervently by the infantry, who were most appreciative of the timely effective artillery support.

Mal Meadows said: 'One memory I'll never forget is a shell landing in front of us. The blast blew me backwards, off my feet, and the flash temporarily blinded me. For the next minute or so I didn't know what was going on. It created an enormous crater in front of my pit.'

The huge explosion rocked the company position, and at the battalion HQ Kim Patterson was asked sharply by Col Adamson what was going on. (A few days later, a visiting battalion commander from Australia came around and Col made a point of showing him the closeness with which heavy artillery was employed in the attacks.)

To the left, on the edge of the gap across to C Company, Neil Weekes' 3 Platoon fought on. Despite the situation, his batman, Schultz, called to the platoon sergeant, who refused to answer so the enemy would not be able to locate an NCO. But Schultz persisted, and finally Bruno Flematti replied, 'What do you want?' Schultz pointed to his riddled shelter: 'I want a new hutchi, this one's full of holes!'

The wounded had crawled to Weekes' platoon HQ area, and he was faced with the problem of what to do with them. Quickly, he decided that he, Schultz and Flematti would carry them to Adamson's HQ, some 100 metres away. Carrying and dragging the wounded, they hurried to Adamson's area, passing many NVA in the intervening space. The NVA paid them little attention, and Bruno Flematti shot several at point-blank range as they kneeled trying to fire RPGs at the 102 Battery position.

Adamson was, recalled Weekes, 'irate that I was at company HQ, but I replied that there was no one else to bring the wounded, and no one else to collect the ammunition needed by the platoon. We returned to the front line and distributed the ammo.'

Ernie Jacobs, the artillery Forward Observer with A Company, relayed the artillery and mortar fire corrections radioed by Weekes. In order to see over the area, Weekes stood by his pit, near a small tree, and walked the pattern of shell bursts back, forth and sideways across the area between him and Campbell's company. 'I simply had to plug the gap,' was Weekes' thought, and he moved the fall of shot with fifty-metre corrections.

When shrapnel hit the tree high, he went to his knees and brought it in until it was hitting the tree lower down, then went to his belly and moved it back out. Later, Jacobs told him he had controlled over 2500 rounds that night.

The scene was lit by the eerie light of parachute flares, and the sharp smell of cordite drifted through the positions. From the far side of the gap, C Company gave good covering fire towards Weekes' position, and one of his M60s, operated by Private Barents, fired thousands of rounds. The gun kept on all night, and when the spare barrel was put on, the hot one was cooled with urine.

TF Commander's Diary:
0330 1RAR to TF: VC attack held off at perimeter of A and B Companies.
0345 Base Commander to TF: All is quiet in the inner perimeter, except for to the north Callsign 1 and 2 of 1RAR receiving sporadic fire.

Some NVA had occupied the pits of the abandoned section area, and into it had dragged a 12.7mm machinegun mounted on wheels. The fire from this was directed into the base, causing some concern at 1RAR HQ. Lieutenant Colonel Bennett came on to the A Company radio net, and asked Neil Weekes what he was going to do about it.

'Quite frankly,' said Weekes, 'I didn't know what I was going to do about it. I thought about it, then asked if I could bring mortar fire on to my own position. He hesitated, and asked if I was aware it would cause casualties. I replied I was;

157

he then asked if I was prepared to accept the casualties; I replied that I had no alternative; and he said he would put the mortar platoon on to me direct.'

When Tony Jensen spoke to him, Weekes explained the situation. The mortars prepared themselves for firing below normal minimum range and launched their bombs. The results were described by Weekes as 'excellent'. The 12.7 was not destroyed, but reinforcements were prevented from getting to it until it was destroyed by Weekes' platoon. Only one of his soldiers had a slight wound in the neck, not serious enough to require evacuation.

The enemy were still coming into the gap, but did not seem to know how to exploit it. Weekes suggested APCs come up to support him, but this was refused because of the large numbers of RPGs there. Also, unknown until next morning, the NVA had 57mm and 75mm RCLs in the ditch, adding their fire to the mortars and RPGs. The M113s would have made good targets in those conditions.

Boxes of handgrenades had been brought back from company HQ, and these were used to throw at NVA creeping into the position through the grass. Despite the noise, the ears of Weekes' group had become so attuned that they could hear the rustling grass under the roar of battle.

Around them was what Neil Weekes described as 'the distinctive crack of the AK47, the 12.7mm machineguns, the mortars coming in on our position, our mortars and 105s going out, Puff the Magic Dragon firing his miniguns at 6000 rounds a minute with a constant stream of tracer coming down—it was more than my mind could take in.'

Behind him, in the A Company HQ area, Col Adamson was calling for APC support and ammunition resupply. The armoured vehicles with turrets were all deployed elsewhere inside Coral, and the ammunition was taken by Land Rover. Company Sergeant Major Jack Cramp, with members of the Company Support Section, did the first ammunition resupply to the platoons. Later Col Adamson himself helped carry ammunition as he went round the position as dawn was near.

Harry Wall, the A Company driver, had attempted to take

ammunition to the company, but had run into the barbed wire, which became wrapped around the drive-shaft and axle of the Land Rover, bringing it to a halt. In a way this was fortunate, as he could have driven out into the enemy. The wire caught under the vehicle was making a clanking noise, which had unfortunate results.

Bob Lowry, in 102 Battery, heard F1 fire from the sentry pit behind him, and asked the gunner there what he was shooting at. The reply was that an enemy tank was out there, and as Lowry peered into the flickering flarelight, he heard the clanking noise of Wall's Land Rover, and realised what it was. The trigger-happy gunner was quietened down, and the resupply to A Company went on.

In the 1RAR echelon area, Ned Kelly was told by Ivan 'Tubby' Skinner that he would have to go down to A Company as Harry Wall had become entangled in the barbed wire. Taking his steel helmet, flak jacket and M16, Ned drove to the 1RAR ammunition point, where he found the warrant officer caterer, 'Hughy' Hughson, barefoot but with jacket and helmet, and they loaded the Land Rover. With Ned was Private Knight, of A Company, taking back with him the M60 from the place where Harry White was killed.

Kelly 'couldn't let them down, so concentrated on getting over there. We couldn't have lights, so drove by the light of flares and what was available. There were still mortars, rockets and small arms fire, and people were challenging me, but I replied it was ammo for A Company, with language I can't put on tape. When I got to A Company, I looked around and saw Bruno Flematti, and told him I had the ammo. The vehicle was surrounded by people grabbing it all, as well as my M16 from between the seats.'

Ned asked if there was anything to go back, the reply was no, and he set off on the return journey, stopping to pick up Harry Wall from a dip in the ground near the ensnared A Company Land Rover. At HQ, he reported back, and was reprimanded for the loss of his M16, but given another. He went back to his pit, finding Bedford and Goodwin there.

Ned Kelly's own brief description of the resupply mission, typically Australian, includes nothing of the courage needed

159

to drive without lights, perched in the high driving seat of an unprotected vehicle, through the base, in the middle of an attack, with small parties of NVA at large, among the incoming bombs and rockets, not to mention the numberless 7.62mm bullets, then go back through it all again. Some armies award decorations for valour for lesser feats. Later, when it was all over, Ned was regaled by stories of the amount of fire, and handgrenades, which had been directed at him, and through which he had driven.

Meanwhile, on A Company's right, Mal Meadows and his batman, Rod Quarrell, had crawled forward to throw grenades into the huge eight-inch-shell crater, as at least one and possibly more enemy had jumped into it, but, to their consternation, the first two grenades did not go off. They threw another one each, and the explosions cleared the crater.

They crawled back, Mal checked the ammunition supply in the sections, and Rod Quarrell went back, collected more, returned and distributed it. Rod was a National Serviceman, and that night left a lasting impression on Meadows of the quiet way in which the young soldiers simply got on with the job, with no fuss or bother. The loud ones seemed to be occupied digging; the others were ready for what might happen.

Meadows was pleased to see the gunships arrive, but less so when they opened fire from behind him, the bullets cracking through the trees above the platoon, and hitting only ten metres to the front, so he called for the fire to be lifted a little.

Neil Weekes had seen a determined fight between a helicopter and an NVA 12.7 machinegun ended when the helicopter hovered, firing, and he saw one stream of green tracer going up, and four streams of red going down, silencing the NVA. Later he was told the gunship took twenty-seven hits, the pilot was wounded, but managed to get to a base for a crash-landing, and later died of wounds.

Over in the TF HQ area, Noel Sproles, in his pit, 'was rained on by spent cartridge cases' as the gunships roared overhead, miniguns firing. For many at Coral, as on the first night, there are vivid memories of the activities of the gunships.

The NVA, goaded beyond bearing by the seeming arrogance, the immunity, of the throbbing helicopters, fired at their tormentors, and drew on themselves the hail of rockets and tracer. A few survivors were awarded the title of 'Brave Destroyer of Helicopters' or 'Determined to Win Hero', with appropriate ceremony.

TF Commander's Diary:
0435 Base Commander to TF: SITREP Inner perimeter, no change.

Those in the forward positions were especially aware, and appreciative of, the amount of artillery support, and impressed with its accuracy.

In the 1RAR CP, Mick Bindley heard an American voice come over the artillery radio net, from a distant heavy battery, informing the Australians that 300 rounds had been fired in support of Coral. Bindley's 'first thought was, "My God, does this mean you're about to turn it off?" He said, in a deep American accent, "I'd just like you to know that I have a whole heap left." That was the type of morale building support, the confidence, that their voices on the radios gave you. Of course, the support they gave was very good.'

To John Salter, 10 Platoon D/1RAR, the heavy shells arriving on target 'sounded like someone driving express trains into the ground alongside you'.

With the artillery, air support was playing a major part in the defence of Coral. To assist the pilots circling in the blackness above, it was decided that the perimeter of Coral would be illuminated by the light of burning Hexamine tablets—the solid fuel supplied for cooking in the front line and on patrol. This worked well, pleasing both the aircrews and staff co-ordinating the defence of the base, but was not so well received by the soldiers who were trying to avoid being lit by the small fires in the bottom of their weapon pits.

Independent thinker that he is, Richo Richardson thought it was 'a bloody stupid idea. You put them in the bottom of your pit, or you dug a little hole alongside and lit this

Hexamine, and the guy's face was above the level of the pit and it was lit up like bloody Guy Fawkes. I couldn't see the bloody point in that. In fact I didn't light any in my section, so that's probably another order I disobeyed. But nobody chastised me for it.'

TF Commander's Diary:
0437 IIFFV to 1ATF: Moonshine 71 arriving shortly until Spooky is rearmed.

At HQ 1RAR, Lieutenant Colonel Bennett was not worried about the ability of the battalion to withstand the assault. He felt that 'there was a lot of confidence in the companies after the first attack, in the intervening days they had several contacts with the enemy, and there was a general feeling of superiority, once we'd formed a tight perimeter around the base. I think we were pretty confident.'

Earlier, a 12.7mm HMG had been detected at grid reference 945289, and had survived mortar and artillery fire, so it was decided to call for an airstrike. Then it was found there were two HMGs in the location.

TF Commander's Diary:
0437 1RAR to TF: CO 1RAR has contacted Jade [Forward Air Controller] reference napalm on HMG pit. Believe Jade will use heavy ordnance as well.

Strangely, one MG was firing into the base, while the other fired outward, back the way they had come. Major Keldie 'could not believe my eyes. I thought it was one of my vehicles firing outwards'. 1RAR reported this, and it was agreed the outward arcing tracer was a guide for other units of NVA, to indicate the place they were to make for. Due to the congestion in the area, the counter-penetration force could not get close enough to attack the 12.7s, so .30cal MG fire was brought to bear.

The artillery and mortars were firing steadily. It was necessary to keep them in action as long as possible, but keep them going in preference to air attack. The Forward Air Controller had his radio-equipped jeep in the position and, smoking a cigar, discussed the attack with the jet pilot. Many cannon were firing into the area of the battle, and the trajectories of the streams of shells had to be avoided, both as the jet approached and departed; the attack had to be accurate as the infantry and other parts of the base defenders were close to the 12.7s; all this was in the shifting light of flares and ever-changing flickering lines of tracer and explosions on the ground.

Jack Kelly recalls the pilot 'brought it down between parallel lines of guns, dropped his napalm on that thing and knocked it out without stopping a single round of artillery fire. That's what we always try to achieve; never done it before or since, but we did it then.'

The aircraft, in the night sky, was unseen by anyone on the ground until it was at the bottom of its diving approach, and Blue Keldie glimpsed it 'leave us, its tail pipes were aglow as it went past, almost on the ground, and then there was this surgical removal of these two, that's the best way I can describe it', and 'as long as one has been in the service, I have never seen greater professionalism in my life. The attack aircraft was in darkness, but at the last moment illumination was provided by Spooky, and the fighter wiped out both 12.7s sitting between the companies.

'Such was the accuracy and determination of the pilots. That remained one of the epic memories of Coral.'

Other soldiers in the base were also aware of the dangerous 12.7s, and from the 1RAR HQ position, John Kearns has a vivid memory of the sudden brightness of the flare, then the shape of the fighter, 'like a giant bat, swooped across from out of the darkness, into the light, and out of it again, and behind it the 12.7s were destroyed.'

Soon after, the FAC jeep was hit by a mortar bomb, but the FAC himself survived. Jack Kelly used the wire running from the jeep to Keldie's ACV as a guide line, and crawled along it to reach Keldie. This was the only personal contact for the entire night between the two HQs.

163

TF Commander's Diary:
0502 Base Commander to TF: SITREP nothing to report.
0505 1RAR to TF: Require F100 strike in A Company area.
1RAR talking to Jade.

As the airstrikes flew in, Col Adamson had a 'lasting, striking impression of them. There were fires all over the place, equipment on fire, grass on fire, the odd tent on fire, and in the fog and confusion, with the parachute flares, there screaming at me, coming out of the north-east, were three jets. I saw the fire reflecting from their bellies and bottom of their wings as they lifted up to drop. They dropped napalm almost on our wire, coming almost towards me. They made another run, from the north-west, strafed across the front. I hadn't known they were coming at all.

'The helicopter gunships were streaming up and down our front. I had the soldiers light Hexamine in mess tins as a minor attempt to show our positions. Just to the north, Spooky was strafing away as well.'

Mal Meadows watched with interest as two F4 Phantoms thundered past, firing Gatling guns mounted in pods under the wings: 'They swooshed overhead, their firepower was awesome, beyond description ... I watched the ground lift fifty to a hundred metres out. There were two of them, one after the other, and they each did two passes. I was very confident once I saw those aircraft come in; there was nothing the enemy could do to take the position.'

The jets passed right over Noel Sproles, still in his pit in the TF HQ area, and he also looked up into the glowing exhaust pipes as the fighters climbed away into the night sky.

In the B Company position, Lieutenant Garry Prendergast, 6 Platoon, noted, 'You could hear them in the air, but wouldn't know that they were right there, until all of a sudden they were sitting on their tails, the afterburners came on, and the bloody bombs went off. You had this huge *clump whump*, the bloody earth would shake, frighten shit out of you, all of a sudden *whrummff*—these things screeching up into the sky, fascinating to watch, with full flames sticking out of an aircraft; fascinating.'

As well as the distant guns and jets, the base defences were firing, and to Bob Hennessy, commanding B/1RAR, 'The noise was incredible. There were 40mm Dusters firing on our right flank, which was wide open. We did not expect anything from the south, but with the Dusters firing, they made sure nobody came from that direction.

'Really, they didn't press us, in B Company. They were pressing their attack along the axis of the track which ran into the A Company area. We had so much firepower it would have been suicide [to attack B Company].'

In the 6 Platoon area, the younger soldiers were reassured by Sergeant Brian 'Jazza' Smith's 'cool, calm attitude which kept a lot of the fear away from us through the night.'

Private Tim Foster, in 9 Section of 6 Platoon, found 'the air was absolutely choking with smoke' as the fighting progressed. As the NVA probed their positions, the Diggers would duck the RPGs which came streaking out of the murk, then pop up again to fire back.

In the distance, at IIFFV HQ at Long Binh, Major Alf Garland had been told that the Australians were in action, so went to the Operations Room. There he saw the Commanding General, Fred C. Weyand, with all the senior staff: Operations, Artillery, Air, Helicopter, B52 Liaison Officer, et cetera. Three radios were tuned to the frequencies used by 1ATF for command, artillery and air radio nets. Weyand sat there, ordering whatever was necessary for the support of the battle at Coral and, in Garland's opinion, more than any US formation could have expected. Nothing was held back.

Previously, on the left flank of the 1RAR position, Tony Hammett brought his tripod-mounted machineguns into action, and believed that the effort was well repaid. The M60s were 'on fixed lines, covering across the company front and across Digger Campbell's front, and I have always claimed that the enemy killed in front of his company were killed by our own guns.

'It was a beautiful machinegun. There was a flat killing ground, and the range was probably up to 300 metres. That's not a bad field of fire, going into the rubber [plantation].'

In that part of the 1RAR perimeter, all were ready for the

expected attack. The sound of the incoming mortars had woken everyone, and artillery Forward Observer Gordon Alexander was trying to make the most of what he suddenly realised was 'a woefully inadequate shell scrape', under the frightening noise of falling mortar bombs.

The mortars decreased, small arms fire began, and above the noise Alexander could hear Tony Hammett calling for him, 'so dashed over to find him, with radio handset, telling battalion what was happening—standing up!

'In retrospect, I'm convinced it was calculated to quell the fear of those around him, because our outgoing fire was beginning to dominate the battlefield. Nevertheless, his behaviour had the intended effect. Everyone became more confident. It was infectious, because I remember Tony and I standing as if we were on the sideline of a football field, handsets in place, with my signaller tugging at my knee, telling me, "For Christ's sake, get down."

'Tony pulled this stunt on numerous occasions during the tour, although on this occasion you could not only hear the incoming fire, which was heavier than usual, but also see it by tracer rounds.'

TF Commander's Diary:
0510 1RAR to TF: More activity between A and C Company. Engaging with mortars.
0515 TF to 1RAR: Check fire on your mortars.
0516 1RAR to TF. There is a thrust between A and C Company. We must have mortars.
0517 1RAR to TF: Engaging A and C Company junction plus 400 with mortars.
0520 US 1 Div LO to TF: I have two more light fire teams on call.
0520 1RAR to TF: A and B Company receiving mortar fire.
0521 1RAR to TF: Correction. Own arty drop short. We are adjusting out.

The Mortar Platoon of 1RAR fired all the bombs stored at their position but, as the storage dump was only forty metres away, simply went and helped themselves, at first carrying the heavy ammunition, later helped by a vehicle. Two mortars were mounted in M113s, the other two were on the ground and had to be rebedded twice, such was the volume of firing required. 750 rounds were expended.

The mortars were controlled by Tony Jensen, Jack Parr and Leigh Boneham from an open fighting pit. Parr was relaying the fire control orders to Boneham, who did the plotting, and Jensen would then call the bearing and elevations to the mortar section commanders.

Over the APC radio net, Gus Ballentine was ordered to take his M113 to collect casualties. The night was 'pitch dark, but lighted by all the tracers, fireworks, et cetera. Blue Keldie called me, and stood halfway out of his ACV, making himself the reference point to his orders on the radio. Thanks to his guidance, it didn't take me long to find, pick up and deliver the casualties to the Dustoff point. Then the incoming fire got even heavier.'

The sight of Blue Keldie, 'illuminated by all the fireworks, standing in his ACV directing the APCs; it's a wonder he didn't get his head blown off', springs to mind whenever Ballentine recalls the battle.

No doubt having attracted attention during daylight, and bulking hugely at night, Keldie's ACV was the object of attack by RPGs. One hit and penetrated thoroughly the 4.2kw generator mounted on it, the noise and shock of the hit giving all five members of his staff a severe headache. In addition, a mortar bomb hit the roof, detonating more or less harmlessly. To cap all, many splinters flying over the forward positions, not hitting anything else en route, were striking the outside of the vehicle.

After this night, every AFV had a protective bund, with screens of cyclone wire-netting erected around the whole, to trap and detonate prematurely RPG rounds.

In the TF HQ CP, Brigadier Hughes noted the smoothly working team there, but 'the unusual thing was in the gunner party. There was a very young signaller, he might have been 18, I suppose, and he was the only one who was perturbed. He was perturbed because he did not know if his rifle would fire or not. He felt that he might have to defend himself in the headquarters eventually, and I think it was Ian MacLean who took him outside and let him fire his rifle into the air. He was happy after that.'

During respites, when the NVA were preparing for another lunge, Keldie's APCs were required to resupply 1RAR with ammunition, and at the same time evacuate the dead and wounded. This had to be done at night, with no lights, through and across an area which had just been the scene of bombardment and ground attack. Communications between the individual infantry soldiers and the crews of the APCs were non-existent. The officer in charge of this difficult operation was Captain Geoff Auhl, who had only his memory of the walk around in daylight to assist him in guiding the bulky APCs. Because the crew commander's position was only partially protected by a shield at the .50cal machinegun, the role of the individual crew commanders was not easy. Much depended on the ability and quality of the drivers and commanders.

Gus Ballentine's APCs were among those ordered to the ammunition dump to collect more for distribution, and 'a darn thing happened to me and my crew at the dump. A lieutenant or captain wanted a requisition form to get ammo! I know it sounds like a tall story, but it was true. We ignored him, of course, and loaded up ourselves. I cannot tell you what action was suggested to the officer.'

Later, the Troop was sent to the south-eastern part of the base, with Col Adamson's A/1RAR on their left, and the US 40mm Duster anti-aircraft guns on their right. Gus had learnt by experience that the infantry always needed machinegun ammunition, so he and his crews 'carried a bit more than we were allowed to. We gave them all our handgrenades as well. We returned fire as fast as we could.

'During our little distributions of ammunition, we were pinned down a few times, and wished we were back in our carriers. I had a private quick O Group with the Duster crew commander, and decided we would watch each other's fall of shot, and it was effective use of co-operation when we needed

168

it most. My .50cals fired at spotted targets, with subsequent Duster shots on the same spots, and vice versa.'

John Goodwin, radio mechanic in 1RAR, had his pit destroyed—luckily while he has away—so he took over the vacant pit of one of the people busy with the ammunition resupply to A Company. He had his own radio, and listened to the conversations between the ground and air. The pilots impressed him as 'brilliant'.

He watched one engagement between the helicopter gunships and a machinegun. 'At the time they were coming in, they had their lights on, and Charlie set up a .50cal out in the scrub somewhere in front of us and opened up. There was a hell of a panic among the gunships, they shot off in all directions, and then I saw one of the greatest things I've ever seen.

'The leader of the gunships came on the radio, organising a strike on the gun; it had hit one of the gunships. He came in with all his lights on, but underneath him he had another gunship, blacked out. When the .50cal opened up at him, the gunship underneath him just let go a full payload straight at the tracers coming up, and that was the end of the .50cal.'

Over in the B Company area, Captain Bob Hennessy was also watching the incident. 'One helicopter suddenly appeared out of the night with all its lights on, lit up like a Christmas tree, slowly spiralling down towards the 12.7. Suddenly the 12.7 opened up. Next to the illuminated helicopter, the darkened ones fired on the 12.7. This was typical American bravery, courage and their gung-ho approach to war. I admired the Americans.'

The machinegun crew would have had one or two seconds to realise fourteen rockets were streaking towards them, barely time for their exhilaration and satisfaction at scattering the gunships to drain away ...

In the artillery positions within Coral, the gun crews had operated throughout the fighting and during the bombardment of their own position, manning the guns after the mortar primaries had been fired, as they knew there were still about twenty or thirty seconds before the bombs exploded, flinging themselves into cover at the last second.

Geoff Grimish, on No. 2 gun, felt that 'we fired so much that the heat from the guns would have given you sunburn!'

Throughout the night, Keldie's only contact with TF HQ had been through the Duty Officer and Artillery Commander, Lieutenant Colonel Jack Kelly. Kelly's Arty Tac HQ had controlled the fire support coming from Bien Hoa, Cu Chi, FSB Echo and other places. To Keldie, the effect of the artillery was 'like living through a continuous electrical storm'.

The sheer volume of noise made normal voice conversation impossible. Keldie wondered how the NVA coped, out there in the storm of explosive and steel.

TF Commander's Diary:
0530 1RAR to TF: Heavy RPG C Company location. A, B, C Company under fire. D Company untouched.
0532 1RAR to TF: Require Light Fire Team.
0535 101 Airborne Div LO to TF: Silver Spurs have Light Fire Teams available.
0535 Base Commander to TF: SITREP, Inner perimeter nothing to report.

Neil Weekes, in the battered but holding position of A Company 1RAR, had to counter-attack into the position of his left-hand section which had been occupied by the NVA. The noise level was so high that his other section commanders could not hear him calling. Weekes sent Schultz down half-way to Corporal Moyle's Section, to relay the shouted orders for the platoon attack on the enemy in the 7 Section pits. This was the only way to get the orders passed.

Weekes shouted the order to advance, nothing happened, he shouted again, still no one moved forward, and finally Moyle yelled that every time Weekes shouted the order, the NVA raked the pits with fire. Finally, with fire and movement in a pincer operation, the enemy in the platoon area were killed.

Another lull developed, and it was thought that, as

Brigadier Ron Hughes (*AWM No. THU/68/656/VN*)

Lieutenant Colonel Jack Kelly (*AWM No. 2000118*)

Sketch of fellow NVA soldier by unknown artist (*Greenway*)

Lieutenant Colonel Phillip Bennett (*left*) and Major Tony Hammett (*AWM No. ERR/68/787/VN*)

Officers of 102 Battery RAA. *Left to right*: Captain Don Tait, Second Lieutenant Bob Lowry, Second Lieutenant Matt Cleland, Lieutenant Ian Ahern, Captain Dave Brook.

Mal Hundt (*Forsdike*)

Andy Forsdike (*Forsdike*)

Top left
1RAR arriving at Coral (*Neil*)

Above
102 Battery arriving at Coral (*Neil*)

Left
Searching out and collecting NVA
dead, 13 May 1968 (*Dellaca*)

Below
The New Zealand artillery
position, 12 May 1968 (*Dellaca*)

Above
102 Battery preparing artillery rounds
(*Floyd*)

Sergeant John Stephens (*AWM No. 200046*)

Below
Sergeant 'Skeeter' Humphry's damaged
105 mm howitzer (*Brooks*)

Left
1RAR Anti-armour platoon soldiers: Private J. Swan (*front*), and Corporal D. Dupille (*Tranter*)

Below
Left to right: Larry Darcy, 'Pommy' Fisher, 'Cossie' Costello, John Burns (*Darcy*)

Bottom
Geoff Grimish listening to the races on Radio Australia (*Grimish*)

Chinook helicopter lifting a
105 mm howitzer and pallet of
ammunition (*AWM No.
COM/69/266/VN*)

Lieutenant John Salter (*AWM
No. 200096*)

Above right
Sergeant Ray Curtis (*AWM
No. ERR/68/505/VN*)

Corporal Paul Richardson

A Company HQ at Coral. *Left to right*: Warrant Officer Jack Cramp, Major Col Adamson, Captain Ernie Jacobs, and Captain Bill Raggatt (*AWM No. ERR/68/483/ VN*)

Second Lieutenant Neil Weekes (*AWM No. 200091*)

Sergeant Bruno Flematti (*AWM No. 200105*)

Collecting NVA dead, Coral 16 May 1968 (*Crossman*)

Soldiers of D Company 1RAR enter the perimeter of FSPB Coral. In the background is the rubber plantation through which the enemy attacked (*AWM No. THU/68/596/VN*)

daylight was fast approaching, the enemy had broken contact. The APCs began collecting casualties for evacuation from the area of TF HQ, and the helicopter gunships were directed on to what were thought to be NVA withdrawal routes. There was sporadic firing from parts of the perimeter as groups of enemy were fired on.

At 0605 a third attack, by an estimated NVA battalion, was flung at D/1RAR. On their left flank was a gap between the 1RAR position and the neighbouring unit on that portion of the perimeter. If the NVA had attacked them, rather than the infantry, they might have had a greater chance of success.

The right-hand platoon of D Company was 12 Platoon, commanded by Geoff Bowcock. They had also watched the 'steady stream of rockets, and regular mortars', passing overhead, as well as small arms fire from the ruins. His right-hand sections were relatively quiet, but the left-most one, near the rubber trees, began to engage enemy in there. Soon they were calling for ammunition, and Sergeant Trevor Warburton took up what there was, then went to company HQ for more.

Before the resupply could be made, and people called they were almost out of ammo, Bowcock loudly called to 'throw bloody grenades!' But, as on the night of the first attack, he still felt a sense 'of distance from it all; a feeling of unreality'.

On the left of the company position, in their patch of dirty rubber trees, John Salter's 10 Platoon lay in their shallow holes underneath all the missiles. Ray Curtis thought he could distinguish the distinctive buzzing sound of 122mm rockets as they flew past.

John Salter also had not made time to deepen his pit, and it was a little too short for his length, so he found himself lying on his back, looking up at the stream of rockets going overhead, with his knees bent and projecting above the ground surface, thinking they would be shot off at any moment. Then he had 'a crazy desire for a cigarette, so called out, "I need a smoke", so Richo [Richardson] came across, gave me one and wandered back.'

The attack on 10 Platoon seemed to be hesitant, perhaps because of the failure of the sappers to locate any fixed defences. However, 12 Platoon received a heavy volume of RPGs, fired from the ruined houses some 800 metres away. The RPG-7 was fitted with a self-destruction fuse, and after passing above Bowcock's men, the missile would detonate somewhere inside the base.

Ray Curtis and the others heard Billy Stinton call out to John Salter, 'Skipper, I can see them coming', and Salter's reply, 'Well, shoot the bastard.'

The advancing NVA were still in darkness, which somewhat puzzled Paul Richardson. The day before, he had helped set over twenty trip flares. 'We set them head height, and five centimetres off the ground, all bloody heights. Not one was set off, which disappointed me greatly.'

Flitting through the gloom, dodging from tree to tree, was a lone NVA, trying to get closer to the platoon. Billy Stinton called out that he could see one. Paul Richardson looked across and saw the NVA as Stinton aimed. A single shot cracked, the NVA was flung back and then burst into flames. He had been carrying RPG rounds and the propellant charges had ignited under impact of the 7.62mm bullet.

Richo saw 'this bloody great white flash, and he sort of disappeared behind the trees, trying to beat himself out. Everybody concentrated their fire on him, and he was being hit all over the place. He was on fire, and he went up in a big flash. We all cheered.'

A piece of rocket shrapnel slammed into the feed plate of Richardson's section M60 machinegun, so it was exchanged for the gun from the section in depth. The damage was repaired in the dark, illuminated with quick flashes of a torch, by hammering the offending metal back into shape with a bayonet butt.

Naturally, the NVA fired at the torch flickers. Richo noticed all the tracer streaking towards the platoon headquarters, and 'kept yelling out to Salter and asking him if he was all right, and he said, "Yeah," and there were bloody torch lights going on, and I didn't know what was going on at that stage. Now I know they were fixing the gun.'

Most of Richo's attention was taken by the activity to his front, where the NVA were keeping a heavy volume of fire going into Coral. 'The amount of bloody tracer that was coming in was incredible. But I find the hardest thing to believe was their shooting. Most of the hutchies were still up, and because of, or despite, the illumination from mortars and artillery, they were firing six to ten metres above the hutchies, from no more than thirty to fifty metres in front of us.

'Why they didn't bring their fire down to ground level has me beat. They probably wouldn't have hit any of us except me, because I was sitting up on the side of my pit, but the rest of the guys were lying with just their heads and rifles above ground. Whether they just ducked their heads and lifted their AKs up and fired, I've no idea.'

Recalling the boost to morale resulting from the order to fix bayonets on the morning of the 13th, for the attack across the open ground near the night ambush position, John Salter decided to do so again, and called out in a voice loud enough to be heard around the company position.

Geoff Bowcock wondered who the hell was yelling that out, and Tony Hammett called on the radio, asking how many enemy were coming for such an order to be needed in 10 Platoon. One bayonet was literally shot off the end of the rifle.

On the left of Salter's platoon area, Squizzy Taylor called to Richardson that his M16 had jammed, and was told to swap places while he cleared the mechanism. Richo 'got up and walked across, and all the pretty green tracer was going everywhere, and Squizzy was like a bloody snake down in the grass. I said, "What are you doing down there?" and he replied, "I'm not getting shot for any bastard!" I asked him if he knew where my hole was, he said he'd find it, and about two seconds later I heard this horrible moan. He'd found it all right, head first into my rubbish pit.'

Richardson stayed there, until Taylor returned, when they fired on two enemy seen crawling into the spot where a rubber tree had been pushed over.

Then D Company began firing M72 rockets back at the RPG launchers, and the resulting back-blast effectively demolished any hutchies behind the forward pits.

Richardson thought that 'they're not really fair dinkum about this attack, so I started to sing "Waltzing Matilda", and the whole section took it up, and I think Bluey McGlerkin's lot in 12 Platoon started. There were rude comments from platoon headquarters, and I think they finally got a message that we were to shut up singing, and we did.'

As the position returned to silence, Gordon Alexander heard a quiet but nervous voice come from behind the company HQ, back where the Engineers were positioned, with 'all the wire in front of them, obviously worried that there was a sudden silence. "D Company, D Company, are you still there?" We decided to keep our mouths shut, to let them sweat for the rest of the night.'

As dawn softly intruded between the tree trunks, the NVA began to withdraw. Richo Richardson noticed them moving back, and called to his section that 'the buggers are pulling out'. To his amazement, the careful infiltrators of the night before 'hit every one of my trip flares on the way out. There were trip flares going off everywhere, and that spurred the guys on. We fired madly, just a sort of tension release that everyone laid right into, firing at where all the flares were going off. I think we did a lot of damage there, but you'll never know because the buggers take their bodies with them, drag them off and so forth.'

'The battle didn't come to a sudden end,' recalled Col Adamson. 'It was more like a whimper. All of a sudden, my company realised that incoming rounds were diminishing, and sort of stopped.'

Neil Weekes' tired men stood in their old position, looking at the dead enemy scattered around, and the two dead Australians, still with weapons in their hands. The platoon was 'raring to go'. Weekes had to be restrained by his medic from going on, outside the perimeter, to find NVA and 'make someone pay for what happened to my men'.

Next to Neil Weekes' platoon, on the extreme left of Sutton's 1 Platoon, Private Martin had been shot and killed. With him was Private King, who did not call out to inform anyone, but crouched there. Three NVA crawled up through the grass, then one must have decided he had crawled far enough, and 'an enemy figure rose immediately to King's front, literally at the tip of his SLR barrel. King pulled the trigger and the man dropped dead. Two others crawled up and knelt by the body, talking, presumably about what to do with the Bangalore they were carrying, looking for the barbed wire barrier they were to destroy. King fired twice more, killing both instantly.' Next morning they were found like that, King and the dead enemy, only one or two metres apart.

Waiting for orders to go outside and continue the hunt chafed Neil Weekes, who later realised that the interior had to be thoroughly checked and secured, and any NVA who had penetrated the base were accounted for. Helicopter pilots reported 'hundreds and hundreds of enemy, ox-carts, women and farmers being used to evacuate the NVA dead and wounded'.

Further away to the south, having been spectators during the night, with only bombardment on their position but no ground attack, was Les Tranter's Anti-armour Platoon. Realising that A Company had been hard-pressed, he had been prepared to move the platoon to assist, but no call came. At dawn, Corporal Murray called that he was going to the latrine. Tranter saw him move, crouching, get half-way and exclaim, turn and come back, saying he would use the fighting pit. Tranter queried him, but Murray said he would show him later. Afterwards, Murray took Tranter to the platoon latrine, and showed what had made him change his mind: clustered around the place were about fifteen hits by mortars and RPGs. The enemy had obviously marked it, and for all Murray knew, were watching it yet.

Not far away, in the A Company HQ position, Col Adamson looked out at the scene. 'As the sun came up, it was a real moonscape. The dust, the haze, still-smoking parachute flares . . . the sun was blood-red. There was a stillness, not a bird to be heard . . . after all the noise and confusion of the night. There was a smell of blood, flies buzzing like crazy. Guys with eyes hanging out, everybody was weary . . . there was no exhilaration . . . that may have come later. Everybody was plain bloody tired and plain bloody thirsty; clean worn out.'

6 Enter the Centurion

Now sways it this way, like a mighty sea
Forc'd by the tide to combat with the wind;
Now sways it that way, like the selfsame sea
Forc'd to retire by the fury of the wind.

King Henry VI, *Part 3 (II. v.)*

IT BECAME OBVIOUS to the Australian commanders that the last attack, so close to sunrise, had been mounted to distract them from NVA activity in clearing the area of the earlier assaults.

TF Commander's Diary:
0645 1RAR to TF: All contacts broken. Light Fire Team gone to open ground as we have no immediate task. Jade 7 looking for withdrawal routes. Casualties light. Total 5 KIA, 8 WIA. Appears A and C Company were attacked by a battalion, and another battalion tried to get through the junction of A and C. At D Company location there appeared a reserve arty regiment suspected but little fire into our area.

In the light of the new day, there was time to consider how well or otherwise things had worked during the night. The defences had stood a severe test. Some in the perimeter did not need to fire a shot. The APCs had proved effective, both in their positions and in manoeuvring at night in the position, but lack of turrets precluded their wider use.

Australian casualties were five killed, nineteen wounded, plus two US artillerymen wounded. Only thirty-four NVA bodies were found, but the numerous blood trails and drag marks testified to the numbers killed and wounded. Later Intelligence information revealed that only about a hundred of the 790 NVA who went into the attacks survived death or wounds.

In the 1RAR area, people were realising that the night was over, they were alive, they had held.

176

Neil Weekes, still emotionally wound-up after the night battle, eager to get out among the retreating enemy, was tasked to sweep the area between the artillery position of 102 Battery and A Company. Then the company front was cleared. At least thirteen, and possibly as many as twenty-seven enemy, were counted dead in the platoon position. (The variation is caused by just what constituted the platoon area.)

Weekes, like the others, saw 'dozens of bodies, and drag marks everywhere'. He believes that if the platoons had been unleashed, the body count would have been at least doubled, as the NVA and local people were carrying off as many casualties as they could, under the eyes of the observation pilots.

Within his platoon position, he found seventy-five craters from 82mm mortar, and at least thirty from RPG hits. Fortunately, on the afternoon before, he had relocated some weapon pits to make better use of his weapons. Two of the old pits had received direct hits.

On the right-hand end of the company, Mal Meadows also cleared his platoon area, then turned the platoon attention to the outside. On the far side of the crater from the eight-inch shell was the first NVA, legless.

He also wanted to press the advantage, but with hindsight believes the decision to consolidate first was correct. 'We had an unrealistic idea of our strength and our ability to do more damage. Half a dozen hot-headed platoon commanders with no idea that what hit us was a regiment, and they could have gone straight over the top of us when we were out there, un-protected.'

Bob Hennessy, with B Company, 'was chafing at the bit, ready to go. We let them get away'.

What would have happened if the companies had gone out looking for the reported enemy in disarray will remain one of the *ifs* of warfare.

The same things were seen by the other rifle companies of 1RAR. The tired soldiers searched the ground in front of their positions, and found 'guys out there with Bangalore torpedoes, the guys coming to blow up the wire [defences], and there was all sorts of blood, and bits of bone, and bellies and Christ knows what. You could see the drag marks through the grass, right through the rubber trees. We'd mauled them.'

The wire in front of A Company was broken in seven places by Bangalores, but Col Adamson doubted whether more than fifty NVA actually passed through the gaps. Six lengths of old signal cable, each about 400 metres long, were found, leading up to the line from which the enemy had started their attack. Adamson had been told by his counterpart in 7RAR of the enemy attention to collecting the cartridge cases of expended rounds, and was impressed by the fact that none were found by his own soldiers. Even in close combat the NVA picked up the fired cases.

It was also noticed that none of the enemy carried packs, which obviously had been left elsewhere, some distance away, and the closest pits dug to A Company were only some forty metres away, yet nothing had been heard. Some could have been dug during the fighting.

Diagonally across the battalion position from Neil Weekes was Geoff Bowcock's position. 'There was a lot of trampled grass, signs there had been quite an engagement. Ammunition boxes all over the place; kit all over the place; tired Diggers; the hasty digging; a pack placed behind a mound of dirt to protect it. Over on our extreme right flank, where the guns were, lots of activity, patrols coming back saying that over there was a body count of at least twenty, significant body counts elsewhere. People started to look around at one another, to notice what was there about them.'

In the uncleared rubber trees, he was surprised at the amount of shrubbery which had been knocked down or squashed by people crawling forward, or dragging backwards through it. On the far side of the road, they found the position where mortars had been fired, littered with cases for the bombs and personal webbing among the trampled waist-high undergrowth.

When the interior and perimeter was checked, it was time to go further afield, and the rifle companies were given orders to do so. Col Adamson, well aware of how his men had been tired out by the night battle, ordered shaving, eating and a cup of tea in the platoons, delaying the move out. 'I remember shouting at Kim Patterson, and him shouting at me, that I'd go out when I was ready, but we were not ready to go out then.'

When the rifle companies swept their fronts, all were surprised to find the large numbers of holes dug during the night, some 200–300 metres away, by the waiting NVA battalions.

Neil Weekes also noted that stakes had been placed in the ground to mark the positions of his platoon machineguns, and that cable had been laid right up to the irrigation ditch alongside the track running into the Coral position. There were signs that the NVA had time for a smoke. In the ditch were also the marks of the NVA casualty collection point: stretchers, medicine vials, blood stains, bundles of equipment and items of clothing.

Accordingly, the machineguns were moved, not much, but enough to take them from points marked by the enemy. Of course, everyone developed an intense interest in digging deeper.

But not all the enemy around Coral were dead, or willing to surrender.

At 0900 Chris Forde's 5 Platoon, B/1RAR, was sweeping the area outside the perimeter, looking for enemy dead and wounded. Six NVA were seen on the ground, and as the platoon began to deploy one of them, with an RPG2, began to move as if to fire it, and was shot by two short bursts of M60. The platoon relearned the lesson of never taking anything for granted when dealing with 'this type of enemy', as Forde described them.

Tim Foster, 6 Platoon B Company, was surprised by 'the enormous number of limbs scattered throughout the bush.' The crushed grass, pools and patches of blood were ample evidence of the number of enemy casualties, and after some experience the Diggers could tell if the NVA had been dead or alive when carried off, leaving bloodstains behind. The soldiers had to overcome a feeling of reluctance to actually grab the corpses and load them on the APCs. Foster had 'a feeling of unreality, of horror, of shock ... can this really be happening? Nobody really wanted to touch the enemy bodies, but it was our job to load them on to the APCs. It was a terrible sight, a terrible feeling.'

Geoff Cameron, GSO2 Intelligence, was sharing a small tent with Kevin Gurney, the Logistics officer. After observing the holes made in their tent by RPGs, it was decided some digging was necessary, and they created two parallel deep pits, which were later roofed with metal posts (star pickets) upon which layers of sandbags were placed. Close by Warrant Officer Bob Kissin dug a very deep pit, well protected by star pickets and sandbags.

Cameron was struck by the type of soldier opposing them. He had previously acquired a large amount of experience in similar field operations, against the VC, in the Australian area further to the south, and during the Tet Offensive and recent fighting. By early 1968 the VC were beginning to feel the effects of the Australian tactics and methods of operation in a counter-revolutionary warfare role. Sickness and lack of food was becoming evident.

But at Coral Cameron found 'these buggers were totally different. Very fit and well equipped. One PW told us they'd start coming towards us from twenty kilometres away, at about 1600 hours, trotting with all their gear until they were within a reasonable distance, then prop. After night fell, they would drop their heavy packs, and come on to within about 800 metres. They would wait there, and at two-thirty in the morning, a battalion would stand up ... and begin the attack.'

Cameron accompanied Lieutenant Colonel Bennett on a helicopter flight over the surrounds of Coral on the next morning. There below them, between 200 and 400 metres from the forward positions of 1RAR, were hundreds of small individual scrape holes dug by the waiting NVA.

Viewing the pits from closer were the soldiers, who 'swept right to the front and found their FUP. It was amazing, because it was no more than 200 metres from my pit,' recalled Richo Richardson, 'and there must have been 300 of these bloody holes, but we never heard a thing. Absolutely amazing.'

However, apart from the easily found bodies and equipment, there was little else of note.

One of the Communist tactics emphasised battlefield clearance after an action, leaving as little as possible for the opposing troops, to create just such an atmosphere of not knowing how hard the VC/NVA were suffering. The cumulative effect of finding little return for such great efforts as repelling heavy attacks was intended to give rise to a feeling of fighting invulnerable will-o'-the-wisps, countered by friendly casualties all too visible.

While this was successful for the VC/NVA against other poorly trained and led allied units, who were content to remain in static positions and bear attacks at times chosen by the VC/NVA, it had little lasting effect on the aggressive and mobile allied formations.

Plans had been made to disrupt the withdrawing enemy, and Blue Keldie's 1 Troop sortied from the base, engaging and chasing an NVA battalion in a pursuit that lasted until 1500, during which the vehicles travelled forty-five kilometres around the neighbouring countryside.

Sergeant Gus Ballentine recalls, 'It was dawn by now, and awfully quiet. After a short trip they dismounted, went into line abreast, and I formed my three carriers with my Alpha [M113] on the right, myself, and my Bravo on the left. The sun was nearly up, and good vision was possible.

'The area was lousy with tree stumps, an extra worry for us, fallen trees, odd enemy bodies, a real Verdun. It all seemed quiet, then directly in front of me a grunt threw himself down and opened up with his SLR [rifle]. We pulled up for a split second to spot what was going on, then all three APCs fired.

'I spotted a figure jumping behind a fairly thick tree and I fired and sort of stitched him up. The grunts did the right thing by us, and stayed put. I am grateful to the grunt who initially opened fire. He spotted something, later established to be a lightly camouflaged NVA, pointing something in our direction, and it turned out to be an RPG.

'We received all sorts of ordnance from the thick wooded area, did not directly spot the enemy, but returned fire without .50cals. The Possum [Army light aircraft] joined us, and told me there were enemy and a bunker on our left, but most firing came from our right, so we continued firing in this direction. My Troop leader came up on the radio and told me to check fire. We used our personal weapons then, because the .50cal bullets were worrying Chinook crews close to the base.

'I spotted movement in thick bush to my right. It all happened at once. I yelled over the radio, "Bob! To your right, depress and fire!" He did that and the NVA soldier just popped out of the bush and collapsed. Didn't look too well after a short burst from a .50cal.

'When we returned to base, the three carriers had enough captured assorted weapons to equip two sections of infantry. Reluctantly, we collected all the intact enemy bodies, and buried all the ones in bits and pieces; they must have been hit by arty, Spooky, et cetera. The method of carrying the bodies consisted of stacking them between the lowered trim vane and the front of the carrier, with the trim vane lowered to forty-five degrees, and secured with ropes.

'I remember my concern for the drivers: they had the bodies right in front of their noses. At times, a body would slip off and have to be picked up again. On arrival we dumped the bodies beside a deep scrape. The intelligence people came along and searched them, and asked a lot of questions. Someone came along also and collected all the captured weapons.'

Ballentine had noticed that many of the AK47s were still in packing grease, and questioned to himself the enemy skills as soldiers, going into an attack with weapons not cleaned. Of course, some of the unfortunate NVA may not have had time to clean their weapons before going into the assault.

At about 0950 Lorne 'Doc' Clarke, of C Company, was standing in the body of an APC, looking around, when he was nudged by another soldier, 'Rosy', who pointed to an NVA hiding near a tree; the infantry had missed him somehow. They called to the APC commander.

Corporal John Flood, in vehicle 13B, had been looking around as the M113s rolled through the light rubber trees, and he glanced down at the base of the tree they were passing, to see the muzzle of an AK47 pointing at him, the weapon held by an NVA. The Vietnamese didn't fire.

Flood whipped out his 9mm pistol from his shoulder holster, and aimed it at the NVA, who was surrendering. Flood remembered too late that because of recent emphasis on snap inspections of the pistols, he had plugged the barrel with a piece of cleaning flannel, so he was 'pointing it at this fellow, and there's a daggy bit of 4 × 2 hanging out of the barrel!'

The NVA was collected, brought into the APC, given food and a cigarette, and accompanied them on the rest of the sweep, being handed to Intelligence when they returned. John later retrieved the AK47, and carried it with him for the rest of his time in Vietnam.

Tales of enemy fanaticism were often recounted but seldom experienced in the first person. On this day, Bob Sutton's 2 Platoon met one dedicated NVA. Wounded in a burst of fire from the Australians, the Vietnamese, one of two, dragged himself some distance away, then apparently realised he was dying. While he had the strength, he placed a grenade with instantaneous fuse under his AK47, and another under his own body, then died before the Diggers arrived.

But his actions had been observed and reported by the circling Army helicopter, and the grenades claimed no victims.

It was decided to rearrange the defences of Coral, one result being that the gap between A Company and C Company was filled by 1RAR's Assault Pioneer and Anti-tank Platoons, under command of Col Adamson. Depth to the perimeter here was provided by the US self-propelled 155mm guns. Adamson found these to be 'pretty damn frightening, because they were firing all the time, and the loading mechanism was such that after firing a round, the barrel was depressed, so pointing at company headquarters, another round was shoved into the breech, the barrel elevated, and fired; rather horrendous.'

So Les Myers was told to take his Assault Pioneer Platoon across to that part of the perimeter. At first Adamson wanted to split up the Pioneers and put them in as individuals to replace his own casualties, but Myers refused this, saying he wanted a platoon position for his men. Adamson agreed.

Myers led his men to Weekes' area. 'When we arrived there it was quite horrific, actually. There was a big tree there, and obviously the NVA had used it as an aiming mark for their mortars, and they [mortars] had decimated the A Company people in that area. There was blood and rubbish all over the place, quite a bit of odour.

'This all frightened hell out of my blokes, and it was about midday by the time we had areas of responsibility sorted out. I had to go to an O Group, and by the time I came back the tree had gone and the platoon had completely dug in. I think they had a bulldozer to knock the tree over, then took to it with chainsaws and axes, as well as anything else in the area that was distinguishable.

'The lesson was clearly there: anything someone could see from a distance was used as a reference point. Camouflage and concealment became very big in the eyes of the troops, who could see what was going on. We went below ground, and from fifty metres away you couldn't see a position.'

Neil Weekes 'never saw a platoon dig in so quickly and thoroughly as the Pioneers, and by the afternoon they were under overhead protection.'

In the weeks to come, Les Myers' Pioneers became slightly irked at their role of housekeepers when companies were away on patrol. At Coral, they occupied five different positions on parts of the perimeter, and in none of them found the pits and defences to their liking, so spent time and effort on improvements, to the delight of the returning 'owners'.

Later, touring the battalion perimeter, Lieutenant Colonel Bennett took Neil Weekes aside and told him that the platoon 'had distinguished itself, because had we not held on, in all probability the complete regimental assault would have come straight through and wiped out the fire support base.'

Another who was complimented was Gavin Andrews, commander of 102 Battery. Remembering the close explosion of the eight-inch round the night before, near A Company, he kept his eyes open when accompanying

Lieutenant Colonel Bennett around the perimeter.

'I did spot it,' he recalls, 'and it was about fifteen metres in front of a platoon machinegun position. It was with some trepidation that I pointed to the hole and asked two young soldiers what they thought when that shell arrived. One soldier recognised me and became quite eloquent: "I don't know how you did it, sir, but that was unbelievable. We had eight or more enemy coming at us, things were looking grim, then this explosion occurred in front of us and we were safe, there were no enemy at all. How you did it, or even knew we were in trouble, I don't know. It was just great." I looked over at Lieutenant Colonel Bennett, and his face indicated that no explanation was required, for the time being, anyway.'

After the tension of the night hours, a natural feeling of satisfaction and pleasure at having withstood the assaults was evident in some of the platoons. John Salter's ebullient fellows were rehashing the events, when Lieutenant Colonel Bennett came by on an inspection, and sharply reminded Salter that his men had not shaved, which 'brought us all back to reality. We cleaned the weapons, picked up the enemy dead and loaded them on the extended trim vanes of the APCs which came around.'

Meanwhile, Ned Kelly, who had driven the ammunition to A Company through the night battle, had been evacuated to a US hospital suffering from heat exhaustion and shock. After improvement in his condition, he was sent to the Australian hospital at Vung Tau, but no one there knew anything about him or his medical condition, so he walked out, got a lift back to Nui Dat, reported to 1RAR and carried on with normal duties.

Assuring themselves that things were quiet in their area, Richo Richardson and several friends asked permission to go across to A Company to visit mates there. On the way, they passed Lieutenant Colonel Bennett, sitting on top of the CP bunker.

'Where are you reprobates going?'

'Going down to give A Company a hand,' replied Jim Daley. 'Looks like the buggers need it down there.'

Richardson did not think Bennett was too pleased with the answer. He, Daley and Dave Cunningham went on, and spent a few enjoyable hours with A Company, swapping yarns and drinking brews.

While all the action had been taking place, Lieutenant John Crossman, of Keldie's APC unit, had been enjoying a few days' leave in the seaside recreation town of Vung Tau. He had arrived in-country the day after the Tet Offensive began, and had been continuously engaged in operations as a Troop officer since then. His leave was terminated when a military policeman came to his hotel room on 15 May, with the news that Crossman was to return to his unit at once. So on the morning of 16 May, John Crossman was at Luscombe Strip at Nui Dat, hitching a ride on a US Chinook helicopter which was going to Coral. But what should have been a normal trip to his unit became something of a nightmare for him.

In Vung Tau, Crossman had collected a dose of dysentery, and 'was not feeling very well at all'. The Chinook is not fitted with any sort of toilet. 'Quite unashamedly, I was dying to go to the toilet, sitting in this aircraft for about two hours, shuddering along through the sky, all I could do was sit there, rifle between my knees, and pray that I didn't disgrace myself!

'There was a very attractive American nursing sister sitting opposite me, trying to engage me in conversation, and I don't know whatever she must have thought of me, as I really didn't do us much credit that morning!

'The thing landed, I sprinted off, went two metres from the back of the Chinook and dropped my trousers. I wondered what the soldiers there thought of me, because right alongside there was a trench into which they were throwing the bodies of the NVA killed in the attack.

'It was totally unrealistic, certainly one of those occasions the Air Force has more often than the Army, where in a very short space of time you go from a relaxed, comfortable, luxurious environment, into something which is quite ghastly. They had these bodies laid out, and were bringing in

186

Private Farrens informing General Westmoreland of the shortcomings of the M60 machinegun (*AWM No. THU/68/565/VN*)

FSPB Coral (*Carbury*)

View south-east over Coral (*Fowler*)

Major John Keldie (*left*), and
Major Peter Badman (*AWM
No. ERR/68/661/VN*)

Captain Bernie Sullivan
(*AWM No. CRO/68/169/VN*)

Tanks moving to FSPB Coral, 23 May 1968 (*AWM No. ERR/68/543/VN*)

Centurion tank at Coral (*Carbury*)

Warrant Officer Wally Thompson
(*AWM No. ERR/68/736/VN*)

Lieutenant Gerry McCormack's
tank moving with D/1RAR to
engage NVA bunker system, 26
May 1968 (*De Jong*)

Major Ian Campbell (*Clarke*)

Lieutenant Colonel Jim Shelton
and Colonel Donald Dunstan
(*AWM No. HAL/68/531/VN*)

Middle
Lorne Clarke (*AWM No. ERR/
68/736/VN*)

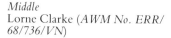

Below
FSPB Balmoral, 28 May 1968;
officers of 3RAR assembled to
meet General Westmoreland.
Back row (*left to right*), Jim
Shelton, Geoff Cohen, Alan
Hitchings, David Candow, Hori
Howard, Ian Hands, Peter
Phillips and Laurie Hall. Front
row (*left to right*) 'Blue' Doyle,
Dick Lippett, Bruce Richards,
Mick Butler and Vince Murdoch
(*Shelton*)

Centurion tank crew members, 2 Troop C Squadron, on the morning after the second attack on FSPB Balmoral, 28 May 1968 (*AWM No. CRO/68/579/NN*)

The killing ground at Balmoral, from D/3RAR position (*Fowler*)

B52 bomb crater, Balmoral (*Butler*)

Corporal Bill Burton's tank, 31B, broken down at the entrance to Coral, 30 May 1968 (*De Jong*)

Part of NVA trench after the battle of 30 May 1968 (*De Jong*)

Private Dick Norden, who won the DCM
for his bravery in the fighting of 14 May
1968

more all the time. I didn't count them, I was too bloody sick.

'In fact, being sick overcame any feelings of trepidation I might have had. Anyway, Keldie took one look at me, and said, "What the bloody hell's wrong with you, X-man?" They always called me "X-man", from "Cross"-man. I said, "I've got a terrible bad bloody stomach", and he appreciated that I wasn't fit to go as liaison officer to Tan Uyen.

'I went off and got some sulphur thiozine tablets, took a whole phial, and they seemed to sort it out, really stopped me up.'

At the LZ, Crossman saw 'a young military police corporal who'd probably been sent up to help take some of these prisoners back. I mean no discredit to the guy, but there he was, in his freshly starched greens, spitty boots and brassard made in Shop 3 in Ba Ria or wherever, and he really looked a right spiv.

'He took one look around, and I heard him say, "I'm not staying here. I am *not* staying here," and he was off. There was a helicopter cranking up on the pad, and he was going to get on it, no two ways about it, and get the hell out of there.

'This was the sort of unreal situation that you had. He might have flown up direct from Vung Tau. Depending on the transport you had, you could go from a semi-permanent camp environment with tutti frutti and what have you, into the middle of a charnel house. There were bodies and bits of bodies everywhere. For most of the soldiers, who were used to being in the field, it was still a shock to them, but nothing like it had been to this young man, and he was off.

'I grabbed him, and I think the Sergeant Major grabbed him, and we had to settle this young fellow down.'

Blue Keldie agreed that Crossman should stay for a day, until he was somewhat better, then go to Tan Uyen, releasing Lieutenant Brian Kollias to return to A Squadron.

John Crossman noticed that the soldiers seemed 'to be a little bit dampened, a little bit subdued. Normally, you could never stop them chiacking, but for many this was the first time they had seen something on this scale. It had been a fearsome fight, which had gone on most of the night under very confused circumstances, and the element of danger was still there. But they were in good spirits, because they realised they'd more than met the enemy on his own terms and given him a hiding.

'They were fairly trying times, and I thought our soldiers held up magnificently. They hadn't really known what they were up against any more than the North Vietnamese had known what they were up against. The NVA 141st thought "We'll hit those blokes on the run, and have them out," and it didn't work.

'I don't think I got a single comment about the fact that I had an upset stomach. Normally, they would have said something like, "Something wrong with you, lieutenant? No stomach for this sort of thing?" They didn't even say a bloody word.'

Crossman spent the rest of the day assisting Keldie in his work around the perimeter. Following the big major around, Crossman saw that 'Keldie absolutely revelled in it, you know. He'd hit his straps, got the scent of something decent in his nostrils, and was away. He was on a high—there is no doubt you do get that way—and he said, "Come along, come along, X-man, and we'll have a look."

'We were wandering around, and in some areas it was still confused. He was striding ahead, crossing this small track, and I had an Armalite pointing over to the left. He went across the track and I caught a movement out of the corner of my eye, to the right. I looked up, and there was a man, one of their North Vietnamese reconnaissance teams, about thirty metres up the track, and I never stopped, the paces sort of carried me along.

'I said, "sir", and the fellow had his AK47 carried like mine, pointing away from me. Keldie said, "Come along, come along," and that was it. I was across the track and the man was gone. You wonder, "Did I see something, is it the product of a fevered imagination?" He was wearing a sort of a greyish-brown type of uniform, some camouflage, no helmet.

'I spent a very uncomfortable night there, very tense, and I wasn't feeling the greatest, so I didn't get too much sleep.'

Next day, John Crossman flew out to the town of Tan

Uyen, on the northern bank of the Dong Nai River, to act as 1ATF Liaison Officer with the ARVN unit there, the 48th Infantry Regiment.

Keldie noticed 1RAR was intent on preparing for whatever might come. 'The professionalism of our infantry came back to me when I noticed a company practising its counter-penetration. Both flanking companies were practising, as their commanders were not happy with what had happened. It was interesting to see them doing it.'

As the day wore on, the tiredness caught up with the soldiers. Richo went around the section pits 'about four o'clock, and apart from the bloke on the machinegun, they were all bloody dead to the world. I don't think anybody had lunch, either.'

At Nui Dat, Second Lieutenant Phil Busby noted: 'Quiet day here, but TF Main has been involved in a lot of fighting up north near Long Binh. They are fighting 141 NVA Regt; good troops and well-equipped. We have lost a few men killed and wounded.'

In Australia, the newspapers reported that the prime minister had refused a request by a Labor member to enquire into claims by the NLF, made in Moscow, that it was not responsible for the deaths of the Australian journalists killed in Saigon, but the South Vietnamese Government was.

It was later shown conclusively that the journalists had been deliberately killed by VC troops, one of whom had shot the wounded with a pistol at point blank range as they called out they were reporters.

After two large attacks, and with the probability of more, not to mention the daily patrol clashes, there was an upsurge of religious belief. Services of all denominations were well attended. Experienced padres had already noted this phenomenon in previous campaigns, and would do so in the future.

Father John Tinkler, Catholic chaplain of 1RAR, was still at the US hospital at Long Binh, and remembers sitting by the bedside of two Diggers, Clelland and Green, who had bandaged eyes, describing the ward to them in detail, relating the events of the ward, and doing this for hours.

He noticed that the presence of a pretty nurse in the ward had a definite positive effect in helping the young soldiers to recovery, and as the days went by, realised that when they began to complain about the US hospital diet, then they were on the road to recovery.

On the 17th, at GR930299, Geoff Bowcock's 12 Platoon found an abandoned mortar baseplate position which testified to the success of 1RAR's own mortar fire, during the attack on the early morning of the 16th. Blood and other signs of casualties were splattered about the four-mortar position, plus twenty-three destroyed bombs. Only two 82mm bombs had been fired, but scattered through the location were the tail fins of 1RAR's 81mm bombs. They had impacted right on target.

Later, moving back to Coral, they found a 500lb bomb, 'in pristine condition', which had obviously been recovered by the enemy, who had fitted ropes of woven bamboo around it in a form of harness for carrying poles, but for some reason the bomb had been left where the Diggers found it. As he had an Engineer team with him, and their explosives, Bowcock decided to destroy the bomb in place.

Looking at his map, he saw that the charges could be placed and the fuse ignited, and the patrol could then move to a creek-line for cover from the explosion. This was done. They waited for the noise of the detonation, but nothing happened. They waited longer to give the fuse more time, then longer for safety's sake.

No one knew what had happened, but Bowcock was now determined to blow the bomb, so decided to call artillery in on the area, and move it back and forth in case the carriers had returned and removed the explosive charge, and were waiting in ambush. So, he called in artillery, first some distance away from the bomb, and began decreasing the range, with a series of 'Drop 100' corrections.

Suddenly, Lieutenant Colonel Bennett was heard on the radio, calling 'Check fire! Check fire!' and demanding to know what was going on, as no contact requiring the artillery shells had been reported. Bowcock explained what he was doing, and that he was about to go back to the bomb.

Leaving most of the patrol in the creek, taking only the Engineers and a couple of others, they cautiously approached the bomb. The fuse had stopped burning a few centimetres from the detonator of the explosive charge. But the Engineers had only a short length of fuse remaining. It was decided to use this, pray that it worked this time, and run like hell back to the creek before the 500-pounder blasted the location. This they did, sliding into the creek just before the huge explosion devastated the vicinity.

Other platoons were having their own excitement that day, and while returning to Coral at 1717 hours. Forde's 5 Platoon, B/1RAR, was crossing an area of thick grass, and nearing the position of a friendly standing patrol.

Then a rifleman noticed a green enemy shirt on the ground, pointed his weapon in the direction and called the machinegun group forward, the gunner saw movement in the grass and fired, killing an NVA. 5 Platoon realised that alertness had to be maintained for the entire period of a patrol, and could not be relaxed when close to base. In fact, B Company HQ tried to halt the firing as it was feared the standing patrol might be in danger, and Forde realised that he should have informed the HQ of the direction of fire when first reporting the incident.

Other patrols in the area produced information about the enemy methods, such as the one by the Pioneers, when Wally Fiedler noticed sticks tied at an angle to trees. When this was investigated, it was found the sticks pointed at Coral, and were to provide a rest and aiming angle for RPGs to fire rockets into the base.

Other hazards became evident. When the patrol returned to the platoon area, Wally was surprised to find that no one was in his weapon pit, but two of the fellows had been manning that part of the perimeter when he left. All was deserted. The two soldiers told him that a cobra had taken up residence in his pack, so they had left the snake in possession of the machinegun pit. Wally took care around the pit, and did not sleep that night, but never saw the cobra at all.

There had been many other sightings of snakes, and this contributed to the reluctance of the soldiers to sleep in their pits, as often the snakes wriggled into them. If it was a choice between being bitten by a cobra or krait which had fallen into one's weapon pit, or by wounding from rockets and mortars, most people chose the rockets.

Paul Richardson, Section Commander in Tony Hammett's D/1RAR, was eating a tin of fruit from the ration packs. Hammett came along, spied the food and asked where Richo got that tin of fruit.

'Out of the ration packs, of course,' was the reply, showing the tin to Hammett. At that instant, Richardson realised he was looking at an officer who was himself realising that his batman had been keeping the best of the rations for himself.

'The last I saw of Hammett that day,' recalls Richo, 'he was running down the track yelling his batman's name!'

Back at Nui Dat, the fighting at Coral had little effect on most things, and it was not until Colonel Don Dunstan, Deputy Task Force commander, actually went to the Fire Support Base, that he realised how intense the fighting had been. Other people were affected in various ways. Because most of the TF support went to Coral, SAS patrols were curtailed for lack of helicopters to insert and extract them. However, COMAFV ordered that SAS would continue to patrol and 1ATF would find the resources, so they went out on foot, in Troop strength.

With the recent intense fighting around Coral, HQ IIFFV demanded the Daily Situation Report (SITREP) as soon as it was available. However, the radio nets were so clogged that IIFFV decreed it was to go by FLASH priority. But there were so many FLASH messages that two higher precedences were introduced: RED ROCKET FLASH and FLASH OVERRIDE. Captain Peter Desmond, GSO3 (Operations), recalls that it was probably the only time a Daily Sitrep, authorised by the Duty Officer, was sent FLASH.

Desmond, communicating directly from Nui Dat to the CP at Coral, recalls a sense of amazement at the jocular attitude of those at the Fire Support Base, who showed no signs of being perturbed by the actions, and could calmly carry on, though they might be perched on a field table, in a hole full of water, at night, co-ordinating fire support with someone a province away.

On 18 May 1RAR HQ, B Company and the Anti-armour Platoon redeployed inside Coral, adopting what became the final positions in the base.

Lieutenant John Crossman had meanwhile left Coral and begun his duties as Liaison Officer with the ARVN 48th Regiment at Tan Uyen. The US advisory team was led by Major Ed Wilkison, who had been there for some time. Wilkison told Crossman that an estimated 5 per cent of the 1000 ARVN were believed to be VC sympathisers.

The 48th were not very active, and had not been out of their encampment for months. On the last foray, they had been ambushed a mere 500 metres from the main gate, suffering about a hundred casualties. So they tended to remain inside.

Crossman, with a radio operator, was to maintain communications to 1ATF in AO Surfers, both to inform them of activity in the area by the ARVN, and vice versa.

While appreciating the finer points of life in the relative civilisation of the Tan Uyen compound, such as living in a brick building and eating off plates, Crossman noted the realities of everyday life in a camp with suspected enemy sympathisers. Recent films were distributed to US units, and these were screened outdoors for all to enjoy. At Tan Uyen, the screen was built near the advisory HQ building, with the advisers watching from one side and the assembled ARVN on the other. The screen was raised above the ground, so that the audience could be watched.

Crossman was surprised at the reaction by the Vietnamese to the final scenes of *Bonnie and Clyde*, in which the bank robbers are machinegunned to death, in colour and slow motion. 'These ARVN thought it was the funniest thing they

193

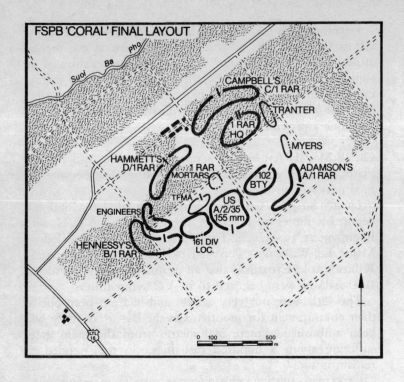

FSPB 'CORAL' FINAL LAYOUT

had ever seen. They were literally falling out of their chairs laughing at this.'

Crossman had another lesson in the unrealities of the location. Deciding to use the running river for a wash and shave in idyllic surroundings, he took towel, soap and thongs and went down the bank to the water, noticing an island in midstream.

'I was dabbling around in the water, dhobi-ing-up, and next thing there was a ripping sound from the island and a few little geysers in the water. I don't know if you've ever tried to run up a mud bank in the nude with someone shooting at you, but it's amazing how you can get toeholds in the bank when the desperation is there ... They thought this was a huge bloody joke.'

In his journal at Nui Dat, Captain John Bullen, Survey

Troop, noted the details of the casualties suffered by each side, with a few relevant comments. He also recorded that an American jeep was ambushed close to Ba Ria, with no casualties but twenty-five bullet holes in the vehicle. More seriously, the nearby town of Long Dien was reported to be 'under Vietcong control for several hours', and much fighting went on, with the airstrikes easily visible from Nui Dat.

Next day, fighting continued in Long Dien, and both the village chief and US senior adviser in the district were killed. Bullen also did his own analysis of action reports, and saw that when helicopter gunships were used, enemy casualties were reported to be up to five times the number when no helicopters were called in. He attributed this to the 'murderous miniguns above the battle', rather than the interference by the gunships with battlefield evacuation activities.

The counter-mortar radars never did achieve acceptance, despite continued efforts with their use. The Engineers dug a pit for the machinery, later realising that the pit must be dug to suit the requirements of the device, not the other way around. While all this was being sorted out, an enemy mortar began firing, and the baseplate position was obvious to all, in plain sight were the bombs sailing through the air. It was a great opportunity for the radar, and George Hulse and his men stood there, watching the radar dish move across the sky tracking the bomb . . . then the operators gave a position for the enemy which was wrong by 180 degrees . . .

In the days which followed, some of the older soldiers at Coral became disappointed at the lack of immediate aggressive and distant patrolling, and noted what some of them thought was a defensive attitude creeping into the manner of the less experienced men. However, once again it was a case of trying to make a pint fit a quart pot, for there simply were not enough men available to protect the base, patrol in sufficient strength at any distance, and have enough in reserve to react to a heavy patrol battle which might eventuate, given the numbers of aggressive and active enemy in the area.

From the 18th to the evening of 21 May, there was little enemy contact, and what there was had inconclusive results.

Patrols did find more bodies and equipment, enemy were sighted, some followed a D Company patrol, but there was little to report.

On the 19th, however, the artillery, particularly 102 Battery, was able to reach outside the normal activity in AO Surfers, to support a battalion of the US 101 Airborne Division's Third Brigade. The paratroopers found themselves heavily engaged in a bunker system, and just as the US guns had fired in support of Coral, now 102 Battery fired in support of the Americans. Over a period of several hours, 821 rounds were fired.

At the end of the battle, the US operations officer offered the Australians part of the bodycount of enemy, but Ian Ahearn refused, saying that was not necessary. The paratroopers showed their appreciation by insisting on conducting the resupply for the guns, and included some beer with the ammunition. As it was a night resupply and the Chinooks used lights, it was received with less than enthusiasm by some at Coral, but of course 102 Battery were delighted. Both the US battalion commander and divisional commander flew in to thank the gunners personally. As Gavin Andrews said, '102 Battery were quite fond of the Screaming Eagles.'

What happened to the beer is another, unresolved matter, as some of the gunners vehemently state that they did not see a beer during the operation.

On the 20th a conference was held at Coral, attended by Major General A.L. MacDonald (Commander AFV), Colonel Dunstan and the unit commanders. The protection of the Fire Support Patrol Bases was discussed. Moving in the heavier armour available, by bringing up the tanks from Nui Dat, was supported by Colonel Dunstan. The characteristics of armour—fire power, protection and mobility—would be of value at the base.

While flying up to Coral, Dunstan had an experience which was amusing years later, but annoying at the time. The helicopter was some ten minutes north of Nui Dat, and in it were Dunstan, his batman and radio-operator. Suddenly, they were told to return to Nui Dat, and when he queried the pilot, Dunstan was told it was to pick up a VIP. Dunstan wondered who this could be, important enough to have called back the machine of the Task Force Commander designate. They landed at the 1RAR pad, and Dunstan saw one of the battalion characters, Stitches Fyfe, so asked him, 'What's the form, Stitches? Who's this VIP we've got to pick up?'

The blood pressure of the normally placid Don Dunstan soared when Fyfe told him it was a CMF (Army Reserve) major who was visiting Vietnam and wanted to go to Coral!

Colonel Dunstan was to take over command of the Task Force when Brigadier Hughes went on rest and recreation leave, a move which had been planned for some time. There had been little happening for some days, and Hughes saw his departure, as planned, to be a declaration of faith in the ability of his subordinates, and of Colonel Dunstan in particular. On 21 May Brigadier Hughes had flown back to Nui Dat, and was preparing to depart, but was still in-country when Colonel Dunstan began making his own decisions about the conduct of operations.

As far as use of the Centurion tanks was concerned, Colonel Dunstan 'just felt that there was a very strong element that wasn't being used, and it ought to be there because it would give us so much more flexibility and fire-power. I couldn't see any reason for them not to be there; I saw it as a level of operation in which tanks could play a role. There's no doubt in my mind that there's many an Australian infantryman who survived that operation who otherwise wouldn't have done so.'

It must be remembered that in the week since the major attack on 16 May, contact with the enemy had been light and fleeting; there were no indications of more such assaults. The wet season was about to begin; there were no maintenance facilities for the tanks at Coral; their arrival would mean an additional strain on the logistics system; the roads and bridges between Nui Dat and Coral were less than good; the prob-ability of enemy action or bogging en route was unknown. In addition, as 1ATF was in the area at the behest of IIFFV, and enemy action seemed to be lessening, the Australians could soon be moved elsewhere. On that basis, there was little reason to call for the Centurions.

There had been disquiet among people of senior rank about the very concept of using tanks in Vietnam, but as Dunstan recalled, 'nobody senior to me resisted. When I took command I spoke to Keldie about bringing tanks up. There was concern amongst other people that the area was very boggy, and it was well mined, but it was really the boggy area that was seen to be very risky. The Americans took the same view, because they'd had some bad experiences. I came to the conclusion I'd really like to have the tanks there, and asked Keldie for his view on the ability to move them around the area. He said it was no worse than Puckapunyal in the middle of winter. That was the thing that made me decide to bring the tanks up. It was in the first twenty-four hours, perhaps the first twelve hours (of my time in command).

'I rang Brigadier Hughes and asked him to send the tanks, but he said I would have to give the order, so I rang Badman and said I wanted him to bring his tanks. There was never any doubt in my mind that I had made the decision, and if it failed I was for the big jump. Since then I've heard other people say publicly that they brought the tanks up.'

The major problem would be moving the heavy vehicles along the Vietnamese roads, through the traffic, to the base at Coral, a journey of some 150 kilometres.

Major Peter Badman, commanding the tank squadron, had already made a reconnaissance of the routes to the area of Coral, as ordered by Brigadier Hughes after the attack on Coral on 16 May. There were only two: one north through Xuan Loc, turning west along Highway 1 to Bien Hoa, then north again to the operation area; the other followed Route 15 north-west from Baria to Bien Hoa, thence to Coral. Because of the number of bridges on Route 15, he opted for the road through Xuan Loc, which also had the advantage of passing through the area of the US 11th Armoured Cavalry Regiment.

However, while waiting to prove themselves, no call had been made for the tanks. The crews knew of the fighting around Coral, and while confident of their ability, were somewhat disheartened by their relegation to sitting around Nui Dat. Despite some enjoyable farewell parties at 2RAR, the 'tankies' could see little prospect of showing what they could do.

Then Major Badman received a telephone message from Colonel Dunstan: 'Come up tomorrow', the only order for the move which he received.

On the afternoon of 21 May, after a day of sporadic contact with enemy logistics groups, it became obvious that the NVA were again reconnoitring the base. Young enemy soldiers would appear in daylight, walking openly up to the perimeter of the defences. It was necessary to call in helicopter gunships to patrol the area and keep the Vietnamese away, hindering their approach through the long grass.

After the attack on the 16th, John Kemp, commanding the Engineers, had used the bulldozer to clear the undergrowth from among the trees, opening up the area out to a distance of 300 metres or so. This removed cover for the enemy, and improved visibility for the defenders. When the night-vision devices were used earlier, the close-in scrub had lessened their effectiveness, but as the bulldozing progressed, the value of the devices was greatly increased.

So much work had been done by now at Coral that when John Dellaca went back there from FSPB Coogee, to rejoin the artillery Divisional Locating Battery detachment, he found it hard to recognise, due to the large number of pits, bunds, overhead protection, wire fences, aerials and tents.

By this time, Father Tinkler had made his way to Coral, when the Australian casualties at Long Binh were moved into the Australian medical system. He found that Mass was well attended, and was able to conduct two a day, on opposite sides of the base. In his constant travels around the units and pits, he came to know many people by name, and more by sight. He realised that some were afraid, but carried on, and some had serious moral problems, mainly whether they could shoot to kill another human being.

He was amazed at how well the soldiers stood up to the strain, and surprised to note no reluctance to go out on patrol. Conversations were lighthearted, with much laughter and joking about events, and Tinkler was proud of them, as there was no recounting of personal exploits, but rather tales of what their mates had done.

During a visit to A Company, Bob Sutton, commanding 2 Platoon, told him how, during a lull in the battle on 16 May, he had been praying to overcome the battle-fear, but had no rosary, only ten cigarettes, so decided to use the cigarettes for the Hail Marys, and really wished for a cigar to mark the Our Father between every ten Hail Marys.

Sometimes Tinkler had stood in a pit to conduct a Mass, so that the ground was his altar. One day he saw a couple of Diggers with a wooden box, and asked them where they were taking it, and they explained it was a new thunder-box for the field latrine. Tinkler commandeered it for use as an altar, but many of the Diggers took photos, and now he wonders what tales were told of the Padre saying Mass using a thunder-box, albeit an unused one.

The Australian casualties did notice differences between the US and Australian hospitals, one of which was the basic construction of the wards. The Americans enjoyed air-conditioned buildings, while the Aussies had walls with a 150mm gap at the foot to allow free air circulation. In the Vung Tau area this meant a constant intake of sand whenever the wind blew, and some of the wounded recalled the beds with a light coating of sand.

The casualties who were evacuated to Australia were partly happy to be doing so, and partly sad at leaving their friends and units. Some hoped to get back after a few weeks in hospital; some did, some never managed to do so. Perry Neil told the medical board that he wanted to go back to 1RAR, and was told that if he did so and was killed or again wounded, 'it would look bad for the government', so he spent the rest of his Army service in Australia.

Back at Nui Dat, John Bullen noted seeing a water tanker driving by with the painted sign, 'H₂O au Go Go'. He also recorded that 'the Divisional Intelligence Unit went rabbiting in Hoa Long and found some burrows, and in one of them they caught the Hoa Long Viet Cong chief, their biggest catch ever. They also caught a VC female Intelligence agent whom they have been hunting for some time. Expected a storm today but it didn't come.'

At 0010 hours, 22 May, a short, accurate mortar bombardment was fired by the NVA, with the bombs impacting in the headquarters area. Radio antennas were damaged, requiring changing, and it was as a result of the problems of command in such circumstances—being well dug-in, but with no communications—that ACVs would be employed in future for TF HQ and Arty Tac.

The mortars were called to action, and Leigh Boneham ran from his pit to the CP, fell mid-way, and when he arrived, found the fire mission being called already, but then discovered he had no pencil. On the spur of the moment, he used his finger to mark the spot on the board, and the rounds were fired.

Phil Thompson calling from C Company, astounded Leigh when he radioed that no more rounds were needed, 'you hit them right on the head!' The approaching NVA had been scattered.

In his pit, Noel Sproles was waiting for his relief from duty, and finally one of the unflappable Diggers went to the officer's pit, ignoring the bombardment, calling out, 'Come on, sir, you're wanted in the CP,' and then indulged his curiosity by strolling around to take in the sights. He returned to tell of the strange noise he heard coming from the nearby artillery area, which on investigation proved to be an artilleryman digging furiously.

An Army Reserve officer, commanding a Reserve artillery regiment in Australia, had arrived earlier at Coral as part of a tour to the forces on active service. He had asked where his pit was, recalled Phil Busby, but on being shown a piece of ground, 'he did not think it very funny, and thought a soldier should dig it for him'. He was told that the soldiers were either fully employed or resting, and not used digging weapon pits for officers. The officer dug a shell scrape, ignoring the presence of the well-developed pits around him. Soon after, rockets and mortars had rained down across the base. By morning he was in a deep weapon pit.

Neil Lloyd-Jones was in the 102 Battery CP during the bombardment when Sergeant Creek came in, looking for and calling out to a Scottish gunner: 'Gunner so-and so, where are you?' A Scottish voice replied, 'In me fookin' hole, sergeant, and it's where I'm stayin'!'

In the CP itself, Colonel Dunstan was 'full of admiration for Gavin Andrews and Jack Kelly, enormously impressed with the calmness and competence of these two fellows handling something like six batteries of guns [with shells falling] right outside the perimeter.'

The mortaring went on for twenty minutes, then was joined by a heavy attack by fire, comprising rockets, mortars and recoilless launchers, fired from the south against the rear-echelon positions in the base. Weak probes were made against D/1RAR, and as the firing went on, an interested observer was George Hulse, in the Engineer position. As a young infantryman, he had practised the 'pepper-pot' type of advance used by the probing NVA, but never had a high opinion of it. Now he saw just how effective it could be, with one or two enemy popping up, running forward a short distance, diving to ground and rolling away while another couple jumped up elsewhere, giving only fleeting dispersed targets to the defenders.

In the attack on the 16th, one of the neighbouring signals unit had been killed by an RPG which streaked directly into the opening of his sleeping bay. The Engineers, among others, were a little angry at this, as the man's bay had been dug exactly the wrong way, with the opening towards the enemy, rather than away from him, in the forward side of the pit. Hulse noticed the sigs took this to heart, and while doing their job well, 'every time they came out of their pits, they were moving at fifty kilometres an hour, body only centimetres above the ground.'

While making the rounds of his position, Hulse met a sig who was called to go on some type of duty, and 'he came out of the ground so fast, it was unbelievable the speed he was doing by the time he connected with me, barrelled me over, not a word of apology, and he kept going into the night.'

D and E Platoon also had to relearn the hard way the old

202

lesson of not firing the machineguns at night unless being definitely attacked. The NVA had forced them to fire by approaching closely and aggravating the gunners, then marked the locations. Hulse and his men were puzzled by the routine of approach; firing, then out in front a babble of Vietnamese and 'chip-chop chip-chop' as a sapling was cut down, silence until it was repeated further away. Later it was found that saplings had very neatly been cut down and arranged to point to the machineguns, for the benefit of the RPG gunners, who chastised D and E Platoon with rockets.

The attack added impetus to the movement of the tanks from Nui Dat to Coral.

Peter Badman had already visited the HQ of the US 11th Armoured Cavalry at Xuan Loc, and been assured of their assistance, as well as the safety of the roads in their area. Not funny at the time, but humorous in retrospect, was the ensuing damage to a tank 'by a bloody great mine' about 200 metres past the entrance to the 11th Cav.

This was somewhat embarrassing to the Americans, as the spot was very close to their base gate, and the mine had obviously been placed there, under their very noses. The tank-dozer had the right front suspension station blown off, and it was towed back into the US camp.

The Centurion design had evolved from British World War II experience, and the suspension items were designed to be blown off without damaging the hull. Accordingly, Sergeant Jock McConnell, the crew commander, set his men to work with borrowed US tools, to remove the damaged parts. Next day, a Light Aid Detachment arrived by helicopter with replacement parts, and that afternoon the vehicle was ready to run.

As Bernie Sullivan put it, 'We were a bit uncertain of its perfection of alignment, but that tank continued to run thereafter.' The Americans were also surprised because if the same had happened to one of their tanks, it would have been a write-off.

There was no other enemy action, but considerable concern was felt when the fifty-ton Centurions had to cross the rusty old Class 30 (thirty-ton capacity) Bailey bridges erected during and since the wars from 1945 to 1968. It was noticed that the thrifty local Vietnamese had removed bits and pieces of the bridges, presumably for home use.

Only one tank at a time could be allowed on each structure, which literally bowed under the weight. Any attempt to correct the direction of the tank when on the bridge—by manoeuvring the caterpillar tracks—resulted in an alarming sway by the whole bridge.

But, at midday on 23 May, Badman's Squadron arrived at Coral: 1 Troop under Lieutenant Gerry McCormack, 2 Troop under Second Lieutenant Mick Butler, and the improvised 3 Troop under Second Lieutenant Wilson.

Welcoming the addition to the defences, Colonel Dunstan told Major Keldie to put them on the perimeter.

Keldie's A Squadron APCs had escorted the convoy on Route 314, during which the commander of the Australian Army 161 Reconnaissance Flight, Major George Constable, was shot down. He was giving reconnaissance cover to a convoy which was returning from Coral to Bien Hoa, and when hit almost crashed into it.

Lieutenant Alan Cunningham, Intelligence Officer at the Australian logistic base at Vung Tau, had gone to Coral the day before to help the Intelligence people at the fire support base, and was returning to Vung Tau with a column of Australian trucks, under command of Major Peter Douglas. Alan Cunningham, who had some pilot training, was in the truck two back from Douglas.

As the trucks neared a road junction some twelve kilometres south of Coral (GR944194), Cunningham became aware of the Cessna 01 'Bird-dog' flying south along the road 'at about 120 metres, going fast, as at the end of a dive, passed to the head of the convoy and gained height rapidly to about 300 metres. East of the intersection he did a steep bank to the right and flew west, down along the road [to the west], and gained height as if to execute a wing-over [that is, to pivot on the wingtip].

'At the top of the manoeuvre, I distinctly heard "bang-bang . . . bang-bang-bang", definitely not automatic fire. The aircraft just seemed to hang there, and I thought, "This is going to be the sloppiest wingover I've ever seen or it's going to be a hammerhead" [stall]. The aircraft did a very peculiar turn and just headed, nose down, directly along the road back to the intersection, and just kept going down, no attempt to pull it out of the dive, it went straight down, which leads me to think the pilot was mortally wounded or shot dead at the top of the dive.

'As soon as he hit the ground, at the front of a house at the intersection, the aircraft burst into flames. I was about 200 metres away. Peter Douglas stopped the convoy, and he, myself and others ran to the site of the aircraft, burning fiercely in the front of this house, and tried to see the pilot and render assistance, but couldn't get within twenty metres. It was burning fiercely, not a thing we could do about it.

'I didn't know it was from 161 [Recce Flight]; it had US Army painted on it. I was shocked to find it was George Constable. Peter Douglas and I looked at each other and realised there was nothing to be done.'

In Cunningham's opinion, if the house had not been in the aircraft's path, it could well have made a type of landing on the open ground at the intersection, possibly damaging itself, but remaining more or less upright.

(Another version of the incident had Constable making repeated passes low across the front of an enemy machinegun firing on the convoy from the high ground west of the road, being hit by its fire, and hitting the ground while making a low turn at the end of one of these passes. Alan Cunningham is adamant that the convoy was not under fire, and nor was fire being returned at the high ground.)

Cunningham noticed the excited chatter and laughing manner of some teenage RF-PF armed with M-1 rifles and carbines from the nearby defence post. He suspected the RF-PF had shot down the plane, but nothing could be done at the time. The Vietnamese merged with the crowd, and the convoy had to move on. Other people in the convoy saw the aircraft making its violent manoeuvres, and some assumed it had crashed because of one of these.

Constable's loss was deeply felt by those who knew him, describing him as a superb pilot who thoroughly understood aerial reconnaissance, an outstanding officer and a good friend.

Peter Spoor was flying back to Nui Dat when he heard on the guard frequency a conversation between rescue aircraft about a Bird-dog down on fire near Tan Uyen, and knew at once that it was Constable, 'the best boss I ever had, civil or military'.

The safe arrival of the tanks at Coral was greeted with relief at Nui Dat. Sending them had been a big decision, and the staff were well aware of the problems and potential for disaster posed by the rickety bridges, deep creeks, bogging and enemy ambush.

The approach march by the tanks was the longest Centurions and Australian armour had made, and certain technical problems became evident. Captain Bernie Sullivan, the Squadron Technical Officer, soon became aware that as the approach march was made continuously on roads, the wheels generated a greater amount of heat than previously experienced. Normally, in training and in operations, tanks advanced by relatively short bounds, as part of the tactical movement required for a piece of terrain. Pauses between the bounds, as other sub-units took up the move, allowed time for the road-wheels to dissipate some of the heat. This had not happened on the move to Coral, and there were many cases of separation of the rubber tyres from the steel road wheels. While spare wheels were carried, the appropriate nuts were not, and both wheels and nuts had to be flown up by US Chinooks. The first lesson in technical problems caused by the long fast march had been met.

The base now had added to it two and a half troops of tanks, 3 Troop A Sqn 3 Cav, plus two US air defence weapons, formidable when employed against ground forces: twin 40mm guns mounted on a tank chassis, called 'Duster', from the Texan 5 Bn 2 Arty. The signals unit was, at last, moved out of the perimeter; there were now two artillery batteries inside; and the perimeter itself had expanded to 850 metres by 700 metres. Coral awaited a divisional attack.

At 0600 on 23 May Tony Hammett's D Company had set off on a move to the north, not without some excitement at

206

the start. John Salter's 10 Platoon was leading, and as Paul Richardson recalled, 'Once again, as you probably guessed, I was in the lead. It was still dark at that stage, we were going out through 12 Platoon's left-hand section, and the buggers hadn't neutralised their trip flares.

'Of course, Squizzy and I tripped every bloody flare they had, which was a pain in the arse. All you could hear was abuse from 12 Platoon and me swearing.'

Some of the non-infantry had time to notice the patrols leaving and returning, the artillery fire called in support during the clashes out there in the featureless scrub and rubber trees, and have some understanding of what it meant to be in a rifle company.

Stan Carbines, battery surveyor in 102 Battery, 'felt for those guys, for they knew that the enemy were beyond the trees and they had to walk towards them. When they contacted the enemy, usually an Aussie was killed, and the artillery fired in support.'

As the platoons stalked north, they found more weapon pits dug, the trench-ditch they had seen on the night of the first ambushes north of Coral, 'with all these holes dug in the side of it and millions of footprints, old bunker systems, new bunker systems that had obviously been used, and you got the feeling the area was bloody well fortified.'

Richardson was leading 10 Platoon, which was leading the company. After some hours, he had words with Salter about always being 'up front', as 'poor old Squizzy was getting a bit tired, and the section was a bit pissed off, and I've often asked that question: why I was always used up front, but nobody could give me a bloody answer.'

It was a case of using the willing horse. When Hammett wanted to cover ground, he used Salter's platoon; when Salter wanted to cover ground, he used Richardson's section.

As they were preparing their evening meal, word was flashed to them from Coral to return as soon as possible. 1ATF had been informed that strong enemy units were in that area, and if the company remained they would be obliterated before morning.

D Company did not know this, and assumed they were

being stuffed around in true Army fashion as they hurried back to the Fire Support Base. Arriving just on dark, they settled back into their old positions.

Earlier in the day, the Centurions had arrived, after their march north, and were dispersed around the base. Plans were being made for Australian armour to burst out of the Cinderella role which had been theirs since the end of World War II. They were about to move to centre stage with the other major performers.

7 Old Faithful

Most opponents are at their best if they are
allowed to dictate the battle; they are not
so good when they are thrown off balance by
manoeuvre and forced to react to your own
movement and thrusts.

Montgomery of Alamein

HAVING BRIGADIER HUGHES' approval to go on with the intended move into AO Manly, on 13 May Lieutenant Colonel Jim Shelton had returned to his battalion headquarters in the rubber plantation, north-west of Coral, and began 3RAR's successful ambushing operations.

Major Ian Hands' C Company established the base, into which the 105mm howitzers of 161 Battery were lifted, and was joined by Shelton's HQ.

Hori Howard's A Company was able to select a good ambush position, and settled down to a series of ambushes. After each, they carefully cleaned the location and waited for the next group of enemy to walk into the killing ground. Wisely, they had located their resupply landing site some distance away, and one night were pleased to hear enemy rockets blasting the vacant area.

Bert Irwin's B Company also had contact on the first night. A and B Companies were being met by the leading parties of 165 NVA Regiment, which was withdrawing into War Zone D after attacks on Tan Son Nhut air base near Saigon.

D Company, under Peter Phillips, was settling into its night position when a group of enemy were seen, coming towards Lieutenant Mark John and Sergeant Peter Lewis, who were emplacing Claymore mines outside the perimeter. Lewis tried to get behind the Claymores, but was hit by enemy fire.

Corporal Dave Mancer, commander of 4 Section, was looking across the clearing, saw Lewis down and wounded, and Mark John on the ground, apparently dead. He wondered what to do, as the enemy were on the other side of John, when he heard him shout, 'Shoot over the top of me, you mad bastards!' The enemy withdrew into the dusk, rapidly moving out of range.

A helicopter was called to evacuate Lewis, but he died of wounds en route to hospital. The skill of the pilot, coming in under the prevailing conditions, and his courage, not knowing where the enemy were, greatly impressed the soldiers, on this as on many other occasions in the war.

Lewis was Mark John's platoon sergeant, and his loss was felt by many. Jim Shelton described him as an 'extremely good sergeant', and added that 'the RAAF helicopter which came in broke all the rules, and this was appreciated by D Company. The pilot had to be talked in.'

Dave Mancer took over as platoon sergeant, but continued to lead his section.

On the 14th and 15th, A, B and C Companies all contacted groups of small numbers of enemy, found camps and bivouac areas, and proved that the Suoi Ba Pho was an infiltration route and staging area. Jim Shelton reorganised the company dispositions to concentrate on this part of AO Manly, and more contacts occurred over the next three days.

On the 17th, at 1700, B Company saw a group of thirty-four NVA moving north, with camouflage against air observation. At a range of 500 metres, they were engaged, artillery was called in, helicopter gunships arrived, and even the CO's Sioux took a part in it.

Peter Spoor was the pilot. On the first pass over the target, high up, he could not see anything, but as they swept back at lower altitude, saw them. 'They were still camouflaged,' recalls Spoor, 'crossing a paddy, but had spaced themselves too evenly. There were seven evenly spaced bushes in an open area. Every battery and mortar in the area wanted to fire on them. I called for three rounds, and then two enemy got up and ran through it all. I couldn't believe it, but it was not the first or last time I saw that. It is amazing how much artillery fire a man can run through and survive.'

Jim Shelton had fired a few bursts with his M16, but decided a more appropriate weapon would be an M60, so the

Sioux returned to the battalion HQ and Private Muggeridge, machinegunner in 6 Section, 8 Platoon, with his M60, flew back to fire at the harried party of enemy. Muggeridge enjoyed himself, and when it was all over, eleven enemy dead were found before dark; there may well have been others. Spooky and artillery gnawed at the survivors during the night.

At 1800 A Company first fired on two enemy sentries, wounding one, then while sweeping through the area met and engaged six, killing one and capturing two. Later, at 2140, they fired on four more.

On the 18th a clearing patrol from B Company killed one NVA at 0630, and later in the day another five bodies were found by the companies at the sites of previous actions.

On the 19th A and D Companies sighted enemy in the distance and called in artillery on them, with no known result.

By now the enemy realised there was a dangerous group active along the banks of the Suoi Ba Pho, and activity ceased, as they probably diverted around the danger zone.

Lieutenant Colonel Jim Shelton, CO 3RAR, made a practice of visiting his rifle companies each day, in the small Sioux helicopter assigned to him. The Sioux would leave him at the location, and fly away, to return and collect him. One of Bert Irwin's soldiers was pondering this procedure, and asked, puzzled, where the CO went at night.

Irwin immediately said that the CO, of course, went back to watch television every night. Every time thereafter that Jim Shelton arrived, Irwin would loudly ask if there was anything good on TV last night, and Shelton, in all innocence believing Irwin was having a friendly dig, would reply he watched some wonderful shows, 'you should have been there to see them'.

It was some days later that the CSM enlightened Shelton that some soldiers thought he spent carefree nights watching TV, not commanding a battalion in the field.

On the 21st one of Bruce Richards' APCs was hit by a command-detonated mine while crossing the Ba Pho, with one man, the Light Aid Detachment armourer, wounded and flown out. The damaged M113 was towed to Coral and later a replacement arrived.

In the evening one of the APCs further added to their bad luck when it caught fire and exploded. Ammunition, grenades, flares, et cetera inside the vehicle began to detonate, giving what was described by Peter Phillips as 'a firework display seen and heard for miles'. People from other vehicles ran across with fire extinguishers, but nothing could be done. One soldier, with a long stick, was trying to push cans of ammunition off the top deck, and had to be called away as the danger grew. Jock Douglas, the M113 commander, was wounded by flying fragments and was evacuated.

Ossie Kleinig, the 3RAR Signals Officer, had been nearby, cooking a mugful of chicken soup, and when the explosions began, dived into his pit without spilling a drop; he thought he must be getting good at taking cover.

The rear ramp of the M113 was raised, and the back door shut. The explosions blew the door off, and the flying chunk narrowly missed decapitating the RSM, Vince Murdoch, who was running over to help.

There was never any investigation into the cause of the accident, because, as David Brooks put it, 'it was just one of those things that happened'. Personally, knowing the history of the M113, he believes its destruction was caused by age-ing ammunition stored inside it. Perhaps the pin on a flare worked loose from the constant jolting and vibration, and it ignited inside the storage bin. When Douglas took over the vehicle, it had been carrying the ammunition and pyrotech-nics in it for about a year, and he had warned Douglas to get rid of it, but with the continuing pressure of operations this had not been able to be done.

A variety of reasons for the loss were given by various people, including an accidental discharge of an infantryman's weapon, a mishap while cooking on a primus, and similar.

Earlier, RSM Murdoch had provided some amusement for the on-lookers when the mortars had a defective round which merely fizzled up into the sky, and began to fall back. The RSM was near the Anti-armour Platoon, and one of the tracker dogs reacted to some piece of canine reasoning, firmly fixing its jaws around the top of Murdoch's boot, preventing him from getting into a pit as the dangerous mortar bomb began its descent. So there were all the personnel, in pits or prone, treated to the sight of the RSM trying to take cover with a dog hanging on to his leg, as Dave Candow puts it, 'not a dignified position for the RSM'.

Three days later, on the 24th, one NVA surrendered at Coogee, waving a Chieu Hoi leaflet.

In the meantime, it had been decided to move the battalion out of AO Manly, to the north-east, and it was here that 3RAR was to meet an aggressive enemy. Colonel Dunstan had visited the Coogee position and, over a mug of tea, both Jim Shelton and David Candow had put in a strong request for tanks. Dunstan agreed.

Colonel Dunstan decided to move 3RAR from its base at Coogee, to a position north of Coral. The battalion was to occupy the position alone, with 161 Battery going to Coral, from where it would still be able to support the battalion. The new position was originally named LZ Sugar, and it was intended to occupy it with a heli-borne 'hot' insertion. A 'hot' insertion was one before and during which air and artillery pounded the surroundings of the LZ to discomfit any enemy there. A 'cold' insertion was one with no preparatory fire.

When Dunstan gave these orders to Lieutenant Colonel Shelton, he saw Shelton was 'very upset about that, he didn't want to go'. A photograph was taken while Dunstan was giving these orders to Shelton, and Dunstan believes that the look on Shelton's face shows how displeased he was. He also wanted 'his' battery of guns, which were to go to Coral, and Jack Kelly pointed out that what Shelton would need would be 'rounds on the ground, not guns on the ground'.

But Lieutenant Colonel Shelton was, first, not happy about leaving the good hunting around Coogee, and second, not keen to take part in an arrival broadcast to the world by artillery, bombs, rockets, jets, gunships and the parade of troop-carrying helicopters necessary for such an event.

'I wasn't enthusiastic,' he said, 'because I thought we were

213

doing pretty well down there [in Coogee], and I thought we were going to do better. Then we were told we were going to move again. We'd been told we were going to do a hot insertion, but it was close enough to do a ground approach, so I suggested we go in on the ground and build up later when we got the LZ secure. We were not taking the guns, so it was really only a battalion advance into a defensive area.

'Colonel Dunstan agreed it was feasible. There was good reason for doing it. I wanted time to get into the area and get sorted out before the enemy were alerted. Having seen them hit the first night at Coral, it was obvious they could react quickly. The first day at Coral showed that they could react quickly, especially if alerted with all the helicopters coming in landing troops.'

The company commanders agreed, preferring a more sedate arrival among the people they were going to hunt. Hori Howard had 'seen the full treatment, with smoke and gunships, and a helicopter lift, and preferred the quieter Australian insertion.'

Peter Phillips' D Company was to lead the move into the new location on 24 May, hopefully by a quiet, undetected approach to secure the position, after which the rest of the battalion would arrive by APC and helicopter. Then the battalion would begin operating from a base within the enemy area. However, the move did not go to plan.

'It was intended to be a silent approach,' he said, 'and we left at three or four in the morning. It didn't become a silent approach, because before dawn we had run into a lot of carriers, who used to take stuff from the villages out to the VC and NVA. It was quite an intriguing sort of morning, but we didn't achieve surprise getting into Balmoral.'

In the dark, the company was moving in single file, at a good pace of 500 metres per hour. The rear platoon heard noise, fired on it, and later found one dead VC and a sack of rice. Then the leading platoon engaged more VC, who escaped but left a large quantity of fresh meat behind. The leaders then had a series of four contacts with VC in bunkers who fled, and escaped no matter how fast the platoon tried to run them down when engaged. Some small caches and bunkers were found.

214

'The contacts we had delayed us,' said Peter Phillips, 'so we had the same problems getting into Balmoral as we had at Coral, and didn't get in until late in the afternoon, rather than, as we hoped, to get in at eight or nine in the morning, under concealment of the scrub, with a nice defensive position established before last light. It was anything but.'

The numerous contacts, some at quite close range, made it obvious that the enemy regarded the area as his own, and that hunting and ambushing could be done successfully. The fortunes of war sometimes fall on the unlikeliest people, and one of Mark John's sentries 'fired from a range of two feet, max, and missed! I don't know who was more surprised, the sentry or the bloke, but it caused some consternation, because at first it was thought the OC's [Peter Phillips] recce party had been fired on.'

In Peter Phillips' opinion, the Balmoral position 'was a pretty good one. It was all low scrub, plenty of concealment, and we opted to put the battalion down where we had a large open space in front of us. There weren't many of these; they were actually dry swampland. In the wet season they would have been wet slush, but we were there in the dry, and it was built like a golf-course.

'Beautiful green rolling dales, and it looked like sand bunkers everywhere, because a B52 had been through about a year before and we had all these huge big bunkers [bomb craters]. We didn't have time to play golf.'

Lieutenant Colonel Shelton and his HQ made the move in Bruce Richards' APCs. Shelton was pleased despite the delaying contacts, as his troops were gaining knowledge of the ground and the area. He kept the battalion back from the open area so that the enemy would have to 'come and find us in the scrub. We dug in and waited'.

Second Lieutenant Bill Studley, 2ic of the Mortar Platoon, had taken two mortar sections in the APCs. He was not perturbed by the move, because from a subaltern's viewpoint 'at this stage, one AO seemed like the next'. He watched as Sergeant Dave Brooks, from the APC Troop, dismounted, went into a patch of shrubbery, and came out again wheeling a well-maintained motor-scooter.

The Lambretta motorscooter was far from the normal area

of civilian travel, so was regarded as enemy. The APCs took it along and had it flown back to Nui Dat by RAAF helicopter, where it was used in the unit. Picture the surprise and disgust of the Viet Cong rider when he returned from his errand or place of hiding to find the scooter gone, and his problem explaining to the relevant Party Committee.

As well as the frequent contact, the well-used trails they encountered warned the Diggers of the large numbers of enemy around them. Travelling with Lieutenant Colonel Shelton's HQ in the APCs, Ossie Kleinig, commanding the Signals Platoon, had looked along a sandy track they were crossing, and 'all we could see were prints of Ho Chi Minh sandals, and we knew there had been a hell of a lot of troop movement'.

LZ Sugar was secured and helicopters flew in the remainder of the battalion. As they approached, the lead pilot called for coloured smoke to be thrown to identify the correct location. He then called to say that he had two clouds of smoke in view; 3RAR 'popped' another to confirm their position, and the air-landing proceeded. It was one sign that the enemy was alert, and listening to the radio.

While the battalion was settling in, Jim Shelton had been visiting the rifle companies. The HQ staff were worried when his radio operator called to say he was 'in strife; I've lost Sunray'. Shelton had kept on walking when the radio operator had become entangled in the scrub, and by the time he had freed himself, the CO was gone. In addition, the soldier was disoriented, and was finally talked back by radio directions. Jim Shelton, of course, made his own way back.

Artillery registering was kept to a minimum, and everything done to deny the enemy easy acquisition of information.

3RAR was now established on an old track complex which the enemy had ceased using for the time, as it was too exposed to the air. Some 1500 metres to the east was the forward command post of 141 NVA Regiment. This command post, in a bunker system, controlled movement and staging through the area. The regiment itself was some 5000 to 10 000 metres further north and east, involved in training the members of seven infiltration groups which had just arrived.

The helicopters flying in to Balmoral had alerted the NVA in the command post, who vacated it and sent reconnaissance groups to the area of the landing.

After the events at Coral, and the numerous signs of enemy along the approach to Balmoral, 3RAR needed no further incentive to dig.

Bill Studley was amazed to see the large open expanse, and as the platoon dug in behind Peter Phillips' D Company, thought that 'no one in their right mind would assault across that killing ground'. The mortars were so close to D Company that they could see the forward pits of the company and the open expanse beyond. The platoon was split into two, so that firing could be maintained from separate locations if one came under fire.

In an effort to confuse the enemy, Jim Shelton had two sections of mortars mounted in APCs, and sent out on fast runs around the area, firing from various locations en route; if enemy were met, they were to go straight back to Balmoral without getting into a fight. These sorties were called 'Shelton's Mortar Marauders'.

Bill Studley took out the first, which was brought to an abrupt, unplanned halt when the APCs 'ran under some trees filled with red ants, which were dislodged by the antennas. They caused havoc in the first three APCs; everyone leaped out and stripped.' He moved the other two M113s up on either flank to give some security, before joining the others in clearing the ants from personnel and vehicles. Studley was not too concerned about enemy reaction, as he thought they would have died laughing at the spectacle.

3RAR continued preparing its position, and on the afternoon of the next day, 25 May, were pleased to see the tanks of Lieutenant Mick Butler's 2 Troop C Squadron 1 Armoured Regiment rolling up from the south, with Bob Hennessy's B Company walking alongside. En route they had fought a small battle with NVA in a bunker system, disengaged and continued on to Balmoral.

Trevor Lowe, commanding Butler's 32C, had never seen infantry give such a happy welcome to armoured crews.

For Lieutenant Colonel Shelton, the tanks 'were a bonus.

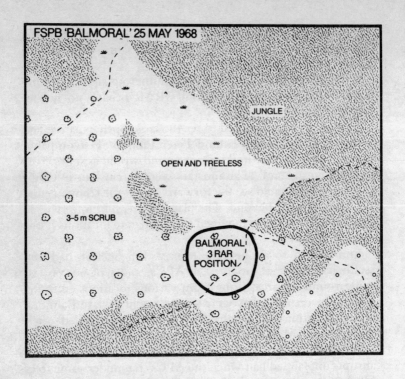

JUNGLE

OPEN AND TREELESS

3–5 m SCRUB

BALMORAL
3 RAR
POSITION

That was tremendous. It was nice to see Butler and the tanks'.

One of the advantages of the relative smallness of the Australian Army was that Shelton, Butler and Bruce Richards, who commanded the APCs at Balmoral, all knew each other from training exercises in Australia, service in armoured units, or recent operations in Vietnam. Mick Butler had already established a relationship with 3RAR during Operation Pinnaroo, when he assisted in the extraction of a rifle platoon in the Long Hai Hills.

Butler left the tanks at the southern perimeter of Balmoral, and walked around the battalion position. Bruce Richards told him that the APCs were interspersed with the infantry platoons, and suggested the best tank position was on the northern side, with fields of view and of fire across the big grassy area. Richards had already suggested this to Jim Shelton, who agreed.

Butler also concurred, but privately thought no one would be silly enough to attack across such a clearing, which looked to him 'like a billiard table'; they would be far better off closing in under cover of the vegetation on the other sides. However, night was falling, and the tanks had to be moved inside as soon as possible.

So Shelton and Butler decided to split the troop into two groups, with 32A (Allen) and 32B (Britten) on the north-west, between D and A Companies, while 32 (Butler) and 32C (Lowe) occupied the north-east side, between D and B Companies. The RAEME ARV was positioned with Butler, and the Fitters' M113 went with Sergeant Allen.

Next day it was intended to cut out routes for the tanks from the present positions to each forward platoon, so support could be moved to them if needed. As darkness settled, the tank crews determined the actual location of the infantry on their flanks, radio nets were established, and they began their duty roster and a 50 per cent stand-to.

Jim Shelton intended to keep the tanks back out of sight during the day time, and move them forward at night. 'What I was looking for was complete surprise for the enemy. It was a trick the British used in Korea; they used to come back behind the ridge, then at night come up on to it. They were tremendous, because the enemy never knew they were there, and before first light they would roll back. They'll draw the crabs—if the enemy know they're there, they'll go for them with rockets or whatever they've got. So it is not just tactics on our part, it is survival.'

One of the drawbacks of being in the Assault Pioneer Platoon of an infantry battalion is that the platoon is required to do several times as much digging as the other soldiers and, as well as their own pits, are tasked to assist in construction of the CP, aid post and other positions. By the end of this day, 19-year-old Wayne Meech was 'knackered, and I had night-mares of bloody shovels for weeks'.

He was sharing a pit with Bill Phillips, from Victoria, and like the rest of the younger members of the battalion, were not sure what was ahead of them. The intense actions at Coral were now over a week in the past, there had been no reaction against Coogee, but it was obvious the senior members of the battalion expected the enemy to move against this new position.

Having spent the last couple of days digging his own and other pits, providing them with overhead protection and sandbagging, Meech 'was not too keen on this night watch business', but settled into his sleeping bay until Phillips woke him for his turn.

8 A Good Little Action

And he is bred out of that bloody strain
That haunted us in our familiar paths.
Henry V *(II. iv.)*

AT 0730 ON 25 MAY Bob Hennessy's B Company 1RAR began escorting the tanks of Mick Butler's 2 Troop to the recently established FSPB Balmoral. En route, they encountered, at GR XT 931311, an enemy base camp, and the action went on for over an hour, until the Australians disengaged, pushed on to Balmoral, and B Coy returned by air to Coral.

For the first time in twenty years Australian tanks had been in action with Australian infantry, in the tropics, and showed what should be done in that type of terrain against a dug-in enemy armed with anti-tank rockets.

Peter Badman called it a 'a good little action. It all happened quickly, and immediately lifted morale of the tank crews'.

It was intended to fly Hennessy's men back to Coral, so its strength for this task was reduced to seventy, comprising two platoons and a small headquarters.

There had been no time to practise moving with tanks in the type of country which the small force would traverse, so after some discussion with his CSM, Laurie Annesley, Hennessy decided to have his platoons leading, with Annesley carrying a radio behind the company HQ, guiding the tanks.

Mick Butler's 2 Troop moved behind Hennessy's HQ, with two tanks forward and two to the rear, called a two-up formation. The Australian group was moving carefully, as all were fully aware of the large number of aggressive NVA in the area.

An Engineer mini-team accompanied them, for the purpose of checking the road they would have to cross, to locate any mines which may have been placed. This all took time, and Hennessy's men noticed the large amount of battlefield debris which now littered the area, as well as the burnt-out wrecks of the destroyed convoy. Finally, the tanks were brought across and the actual move to Balmoral began.

Garry Prendergast's 6 Platoon began to notice that the tracks they came across were quite wide, enough for two people, and so used that the surface was literally powdered. This reinforced the knowledge that the enemy were numerous.

Footslogging infantry easily believe that anyone who rides has a good life. However, the tanks found the going difficult, because of the short range of visibility, the bamboo, which was thick enough to have a tank stuck on a clump of it, and, as Trevor Lowe describes them, 'the dreaded red ants. These would get inside, down your tank suit, and they were very, very unbearable. You'd break out in lumps; they were very annoying and painful.'

At 1058 the forward scout of 6 Platoon saw two enemy in an open space. They were dressed in green clothes and hats, with camouflage on their hats and rifles. He fired at them, and they fled north, but were suspected of having gone to a flank. Hennessy put 6 Platoon on the left flank of the axis of advance, with 5 Platoon on the right and rear, and the tanks in the centre.

At midday, 2500 metres north of Coral, the infantry were passing through some light scrub, and 6 Platoon engaged one enemy trying to get closer to the column, went after him, and received machinegun fire from bunkers in the jungle. At once Hennessy wheeled to attack, and the leading two tanks swung after him, while the others began to put down covering fire.

As they began to move forward into the trees, Tim Foster saw 'the first weapon pit, and called out (to report it), then two arms holding an AK47 appeared over the top, and sprayed the area with fire. I ducked behind a tree and returned fire before the enemy pulled the AK inside. I was so close I could hear him breathing and changing magazines.'

Foster was in a slight hollow, and as the firing increased all around found that he could not move in any direction without being hit. Eventually, in the confusion, he began wriggling backwards, but his webbing belt began catching on grass and other obstructions, and 'ended up around my neck.'

Foster found himself next to Allen Green, and then tried to lob a grenade into the pit, but they were called back to the edge of the trees. All the while, a large volume of fire from the enemy had been cracking and snapping past and overhead. The sole casualty was a wound in the foot, suffered by Mick Sargeant.

The tanks began using a new technique for placing fire in support of infantry in jungle, using the hand wheel and turret traverse indicator in the turret to correct line and distance of the fall of shot. The technique was necessary, as the tank commander's eyes were some four metres above ground level, and he was thus looking down on the vegetation, not through it as an infantryman can do.

The tanks on the flanks, supporting the attacking infantry, did not see them throughout the assault. Their fire was controlled and corrected by radio, keeping the machinegun fire just in front of the leading Diggers.

The leading tanks fired canister from their twenty-pounder cannon, the thousands of small shot clearing away the shrubbery to reveal bunkers and trenches.

As Hennessy's men fought their way into the bunker system, it became obvious to him that what was first thought to be a platoon position was in fact a part of a much larger complex. He therefore changed his direction, and fought clear of the position at an angle.

'It was quite obvious to me that it was a big position; there were machineguns in depth firing at us. Pepe Prendergast also said it was a big position. I did not intend to get involved there, but had to get on to Balmoral.'

However, his artillery officer, Captain Don Tait, did not agree that the enemy were there in larger groups than a platoon, and the differing estimates of enemy strength, when reported back at Coral, led to Tony Hammett's D Company having an exciting day on the morrow.

The NVA withdrew ahead of the attacking force, though

resisted as they did so. Hennessy moved back to the clear area, and requested a Dustoff for one wounded Digger. He was surprised when Battalion Headquarters told him to take the Dustoff in place; he had wanted to move away from the immediate area of action.

In order to give the helicopter as much support as possible, Hennessy placed the tanks to open fire on the jungle when the pilot touched down. It was an RAAF machine, and the pilot later told Hennessy that it was the best organised Dustoff he had experienced. As ,it arrived, three tanks fired, what Hennessy called 'giving the helicopter a royal salute'.

In that second, the first enemy soldier killed by Australian tanks since 1945 was unfortunate enough to show himself some forty metres in front of Sergeant Len Allen's cannon, and died instantly in a blast of canister. The effect on his body of the shot was such that a shovel had to be used to turn him over when the crew searched him later. Two other enemy were found dead.

The infantry began to realise that the 'turret-heads' and 'gasoline cowboys' were of some use, and the tank crews themselves felt a surge of confidence. One of the other unkind labels, 'koala bears' (not to be sent overseas or shot at) began to fade forever.

In the enemy position, it would be reasonable to assume that the NVA were also congratulating themselves, as from their point of view they had engaged an enemy force of infantry and tanks, and chased them away.

Hennessy then directed an airstrike on the position as the small force continued on its initial mission, moving to FSPB Balmoral. Lieutenant Bluey Forde's compass had been affected by the metal mass of the tanks, and instead of moving away from the bunker system, they were paralleling it. This resulted in some large pieces of bomb shrapnel whizzing over, as the airstrike fell closer than originally intended.

The platoons began to find lengths of newly laid communications cable leading towards Balmoral, and short patrols could not locate the end of it, so it was ordered cut, and they moved on. More was found, all running towards Balmoral. It was obvious the enemy were intending something serious, and soon.

As the force drew close to the new position at Balmoral, Corporal Trevor Lowe, commanding tank 32C, heard 'chanting and cheering. It was the battalion, lined up along the fence, clapping and yahooing, because they were very pleased to see us. Some of them came up and shook our hands, and said they were pleased to see us.' In an infantry-dominated Army, such expressions of welcome made a lasting impression on the tank crews.

By the time all had arrived at Balmoral, it was again late in the day, and Hennessy's men were to be flown back to Coral. Garry Prendergast saw a fellow graduate from Portsea OCS, Rod O'Leary, commanding a 3RAR platoon, and commented to him that 'better you than us here'.

This was Howard's A Company, and Bob Hennessy told him, and Lieutenant Colonel Shelton, of the numerous signs of impending attack, predicting that it would come from the south-east.

The 1RAR soldiers, safe in the knowledge that they were soon to fly back to familiar Coral, began needling the 3RAR men who would remain in the patch of jungle, reminding them of the many signs of heavy enemy presence, the scrawny wire defences at Balmoral, telling them to dig deeper, and generally enjoying themselves as they were soon to depart this place which was quite probably going to be attacked.

But it grew closer to darkness and no helicopters came. The 3RAR soldiers began to return the remarks of the previous hour. 'Here's a shovel. You guys better start digging.'

To the great relief of B Company 1RAR, the helicopters arrived and they climbed in for a dusk flight back to safe, familiar Fire Support Base Coral.

Bob Hennessy reported the actions to Lieutenant Colonel Bennett, who seemed to reject the estimate of the enemy bunker position being of at least company strength, and accept the estimate of platoon-size made by Captain Don Tait, the artillery officer.

The Australian newspapers reported the death of Major Constable in the air crash, and the exploit of three AATTV members, Captain John White and Warrant Officers Frank

Lucas and Don Cameron, in extricating a 'battered mobile strike force' from their camp near the Laotian border, after suffering heavy casualties in a North Vietnamese attack. Ninety-eight of the 178 men in White's force were killed or wounded.

Haggling at the Paris Peace Talks continued, and it was announced in Saigon that the US forces had suffered their worst casualty toll of the war in the past two weeks, with 1111 killed, bringing the total dead to 23 500.

VC/NVA losses for the week 12–18 May were reported as 4765.

Australia announced a further $200 000 in emergency aid to assist refugees in South Vietnam. Most of these had been made homeless in the intense fighting around the major cities since the Tet Offensive in February and the later smaller offensives.

At 2330 on 25 May John Bullen began a shift in the Nui Dat HQ and the first hours passed serenely, apart from six engineers reported absent without leave in Vung Tau. Then, listening to the radio frequencies used by the forces at Coral and Balmoral, Bullen heard the conversations of the units under attack.

At thirty minutes into the new day a heavy twenty-minute attack by fire was directed at the artillery positions in Coral, and then Balmoral reported the signals denoting a ground attack on their base. By now the Aussies could read the signals as well as the Vietnamese.

The NVA, of course, were quite well aware of the fire support available from Coral, so adopted the obvious tactic of attacking both at once, concentrating on the artillery at Coral while they mounted a ground attack on Balmoral.

The artillery radars had been affected by the concussions and vibrations at Coral, and a technical sergeant was sent up from Nui Dat to repair them, being rostered for duty in the artillery CP during his stay. He had never been under fire before. Thinking that the NVA might be using the interior illumination as a target reference, and acting decisively and swiftly, the sergeant shot out the CP light, to the consternation and amazement of all around him. His action was not well received, and it was explained to him in short sentences why the counter-bombardment processes required light.

Because of the pressure of immediate events, no report to Nui Dat was made for an hour. Bullen decided not to wake the GSO3 (Operations), Captain Peter Desmond, as there was nothing anyone at Nui Dat could do for the people in combat, not even having, as he noted, a Red Phone for Dial-a-Prayer.

However, as the GSO2 (Operations), Major MacLean, was awake under the bombardment, he was, in Bullen's words, 'viewing the world somewhat sourly', and chastised him for not calling Desmond to the CP. Bullen thought he was damned if he did and damned if he did not; waking Desmond could have been seen as an act of panic, while not waking him was seen as not recognising a serious situation in the field units.

Also in his journal, Bullen noted that 'to the complete disgust of all', the film screened for the troops remaining at Nui Dat was *Tammy*. He commented that if revolution was wanted, then *Pollyanna* should be screened, and wondered at the inept selection of films for showing to soldiers.

Meanwhile, more serious matters were concerning those in the fire support bases. The mortars had also exploded among the TF HQ tents, killing Private Thomas, a member of 3RAR forward echelon at Coral. It was only when he did not relieve his predecessor on the machinegun that a search was made for him, and he was soon found, killed by a fragment of shrapnel. He had been carrying his flak-jacket, not wearing it.

Father John Tinkler was in a dugout with Captain Barry French, 2ic Administration Company, and when told of Thomas' death, went to the soldier, despite French's objections, and 'walked over, though terribly scared' of the bombardment, and anointed Thomas, not knowing the soldier's religious denomination. Later, he wrote to Thomas' family, explaining what he had done at the time of their son's death.

Father Tinkler anointed anyone, without question about religion, including VC and NVA.

Over in the Engineer position, George Hulse had found

himself edging back, deeper and deeper into his pit, until he was huddled at the very back, telling himself that he could see better from there. He became aware of a smell, and then found it was his own sweat, permeated with the very odour of fear, and he could 'feel fear welling. It seemed to be inside me but didn't belong to me. This thing was getting hold of me, a very powerful urge to blow my cool or get up and run for my life. I knew it had to be suppressed. The other half of me was giving inspiration: I was an OCS graduate: I was 1 Troop leader and they needed me; I was responsible to other people for the defence of this area; and finally, that I was an Australian, an Australian lieutenant, and we were not going to buckle under any circumstances. And as silly as it seems now, all this was helping, all these lofty things, and I drew fantastic inspiration from that.

'I then went forward, got my head up, tried to see if I could spot anybody coming in after the barrage, got my corporals on the phone—all of them were in the bottom of their pits— and got them to look as well. After the bombardment, I got out and checked the Diggers.'

Some rounds were still coming in, and as he was walking around, an RPG came whistling in, exploded a few metres away, and the blast knocked him flat. It was so close that he was stunned but alert enough to realise that he should have been hit, so he began feeling and clutching himself all over, looking for wounds. Two sappers ran over and told him to move his arms and legs, which were unharmed. Then one asked what Hulse was doing, still grabbing at his body, and when told it was checking for bleeding, replied, 'Ah, blokes like you don't bleed!'

Still slightly stunned, but thinking this must be a compliment, Hulse asked what he meant. The sapper patted him on the shoulder, and said, 'Don't they tell you blokes anything? Officers don't bleed, they're full of shit.'

That evaporated any tension, and the three of them lay there, under more rockets, roaring with laughter.

In the A Company 1RAR position, Major Col Adamson 'distinctly saw an RCL firing on the old company headquarters position. Ernie Jacobs and I could see the blast-flash quite clearly, and brought guns and mortars in on that, stopped them in about two minutes. A search next morning found no bodies, or weapons, but lots of shell cases.'

In fact, 2 Platoon found thirty-three nosecaps for 60mm mortarbombs, and cases for fifteen 75mm RCL rounds.

Meanwhile, Balmoral was under attack.

9 In the Killing Ground

*In cases of defence 'tis best to weigh the
enemy more weighty than he seems.*

Henry V *(II. iv.)*

EVEN BEFORE ARRIVAL at Balmoral, Lieutenant Colonel Shelton had 'looked on this as a straight defensive position; let the enemy attack and we'll deal with him'.

It soon became obvious that the enemy were up to something in the area, possibly intending to attack. The same signals seen by the defenders of Coral were noticed and reported. From soon after 2000, the APCs and rifle companies noticed tracer rounds and shots, and then at 0330 mortar primaries were heard, and bugles sounded.

Second Lieutenant Bill Studley, 2ic of the Mortar Platoon, was on duty in the mortar CP, heard the primaries, and thought it took forever for the bombs to arrive.

Wayne Meech, in the Assault Pioneer Platoon, had just been woken by Bill Phillips, and 'scrambled out of my sleeping bay and fighting pit for a leak, and spotted this green flare. Then rifle fire, rockets and mortars hit us.'

He dived back into the pit, under the overhead protection, wishing it were ten times thicker, hoping the enemy mortar crews were poorly trained and inaccurate, but 'that idea was put to rest, as a mortar exploded so close that dirt spattered down into the pit, on to my boots, and Phillips called out to ask if I was OK. The mortaring seemed to last for hours.' When it ended they manned the parapet of their pit, rifles ready. No one had been hurt, but the foliage in the area had been 'quite broken up'.

In the 8 Platoon, C Company area, Peter Geil had recently come off picket, and gone to sleep in his hammock, but heard the mortars and dived into his pit. Previous bombardments

230

had been by what he termed 'friendly VC in Phuoc Tuy', who had trouble getting a round on target, but this night he was impressed by the accuracy. One bomb hit the webbing of a soldier who was in a pit. The smoke grenade attached to the harness ignited and began hissing out its cloud. Still deep in the pit, the Digger reached up and began groping about, checking on the ammunition and handgrenades on his belt. It was all right, but next day he drew comment on his brilliant purple forearm, which took a long time to fade.

There was some movement in the jungle in front of C Company, but nothing to really worry them for the rest of the night.

In their APC in the A Company position, Geoff Murray, driver, and David Brooks, vehicle commander, were asleep, but the noise woke them. Murray asked, reflexively, what the noise was, to which Brooks gave a one-word answer: 'Mortars!' Murray reached out to shut the door, and saw the bright flashes outside as the bombs exploded, then heard an infantry soldier call, 'Here they come!'

NVA were able to get up to the wire, and blew a hole in it with a homemade Bangalore, but no effort was made to exploit this gap.

Looking to the front, Geoff Murray was surprised to see a group of NVA run in the gap in the wire through which the armoured vehicles passed, then turn and run out through the narrow gap used by the infantry patrols. 'There were only six or seven. I'll never forget it. One was a fat so-and-so, who kept kicking them, urging them to go in.'

Brooks and Murray had adopted a personal method for keeping their .50cal machinegun supplied with ammunition: rather than rely on boxes of linked belt rounds attached to the side of the gun mounting, Murray would sit below Brooks and link one belt after another to the one in the gun, so that it was fed continuously from inside the vehicle.

Howard's men fired Claymores, and the battle began. After a weak effort on Howard's front, the real attack developed to the north, across the open grassy area. This was probably the NVA commander applying the enemy tactic of 'make a noise in the east and attack in the west'.

D Company, commanded by Peter Phillips, reported receiving fire from the north and north-east, and the APCs radioed that the enemy were firing machineguns from bomb craters on the north-east.

Jim Shelton thought the NVA might have had a better chance if they had pressed their attack through the close country around Hori Howard, but also felt that 'it's nice to know you've got your defensive position laid out and the enemy attack you where you want to be attacked.'

As it was, the rockets and mortars preceding the attack woke everyone completely, and the Diggers were ready all around the perimeter.

The 3RAR mortars were firing back, and the concentration required of the crews tended to take their minds off the action around them, though they were aware of the noise, lights, tanks firing, D Company in action close by . . .

In the battalion HQ area, Ossie Kleinig, the Signals Officer, noticed an RPG going overhead, and thought it would hit or damage the 292-antenna and destroy communications. He left his batman, Snow Hill, in the pit and ran to the HQ. He arrived by falling down the stairs into the small crowded room, which was a 'hive of activity'. He noticed the smoothly working members of the staff there, and in particular what he termed 'the amazing co-ordination between the mortars and artillery'. This, with each complementing the other, he ascribed primarily to the personality of Bluey Doyle, the mortar commander.

He heard Doyle and Mark John, commanding 10 Platoon on the perimeter, discussing bringing fire on to enemy in a B52 crater close to the wire. 'There was a bit of money put on whether it could be done, and Doyle got his crews to put a bomb in the crater.'

David Candow was busy co-ordinating the support from outside, and in direct communications with the aircraft commander, requesting fire be placed on the enemy side of the grassy clearing, and the placing of flares to illuminate them for the battalion defenders.

Peter Phillips, commanding D/3RAR on the edge of the clearing, was aware of the mortar rounds suddenly ex-

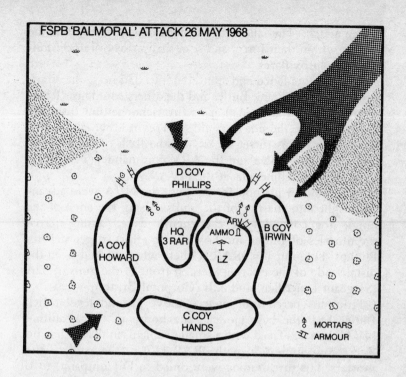

FSPB 'BALMORAL' ATTACK 26 MAY 1968

D COY
PHILLIPS

A COY
HOWARD

HQ
3 RAR

ARV
AMMO
LZ

B COY
IRWIN

C COY
HANDS

↑ MORTARS
⚒ ARMOUR

ploding, and was impressed by the ability of the NVA to 'put their first rounds right on us'.

When the attack began, Mick Butler and his gunner, Bob Gould, were asleep under the Centurion tank, while the driver, Blue Dyson, and the loader/radio operator, Jervis, were on duty inside it. Butler slept through the mortaring, and Gould woke him. As Butler was scrambling up the right side of the tank, he noticed the machinegun fire from both sides, saw some NVA approaching the barbed wire, and at that instant Jervis fired the twenty-pounder cannon.

The tank turret was quickly traversed right so the driver could climb down into his seat in the front of the hull, and a radio check made with the rest of the tanks and the neighbouring infantry companies.

But for some reason, after the initial mortar bombardment and sighting of enemy near the wire, there was a pause in the

NVA attack. This allowed the defenders to carry out the checks within their force, and scan their areas of responsibility, now lit by flares.

As the lights faded and sputtered into darkness, the attack began. Inside the tank Butler and the others could hear RPGs flying overhead and small arms fire richochetting from the armour. Off to the side he could see Trevor Lowe silhouetted on the top of his turret in 32C by the flash of the twenty-pounder. Both Lowe and the ARV commander were firing their .30cal machineguns at the NVA.

Assaulting in platoon formations, the NVA were advancing right into the fire of the tanks. Using the edge of the jungle for concealment, the enemy were passing across the muzzles of Butler and Lowe in an effort to get at Peter Phillips' D Company 3RAR. Others who attacked from the distant side of the clearing were in front of the guns of 32A (Sergeant Len Allen) and 32B (Corporal Britton).

From his perch four metres above ground level, Mick Butler had 'the best view in the house of the assaulting NVA', but was faced with a small problem, in that he had no direct communication with 3RAR HQ or the artillery and mortars. His three radios were tuned to D Company, to B Company and to his own C Squadron nets. His B Company communications were by an AN/PRC 25 set sitting on the turret behind his cupola lid, so he decided to flick off the B Company frequency on to the 3RAR battalion net, pass corrections for the artillery and mortars, then flick back to B or D Company. This he did for the remainder of the action.

As well as this activity, Butler was also controlling his Troop's fire, relaying messages between the tanks and their nearby infantry, and firing his personal commander's machine-gun, mounted on a pintle at his turret hatch. Inside the tank, the driver and loader were identifying targets and giving directions to the gunner.

Artillery from Coral and 3RAR's own mortars were firing in support of Balmoral, though Coral was itself under fire. Because of the need to fire high-explosive and illumination rounds, there were periods of darkness outside the bases, and the enemy used these to clear the battlefield.

To make best use of the tank armament, they were very close to the perimeter, between thirty and fifty metres, which was handgrenade range. So placed, they could fire across the front of the rifle companies, over the open expanse before D Company.

The tanks tried to make up for the lack of light by using their searchlights, but these drew immediate retaliation from NVA machineguns and RPGs, so the tanks alternated their use of the white light.

The artillery defensive fire was right on the wire fences, and the unfortunate attackers were caught by it. Fire from the infantry lashed them, and added to it was the helicopter gunship machinegun and rocket attacks.

0411 A Company to HQ: Callsign 12 [2 Platoon] left pit, 1,000 metres, [bearing of] 3200–3400 mils, heard voices screaming.
0412 A Company to HQ: Callsign 13 [3 Platoon], 200–300 metres, voices to south.
0412 D Company to HQ: VC on callsign 43 [12 Platoon] perimeter but not inside.

As the attack went on, Peter Phillips formed the opinion that Balmoral was being assaulted by 'a fairly foolish enemy, attacking with nothing else than the mortars and the RPGs, which they used to shoot up into the air so it would come down with the same effect as an artillery shell.

'They were foolish to press the attack as long as they did, because we had a couple of machineguns which had the whole open area covered and they took a lot of unnecessary casualties.'

In the battalion CP, due to the lack of space, Ossie Kleinig was told to leave, so went back to his Signals Platoon, pondering Jim Shelton's remark that despite the RPG explosion effect on the antenna, 'it's the best comms we've ever had!'

Ossie did not go straight back to his own pit through the bombardment, but waited for a while in Shelton's pit, then covered the rest of the distance to Tony Zammitt's position. There they saw, silhouetted against the battle lights, some shadowy figures approaching. Enemy or friendly?

Because of the lack of radio sets, Kleinig did not have one himself, and so none of them knew if enemy had broken into the position. Then, 'one shadowy silhouette stood to his full height, and we realised no Vietnamese could be that tall.' It was WO2 Lofty Eiby, CSM of Phillips' D Company, assisting the wounded back to the RAP.

One of the wounded was Lieutenant Rod O'Leary, hit in the arm. Kleinig went to help, and unknowingly did so with O'Leary's injured arm, which caused him to be what Ossie recalls as 'uncouth to me'. To placate O'Leary, he gave him a packet of Benson and Hedges cigarettes, which he noted had never been returned (up to mid-1986).

Later, Kleinig returned to his own pit. He could not see Snow Hill anywhere, and with sinking heart began to think Hill had been hit while he had been away. Sure enough, there in the darkness were boots sticking out of Hill's sleeping bay. Expecting to see a mangled body, he bent down and looked in, as Hill sat up and said, 'What's up? Is it breakfast time already?' He had slept the time away.

The problem of identification between friend and foe had also worried other people in the nearby pits. Wayne Meech, in the Assault Pioneers, had been listening to the battle, to the voices calling on the perimeter, was told the NVA had been repulsed, but wondered how he would have been able to know who were enemy, if they had managed to get inside.

Mick Butler had taken this aspect of the defence into account, and ordered his crews to close their hatches and 'hose down' their neighbouring tank with .30 calibre machine-gun fire to clear any enemy from it. On no account was .50 calibre fire to be used against another tank, as on an earlier operation the 100-gallon external tank on a tank had been hit by .50cal, with dramatic and fiery results.

Lieutenant Colonel Jack Kelly, commanding the artillery regiment at Coral, much preferred to keep the guns firing so that the enemy were unable to clear the battlefield effectively. As the artillery had to stop to allow aircraft in to make their passes, the NVA were given opportunities to remove casualties and equipment. Jim Shelton, CO 3RAR, agreed, as there was always a delay between the time the guns stopped and helicopters began firing, and in the dark it was often difficult to give the pilot adequate and accurate directions to make the delay as brief as possible. However, if gunships could be brought in, so could Dustoff, and this aspect was considered an advantage by the ground defenders.

And, as Jim Shelton said, jovially, 'It's good for morale to hear those gunships coming in. Like a regimental march on a parade ground, it does your heart good!'

Two helicopter fire teams and a Spooky were active around the battle area, mainly concentrating on the area to the north-east, where it was deduced the enemy mortars, anti-aircraft and FUP were located.

The casualties were to be evacuated by Dustoff, and all illumination was ceased to allow the helicopters to fly in and out without drawing enemy fire. Seven wounded were to be taken by the first sortie, five by the second. All the companies were warned of the arrival of the Dustoff, at 0525.

Perhaps taking advantage of the lull and the darkness, at about 0530, the NVA began to withdraw, and were able to carry off almost all the casualties. At 0630, when infantry patrols moved out and swept the surrounds, only six bodies were found, but many signs remained of dead and wounded being carried or dragged off. Blood pools and other signs showed that at least thirty wounded NVA had been carried off the battlefield.

While many of the Diggers realised that the attack had not been really pressed home, they also understood, like Dave Mancer's section, 'just how vulnerable we were', and digging went on more energetically.

As soon as possible after clearing the frontal area, the tanks rolled back from the more exposed night fighting positions into their day hides, some fifty metres inside the position. The tanks were checked and an ammunition resupply was made. Butler and Lowe fired about two-thirds of their rounds, while Allen and Britton expended about one-third. A Centurion in Butler's Troop carried sixty-two rounds of twenty-pounder, 4000 .50cal and 9000 .30cal.

As Butler pointed out, a tank Troop possessed a lot of combat power, for a jungle war in 1968. A Troop had the machinegun firepower of an infantry rifle company, and two-thirds the punch of a Field Battery of artillery, with more first-line ammunition than either.

The simple phrase 'ammunition resupply' does not convey the activity involved and the sheer physical labour necessary to rearm the tanks. Bernie Sullivan, Technical Officer of the tank squadron said: 'Ammunition handling was a problem, of course. The bloke who earned his weight in gold was Peter Simpson. His main task was handling ammunition. The tonnages of ammunition that he and his two offsiders moved in a very short period of time were quite incredible. Twenty-pounder ammo came in a steel container, and it weighed as much as the round itself, a total of about forty-eight kilos.'

There were no front-end loaders available, partly because of the tactical layout of the bases, which prevented heavy vehicles driving back and forth through infantry company lines and positions. Sullivan continues his description: 'Most of it had to be done by hand. When we could, we would move the tanks to the ammo point, but the round still had to be manually loaded from the container into the tank. The crews had to stow it in the bins, and on occasion those bins got way down.

'It wasn't just a case of opening the container and removing the round. It had dehumidifier bags to condition the air inside the container, and there was all sorts of packing that had to be picked up afterwards. The last thing we wanted was to leave a place floating in paper and wooden packing. They were a pain, but the beauty of the system was that when you actually got the ammunition, it was reliable; a thing you could be sure of.'

Others busy cleaning up were the mortar crews, who also had masses of cylinders which had contained bombs.

Lieutenant Colonel Shelton was under no illusions that the NVA had given their utmost. He thought they had not pressed the attack, and were preparing for a bigger assault as

238

soon as possible. What had occurred on that night was the result of the enemy surprise at the move into their area, the difficulty of gaining accurate information about the position, and the need to test the intruders, an exploratory punch to see what would be needed.

During 27 May a small bulldozer was flown into Balmoral and went to work making bunds 1.5 metres high for the tanks' fighting positions, as well as digging a trench for 600 rounds of tank ammunition storage near the helicopter landing pad. The bunds were to be invaluable when the NVA returned.

Sergeant David Brooks, of the APC Troop, taught himself how to use the bulldozer, and dug pits for all his section, then passed the machine on to the other sub-units. He positioned Corporal Rex Warren's M113 where it could best watch over the sector, as Warren had a turret with twin .30cal machine-guns fitted, and observation and fire could be done from in it, whereas the others had the more exposed position behind a .50cal with a plate shield to the front.

The Armoured Recovery Vehicle contributed little to the firepower of the position, so was stationed near the ammunition trench. If necessary, it and the M113 RAEME fitters' vehicles could be called on to perform casualty evacuation and ammunition resupply tasks.

It was obvious that the enemy in the area were not exhausted yet. Patrols and positions reported many sightings of enemy active in the area, fleeting glimpses of Vietnamese busy among the trees and foliage.

During the morning, sitting on the edge of the pit he shared with Lieutenant Colonel Shelton, David Candow wrote on the top of the sheet from the War Diary: 'Balmoral attack number one'. Shelton asked what he meant by 'attack number one', and Candow replied, 'We're going to get a second attack for sure.'

When the bombardment of Coral ended, Colonel Dunstan left the CP and walked back to his sleeping area. There, in the dawn light, he found his batman sitting beside the shrapnel-riddled hutchi. He looked up at Dunstan and said, 'You know, sir, I reckon I ought to go back to Nui Dat. I'm bored stiff out here.'

At 0600, from Coral, Tony Hammett's D Company 1RAR left the perimeter to engage the enemy met by Hennessy's force the previous day, while en route to Balmoral.

10 A Little Classic

> *I think it is the weakness of mine eyes*
> *That shapes this monstrous apparition*
> *It comes upon me. Art thou any thing?*
> *Art thou some god, some angel, or some devil,*
> *That makes my blood cold and my hair to stare?*
> Julius Caesar *(IV. iii.)*

FOLLOWING THE INCONCLUSIVE CLASH between Hennessy's company, the tanks and the enemy on the afternoon of 25 May, Tony Hammett was called to 1RAR HQ. There he was told by Lieutenant Colonel Bennett that Colonel Dunstan's neck was on the block, as he believed that neither General MacDonald nor Brigadier Hughes thought he should have called the tanks forward to Coral, and that Hammett and Gerry McCormack were to go to the area of the Hennessy contact. If there was a contact, he wanted them to show what the tanks and infantry could do together.

Hammett asked Mick Bindley for a phone line to D Company, and gave the CSM, Ron Pincott, a warning order for the next day's operation. Hammett intended to have 10 Platoon as left forward platoon, 12 as right forward, with 11 bringing up the rear behind the tanks. He could sense the lack of enthusiasm in Pincott.

While walking across to the helicopter pad, where he was to meet McCormack and go on a reconnaissance flight over the area of the bunkers, Hammett tried to recall the lessons of previous tank battles in jungle, particularly against the Japanese at Buna, in New Guinea, and apply them to the limited experience he had had with tanks in Australia.

En route, he met Colonel Dunstan, walking along swinging a stick. After greetings, Dunstan said he heard that Hammett was going out on 'a bit of a stunt tomorrow', and, when Hammett agreed, went on to say that this would be the first time since World War II that Australian infantry and tanks were going into action together, while he himself

241

might have been the last commander to use them in that conflict, on Bougainville, in August 1945.

Colonel Dunstan then added that there were 'a couple of things to remember: the tank telephone never works; and take a tank liaison officer with you, as you'll need his radio, and they are also useful to recce the way for the tanks.'

Flying over the area, piloted by Glen Duus, all aboard the helicopter were peering down at the ground, when Hammett looked up to see that they were heading straight for a larger than usual tree poking up out of the jungle roof. He called a warning and they just avoided it.

Later, briefing the company, he could again sense the lack of enthusiasm from the platoons. There would be no practice, no rehearsal; they would be going into action with a unit they did not know; and had a low opinion of tanks as jungle weapons. Hammett repeated the dispositions he had given Pincott on the phone, then gave examples of lessons of infantry—tank co-operation.

Some of the company had worked with tanks before, in the Puckapunyal area of Victoria. The terrain was very different, and many reservations were held by the individual infantry soldiers about actually going into combat with tanks.

The operation was divided into three phases: one, move out of the company position and meet the tanks; two, the approach march to the bunker area; three, the battle. There were no details for Phase Three, because no one knew what would happen then. Also, there were no disengagement and withdrawal phases.

During the night, there were many sleepless people in D Company, and to add to their discomfort, the base was mortared early in the morning. However, the soldiers prepared themselves for the day, and were ready to move at the right time.

What Hammett described as 'twenty eager volunteers' from the company were to remain and man the vacated perimeter while the rest went out to do battle. After his own sleepless night, 'biting nonexistent fingernails', he received a typical soldier's farewell from Major Digger Campbell: 'Cheerio, matey, I'm glad it's you and not me!' In addition, it was the birthday of radio operator Ross Coulter, in Hammett's HQ group.

Hammett had two platoons abreast, then the tanks, followed by the third platoon. McCormack had three tanks abreast, then the Armoured Recovery Vehicle (ARV) and the M113 equipped for use by RAEME mechanics and tradesmen, with his Troop Sergeant bringing up the rear. The tanks moved close together, sometimes only a metre apart.

On the left of the company, John Salter's 10 Platoon were pleased to find that the engine noise of the tanks behind them was audible only as a 'rumble, but it was hard to tell where they were'.

After moving a short distance, the force met its first obstacle, a steep ravine, which could have been difficult for the tanks to cross. After the infantry secured the far side, McCormack sent the lighter ARV across first, so its winch could be used to haul the tanks up if needed, but the heavy vehicles successfully negotiated the sides and lumbered up on to the level ground.

It was here that McCormack had a pleasant surprise, when he saw Hammett's artillery Forward Observer, Gordon Alexander. They had been school mates, and last seen each other when leaving the examination room for the 1962 Leaving Certificate.

Carefully, they pushed on into the greenery and shadows, the leading infantry alert for sign or sound of enemy. It was found that though the tanks did make noise, it was difficult to pinpoint their location, direction of travel, their numbers, or even identify them as tanks. The leading soldiers realised that they could advance, listening and scanning for enemy, as normal.

However, in general the infantry still were pessimistic, with comments such as 'What are we doing? We'll draw every crab for miles. We might as well be banging drums.' The entire expedition was alien to the way the infantry had patrolled for so long, with as much stealth and quiet as they could muster.

Paul Richardson again had a leading section, and though two fleeting sightings of enemy were made, there was no contact. Carefully and quietly, the infantry pushed forward.

Hammett stopped at 1030, to allow a brew-up, and to allow a strike by B57 Canberras on to the target area, then pushed on. He halted again for short rests at 1130 and 1230, and they began moving once more into the very thick jungle.

Almost at once, Richardson heard noise to the left front of his scout, so stopped his section, and walked up, to the left of Squizzy Taylor, carefully looked around, in time to catch a fleeting movement of what seemed to be someone running.

Richo made the field signals calling Salter up to him, and as the lieutenant came forward, something else moved away through the jungle. All senses were alert, everyone straining to see the enemy they all knew to be close by. The impenetrable green enclosed them.

With one section holding a piece of ground, Tony Hammett decided to move 12 Platoon up through it. At the same time, John Salter decided to move another section up to take over the lead from Richo, so Kevin Mathewson's men began to file carefully past, attention concentrated to their front.

Mathewson's machinegunner, Littlejohn, squatting behind his M60, looked behind him to see an NVA coming down the track a few metres away, obviously puzzled, peering at the stranger. Littlejohn reacted at once, letting out a scream that momentarily paralysed the Vietnamese with fright—and stunning nearby Aussies—swung the heavy M60 around and shot the NVA.

At once several things became obvious: there were NVA in bunkers very close by, they had not realised the Australians were upon them, but they were reacting with speed.

The forward scout of Geoff Bowcock's 12 Platoon was just moving past Richo. Then, from an undetected bunker only three metres to their front, came 'this great burst of AK rounds and the bloody scout shot up into the air, and I thought he'd been hit. He went down to the ground in a great cloud of dust, did a big para roll and came up firing again. I thought, "Christ, he's all right",' recalled Richo.

To Salter it seemed as if the scout 'leaped over the tracer stream' and went to ground. Then there were two platoons mixed up on the same piece of ground, and other bunkers started firing from the flanks.

Another NVA appeared at the other side of the bunker, firing at Richardson, forcing him to stay in a small depression. Simultaneously fire from yet another bunker was beating around the machinegunner, while yet more was directed at Mathewson, just to Richardson's left front.

Fire was being exchanged at a range of not more than twenty metres, mostly by engaging the area from which fire came.

To the rear, in his tank turret hatch, Gerry McCormack heard the firing, and some light banter over the radio. 'The spirits were up,' he recalled, 'and the adrenalin was flowing a little bit, when all of a sudden there was a lot of machine-gun fire, a lot of rifle fire, of a type I hadn't heard before. Hammett ordered me to move front left and take over the contact.'

The NVA were raking the jungle to their front, and neither side could really see each other. Paul Richardson: 'We didn't know which way to move first, so Kev Mathewson sort of moved out to his left and did a sweep and cleared out a few bunkers out that way.'

The enemy firing at Richo's gunner, Gill, kept putting his head up, so Gill called Richo forward, with, 'Have a look at this bugger.'

Richo looked, and 'could see him as plain as day. He was a huge fellow and looked very Chinese to me. He had on a blue-coloured uniform, like scrubbed denim, with a high collar, like our patrol collar on blues, but a soft-looking material. He had a dirty yellow armband on, I think, his right arm. No hat, but a brown leather strap across one shoulder. He was firing a short, snub-nosed weapon, automatic, but not an AK, as the noise was different. He was a large man, pale-skinned, with glasses. He seemed to be on his own.

'He kept bobbing up and down, and we'd fire a burst at him, but he was very dodgy, this bugger. The only way we could get rid of him was with grenades. Slug Lewis and I went forward, and in front of the bunkers was a foot pad, on an incline. So we rolled two grenades down, which went off in front of the bunker without seeming to affect it.

'Slug said, "Oh, bugger this, I'll throw one," and his first one went straight into the bunker and that was the end of the

245

Chinese guy. We never went right up there to make sure, as fire was coming from everywhere. We went back to the platoon, where the headquarters was taking a fair bit of fire from the bunker which fired on 12 Platoon, but they were pushing forward.

'Salter was running around, doing a magnificent job, calling the tanks forward.'

Moving alongside Gerry McCormack's tank, Gordon Alexander still recalls with amusement the speed with which McCormack ducked down into the turret when an RPG hit the front of the armour, luckily not wounding any of the infantry HQ party. McCormack pushed on into the fight, leaving the HQ group more worried about being run over by the following tank than the enemy fire.

When the RPGs were fired, and the warning cry went over the tank radio net, 'hearts went into mouths' back at Coral, where the armoured people were listening. The RPG was an unknown quantity in its effect on the elderly Centurion.

The tanks arrived at the platoon area, and Salter's men 'were all terrified of being run over or shot by a tank. We soon found that fire control orders using the axis of the tank's main gun barrel or the axis of the tank itself were a bit hard when you could not see the tank or the barrel.'

McCormack, in his fifty-two-ton monster, had 'crashed forward through the scrub and got into position, so I thought, behind the platoon, and the platoon commander said we were right in among his men, and to stop there, as he hadn't been able to locate one of his sections. So we paused there, and eventually the section was moved out of the way.

'However, while this was going on, we came under aimed fire from the NVA, who were in pits not very far to our front. Not having permission to fire, and being subjected to this small arms fire, was uncomfortable. Corporal Bill Burton, on my left, was saying that he could see a fellow actually sighting his weapon, and could he fire?

'I said no, we did not have clearance from the infantry, and Burton came back and said the fellow had an RPG, have I got permission to fire now? Once again I had to say no, but within two or three seconds we got word from Hammett that everyone had been accounted for.

'All three tanks fired two rounds of canister, which is like a big shotgun shell. They knocked over a lot of the scrub and undergrowth, clearing the camouflage the NVA had over their pits. It left four or five obvious weapon pits with over-head protection in front of us, each with two men in them, some a bit more dazed than others, but with spurts of fire coming from them all.

'We then fired an armour-piercing round, called APCBC —armour-piercing capped ballistic cap. It is a full bore 84mm round that travels about 800 metres a second, and the kinetic energy, the concussion that it would give to weapon pits at a range of twenty to thirty metres, was fairly devastating. We would also engage with machinegun fire in case anyone was still there.'

Richo watched with interest as the tank 'came up to this bunker system, lowered its barrel, couldn't have been more than bloody seven metres away from me, fired and blew the top off the bunker, then went forward and did left-right-track on top of it, and it all caved in. Obviously we had no idea who was inside.'

The tanks crunched forward on to the area they had just cleared, but again the dense jungle obscured vision, so more canister was fired, revealing another series of weapon pits.

The problems of observation from a tank in these circum-stances were made clear, when a pit behind McCormack came to life again. It had not been hit with an APCBC round, as it was too close to his tank, and he 'hadn't seen it, as it was just in front of my driver, and when we went forward we drove over it, but it left the fellows inside still very angry.

'Anyway, we put the tank into reverse, backed up, I told the driver to close [his hatch] down, and we withdrew with the gun on maximum depression. I told the loader to look down the barrel, and when he saw the pit, we would hold it there and decide what we would do.'

With the long barrel pointing at the pit, an APCBC round was loaded, and McCormack called out to the NVA to sur-render, using the words *Chieu Hoi*, the title of the surrender programme of the Saigon Government. Millions of leaflets and many radio broadcasts had taken the programme to the enemy areas, and thousands took advantage of it to leave the VC/NVA. McCormack thought the NVA menaced by his 84mm cannon recognised his call, and wanted to surrender, so he radioed Tony Hammett. Back at Coral, the battle was being followed on radios there, and the possibility of capturing enemy raised the excitement level.

Hammett's first knowledge of the imminent surrender came when Ross Coulter, his radio operator, told him that battalion HQ 'want that Chieu Hoi', to which Hammett replied, 'What Chieu Hoi?' He was annoyed at this 'back-seat driving' from people listening to the radio nets back at Coral, and asked Salter what was going on over there in the 10 Platoon area.

Corporal 'Greasy' Jones, commanding a section of Salter's 10 Platoon, was sent forward to take the prisoners. John Salter saw him, and called out to be careful. Salter could see 'these three heads, with big eyes, looking at the two tanks pointing cannon at them'.

McCormack had received a radio message from Peter Badman, the tank squadron commander, to the effect that 'faint heart ne'er won fair maiden', and he was 'trying to think of something very clever to say'.

John Salter 'heard Jones call out "Chieu Hoi, come out", and they sort of looked at him, blinked, saw him as someone they could shoot, ducked and came up firing ... Greasy went to the right and the two tanks went BLAM! The NVA would never have known what hit them.'

The bullets had actually nicked Jones' webbing and shirt, but he was unharmed. Hammett had heard Jones call out, then the burst of firing, and finally some very bad language from Greasy.

There was little else that could be done by D/1RAR or the tanks, but it is unlikely that three young NVA, newly arrived in the South, would have understood the call to surrender by non-Vietnamese, if indeed they even knew of the Chieu Hoi programme, under which they would be welcomed with 'Open Arms' by the people and government of South Vietnam.

McCormack moved forward again, back to the pits which had been uncovered but not eliminated, and methodically fired into each.

One of Salter's machinegunners, 'Pommy' Nation, thought that the bulk of a tank would be a good thing to provide protection while he fired his M60 at targets. He moved behind one. After a few minutes he came back to Salter, saying, 'I'm never going to go near one of those things again! Everyone shoots at 'em!'

As the fighting went on, Sergeant Ray Curtis recalls, 'you'd be lying there and hear a clang! and it would be an RPG deflected off the tank, and the bloody rocket would whiz off into the scrub . . .' to the discomfiture of the surrounding infantry, and presumably of the NVA.

There was a pause while the bunkers in the immediate area were checked, but there was little left after the arrival of an APCBC shot and a fifty-two-ton tank had rolled over the top. McCormack sent a brief radio report back to Coral, and moved on behind the infantry.

The company HQ party came up to the scene of fighting, and Forward Observer Gordon Alexander looked around at the wreckage, tank tracks, dirt and severed branches, seeing 'amongst the dead this NVA who was huge. Normally they were little fellows, but this guy was well over six foot, dead as a doornail, but as we looked at him some reflex action made him kick, and we nearly jumped six feet!'

Geoff Bowcock's 12 Platoon, on the right, was now fired on, and McCormack's tanks swerved in that direction without waiting for orders. Bowcock quickly accounted for his men, and this time the tanks were cleared to fire as they arrived in the platoon area.

Bowcock noticed the foliage gradually being shot away by fire from the bunkers, his men and the tank canister rounds. A bunker was seen by the infantry, and directions called to the tank crews, 'bring the barrel down, there's a bunker right there', and the reply came that solid shot would be fired.

Bowcock thought this would be interesting, and his Diggers scuttled out of the way as the tank manoeuvred to bring the cannon on target. The long barrel dipped, there was

249

a ka-boom! and today, years later, he can still see 'the round impacting, the earth convulsing—you could feel the concussion in the ground—and the enemy fire paused. I went forward to have a closer look, and thought the tank had made a hell of a mess. I could see where the ground had collapsed into the bunker, and part of a body, half in, half out, caught in the wreckage.'

The Centurions 'crashed through, firing on the move once again, fired canister to clear the scrub and camouflage, and picked off the bunkers.' To Gerry McCormack, 'very quickly it became obvious that this was a different sort of layout. There were two very large bunkers in among the smaller ones. I think we had got through into a large communications or headquarters area. We put a number of rounds into the large bunkers and drove past them.

'This meant that Sergeant Nev Callis and the RAEME vehicles moved up, and were either side of the large bunkers, when all of a sudden small arms fire came out of them and scared the RAEME people to death. Quick as a wink, though, Sergeant Peter De Jong, commanding the ARV, got the infantry flamethrower operators, riding on his vehicle, into action, and I glanced around to see this sheet of flame coming out of the side of the ARV, disappearing down to a couple of holes into these bunkers.

'It was probably the first and only time we had armoured flamethrowers in action in Vietnam.'

Sergeant Major Ron Pincott, distributing ammunition to the forward sections in the 10 Platoon area, on the left, came across Paul Richardson and Gill sitting in a small depression, casually eating a tin of ham and lima beans, one of the more detested items in the US field ration spectrum. About twenty-five metres to their right was 12 Platoon, fiercely blazing away at bunkers. Nearby were the hulking Centurions, methodically firing at targets.

Richo had assessed the situation, and decided there was not much he could do, as 12 Platoon were controlling the situation, so had turned to Gill and suggested 'a bit of tucker', as they had been moving and fighting since 0630 that morning. 'So Gillie and I decided to have something to eat, with all this going on, canister firing and bloody RPGs bouncing off the tanks. That's when the old Grey Ghost appeared out of the jungle, with sandbags full of ammunition, dropping them off here and there. "What the bloody hell are you doing?" I said, "Having my lunch. None of these bastards here know what time it is. It's lunch time." So he went back into the jungle mumbling under his breath.'

Tony Hammett also appeared, having come up to congratulate people on their work so far, and commented that 'I'm glad to see you've got your priorities right', to which the diners agreed.

The rest of the day for Richardson became a succession of attacks on bunkers, to his left and right, working with the tanks, in a welter of foliage and dirt, fire from small arms, tank and RPG, and, later on, rain.

One NVA, bravely or foolishly, jumped up in front of a tank and fired at it with his pistol. The tank crunched on irresistibly.

Vehicle crews, and AFV crews in particular, were always envied by the infantry because of the relatively large amounts of food, bedding and luxuries able to be loaded on and in the M113s and Centurions. In the midst of the flying tracer, shot and shell of various calibres, falling branches and pieces of tree, some of the infantry noted and took 'some consolation from the fact that the bins and containers on the tanks, which carried all their clothes, extra rations and so on, were being removed by the vines and branches or NVA fire. It was the highlight of the day!'

Gerry McCormack himself noticed that the searchlights, which were carried in baskets on the back of the turret when not in use, all seemed to be bullet-damaged, and briefly wondered what would happen if they had to stay out at night, with no light to illuminate targets.

Geoff Bowcock's 12 Platoon became embroiled in a cluster of bunkers on their right, while Richo was eating lunch, and Hammett moved over there, following the tanks. He saw one of the Diggers call out, 'There's one over here!', dodge a burst of close-range fire, get himself behind an anthill and continue to call fire direction to the others.

While all this was going on, Gordon Alexander, for the artillery, and Bluey Skeen for the mortars, were calling down and adjusting fire along the axis of advance. Ross Coulter was sending situation reports back to battalion HQ, freeing Hammett of that necessity, and relaying to him messages from them. Hammett himself did not need to speak to Lieutenant Colonel Bennett.

A particular bunker was discovered in a position where the tanks could not bring their cannon to bear, and it was decided to bring up the flamethrowers. The Assault Pioneers carrying them jumped off the ARV and came forward, got one ready, then stood up and fired—nothing happened. As soon as possible, the other was brought up, and worked, destroying the bunker.

After some four hours of fighting their way into the bunker system, it became obvious that the force of one infantry company and four tanks was not enough to destroy them all. The interconnected system seemed to be endless.

Ray Curtis realised that 'there was no end to the bunkers. You'd take one out and there were more'.

Tony Hammett, no less than his soldiers, had the feeling that they 'were a small wedge driving into a much larger position than we had anticipated.'

At about 1530 rain began to fall, and Hammett had to consider what to do in the remaining period of daylight. HQ 1RAR ordered him to break off the contact and return to Coral.

They had been in action, at close range, for three and a half hours, and despite some close shaves no one had been hit. The adrenalin had been flowing, they were all dry and thirsty, and the rain at least began to cool them down, though it also reduced visibility.

Hammett was very conscious of the danger posed by returning the way he had come. The NVA could be assumed to have at least placed mines on the clearly marked path of advance, and possibly would be placing an ambush on it. He thought of pushing on to the east, to a patch of open ground there, about 1000 metres away.

This would have offered a faster and clearer route back to

Coral, and was close to the route followed by B Company the previous day. However, above the action was Captain Don Tait, the artillery Forward Observer from B Company, in an Army Sioux helicopter. He advised Hammett not to go on to the east, as this would result in D Company moving further into the mass of bunkers, and possibly end in the Australians being swallowed up in it.

Hammett and McCormack had a brief discussion about the best way to extricate themselves from the contact. Common sense advised against going back the way they had just come and fought, through the bunkers, but it was decided to do this, with a platoon scouting the edges of the tank-made route through the jungle back to Coral.

The company and tanks then made a 180-degree turn, while in the presence of the enemy, and faced back the way they had come.

As dusk was deepening, and in the falling rain, they moved back through the splintered and fallen trees, crushed muddy bunkers, shiny-wet leaves, darkening shadows, smell of the jungle and cordite, to the open ground.

Using the power of artillery to assist the move back, Gordon Alexander kept the fall of shellfire some 100 metres behind the company, to prevent NVA from following along the tank-made paths, 'so there was still dead shrapnel flying through the trees, raining down on us, as we moved back'.

Morale was quite high. There had not been a single Australian casualty, despite the close contact and duration of fighting. The infantry had seen what tanks could do, and they all realised the price in flesh and blood which would have been paid in order to destroy those bunkers without armour. The tank crews had shown what could be done, and swept away what reservations and doubts they might have had themselves.

The effect of the artillery could not easily be calculated, but Tony Hammett presumes it had some effect on preventing the enemy from reacting as they normally did, attacking the flanks of intruders. Later he found that just over 1000 rounds were fired that afternoon, which was more than the Australian 7th Division had for the attack on Buna.

'There was a little banter over the radio,' says Gerry McCormack. 'We were pretty cock-a-hoop at this stage. I looked out and noticed the guide roller on Corporal Bill Burton's tank wasn't moving. The guide roller is a small wheel high up on the tank hull, a balancing wheel, and the track rolls along it before it goes down on to the ground. It has to be greased every night. I asked if he did this, and he replied, with a very forlorn look on his face, but politely, "Of course I greased it."'

Later it was found an RPG had hit the roller, and jammed it, but the tank still functioned.

Conscious that the NVA might try to follow them, or indeed had already gone ahead closer to Coral to prepare an ambush, Hammett kept his force alert all the way back, leaving a section of 11 Platoon to ambush any pursuers. None came.

As they entered the base, Hammett was aware of 'a tremendous feeling within the company. The soldiers were on a high. We'd been in action for three and a half hours, we'd destroyed at least fourteen bunkers; we did not count them. I had no interest in the enemy dead, only in the ones still alive and causing us problems. We didn't count the dead for the very good reason that the tanks had crushed the bunkers. All the bunkers were occupied, and firing at us.

'The tanks saved the day. Soldiers were going up to these tanks and patting them, giving the thumbs-up to the crews, saying, "Great, good on you." The fellows were ecstatic that we'd been out and done something, and not had one single fellow receive one single scratch. That is thanks to the tanks, and to the fine group of soldiers we had, the abilities of the platoon commanders, and as importantly, the section commanders, like Richo, Jones, Logan.

'It really was a successful operation. After that, the Diggers always wanted to know if the tanks were coming with us.'

On arrival back in the company position at Coral, the Diggers, in Paul Richardson's words, 'sort of sat down in utter amazement that the day had gone so fast'. Later, thinking about the battle, he thought that the NVA did not realise D Company was actually inside the outskirts of their bunker system. Obviously, the sentries would have heard the rumbling of the tanks, but would not have been able to assess accurately what was happening. The sentries would have gone back into the bunker system to report, and this could well have been the movement seen by Richardson's section just before the firing started.

While the sentries were away, the Diggers moved up and the change in platoon dispositions was begun, then the NVA soldier walked back down the track on to the machine-gunner, who shot him.

Initially, the NVA were aggressive, coming out to fire and fight, but as the attack was on a broad, two-platoon front, supported by mortars and artillery, always punching forward, it was D Company who held the initiative. They never lost it.

B52s were later targeted on to the location, and when D Company returned the position was unrecognisable.

McCormack's men checked the tanks, and found very little damage despite the intense fire directed at them. The small arms had penetrated the bins, destroying McCormack's favourite part of the rations—the tin of pound cake. The feared RPG had been shown to be unable to inflict much damage, seeming to be detonated by the shrubbery or external fittings of the Centurions.

As the tanks came rolling back to their position in the Coral base, Ian Ahearn, Gun Position Officer of 102 Battery, 'distinctly remember[s] Gerry's tanks coming back. They'd been engaged with RPG2; we had fired very close to them as they withdrew and most of them had superficial damage; most of the bins on the outside had been taken off by RPGs, and on Gerry's tank itself, he had an umbrella over the cupola which was in mint condition when he went out, but when they came back it was simply the skeleton of an umbrella.

'He was very impressed with the fire support the battery gave him. He walked around the position and talked to the gun detachments, giving them a description of what had happened, and how accurate and responsive their fire had been.'

Bill Burton knew that he had taken several RPG hits

during the action so, with Bernie Sullivan, the technical officer, went over the tank. They worked out in what position the tank had been when it was hit each time, and counted seven hits across the front of the turret and along the length of the track. None had penetrated the tank. The most serious hit was one which had detonated into a road-wheel hub, and somehow the jet of molten metal had passed through the hub and out the back. There was no spare suspension unit.

Bernie Sullivan solved the problem temporarily with a bit of bush carpentry. 'The best I could do was to cut two green-stick wooden plugs which I hammered into the exit and entry holes in the hub, had the driver pump it up with grease until my little plugs just started to move, and hammered them in again, then put him on pain of death if he lost the plugs or did not check regularly that the grease was up to it.' Some parts were flown up a few days later from Nui Dat. Shock absorber parts were not available, so Bill Burton ran his tank for the remainder of the operation at Coral without one set.

Night at Coral on 26 May 1968 fell on soldiers of three arms who had greater confidence and respect for each other.

In the darkening bunker system, among the collapsed fighting positions, the mud, fallen branches and foliage, the NVA searched for their casualties. Using the unaccustomed light from above, through the new holes in the jungle canopy, they poked and probed into the dirt and splintered wood, hoping to find the remains of friends and comrades. As in every group of soldiers, there were the frightened and worried, appalled at the destruction and wondering what would happen if the enemy returned. There would be the others, mouths set, eyes alert, pondering the lessons of the action, what advantages they could use against these new tanks, how to find their weak points.

Scurrying back along the network of paths, stretcher bearers were trotting with the wounded; others carried salvaged weapons. Lit by small lamps, the commanders assessed the situation, discussing whether to remain or to evacuate the position. One thing was certain: the superior firepower of the enemy would be brought to bear; the sector which had been fought over should be abandoned.

The commanders and political officers already knew how they would talk to the comrades about the afternoon's combat: they had bravely held the position and fought off a very strong force of enemy, causing heavy losses and forcing them to flee; citations and commendations would be made; recipients would relate their exploits to groups not engaged in today's fighting; group discussions would decide on new tactics to be tried, reducing the menace by open talking of it; morale would be raised.

But now, around them it was dusk, in the rain and mud of the shattered bunkers.

On 27 May Digger Campbell's C Company patrolled all day, engaging an NVA squad, with three Australians wounded and one NVA killed.

Neil Weekes also engaged a group of NVA, and was reminded—though he had not forgotten—of the calibre of his foe. The enemy were seen some 600 metres away, and then fired on. The NVA went into a contact drill, and then Weekes 'watched in horrified posture this enemy platoon coming straight at me. There were very few trees around, but what there were had been used as targets for the RPGs, and rockets were exploding in the trees above us, which took the initiative away.'

Artillery was called in, and stopped the attack, after which Weekes moved the shells back and forth on the distant tree line. 'It was not a place to stay overnight, or to get into an area you didn't know, or get into thick scrub, as there were so many enemy about and they were very good.'

The allied commander in Vietnam, General William C. Westmoreland, came to visit the Australians. He was soon to go back to the US to brief President Lyndon Johnson. As the Australian Prime Minister, John Gorton, was also to visit the President, Johnson had asked to be brought up to date with the activities of the Aussies, who had been so recently in contact.

On the tour around Coral, going from unit to unit in an

M113, Westy remarked several times to Colonel Dunstan that the Australian equipment was, in general, better than the American. When Dunstan pointed out that much of it was American in origin, Westy insisted that what was Australian was better. So the visit progressed.

In the course of events, he came to Geoff Bowcock's 12 Platoon, which was in the open on the right of D Company 1RAR. As in any large organisation, word had been passed from higher level about the visit, and where the visitor would be taken, what the soldiers were to do and wear, and so on. The platoon area was to be clean and tidy, the Diggers were to wear shirts and hats, and everyone was to know the military details of the location, such as arcs of fire, flanking sub-units, et cetera.

Bowcock saw 'a conga line of dignitaries wending their way to the position'. The visit went well, and the Diggers spoken to by the general made a good impression. The conga line seemed to be pleased too, and Bowcock began to relax. Then 'Westy turns from the left-hand gun pit, and starts walking to the depth gun pit, which was quite a large bunker with a hutchi slung low over it. Westmoreland walked up to it, looked down below it and pulled up the edge.

'Here are two of my soldiers—without shirts or hats—sitting in there cleaning their GPMG M60, all laid out on another hutchi, in hundreds of pieces. The whole conga line stops. Westy is standing there looking down, but there is no sign of recognition from the Diggers, and they're cleaning away. Private Farrens had got the cleaning rod going up and down the barrel.

'Westy is a little taken aback, because these guys are not paying him any attention at all. I'm getting hot under the collar; Bennett's looking at me; Hammett's looking at me as if to say, "Bowcock! What have you done to these people?" and I'm thinking, "Shit, what am I in for now?"'

'Westy thinks he'd better break the ice, so says hello. They turn around and say g'day and keep on cleaning. Westy thinks, "What am I going to say now?" so he asks what they think of the GPMG M60 [a piece of US equipment!].

'Farrens turns around, not missing a beat scrubbing out the

barrel, and says, "The damn thing's no good." Westy takes a step back, Bennett's getting hot under the collar and Hammett's giving me threatening looks. Westy asks why that is, and Farrens tells him we were out in a contact yesterday and "the bloody thing stopped!" Westy says that is no good. He could see he wasn't making any progress, so he left them. We walked off, and Bennett and Hammett overtook me and said, "That'll be enough, then, Bowcock." Westy said farewell to me and left, with all his brass trailing along. A very vivid memory.'

Not only a vivid memory for Geoff Bowcock, but also for Colonel Dunstan, who thought it hilarious, and who can be seen grinning in the background of the photograph of the occasion.

As evening fell, the signals for attack again rose from the darkness outside the perimeters.

Balmoral was attacked at 0235, and Coral also stood-to, as it seemed likely the enemy would attack both places. Unable to mount a ground attack on both, the enemy mortared and rocketed Coral in an attempt to distract the defenders, while the main effort was applied at Balmoral.

In his pit Noel Sproles could hear the crumping bombs walking closer and closer across the base. Then one exploded so near that he saw the flash from inside the bunker.

It had landed near the pit occupied by Geoff Cameron and Kevin Gurney. Each thought the other had been hit, and after calling and finding neither was injured, decided to see if anyone had been injured. The next pit was deep and well-constructed, built by Warrant Officer Bob Kissin, who was absent at the time. Warrant Officer Brian Knight was the unfortunate temporary resident, and had received the full impact of the concussion and shower of dirt when the bomb scored a direct hit on the roof.

The two majors pulled Knight out, checked him over and gave him a drink. After a few minutes he was well on the way to recovery. Then the officers found that the blast had destroyed Gurney's personal and expensive camera equipment, as well as riddling their packs, which contained a large quantity of toothpaste. Other members of the HQ found the sight of the whiteness oozing out of the bags quite funny, but Cameron had already lost one set of personal equipment to mortars in an earlier operation, and was to lose a third later.

It was also discovered that the mortars had been 'stepping' across the base at regular distances. At the exact number of metres from the final crater, where the next round would have landed, was the sleeping pit of one of the CP staff.

The bombardment at Coral lasted sixteen minutes, hitting mainly the artillery positions and C Company 1RAR. In the infantry position, Doc Clarke was alone, as his partner had gone on leave, part of the rostered rest and recreation break from duty. As the mortars crumped across the base, 'suddenly the world exploded on me. I don't remember too much, I must have been unconscious for some time. I'd taken a direct hit. I remember waking up and feeling my face, which was covered with mud and clay, but I thought my head was blown off and all I was feeling was gore. I pinched my ear, it hurt, and I thought things aren't supposed to hurt when you're dead, and I realised I was alive. I spent the rest of the night praying. I don't think I've prayed so much in my life.'

Next morning, CSM Wally Thompson found Clarke in the middle of a crater, with everything destroyed: food, medical supplies, personal equipment, and the two tins of Coke which had been delivered the afternoon before. Doc had carefully wrapped them in wet sandbags to cool them, but they were riddled with holes. It became a company joke to enquire if he had his Coke yet.

Clarke found the actual fin of the mortar bomb, and has it today as a paperweight. He redug his pit in the same place, acting on the belief that lightning does not strike twice in the same spot.

Later, Doc Clarke found a baby squirrel. No trace of any mother could be found, presumably destroyed by the bombardment, so it was adopted and fed on diluted condensed milk. Later, named Skeeter, it ate biscuits and nuts, but unfortunately died of what was presumed to be a snake- or spider-bite.

One of the corporals, a veteran of the first tour by the battalion in 1965–6, came to Clarke and told him that he could not urinate, but after much effort, a drop or two of blood would appear. After ascertaining that there had been no contact with the local damsels for the appropriate period of time, and thinking about it, Doc suddenly realised what was wrong.

He told the Digger to open his fly, sit down and grit his teeth, 'because this is going to hurt you a lot more than me!' Taking a pair of long-nosed forceps from his medical kit, Doc then, to the acute discomfort of the patient, removed a leech from inside his penis.

The Aussie sense of humour was further exercised by the sight of the patient experiencing 'scalding' when he did urinate.

A popular comic strip of the day was 'Wally and the Major', and this was applied to the CSM and OC C Company, Wally Thompson and Digger Campbell. The title was given with affection, and Clarke acknowledged that the two 'were a source of inspiration for us, so cool, level-headed, always knew the right thing to do at the right time.'

In the artillery position, a gunner had an equally close shave: the mortar bomb hit the roof of his pit, penetrating the sandbags, but did not explode. The man looked up to see the nose of a mortar only 130 millimetres from his head.

Bob Carbury, 102 Battery Q-store man, had twice had much of his stores destroyed in the attacks, but was pleased to find that his job was understood by the quartermaster sergeant, Staff Sergeant Bushby, who sent up from Nui Dat all the requested items, with no red tape involved for Carbs. When he could Bushby also included beer and soft drinks for the gunners.

By this time Dr Neville O'Connor had his medical centre well established. Casualties were reported to him by telephone and, when necessary, brought by APC. His assistants 'were rough and ready, but highly competent and quite brave, the way they would head off into the pitch black with rockets going, administer and return. The US Army ambulance companies did a sterling job, always prepared to come in, and provided tremendous morale for soldiers in the field.'

He was impressed by the professionalism of the Army, both Regulars and National Servicemen, especially with the confidence and maturity of the latter, selected members across the range of society. He attended the Orders Groups, and noticed that in spite of all the action, medical aspects were always in the mind of the TF Commander and Deputy Commander, and they visited his RAP daily. This awareness extended to the battalion and company commanders, some of whom he knew from meetings in Australia. The malaria discipline was quite good.

O'Connor decided on the evacuation priority, and this was followed. He was aware that such medical evacuation systems were not available in civilian life, backed up by the first-class American surgical system, which was second to none. A major difference in the Australian system was the presence of doctors in the field; Americans had to leave the forward area to be treated by a doctor.

He did note that the US troops seemed to be 'ignorant of foot hygiene', suffering many infections. This was in contrast to the Aussie, who seemed to take every opportunity to look after his feet—perhaps a lingering legacy of an infantry-oriented Army. This ignorance puzzled O'Connor somewhat, as all the foot powder available was US issue.

Dr O'Connor recalled that his biggest problem was not the supply system—which was adequate—but in keeping the redoubtable medical officer from 8 Field Ambulance out of the field. Digger James, known to all, had been told not to go into the field, but did persist in 'visiting', on one occasion bringing a parcel from Mrs O'Connor; chocolates, which were enjoyable, even though melted. James was admired by all who met him, for triumphing over the loss of both legs, and insisting on leading an active life.

Like everyone else, O'Connor watched the bombardments, the awesome fire support, and one of his most vivid memories of the time is 'sitting and watching Spooky send a stream of tracer to the ground; most impressive'.

Two of the casualties remain in his mind: a soldier who was asleep in his pit, feet up on the edge, when a rocket impacted close by, destroying the boot, but only inflicting a shrapnel wound to a foot; and a signaller, in his pit, under bombardment, developed hysterical paralysis and became rigid as a board, was evacuated, treated for shock and back on duty that evening—the technique of returning the patient to his unit and mates as soon as possible.

Neville O'Connor went to Colonel Dunstan, and suggested a ration of rum to the soldiers, for medical reasons. Dunstan replied that he did not think the Aussies would like rum, and asked if beer would do. The doctor agreed that it would have the same effect, so next day Dunstan spoke about it to the relevant officer, Major Kevin Gurney.

Gurney replied that on the orders of the Task Force commander, Coral was to be 'dry'. Dunstan reminded him that *he* was now commanding, and beer was to be brought in. Signals flew between Coral and Nui Dat, and some time later Gurney told Dunstan that a Chinook was approaching, and if they went to the heli-pad, they should receive the beer.

Dunstan, Gurney and a group of expectant people walked across in the hot sunlight and endured the dust of the landing, while Gurney eagerly walked inside the big helicopter. He returned, walking more slowly, and Dunstan asked if there was no beer aboard. Gurney replied that there was, but it was root beer.

Dunstan said that was all right, as long as it was beer, then asked what root beer was. Geoff Cameron has vivid memories of the explosion which followed. 'Sarspar-bloody-rilla! Get it out of here!'

The Chinook lifted in a cloud of dust; more signals flew between the camps; a Chinook flew in again, and unloaded cartons of one beer Colonel Dunstan detested: Resch's Diet Ale.

In theory, there was enough for one can per person at the bases, but at time of writing some people deny ever receiving a beer in the field.

263

Father Tinkler's work in the base had attracted quite a few regular attenders, including a US artilleryman. One day, after the operation was over, the American met Tinkler in the marketplace at Baria, and insisted on buying something for the chaplain, as an expression of his appreciation. Tinkler did not want to insult the man by refusing, so selected an inexpensive pillowcase decorated with the Australian flag.

The American bought two, offering the second to the Catholic chaplain, with; 'Father, I'd like you to have one for your wife as well.'

The pillowcases were stolen by local children before Tinkler left Baria that day.

11 Looking Death In the Eyes

Make a noise in the east, attack in the west.
Mao Zedong (Mao Tse Tung)

SINCE THE MORNING of 26 May 3RAR had put more effort into developing its defences, and was much stronger. The Diggers had been told they were 'a thorn in the side' of the enemy, and more attacks could be expected. Like the rest of the Diggers. Dave Mancer and his section were aware by now that they were 'in a position where anything could happen'.

'Shelton's Mortar Marauders' charged out and about, firing salvoes of 81mm bombs, and returned unscathed to the position.

Naturally, the battles brought several visitors of high rank. General Westmoreland arrived from Coral. Jim Shelton was nonplussed when Westy asked how old the NVA were; to him Asians were either very young or very old; there seemed no way to tell their age accurately.

When Westy arrived, Peter Geil, with 6 Section of 8 Platoon, was some 600 metres to the front of the perimeter with a section standing patrol, all aware they were in tiger country and all alert. Then, over the radio, they heard the battalion called to stand-to. Peter never saw a section ready to move so quickly, nor cover the ground back to the battalion position so swiftly ... to find the stand-to was not due to imminent enemy attack, and they were not required back there. It was so that everyone would be in their pits and dressed properly when Westy came by. A nervous section breathed easier.

On the afternoon of 27 May one visitor was a senior Australian general, who insisted on wearing his red-banded cap and on being shown the forward positions. The Diggers had become acutely aware that to be seen by the NVA was to have fire directed at the position, and were less than pleased to have a person with a bright and distinctive hatband standing near them.

Jim Shelton, of course, knew he was responsible for the visitor, and if anything happened to him, no excuse would be good enough. 'I tried to stall him, and kept talking and asking questions, but after twenty minutes he said, "You're just stalling me, and we are going around the perimeter."'

As they did so, gradually moving south, Shelton began receiving reports of sightings of enemy in that direction. Then they came to the southernmost company, Howard's A Company. The position was somewhat untidy, as part of the mortar bombardment had fallen on to the boxes of rations which had been delivered the afternoon before, but not issued, and tins, paper and debris were scattered around. This annoyed the general.

Then he walked up behind a soldier, in his pit, engrossed in cleaning his handgrenades for the coming night's expected activities. The Digger looked up to see a bunch of senior people, including a general, looming over him, and dropped the grenade into the pit. This did not impress either the general or Jim Shelton.

The general wanted to look at Howard's position from the enemy side, but as a patrol had been chased back by about half a company of NVA recently, no one was going to have any part of that. Enjoying his off-duty time from the machinegun watch, a Digger was sitting in a position where he could not be seen by the enemy, reading the Army newspaper. The general walked up behind him and asked what he was doing. Without looking up, the soldier replied, 'Reading the bloody newspaper. What does it look like?'

Howard's barbed wire defences next attracted attention, and were criticised as being 'not effective', but while moving between platoons, the general tripped in it and fell over. While this had been going on, nearby a Digger had tripped a flare-wire, as a final incident during the visit. All heaved a sigh of relief when the visitor was gone. Jim Shelton later received what he described as 'quite a rocket on behalf of A Company'.

So the defenders of Balmoral, confident in the tested strength of their position, settled down for another night, and whatever it might bring. The early hours passed without incident, but from about 2200 to midnight, movement and lights were seen and engaged with artillery, and at about 0130, Howard's A Company reported what sounded like digging noises. It was obvious that the enemy were active, and another attack was expected.

Out in the darkness the newly arrived men of the NVA Infiltration Groups were being led to the positions from which they would begin the attack. Some were not told until they were actually in location that they would soon be assaulting an enemy position, but others were informed that the attack was necessary to affect the talks in Paris. None were told that tanks were in the objective position.

They were simply brought into place, told what they were to do, and ordered to rest until the assault began. Around them the more experienced mortar and reconnaissance teams were active, commanders in small groups making last-minute decisions, guides walking by with their attendant groups, and the young boys from North Vietnam waited.

But the same old signs of assembly and preparation for battle were seen sailing up into the sky, and Ian MacLean, at TF HQ at Coral, was talking to Lieutenant Colonel Shelton at Balmoral, warning him of the impending attack. Shelton replied his people had seen them, and were also waiting for the attack to begin, when the first mortars were heard, and Shelton could say, 'Oh, there they are now,' as if expected but tardy guests were just arriving. It was 0230.

Bill Studley had rostered himself for the 0030 to 0230 shift on duty, in what was now called 'The Bomb Run' period. He was walking back to his pit when he heard the primaries, and noticed that the noise silenced the chirping crickets. He had to decide to run to his pit, which seemed safer, or to the APC, from where he would be passing fire orders to the mortars.

267

He chose the APC and dived in as the rounds exploded. He thought that the sound of the primaries came from the south, and at first return fire was in that direction.

At Coral, Peter Badman, in his ACV, looked up through the open hatch, still awakening from sleep, to see 'a fire-cracker going overhead, trailing sparks, and thought how pretty it was, then remembered where I was.'

With all the ACV crew and the tanks awake and manned, Badman then realised one drawback of the ACV: it had no episcope or periscope, so the only way to see out was to put one's head out for a look. So he opened the hatch a little and peeped around, noticing all the activity, and then thought, 'By gee, this is a large slabsided vehicle', and began to feel vulnerable as they 'were sitting out in the middle of the fire support base in a thing as big as the Hilton Hotel.'

The bombardment of Coral was to occupy the defenders and their artillery, while a bigger attack was made on 3RAR at Balmoral.

By this time the Australians, suppressing disbelief, realised that the NVA leadership were creatures of habit, and would continue to commit assault forces to the routes they had selected, and over which they had suffered heavy losses. In a smaller way, they showed the same inflexibility as their counterparts in the British Army of World War I, sending units and more units to destruction.

The only thing to be said in their defence is that perhaps they believed they were inflicting heavier losses on the de-fenders of Coral and Balmoral, but since they had no pris-oners, little if any captured equipment, and had never actually seized and held either of the bases, it is doubtful they could have believed they were causing more damage than they suffered. They persisted in sending young men to their deaths in the storm of fire around the bases.

Presumably the leaders believed that the pressures of combat around Saigon would lead to concessions in Paris. Their own casualties, as such, had no significance in terms of lost manpower. General Giap is supposed to have said that tens of thousands of people die each year in accidents of normal living, so if those deaths are incurred in the service of revolution they will have been of some use.

On the southern side of Balmoral, Howard's A Company, an attack had been made. The NVA again had destroyed the wooden knife-rest gate by using a Bangalore torpedo. This act had annoyed Howard's CSM, Snow Purdon, who took a personal interest in the construction of the gate.

Close by, in his APC, driver Geoff Murray had jumped out of the vehicle, in time to see a series of red-white flashes, which he soon realised were RPGs aimed at the .50cal machinegun on the M113. He climbed up behind it and began spraying the area from which the NVA were firing.

In the meantime David Brooks, the vehicle commander, had been running back to enter the APC, but slipped on the earth side of the bund and fell between it and the vehicle, finding himself trapped. He called to Murray, who had shut the hatches and was enjoying himself on the machinegun, so Brooks was held there, watching the RPGs flashing overhead, listening to the mortars, finally freeing himself and taking over the gunnery.

After ten minutes, Howard informed battalion HQ that the attack seemed to have ceased, with only light movement heard to his front. But almost at once, from the opposite side of the position, Major Peter Phillips' company was mortared.

The bombs were exploding in the platoons, and Dave Mancer heard one coming down, knew it would be close, and it detonated where he knew 'Dubbo' had his pit. Amid the noise, Mancer called out, asking if he was all right. 'Of course I'm all right. They gotta be more accurate than that!'

Mancer settled back, thinking, 'That's Dubbo, all right.'

0244 D Company to 3RAR HQ: Incoming mortars from north-east corner as before and 60mm mortar from north. No ground attack from this end. Have 1 WIA.

Lieutenant Mick Butler's tanks were in position, cannon covering the expected avenues of approach. He had been relieved from duty in the turret by Trevor Lowe and an infantry soldier from B Company, and had climbed down to the scrapes dug under the tank hull, but not gone to sleep. He

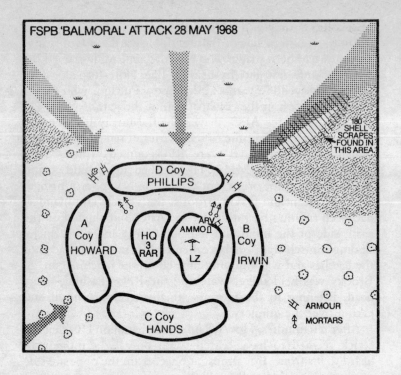

FSPB 'BALMORAL' ATTACK 28 MAY 1968

180 SHELL SCRAPES FOUND IN THIS AREA.

D Coy
PHILLIPS

A Coy
HOWARD

HQ 3 RAR

ARV
AMMO
LZ

B Coy
IRWIN

C Coy
HANDS

ARMOUR

MORTARS

distinctly heard the mortars firing, and training compelled him to count them.

He reached twelve, and thought in quick succession: 'twelve—something's happening ... we do not have twelve tubes ... that is enemy.' Then he told Trooper Gould, his gunner, to wait for the explosions, then climb back into the turret, adding, 'You beat me the other night, this time I'm going to beat you'.

The bombs exploded all around, they were up and on to the turret, Butler jumping through the hatch—on to the shoulders of the infantryman, sitting in the commander's seat. Butler pushed him forward, on to Trevor Lowe, and felt a tap on the head—Gould wanted to get in! Jarvis, the radio operator and loader, was going in through his own hatch.

Butler got back out and sat on his cupola lid as Gould went in headfirst and a Chinese Communist 82mm mortar bomb

270

exploded behind them on the right-hand transmission deck, blowing off the muffler, track guard and other small items, wounding both of them. It was the second salvo detonating all around them.

The normal crew plus two others crammed into the turret and the hatches slammed shut. Trevor Lowe, squeezed behind the cannon, called out not to fire it, 'otherwise I'm a goner!' Lowe and the infantryman crawled under the gun to Jervis' side, the radio was netted-in, and as the mortars moved away, the hatches were opened. Lowe and the infantryman climbed out and dashed to their own tank and pit.

Corporal Britten, in tank 32 Bravo, radioed to Butler that he could see a sapper team of six or seven men with Bangalores at the wire. He fired as a salvo of mortars landed, and the canister round at a range of 40 metres from the tank felled the entire sapper group.

Peter Phillips was impressed with the enemy mortar barrage 'because it was so accurate. We found out later that they had actually crawled up with lengths of string and measured the distance from the base plate position to the target. Not like us, with a few ranging rounds. They had actually measured the distance, to the last bloody centimetre. That was why they got such incredible first round accuracy.'

Spooky was requested and agreed to, as well as artillery flares. C Company reported all quiet, then the APCs radioed that a segment of the fence may have been blown. The activity to the south, in front of Howard, seemed to cease, and then the real attack began from the north.

0301 D Company to 3RAR HQ: No ground attack but troops moving into the area in front. They must be the support element firing RPG.

Major Phillips' D Company was facing out across the expanse of 'golf-course', along which the previous attack had come two nights earlier. It had not really been believed that the NVA would merely repeat their earlier unsuccessful attempt, so only one platoon was actually covering the grassy area, and within the platoon, only one section was positioned

271

to bring fire to bear. The others were prepared and positioned to repel an assault through the bush on the flanks.

The platoon facing the open area was 11, commanded by Mark John. 'The first thing I remember was the mortars hitting us, and that woke us all up. I was just about to stick my head up out of the pit, and the whole side of the sandbag ripped open, when an RPG hit the tree just by me. It wasn't unusual, but I thought to myself. "Oh Christ, this is a bit serious." I wasn't really game to stick my head out until I knew what was going on.'

Dave Mancer and his 4 Section had heard the Bangalores blowing up the wire, and prepared for action to their front. Then the tanks fired canister, the deadly hail of steel pellets clearing the enemy.

Mark John: 'All sorts of stuff was coming over the radio, and I was trying to tell the company what was going on. At that stage, Corporal Mancer appeared, saying words to the effect of, "We need you on the radio, or the radio." I thought it was probably about time I went out and started controlling this thing.'

Not far behind them, in the mortar position, Bill Studley recognised mortars, RPG, machinegun and small arms fire raining into the position, 'louder and more devastating than anything I've experienced before or since. Shrapnel was whistling everywhere and tree branches were disintegrating; most of the enemy fire was high. The tanks and D Company were firing, and our own fire missions came in thick and fast.'

When he put his head up to shout orders to the mortar crews, he saw 'a mass of tracer and flashes; the whistling and cracking was deafening.'

Very quickly, the artillery flares were lighting the area, then Spooky arrived, followed by helicopter gunships. The NVA, using the B52 bomb craters as cover, were firing both at the ground position and the circling aircraft.

The 3RAR Operations Log shows the intense activity:

0332 D Company to HQ: On north-east corner of B52 crater at least six VC there, to right, one VC firing RPG at tank.

0332 B Company to HQ: Continual fire from HMG at aircraft.
0333 B Company to HQ: Miniguns firing into our area.
0333 Pioneers to HQ: Took burst of fire from miniguns into our positions.
0336 tanks to HQ: Would like illumination into our area; I think they are trying to blow wire to our front and the attack to come in from there.
0337 B Company to tank 32: Enemy in crater to your front.
0339: tanks to HQ: Light Fire Team to come across clearing from our side.
0340 B Company to HQ: Aircraft receiving small arms fire from crater in north-east.
0341 D Company to HQ: Light Fire Team move further to east, that is, continue further to the east.
0343 A Company to HQ: 1000 metres [away] small arms firing at helicopter.
0344 tanks to HQ: Light Fire Team are on to the bloke; throwing lead at him, if they come to the west they will have him.
0345 D Company to HQ: Enemy MG in crater 50 metres north-east of my location firing at Light Fire Team.
0346 tanks to HQ: Back vehicles are illuminating area into which Light Fire Team should engage.

While all this was going on, the tanks and infantry of Phillips' company were firing at the enemy seen in the large clearing, and artillery was being called in.

Compatibility of infantry–tank radios was a problem solved by using extra sets. Behind his commander's cupola, Mick Butler had two extra PRC25s, giving him a total of four: one on the tank squadron net, one to 3RAR HQ, and one each to B and D Companies, the infantry units to either side of his Centurion.

Butler and the tank crews 'could see the enemy quite clearly. We had no problems illuminating them. I remember shooting with my .30cal machinegun at enemy on the wire. There was one pair trying to haul away wounded comrades.'

Once again the main thrust of the NVA attack was coming along the sides of the tongues of bush, from the north-east and north-west, in the exposed open ground. When flares

273

ignited, Dave Mancer's section had a clear view, particularly from the machinegun position, and soon ammunition was being supplied to it from nearby pits.

He lost count of the number of rounds, knowing only that it was 'thousands', including that from the other pits nearby. Like the others, he was impressed by the amount of support from artillery and air, as well as the effect of the tanks.

'If they'd got through that wire,' he recalled, 'and we didn't have that tank there, it would have been a completely different story for our platoon.' For him, the night's combat was the most intense of the tour, like 'looking death in the eyes'.

Paul Donnelly was the machinegunner. The M60 was firing continuously, and it was not designed for such work. Its original form was as the German MG42, and it had been produced in its present form by US designers, who could not be satisfied with simply reproducing a foreign weapon. It was generally agreed that the older German weapon would have been superior. (In later years, a West German design for a standard NATO machinegun was entered into a competition with the stipulation that if it was selected, it would be produced as it was, and the US Research and Development organisations be prohibited any work on it.)

Despite the ground activity, the US Dustoff crews flew in to lift out the casualties, and Mick Butler, in his tank, has clear memories of the helicopters coming in to land, through a hail of green tracer, with their reference point a torch held by a soldier from 3RAR. Most of these casualties were men who had been asleep above ground when the initial mortar bombardment began.

It was agreed that the tanks and infantry would fire at maximum rate, a 'mad minute', to the north-west, north and north-east, while the positions on the southern side of the perimeter would hold their fire, thus creating a 'safe' route into the landing zone for the helicopter. It would also take-off and fly away to the south, over the 'no-fire' alley.

As the waves of the NVA were shattered by the blizzard of fire, many of them were driven into the B52 bomb craters to escape the bullets and shrapnel. Mark John was eventually outside the pits, radioing corrections to the mortars, trying to bring the falling bombs into the craters. Next day he was reprimanded for trying to adjust the fall of mortars by 25 metres, too small a correction.

Bill Studley was relaying the orders to the mortar crews, and as the bombs were being called in closer and closer to Mark John's positions, he did something he had not done before, or since: removed the centre screw in the plotting board to enable bombs to be dropped the extra ten metres requested. It was obvious to him that the bombs were falling very close to, or in, the perimeter; the mortars were firing almost straight up, and the noise of the explosions was deafening.

When nothing seemed to be working to clean out the groups in the bomb craters, Corporal Mancer went forward, alone, with grenades. Mark John saw him 'down there, throwing grenades into it, at the height of it all. He was absolutely mad.'

From his vantage point up in the tank turret, Mick Butler also tried to call in the mortars, but the range was too short for accurate high-trajectory firing. Then helicopter gunships were tried, and they 'provoked quite a reaction. The 12.7s opened up on them. We were trying to guide the gunships on to targets to my front, and the NVA team had got themselves into a crater. Finally, we asked the gunship to fly by, and laid two tank cannon on the spot. Bruce Richards, of the APCs with 3RAR, said he could see them and so could a machine-gun from B Company 3RAR. The next time the helicopter flew by and this fellow opened up, two tanks, two APCs and two M60s, and some others, all had a mad minute in the direction of this fellow and he didn't open up again.

'Next day they found the remains of the machinegun, but no bodies.'

Howard's A Company, in the south, was waiting for any attack through the bush into their position. From the far side of the position, they could hear the noise of mortars, RPGs, tank cannon and .50cal machineguns, small arms and grenades.

Not sure of what was happening behind him, but confident

that no real threat was posed to his own front, Howard turned his rear platoon around, preparing it for a break-through by the enemy from that direction, or to be used as a counter-attack force if need be.

His artillery Forward Observer called him over, saying he would not hear anything like it for a long time: on the radio they could hear the massive Corps artillery around Bien Hoa firing on the orders of the 161 Battery commander.

At one time, during a pause in the illumination, Bruce Richards, in his APC, radioed that he could see a couple of enemy on the wire outside B Company, Mick Butler scanned the area, but could not sight them, and Richards opened fire. The figures were still there, so Richards fired again, and again, then the lights revealed he had been hammering a cluster of star pickets.

David Brooks had also been trying to see these 'enemy', but could not, and still laughs at the memory of the riddled star pickets. Such are the anecdotes of night-fighting.

C Company were aware of movement to their front, this time enough to call in a close artillery salvo, but little else of note occurred. The platoons watched and waited.

Further inside, around the battalion CP, the defending platoons of Support Company again had to sit under the mortar bombardment, which Wayne Meech, in the Assault Pioneers, thought was more accurate. For the other soldiers like him, the actions at Balmoral were not only frightening, but frustrating, as they were not busy, firing or calling down fire, but were forced to wait while the action went on around them. So they endured the incoming rounds, with orders not to fire unless fired upon, listening and peering in the frag-mented flare-light as the wounded were brought back to the aid post.

Marking targets for the circling aircraft had been a prob-lem, and it was decided to try the .50cal machinegun which was coaxial to the tank's twenty-pounder cannon. This machinegun was used to find the range to the target, as its rounds were white phosphorus and gave off a white puff when they hit; as soon as puffs were seen on the target, the main armament was fired and the round flew to the same point at 3750 feet (1140 metres) per second. At night, the .50cal spotting round gave off a brilliant greenish flash, and this was easily seen from above. So the .50cal was fired in bursts of three to indicate to the pilots where targets lay.

Mick Butler thought he knew the NVA mortar baseplate position, and also the mortar observer's location, in a tall tree, some 800 to 900 metres across the clearing. He decided to fire some armour-piercing rounds at the tree, as his high-explosive rounds had been expended, and this seemed to have some effect. Even the noise of a twenty-pound projectile crashing through the shrubbery at 3750 feet per second, sounding like an express train roaring by, must have been frightening.

It fell to Trevor Lowe to control the artillery fire on to the mortar position, and he gave his corrections to Mick Butler, who passed them on, thinking that they had what amounted to a Divisional fire mission being 'marched across the countryside' searching for the mortars, directed by a mere 'corporal of tank'.

Butler, looking around from his tank turret cupola, was busy talking to the rifle companies, co-ordinating the tank fire, keeping Lieutenant Colonel Jim Shelton briefed, keeping Major Peter Badman (at Coral) briefed, as well as using his commander's .30cal machinegun. Butler appreciated the Badman trait of allowing him to 'get on with the battle, and every hour or so would ask for a sitrep'.

The hail of RPG rockets persisted, and one struck the top of the earth bund in front of Butler's tank. Most of the force and molten jet was dissipated, only minor pitting being caused to the gun mantlet. If the rocket had flown a little higher, the full force of the missile would have penetrated the mantlet and wrought havoc among the turret crew, and possibly the ammunition.

Not all the artillery was falling exactly where it was called for, and on one occasion Mick Butler saw 'a blinding flash and enormous concussion' from a salvo arriving just in front of his tanks. Later he was told that there had been an error of 1000 mils in laying a distant battery of 155mm guns, for a battery fire mission.

277

As the battle waxed and waned and waxed again, the tank crews were able to enjoy some of the amenities of their big vehicles. They were able to smoke—Mick Butler used a packet of cigarettes during the hours—and make coffee, while the irrepressible spirits (Dyson) told jokes. Having a searchlight, three machineguns and a cannon, they were not particularly worried by the outcome, especially when the enemy were seen to be repeating their previous effort, and being slaughtered in the open ground.

However, Butler was aware that if the NVA had got through the wire, and on to the tanks, then things might have been very different, particularly as the Centurion used petrol. It would not have taken much investigation of the huge vehicles by the enemy to realise what catastrophic fires could be ignited. A hundred gallons were carried in an external tank mounted on the rear of the tank hull.

Now, in the 3RAR companies, the unremitting insistence on keeping all weapons clean, and really in operating condition, paid off. Paul Donnelly's M60 fired and kept on firing throughout the action. Mark John: 'We never had any problems with our guns because we had people who were really dedicated to keeping them clean. The M60's quite a good weapon for that sort of thing. It certainly came into its own. We could just sit there and let her rip. During the night we had to pull ammunition from other sections to keep the gun going, and we got ammunition from Company Head-quarters.'

However, it was not as simple as that. Donnelly and his No. 2 were forced to get the spare barrel from a neighbouring gun, to try to cool the very hot barrels on their own by pissing on them (urinating is too sedate a term for the situation); they were using the bolt from the other gun; they developed their own drill for clearing the stoppages: Donnelly would simply cock the gun, then swing it around, loaded, to point at the No. 2, who had the cleaning rod ready, which he shoved down the barrel and slammed to punch out the shell-case, whipped out the rod, Donnelly swung back and went on firing . . .

Peter Phillips was 'particularly concerned about my CSM,

Lofty Eiby, who showed tremendous courage getting ammunition out and casualties back. It's lovely sitting back in a command post directing fire and so on, but bloody hard when you've actually got to scrabble through the bush in the dark and get ammunition up, and casualties back to the aid post.'

The attack petered out, and much effort was devoted to wiping out the pockets of NVA in the craters. Some continued to fire into the position and at the aircraft, others tried to carry away the wounded and dead, and yet other groups began to withdraw. Sensibly, the NVA waited until the flare light flickered out, then made dashes from cover to cover in the darkness.

Those in the craters must have been concerned when they realised that time was passing, daylight was approaching inexorably, and they had to find cover of some sort or be obliterated. For many of the young NVA, experiencing battle for the first time, reality must have been sobering. The speeches by the Political Officers, and the exploits of the heroes they were to emulate, evaporated, and were replaced by two facts: immediate survival meant staying quietly in the crater; longer term survival depended on safely leaving the expanse of grass and getting into the distant bush.

At about 0540 more NVA mortars began falling along the 3RAR frontage, and, apparently acting on a red flare as signal, the groups in the clearing and along its edges tried to withdraw. A hail of fire was directed at them. Some were seen crawling away from the wire fences, where they may have been waiting for quite a time.

As dawn approached, Mick Butler offered to take two tanks out of the perimeter and sweep the clear grassy area, rather than risk the unprotected infantry soldiers. Lieutenant Colonel Shelton agreed to what Dave Candow called 'let the tanks have a run'. So when the gunner was able to discern targets by natural light, the wire defences were shot away with canister and Butler and Lowe moved forward. At about 0627 they pushed the remaining wire aside with the heavy gun barrel and rolled out among the craters. They turned left and began to check the battlefield.

An NVA soldier stood up in front of Trevor Lowe's tank, calling 'Chieu Hoi', and Lowe repeated the words. Then the enemy quickly grabbed a grenade, but without waiting for an order, Lowe's gunner, looking through his sight, saw it, and fired the .30cal machinegun, knocking down the Vietnamese.

No one else seemed to be moving, so they radioed that all the NVA seemed to be dead, and offered to clear the entire open space. This was accepted, and the two Centurions, with cannon pointing to the tree line, rumbled around the edges of the 'golf-course'. It can only be imagined how many NVA were in the shadows, watching ... but nothing happened.

As soon as a clearing patrol from 3RAR began to walk out to search the bodies, small arms fire came from the enemy 'dead'. Rather than risk useless casualties, the patrol was withdrawn and the tanks gave the battlefield a closer inspection. A few live enemy were killed, and Mick Butler realised that the only way to thoroughly check the field was to fire at each corpse.

However, Dave Mancer's section went out and began checking the bodies. With them, in direct disobedience of his commanding officer's orders, was the Medical Officer of 3RAR, Dr Dick Lippett. Mancer was leading his troops, 'happened to look around, and there was Doctor Dick. Nothing strange; he's come to look for enemy wounded.'

Butler's tank was a few metres from a B52 crater, which was littered with NVA dead and wounded. Lippett was at the edge of the crater, examining a wounded enemy, when Butler noticed another NVA bring his right hand out from under his body, and raise it to throw something—grenade or RPG igniter—and Butler called a warning to Lippett, who looked up and stepped back as there was an explosion and Lippett fell, wounded, as fire from several points slammed into the NVA.

It seemed that was the signal for more firing from around the field, and the infantry withdrew again, with the wounded doctor, while Butler and Lowe began to fire at each body. Then, Butler thought it 'was absolute magic! The dead NVA started to come alive. We ended up rounding up seven wounded prisoners, people we thought were dead.

'One fellow was walking towards me with his hands behind the back of his head. I was acutely aware of my own head sticking up above the turret, among all these bodies, and I had the feeling I was naked, that I was going to get a bullet in the back of the head from one of these NVA who was playing possum.

'I remembered Gerry McCormack telling me of the problem he had two days earlier in the bunker contact with Tony Hammett's company, when a fellow had come to give himself up, hands behind his head, then pulled out a pistol and squeezed off a couple of shots at McCormack. I wasn't going to let this bugger do it to me.

'I put my hands out to say, "Stop, don't come any closer", but he kept walking and I thought, "How do you get him to stop? I don't know the lingo." All of a sudden, a scene from a movie struck me, and with my machinegun I fired a burst two or three metres in front of him. He thought that was it, that I was going to shoot him. He fell to his knees and started pleading.

'I wasn't going to shoot him unless I had to, but I wasn't going to let him get close enough to shoot or throw a grenade. It had the desired effect and stopped him.'

When the other wounded saw they were not going to be killed, they got up. By using hand signals, Butler and Lowe herded the seven into a group, and the infantry came out and collected them. All were wounded and some had to be helped along.

Dave Mancer, meanwhile, thought he would be blamed for the wounding of Dr Lippett, but later Lippett wrote and explained he should not have been out there. No one blamed Mancer. Like everyone else in 3RAR, he had a high opinion of Lippett: 'A very genuine fellow, Doctor Dick, and I had a lot of time for him. One of those fellows who spoke our language.'

Dr Dick Lippett died a few days before Anzac Day 1986. Jim Shelton wrote of him: 'Dick Lippett was not a conventional Regimental Medical Officer. He believed he had the discretion to leave his Regimental Aid Post to seek out wounded. The more dangerous a situation, the more he felt compelled to get himself involved. There is only one doctor in an infantry battalion, so 900 soldiers depended on my ability to keep Dick out of trouble. But I also had to satisfy Dick's conscience. Dick did not see his action at Balmoral as "direct disobedience"—he felt it was his duty. You do not throw the book at a man like that. He earned his Infantry Combat Badge the hard way, and that is how he is remembered in 3RAR.'

From the mortar position to the rear of D Company, Bill Studley was able to see through the trees, out across the clearing, and 'it was a strange sight to see Centurion tanks pulling up cautiously to a crater, depress the gun barrel as low as possible, and in some cases, a little figure with hands up popping out of the crater.'

By now, the adrenalin had begun to wear off, and the resultant tiredness seeped into Butler and his men. From his turret four metres above the ground, Butler looked down on the enemy dead: '. . . a bit of a shock to me. Then I took a real good look at the enemy. It was hard for me to look at them. They were so mutilated. The canister round—550 cylindrical pellets—makes a mess of a man. We had been using the .50cal as a back-up whenever the .30cal was being oiled or a new belt was being fed in, and the .50cal projectile exploded when it hit something.

'The thing that struck me was the devastation these rounds caused and I found it very difficult to look at the enemy dead. I had no hatred for them, or anything like that, and in some way I felt ashamed that we'd done what we did. The bodies were in grotesque shapes and positions, chunks missing, some smouldering, probably from the white phosphorus .50cal round. Such devastation.

'It affects different people in different ways. The infantry pulled this body over; as they pulled the top of the skull fell off and the brains fell out, and this soldier made a joke of it. I tend to think this is a shock reaction to the devastation and what they had just been through. I never heard anyone make a joke like that in my whole time there [in Vietnam].

'The other thing that struck me about the NVA was that every second man carried an RPG, and almost everyone carried one or two projectiles for it. It was incredible, the number of RPGs and projectiles lying around. Prisoners said the allocation was standard, that there had been no increase to cope with armour. They did not know the tanks were there.'

Peter Phillips also was affected by the NVA casualties. 'They were young conscripts, and we saw a lot of them subsequently. I think it's rather sad they were manipulated in the way they were. It's sad to see young fellows used as cannon fodder. Certainly, we would never consider pressing an attack under the circumstances that they did.

'I understand their aim was to divert attention away from infiltration in and out of Saigon, but to waste all that young manpower seemed to me to be criminal ... It's a measure, I guess, of their skill, that they were able to indoctrinate these young kids. I never saw the grey eminences who were directing them; we only saw the young kids who were captured and wounded and so on.'

Many other Australians were similarly saddened by the sight, and also noticed the large number of RPGs carried. Geoff Murray also was interested in the variety of weapons from the Communist bloc: particularly the number of Chinese, Russian and Czech AK47s, RPDs and RPGs. Many of the Australians commented on the newness of the weapons; some had obviously never been fired.

Some of the younger Diggers had a different perspective on the events. In A Company's 2 Platoon, Howard noticed one of the young National Servicemen who had returned from leave in time for the battle. He asked the Digger how he was, to be told that 'I had my first naughty on R and R, and not been killed in the battle, so I guess I'm all right.'

Dave Mancer, who had been at the centre of things, 'felt a sense of achievement. I can never speak highly enough of that section I had. I tried not to be one of those corporals who ruled. I tried leading by example.'

Nineteen-year-old Wayne Meech, the Assault Pioneer, was not deeply affected by the sight of the enemy casualties. To him, service in Vietnam was much like hunting. The mass graves of the NVA killed did remind him of documentaries of World War II, and he thought the front of D Company was 'like a scene from a movie—the concentration of craters which the NVA had used for cover'.

While passing through the centre of the battalion position, Meech saw two of the prisoners, and was struck by the youth of one. He 'was very young, much younger than I, the other was much older and tougher, a mean-looking guy. But this young bloke—I just stopped and stared at him, fascinated by his youth, wondering why in hell he was caught up in this sort of business.' One of the battalion interpreters began asking questions of the young NVA, but 'the older guy became aggressive, and started kicking at the younger guy', and Meech was surprised at the older man's attitude, though a prisoner.

Bill Studley also noticed the youth of the prisoners, and that they seemed 'dazed, like frightened sheep'.

Re-examining the events of the night, Mick Butler believed the NVA used the treeline to cover their approach to the 3RAR position, then swung the attacking platoons out from the trees, like a gate, into assault formation, as they reached the attacking position. About 180 pits were found on the B Company side of the clearing.

The enemy were dressed in khaki, some in long trousers, some in shorts, with simple webbing equipment to carry their weapons and ammunition, a waterbottle, and little else. Some had pith helmets, others had bush hats similar to the Australian issue. Compared to the southern Vietnamese, these northerners were taller, larger framed, with lighter skin. It was found that the average age of the attacking battalions was 16 or 17, and that 15-year-olds were beginning to be drafted in the North. Political and military necessity forced Hanoi to draft youths of that age, but even in the West it has been found that the best assault troops are males in their teens. Military exploits and battle honours achieved by elite units such as the marines, airborne, commandos and Germanic units of the Waffen-SS were won by battalions and regiments with an average age of 19 or less.

One VC, in his black clothes, was noticeable among the differently dressed NVA. Possibly he was one of the battlefield clearance detachments.

Despite being wounded at the beginning of the attack, Bob Gould, gunner in Mick Butler's crew, had fought on for some five hours, and was finally evacuated when the medics had time to examine him. He spent two weeks in the US hospital at Long Binh, then rejoined the unit.

With the tanks back in their daylight hide positions, and breakfast, shaving, et cetera in progress, Mick Butler produced the bottle of rum he carried. For the first and only time, it was emptied, by generous dollops into the morning brew of each tank crew.

In daylight, and in retrospect, Butler thought that the battalion position could well have been penetrated by the enemy, but for the decisive effect of the tank canister fire across the open area, into the faces of the assaulting NVA platoons. Without it, the masses of enemy may well have forced their way into the interior of 3RAR, negating the advantage of air, artillery and mortar support available to the Australians, and involving them in vicious close-quarter night fighting in the trees and scrub.

Certainly many more casualties would have been inflicted on 3RAR. A reinforcement or relief operation would have been difficult to execute, given the limited amount of infantry, armour and helicopter troop lift support available to 1ATF, with Coral requiring defence as well. Almost surely, a helicopter landing or armoured thrust with APCs would have been met by NVA either pre-positioned or moved to counter them.

However, this is speculation, and the known facts are that 3RAR was experienced, in a strong co-ordinated position, with a great weight of artillery and air support available. The NVA showed themselves to be inflexible, and made little use of the advantage offered them by the trees and growth.

Jim Shelton went up in the Sioux helicopter, and below them saw the mass of NVA shell scrapes, 'beautifully dug, right where the DF was tasked, a couple of hundred metres out'. The high explosive had arrived exactly on the NVA preparing to go into the attack.

After the bodies had been searched and stripped of weapons, equipment and documents, there was what Peter

Phillips recalled as 'the dreadful business of all those dead mangled NVA, from our artillery defensive fire concentrations; scooping them up on the end of a bulldozer and burying them. It was rather sad, but there was no other way we could deal with the large numbers in that situation.'

The M60 machinegun used by Paul Donnelly was deemed useless. The constant firing had worn it out. It had consumed 5000 rounds in something like three hours. The barrels had sagged; the machining at the breech end had changed beyond acceptable standards; the bolt was worn; the weapon itself was finished.

As Operations Officer, David Candow also regarded the battles as an opportunity to increase knowledge of the enemy. He thought they had shown themselves to be 'predictable. They showed a lack of imagination and flexibility. They didn't do a close enough recce. They knew where we were, but not who we were or what we were. They got quite a surprise when they came up against a battalion defensive position. I've got a feeling they thought we were a company, or a bit more, and they could knock us off easily.'

To replace the wounded Lippett, Neville O'Connor was sent from Coral, arriving at about 1000, taking over as medical officer.

Jim Shelton began planning company-sized patrols out from the perimeter, to harass and discomfit the enemy. 3RAR was going to dominate the surrounds, and seek out the VC and NVA.

After the second attack on Balmoral, during a rainy night, Colonel Dunstan was sitting in the CP at Coral, 'with water running down the back of my neck, the phone rang, and someone from Saigon said they had the White House on the line. The President wanted to know the name of the battalion commander at Balmoral, and the name of the doctor.'

The information was duly given, and Dunstan realised that this call was to get detailed information for the meeting between President Johnson and Prime Minister Gorton. (When Gorton later came to Nui Dat, Dunstan asked how the meeting had gone, and Gorton told him that before going in to see Johnson, he had asked the White House staff what the President had been told recently that Gorton might not know; they told him, and he went in to meet Johnson.)

On the 29th C/1RAR, with 2 Troop 3 Cav, moved south, looking for the HQ of 7 NVA Div. Nothing was found, but next day Campbell's company was to encounter all the Vietnamese they could wish for.

Also on the 29th people were told at O Groups that they would be leaving Coral on 6 June; the operation had achieved its aims.

Close to the relatively simple life led by the infantry, the tank squadron members were struggling to keep their vehicles operational in the muddy wet conditions, at the end of a nebulous supply line in which all air transport had to be requested from non-Army sources, either the RAAF or the Americans.

Bernie Sullivan, the Technical Officer, had a favourite saying: 'the British positioned the crew and the critical items, like the gun and engine, and built the tank around them'. He adds, 'Nothing was easy, and an engine change was no simple task. Before going to Vietnam, if a tank needed an engine change, it went into workshops and you didn't see it for a fortnight.'

However, actually on operations, no one wanted to have an immobilised tank for any reason, so at Coral, working in the mud and slush, under canvas at night to prevent light showing, Bill Burton's crew, working in conjunction with a team from 106 Field Workshops, achieved a record: an engine change in ten hours. This is something that can only be appreciated by those who have worked on the Centurion.

Of course, working in the conditions at Coral, with the constant shortage of water, meant one showered when one could, and people tried to take advantage of the rain, using a canvas or hutchi to collect and funnel water. But the tropical rainstorms often end as quickly as they have started, and more than one Aussie found himself all soaped up, but the rain had stopped ...

The rains turned the dust to mud, and the sun reversed the

process, but as the wet season really began, the mud lasted longer, and was churned by the constant passage of vehicles. Bernie Sullivan asked his wife to send a pair of gumboots, which he wore in company with a pair of shorts and a beret. The soldiers quickly changed his radio callsign from '39 Charlie' to '39 Gumboots', and years later, when leaving the Armoured Centre, he was ceremoniously presented, in the Sergeants' Mess, with a pair of gumboots and a towel.

By this time, the enemy had been forced to swing away from the bases, flowing north, west and south of them.

It was becoming obvious that the May offensive had been broken, that they were no longer seeking ARVN or allied units to do battle, and the NVA intention of attacking Saigon had been thwarted at great cost to themselves.

But while they may have been wary of contact in the area of Coral and Balmoral, those who were found were often willing to fight, and if they perceived that the tactical advantage was theirs, grabbed the opportunity with both hands, as Digger Campbell and his company were to find next day.

12 Centurion Salvation

*'tis true that we are in great danger; the
greater therefore should our courage be.*
King Henry *(IV. i.)*

BY THIS TIME, the new-found popularity of the tanks had
resulted in a need for maintenance as a result of the daily
patrolling. Gerry McCormack's 1 Troop, at Coral, required,
in his words, 'some fairly major servicing. Spark plugs had to
be taken out, filters and fan belts changed, and it was decreed
we would have a day set aside for this. It just so happened
that was the day Major Digger Campbell's C Company
[1RAR] was heading off on a patrol.

'Now, Digger Campbell was an instructor at Duntroon
when I was there, and a very popular instructor he was.
Young, fit, and very aggressive, a captain, cheery personality, magnificent smile and kind word, he appeared as a ray of
sanity when everything else seemed to be going mad. He was
held in high regard by all of us at Duntroon about that stage.
I was very disappointed that he was going out on patrol
and I wasn't going to be able to go with him, for two
reasons.

'Firstly, [I wanted] just to go on operations with him, but
secondly, he was going to an area where we all reckoned
there were likely to be lots of NVA. Anyway, he was to go;
nothing could be done. Even so, I would not pull all four
tanks down at the same time. I decided to take one down
at a time, and use the whole day, so we would have at least
three tanks ready, and the squadron commander said we
could probably take one from his headquarters if we were
scrambled.'

So while Campbell's infantry were moving out, McCormack's men were working on the Centurions.

At his Orders Group the day before, Campbell had gone into detail about the aspect of 'marrying-up' with the tanks, and infantry–tank communications. Then, next morning, he was told they were not available due to the need for servicing, and was 'feeling almost quite let down. I was looking forward to having that direct fire support'.

His platoons climbed aboard the APCs and were carried away to the edge of the thick jungle which they were to search. He dismounted his soldiers with something of a sense of relief, as while travelling in APCs he 'always felt somewhat a prisoner, not in control of what was happening'.

The armoured vehicles turned back, and the infantry filtered into the green mass before them.

At 0840, 9 Platoon made contact with three enemy, then almost at once were fired on by several weapons in a bunker complex. The leading section was pinned down by the hail of fire.

When the heavy fire lashed the jungle, Sergeant Phil Thompson, the MFC, dived head-first into a nearby empty trench, closely followed by the medic, Doc Clarke. But Clarke was caught around the waist by his webbing, and decided to climb out. Thompson simultaneously tried to help him into the pit by pulling on his legs, and Doc thought he was being torn in two, finally deciding to lie flat along the ground, leaving his legs in the pit.

Campbell sent 7 Platoon to the left, to assault and clear the front of 9 Platoon, but 7 itself was heavily engaged. Bullets and RPGs lashed and shattered the shrubbery and trees.

Murphy's Law exerted itself, and Campbell had communications problems with 1RAR HQ. He tried to use the mortar radio to talk to 1RAR, and at one stage found himself and Phil Thompson 'doing a circus act scampering around an anthill' trying to seek cover but be able to retain contact with 1RAR.

At 0855 small arms and RPG fire from the aggressive enemy was pouring across the company, then mortar fire began falling among the Australians, crumping and slamming among the Diggers. Sergeant Major Wally Thompson said to Phil Thompson, with a questioning note, 'Those bloody mortars; we're not firing mortars,' to which Phil replied, 'No, that's their mortars.'

Campbell was trying to get his platoons into a circle, as the enemy were 'moving freely around us', and he decided to stay in the trees, where there would be some cover, rather than pull back to the edge of the open area they had crossed in the APCs. Soon the NVA were firing from all around the company. Campbell thought that the enemy had seen his arrival, pulled back their sentries and waited for his company to walk into the bunker system.

1RAR was keeping 1ATF informed of the action.
0855: C Company being mortared, and request Light Fire Team.
0903: C Company being mortared again.

The fighting was at such close range that artillery and mortar fire from Coral was falling very near, and two Aussies were wounded by it. The NVA had achieved one of their constant aims in such combat, having both sides in such proximity that the superior weight of allied firepower could not be used.

The thick jungle and nearness of enemy made it hard to identify the friendly position for the helicopter gunships which arrived overhead; their radio callsign was 'Playboy 13'. The call to 'throw smoke' for the forward platoons resulted in RPGs whistling in at the spot, and a call to 'throw again' got a 'not on your life!'

0912 TF Forward to Nui Dat: Contact with C/1RAR is much larger than expected. They have been mortared twice now. LFT and airstrike now going in.

Lieutenant Colonel Bennett realised Campbell needed fast, decisive assistance which could best be provided by tanks, so he rang Colonel Dunstan and alerted him to the situation.

At 0915 Campbell asked by radio for armoured support, and at Coral the tanks were called. Dustoff was also called for two wounded.

0921: Major Keldie's A Squadron reported that it had a

troop ready to move in three minutes if required.

0930: Jade FAC requested clearance for airstrike on GR 965348.
0935 1RAR to TF: 7 Platoon completely pinned down and contact
very close.
0937 1RAR to TF: C Company advises enemy closing in on right
rear.

Colonel Dunstan radioed Major Badman, and told him to
send the tanks out to Campbell, to which Badman replied
that they did not operate in less than troop strength, and not
all the troop was ready. Dunstan told him to send what he
had.

Gerry McCormack was alerted to go out to the contact.
Sergeant Nev Callis' tank was non-operational, but McCormack moved out with the other three: his own and his two
corporals, Bill Burton and Sleepy Tregenza, followed by the
ARV and fitters' M113, which were commanded by Sergeant
Peter De Jong. Passing through the perimeter, he looked
around to see Bill Burton waving his arms, signalling that his
radios had failed, so reducing the troop to two fighting
vehicles. It would have been useless to go into action with no
communication.

McCormack radioed squadron headquarters of his situation, and Sergeant Phil Reeves came forward with his tank
from squadron headquarters. The small unit rolled on, but a
short distance later, Sleepy Tregenza ground to a halt, having
lost engine power.

McCormack was down to two tanks and two RAEME
vehicles. Peter Badman, from squadron headquarters, called
to ask if he wanted to continue. The reply was, '"Most certainly," because I knew we could get out there and do something that would upset the NVA, and besides, it was Digger
Campbell in a bit of trouble.'

At 0945 C Squadron informed TF HQ that McCormack
was departing for C Company's location.

Diverted from another task in the 3RAR AO, Peter Spoor
flew his Sioux helicopter to the scene. His Corps was Armour, but he had not seen a Centurion until Vietnam, and it

was 'a very impressive sight to see the armour charging across the paddy fields to get to the area'.

Gerry McCormack arrived at the spot where the APCs had dropped Campbell's men at the same time as the APCs themselves returned there. The jungle was thicker than any previously entered by the armoured vehicles, but the APCs said they would lead the way in to the contact.

It soon became obvious that the lighter M113s were being held up by the jungle growth. While watching one APC trying to get through, but finding itself pushed up on the bushes which would not break, and with the machine about half a metre off the ground and climbing higher, McCormack radioed that he would break the trail. He called Sergeant Reeves up abreast, and the two Centurions went around the M113s, forward to the sound of battle.

Meanwhile, in the restricted visibility and clamour of the close-quarter contact, now almost all around him, Digger Campbell 'still did not know what we were up against. The complex was fully occupied, the enemy certainly had mobility through the trenches. My main concern was to get proper control of the company.' 7 and 9 Platoons were still held by the heavy fire from the bunkers.

At 1018, in his Centurion tank, Gerry McCormack 'got to where the firing was, and it all looked pretty confusing. I tried to flick my secondary radio on to the infantry company radio net, but the frequencies weren't compatible, so I had to put a main set—the squadron command net—on to theirs; this caused a bit of delay.'

The embattled platoons knew the tanks were closing, and McCormack knew he was near them; he did not want to run over anyone friendly, but did not know exactly where he would see the first Aussies . . .

McCormack was carefully looking out, past his machine-gun, and 'we'd gone about thirty or forty metres into the scrub, when I saw a man in green jump up in front of me and wave his arms. It was a section corporal telling me to stop, two of his wounded men were on the ground right in front of the tank, and as he stood up talking a burst of machinegun fire came through and he dived to the ground.

293

'We decided the simplest thing was to edge forward until the driver could see them, then without the corporal having to stand and show himself again, we would go around the wounded. We did this, stopping in front of the casualties, who then were able to be picked up and put into the APCs.

'We had clearance to fire, and I was giving orders to Sergeant Reeves—on my left—to fire to his front left; I'd fire to my front right; and then both together into the centre, clear the scrub and then we'd pick out the bunkers. All of a sudden, two or three NVA on the other side of the clearing jumped up and started running towards us. I was looking down, trying to work out why the radio wasn't working, and as these fellows came forward they fired an RPG which scared the daylights out of everybody, themselves included, as it went off in the trees just in front of us. Reeves fired and killed them.

'We then cleared the bunkers which were obvious, and went forward, at which stage a burst of machinegun fire right alongside scared me, and I asked Reeves to cover to the front while I found out what the hell was going on. At first I thought it was our infantry firing, but over the radio was told it wasn't, it was an enemy right about where I was. I asked the infantry if they could see where it was coming from, and they said, "You are sitting on it."'

'We'd been so careful about getting forward of our infantry casualties that we'd actually straddled an enemy pit, and when we moved sideways to deal with the fellows who came running with an RPG, we'd released part of the entrance to their bunker. We couldn't reverse off, because we still had the casualties behind us.

'I picked two handgrenades out of the inside of the turret, and by a bit of judicious poking my head over, found out where the devil he was, then positioned the tank so I could just drop them over the side. They went into the pit, and that silenced the machinegun.'

1035 1RAR to TF: OC is calling back C Company and wants airstrike. 7 Platoon are tied down but as soon as possible will pull back 500 metres, then airstrike and gunfire team will take over.

Circling above the battle, Peter Spoor in his Sioux had watched the tanks swallowed up by the thick growth of vegetation, but then 'in a few minutes you could see the jungle being laid down by the tanks' canister—whole swathes being levelled out.'

On the ground below him, the soldiers were well aware of the value of the Centurions. In Doc Clarke's opinion they 'changed the situation dramatically. As they came to each bunker, they were just dropping the barrel of the gun and firing at point-blank range.'

But Digger Campbell, commanding the company, doubted that the initiative had been regained, even with the tanks. The enemy were still firing and manoeuvring around the Aussies. Even though eight bunkers had been destroyed in front of 7 Platoon, the size of the complex was unknown, and 9 Platoon was still under fire.

It was no mean feat, in the conditions of thick jungle, close contact, uninterrupted enemy fire, ceaseless noise, with casualties to be removed almost under the noses of the NVA, and everyone to be accounted for, to break contact and move away from the bunker complex. Keeping the APCs to the rear, as a reserve, Campbell pulled his platoons back.

There was a bit of a delay until the last man was located—Private Barry Herkins, a platoon medic, was temporarily lost in the jungle, but found his way back.

1050 TF Forward to Nui Dat: C Company in heavy contact and are pinned down. Have sent A Company 1RAR plus troop of tanks and troop of APCs to assist. Contact continues; unable to extract C Company at this time.

An NVA managed to get close enough to fire an RPG at the M113 into which the wounded were being loaded. Doc Clarke saw the explosion of the rocket, which 'pierced the side of the APC. Fortunately it had four or five jerrycans of water strapped to the inside and they took the full force of the rocket. The tailgate dropped and the people inside spilled out, totally deafened, not knowing what was happening. Fortunately there were no severe injuries and in a few days they all got over the deafness and concussion. They had to be lucky guys.'

Gerry McCormack, just in front of the APC, was also impressed by the way everyone remained 'very quiet and getting on with their business as if they had been at the Puckapunyal range, and something had gone wrong with the practice', despite the spattered water, smell, dust and smoke.

McCormack was shifting his tank around the edge of the clearing, trying to widen it a little, when he heard the distinctive woka-woka sound of Huey helicopters. Over the tank squadron frequency came a Texas accent, 'Say, Aussie tanks, this is Playboy 13. Where do you want me?'

McCormack told the gunship commander to remain ahead of the tanks, to try and see anyone coming towards the ground force. The Texan accent acknowledged, and then 'he disappeared. He was firing, rockets and mini-guns everywhere, he had seen another group moving up to counter-attack.'

Artillery observation was difficult on the ground, amid the dust, leaves and smoke, so McCormack, perched a little higher in his turret, was asked if he could direct the guns. 'I hadn't taken too much notice of definite compass bearings, so my only artillery fire orders I ever gave in action were, "Can you take it north about another 200 yards?" to get it away from us, as it was bursting on the edge of the clearing just in front.'

McCormack moved forward into an area of bunkers cleared by his canister and artillery, to see 'a strange-looking one, that had some overhead protection which ran off at a bit of an angle. People were firing from it, so we put an armour-piercing round into it. It turned out to be a zig-zag communication trench, and as the round went through the ground it opened up the zig, of the zig-zag, and uncovered a number of people in the trench.

'That explained how we could keep firing at these people in

pits and never seemed to hit them. They would take their casualties out the back of the zig-zag and move the next lot forward. It caused some concern.'

At one time, McCormack was standing in his hatch, looking back towards the friendly forces, talking to them on the radio, when Jack Luff, the gunner, grabbed him by the knee, shouting into the microphone, 'There's a bloke, there's a bloke!'

Through his gunsight, Luff could see an NVA aiming at the tank, but the gun was unloaded and Bavistock, the loader, was down in 'the bowels of the tank, trying to get some more ammunition. I flicked around with the machine-gun, but Reeves shot him.'

Behind the tanks, the infantry platoons were gathering, making sure no one was left behind, but keeping the aggressive NVA from moving with them. The NVA called the tactic 'hanging on to the enemy's belt'.

Off to one side, Gerry McCormack saw an NVA trying to aim an RPG at the tank. The turret began to pivot towards the man, the long 84mm cannon swinging around on to him. McCormack could see the RPG wobbling as the shaking NVA tried to aim, wobbling so much that it went off into a tree just in front of the man.

When it became obvious that the pressure on Campbell's company was being eased, Peter Spoor in his Sioux was sent to look for any NVA withdrawal routes, and he soon found them. There was plenty of artillery, and he began calling it in on the enemy below. 'One of the techniques I used was to get in immediately after the last round went off, to see what damage was done and where I should put the next lot of arty down. Hopefully, the enemy would still have their heads down and have little opportunity to fire at me.

'Well, it didn't take them long to wake up to this, and they weren't terribly interested in having a go at me, more in using the time free of arty to move out. As usual, they were carrying dead and wounded. This worked well in their favour and in my favour for a while. Then a team of gunships turned up, and it was all my way.

'As the enemy heard my little chopper move in, they'd be

297

up and off. But immediately behind me were the two gun-ships, and they played merry hell with them for a while, until the enemy moved into the denser jungle.'

Spoor also controlled a flight of Phantoms, and his opinion was confirmed that the big F4 was the most inaccurate fighter-bomber in Vietnam. Best were the little A37 Dragonfly, and the propellor-driven A1 Skyraider, then the F100, and last the Phantom.

Digger Campbell called Gerry McCormack, busy wreaking havoc up forward in the midst of the bunkers, to inform him that the casualties had all been retrieved and the force was ready to leave. McCormack suggested that once again the vehicles return along the route made on the way in, but everyone should be alert for enemy on the flanks.

At 1115 the APCs reported the tanks had finished their sweep and were moving back to C Company; the entire group was then to move to their left rear.

Five minutes later mortars began to fall on the Australians again. Gerry McCormack asked the Playboy helicopter gunships if they could locate the mortars. By now two helicopter teams had used up their ammunition, and a third was requested. As they moved away, mortars began impacting in the positions just vacated by the people treating the wounded and in the company headquarters.

1140 1RAR to TF: C Company disengaging and will move to XT955290.
1147 TF Forward to Nui Dat: C Company contact continues, breaking contact to allow airstrikes to go in, then will resume contact, 12 VC KIA (BC) so far.

Again, the tanks had proved their worth. After their arrival, there were no further infantry casualties, and McCormack believes that the tank fire to the flanks kept the aggressive NVA in their pits and bunkers, unable to move for a counter-attack.

C Company lost one killed and seven wounded, plus leaving an M60 machinegun behind at the scene. Digger Campbell's opinion of the tank support is that 'without

298

their assistance, contact would have been greatly prolonged, and was a very difficult one from which to extricate [the company].'

Colonel Dunstan's comment is, 'There were only two tanks in that operation, but they probably saved many lives; one couldn't estimate the number of casualties which would have been caused otherwise.' Dunstan has always assumed that the numerous and aggressive enemy contacted by Campbell that afternoon were positioning themselves to attack Coral later that night or early next morning.

Some weeks later, Campbell was spoken to by a much more senior officer, and 'told in no uncertain manner that to lose a machinegun in action was quite unforgiveable'. Personally, Campbell thought that he would have failed had he left a dead machinegunner behind, rather than the weapon, and rejected the other line of thought. He later worked closely with the senior officer, and admired him for his abilities.

Blue Keldie's APCs had sortied from Coral, with a platoon from A Company and the Assault Pioneers, and gone on out to the point of entry into the jungle. Keldie saw a tank coming through the trees, 'looking as if it had been sandpapered', with all the external fittings torn off or shot away. It was Gerry McCormack. The volume of fire which had been directed at him must have been enormous, and Keldie thought McCormack would have been deaf for days.

When the company arrived at the open ground, the ever-present Dustoff helicopters flew in to take all the casualties. McCormack had called for an ammunition resupply, as he and Reeves had fired almost all their sixty rounds of main armament in each tank. Soon two US helicopters flew down, and he ran across, thinking it was the ammunition. But the crews slid out great blocks of ice, with beer cans frozen into them. There was nothing to do but wait for the ice to melt, hoping to get a beer later. However, the ammunition soon arrived, and in the process of loading up the tanks, McCormack did not get a can.

Campbell, in real infantry fashion, wanted air and artillery to pound the bunker area while he reorganised, and then go back in again, with the armour and other elements of 1RAR which had come out to the scene of Keldie's APC force, to really get stuck into the enemy. Gerry McCormack, after a brew, was ready to lead the assault, as he knew exactly where the trenches and bunkers were.

The CO, Lieutenant Colonel Bennett, vetoed this, and it was decided against renewing the combat, so McCormack and the armoured vehicles went on back to Coral. Once again, the RPGs had very little effect, the small arms fire had bounced off, and the tanks had reproven their worth.

Again, for Gerry McCormack and the other tankies, 'the thing that really did amaze us was how well we had applied our training, how appropriate it was, and how easy it was to apply it.'

Digger Campbell sought out the Sioux pilot, Peter Spoor, to express his thanks for the work done that day. This thoughtfulness impressed Spoor.

But after the two previous contacts on 25 and 26 May, and the role played by the tanks at Balmoral on 26 and 28 May, the old infantry distrust of tanks was gone, swept away almost literally by the canister and solid shot pumped into the bunker positions. The grunts realised what a friend they had in the turret-heads.

Of course, human nature being what it is, the pendulum swung the other way, and as Peter Badman found, not only did every infantry company want tanks in the future, but they became armoured experts overnight, and he had battles of a different nature on his hands!

On the 31st A and D Companies patrolled to the north-east and south-east, with Neil Weekes' platoon having the sole significant contact of the day.

The platoon had discovered freshly used footpaths, and at the end of a patrol leg had gone into all-round defence on a track junction. Then voices speaking Vietnamese were heard, and a single enemy, casually dressed in only shorts and boots, came walking along the track. When he was 15 metres away, he was shot dead, and Weeks moved two M60s forward, past the body, but no more enemy were found.

He then called in artillery, but considered it took too long to arrive on the suspected enemy position, because of delays in getting clearances to fire from the Air Force.

It was obvious from this and several earlier contacts that the VC and NVA became complacent, even though they must have been aware of the patrolling from the bases. But slowly they and their leaders were made to realise that they could be attacked at almost any time in the neighbourhood of Coral. To that there was only one answer: move away.

13 Finale

Our gayness and our gilt are all besmirch'd
with rainy marching in the painful field.
Henry V *(IV. iii.)*

WE ALL KNOW that with good tactics a certain number of troops can defeat the enemy, but if the tactics are bad, these troops can hardly be victorious and sometimes sustain losses.

Vo Nguyen Giap

BACK AT NUI DAT one of the unpleasant jobs which had to be performed by people such as Terry Loftus, COMS of B/1RAR, was identification of the dead Australians, often their friends. Fatalities were taken to the morgue run by the Americans, at Tan Son Nhut air-base. Even today the effect of this place is still strong for Loftus.

'The Yanks had everything pretty well organised,' he remembers, 'and they had taken more casualties than in the Tet Offensive. The place was just overflowing, no matter which way you looked. It was very efficient. They even had a diagram which showed where the fellow was hit, for example, if he had a head wound, and half his head was missing. They cleaned their teeth, and combed their hair and shaved them, polished their fingernails, reshaped their skull, if they could. They had twenty-six procedures they had to do before the body was cleared for shipment back to the States or wherever they may be going. It was a shocker block, and it stank of embalming fluid.'

While the operations in AO Surfers continued, so did life at the Nui Dat base, with patrolling and other normal military activities in the province. To keep people informed of the activities of other units, and the situation in Phuoc Tuy and country-wide, briefings were given, usually at the beginning of the working day, often by Intelligence staff who were trained in such matters.

Brian Tobin, a 1RAR character, was the Intelligence Sergeant. 'Tobes' was known for his liking for the amber fluid, and for a remarkable recuperative ability which allowed him to wake up in time to give the morning Intelligence briefing. One night, at Nui Dat, there had been a generator failure so for some hours no lights had been available. The audience for the morning briefing gathered in the room separated from the Intelligence Section by a thin wall, sitting in the gloom. Not being in any condition to know of the absence of lights because of the night before; Tobes entered, stumbled in the dark, raised a fist and pounded on the partition, yelling 'Lights!' Simultaneously, in the distance was heard a roar as the generators began as if on command, the lights came on, and the audience collapsed in gales of laughter, with Tobes standing in puzzlement at the hilarity.

Meanwhile, John Dellaca, of the detachment of 131 Div Loc Battery, had already returned to Nui Dat, and was surprised to find that some people there did not realise the large scale of the actions being fought by components of their own formation, 1ATF, at Coral.

As the rains continued, Peter Badman seriously began to think the tanks might have to be abandoned, stuck in the mud of Coral, set in their dug-in positions in which the mud came over the top of the roadwheels. Maintenance still had to be carried out, with the crews in the mud over their knees, feeling around in the porridge for the greasing nipples.

Colonel Dunstan had inherited the commander's caravan, but did not occupy it at night. The engine for the airconditioner drowned some of the outside noise, including the important sound of mortar primaries firing, and in addition its size and shape made it a good target. What he did use it for was to send into it for sleep during the day those people such as Duty Officers who by necessity were awake most of the night. 'It was a very dangerous piece of kit,' he recalled, 'and I kept well clear of it at night.'

The different methods of the Australian and American

armies often provided a basis for discussion and comparison among the Diggers, one of the most noticeable being their ways of checking that their positions were clear of enemy.

The Aussies went out and physically walked through and across their unit frontage, in the well-known patrolling and clearing-patrol activities. But the Americans merely gathered along their perimeter and fired into the scrub, hosing down their surrounds with a rain of automatic fire from weapons of various calibres. The 40mm Dusters were particularly impressive, as the great glowing rounds flashed out into the scrub. Stan Carbines, 102 Battery, thought this 'seemed like a great waste of ammunition, but lots of fun'.

From an infantry platoon commander's point of view, Mal Meadows perhaps best sums up the opinion of the Dusters as base defence weapons: 'Spectacular. They were devastating, and within a matter of seconds of being brought into action, everything had died down. We were all impressed; they were a talking point. The most effective suppressive fire I've seen.'

On 1 June it was decided by the US Command, IIFFV, that the Australian effort had succeeded, and 1ATF blockage of the NVA corridor to Saigon had greatly lessened the effect of the offensive on Saigon. ARVN units could now be deployed in the area.

On that same day B Company and the tanks swept the two grid squares 9431 and 9531, while other companies carried out local patrolling. Next day, C Company, with tanks and APCs, returned to the bunker system where they had fought on the 30th. It seemed as though nothing had been touched since that day. Five NVA bodies, an RPG, an AK47 and an AK50 were still there among the debris. The artillery and airstrikes had hit the position accurately, collapsing bunkers and trenches. The M60 lost in the action was also recovered.

Digger Campbell and his men were able to examine the defences in a more leisurely manner than during their first visit. Campbell reported later that the 'enemy made good use of communications trenches for alternative fire positions. The enemy positions appeared to overlook tracks and clearings, were well camouflaged from the air, dug in with overhead protection, and had communications trenches linking the main position and standing patrol positions.'

The standing patrol positions were at all four corners of the main position, and were connected by zig-zag trenches back to it.

On 2 June the last prisoner taken on the operation was captured by 2 Troop of the APC Squadron, with D Company 3RAR, north of Balmoral. The APCs had dropped off the infantry, then reversed into some scrub to watch over an open area. The M113s were spread out, some forty or fifty metres apart, and the guns were manned.

Diggings had been noticed in the position, and Dave Brooks told his driver, Geoff Murray, to take the sandbag of rubbish from the APC and throw it in one of the holes. Geoff was cooking breakfast, and waiting for the water to boil, so he walked over to one of the holes, first checking it with F1 submachinegun in hand for unfriendly occupants, then returned to the vehicle for the bag, leaving the F1 in its place. He had noticed another hole, covered with cobwebs, thought there was nothing to worry about, and threw the contents of the bag in through the webs.

'To my great surprise, an NVA popped his head out! All I could think of was to throw the bag at him, and took off back to the APC, yelling "Charlie! Charlie!"'

Brooks asked what Murray had seen, and was told there was a VC in the bunker, then told Murray to wait a bit, as Geoff wanted to call on the radio for a variety of heavy support. Brooks realised that the other holes could not be occupied, or the vehicles would by now be involved in a battle. He called Peter Malone, commander of 22 Bravo (later killed in action), and together they returned to the hole.

Murray was covering them from the back of the M113, and Brooks had a grenade ready to throw. Peeping in, he could see the NVA—not VC—had his hands up, and together he and Malone coaxed and pulled the Vietnamese out of the small hole in which he had hidden. They took him through the bush to D Company HQ, and handed him over. He had been wounded in the attack on 28 May, and been left behind, unable to walk with much of his heel shot away.

One of the outstanding recollections of the Balmoral operations for Peter Phillips, OC D Company, was the capture of this wounded NVA soldier. 'The thing that sticks in mind is that his wounds were fly-blown, but he'd been so debilitated that he couldn't attend to himself. I remember that Jim Litchfield was the only one who had the guts to do it, to clean this fellow up and get rid of all the maggots. The NVA smelt to high heaven, as most of them did anyway, but I thought that was not something that many of us, even the medical orderly, were inclined to take on.

'Jimmy Litchfield attended to this fellow, who was taken off as a prisoner, and I remember that within a few hours he was wolfing down Australian rations with great relish.'

As the possibility of enemy attacks in the daylight hours receded, the fit young men at Coral began to kick a football around to expend some energy. However, Australian and American codes of football differ greatly, and the games dissolved to what Stan Carbines, 102 Battery, recalls as 'mainly kicking and throwing their ball to one another'.

Another American attraction was their food. They had brought a kitchen and cooks to prepare meals, while the Australians ate from cans. First a few, then more Aussies joined the end of the US meal queue. With their usual generosity, the Yanks fed all those who appeared.

Alan Floyd, guncrew member, was surprised at the American methods and largesse. 'They had some food left over, and rather than throw it away, called, "Any of you Aussies want any food?" Well, you've never seen 120 men move so fast. Heaps of food; sliced warm meat, potatoes, cabbage . . . and to our amazement, litres of flavoured milk.'

The TF After-action report referred to the unsuccessful result of attempting to provide one fresh meal a day per man to those at Coral, with the other two meals being a mixture of US and Australian rations. The idea of a central kitchen proved unworkable, and it was decided to use unit kitchens in the future. Naturally, the good intentions of the staff were ignored and customary Australian mutterings about cooks and rear echelons went on.

As is usual in such situations, rumours abounded. Repeatedly, it was said that NVA tanks and even bigger rockets were being prepared for use against Coral. For some people, the strain of the operation proved too much, the daily waiting to be bombarded nibbled away at their composure, and their behaviour altered in ways that were sometimes noticed by others.

Every night, an artillery senior NCO would go around the position, morosely warning the gunners that 'this is it. This is worse than Korea or Borneo. They're gonna hit us. We've had it ...' Bob Carbury thought that this unnecessarily frightened people, but there was not much he could do about it.

Colonel Dunstan toured the forward positions to keep in touch with the rifle company Diggers, and one day was informed of their opinion about the tinned rations supplied. He asked someone in B Company 1RAR if there was anything the soldiers wanted done, and immediately was asked about 'this bloody tuna, sir? We've been eating it for three bloody weeks!'

In D Company 1RAR Tony Hammett kept his soldiers busy with a system of inspections of various items of weaponry, personal equipment, pit construction, hygiene and so on. The Diggers were quizzed about the capabilities and characteristics of their own and enemy weapons, what they thought the enemy was doing now, what could be learned from him, and similar questions designed to keep the men thinking and conscious of the situation. Naturally there was grumbling about some of it, such as putting polish on boots, but it was insisted on, if for no other reasons than a good soldier looks after his gear and polish preserves boots.

Much of the area of Coral was treeless, open grassland, and a direct contrast to the jungle vegetation usually encountered by the soldiers. A platoon of 1RAR had a platoon commander not known for his sense of humour, but that did not stop the young Diggers from skylarking and playing jokes on each other. One day the platoon commander called an O Group, and one of the corporals picked up his machete, then began hacking his way through the non-existent thick vines and branches of the imaginary jungle between them. The platoon thought it funny, and even funnier when the platoon commander's face registered the range of expressions from surprise to dismay in the presence of an advancing madman wielding a sharp machete—and reached for his rifle.

Geoff Grimish, 102 Battery, who had taken the red and green tracer as an omen, and bet on South Sydney to win the Rugby League premiership, was also the battery bookmaker. 'After having lost most of my pay to the bookmaker during the two years I served in Malaya, I decided to run the book whenever we were able to get the race fields over Radio Australia. At the end of the tour I had accumulated a good deal.'

At the end of the battery's tour, while waiting to be flown out of Nui Dat, Geoff decided to run the books one last time. Sergeant Skeeter Humphry was known as an astute judge of horseflesh, and bet on 'Bright Promise', at 33/1; everyone followed him; the horse won; Geoff returned to Australia broke.

At Tan Uyen, Lieutenant John Crossman was carrying on as Liaison Officer. Life there with the US Advisory Team to the ARVN 48th Regiment had numerous examples of a certain unreality. Rockets would be launched by the VC or NVA out in the scrub, and the missiles would pass over the town or encampment en route to their allied targets. He knew that 'if you went outside the gate after dark, your chances of surviving for very long were minimal. It was tiger country. When there had been a bit of a disturbance, or some shooting, I found myself wishing I was back with my own, because at least you know then that the man next to you is going to back you up, not necessarily pitch a grenade in your bunker and go his merry way.'

The enemy in the area, in Crossman's opinion, 'had realised that the 48th Regiment, given its bloody low state of morale and efficiency, was no real danger. By leaving them alone, they probably got more information from them. If they attacked, God knows, some of them might get angry.

'The South Vietnamese units, to a much greater degree

than our own, used to reflect the style, personality and leadership of their commanders. If their commanders were good,
they were as good as any soldiers I've met, and there were
some magnificent ARVN units. In this case, the leadership
was not dynamic, to say the least.

'Morale was poor, motivation was low, and I think the
previous beating they'd had probably affected them badly.

'While I was there, they had a Hoi Chanh [surrendered
enemy]. I had the opportunity to talk to him, and it was a
very interesting experience. He was a North Vietnamese, a
young fellow, about 21 or something of that order. I noted,
firstly, that the South Vietnamese deferred to him a bit. They
gave him a ration pack, they had cigarettes, that sort of
thing.

'Whether that was because he was a North Vietnamese,
or a bona fida Hoi Chanh and they were playing the rules
straight for once, I have no way of knowing. Anyway, I went
over there, I had an interpreter, and was talking to him.'

Crossman noticed the smell peculiar to the VC/NVA who
lived in the wilderness. 'They smelt like a fox; the smell of
the wild; way past what you and I would call body odour. An
all-pervading smell, from their diet, living conditions and
everything else.'

The North Vietnamese told Crossman that he had malaria,
had been suffering with it for three months, with only aspirin
for treatment. He had been a farm worker near Vinh, in
northern central Vietnam. He had a few weeks training on
infantry weapons, then walked down the Ho Chi Minh Trail,
during which the group ahead were caught and annihilated
by a B52 strike, and since arrival in the South had been
carrying supplies for the armed forces, living in a hole in the
ground which he could not leave for fear of artillery and
gunships. The routes followed on the carrying tasks were not
known to him, as they were taken hither and yon by guides.
At the time Crossman was talking to him, the man did not
know the time, the date or where he was.

At one stage, John Crossman recalls, 'I said, "Who is going
to win this war?" He said, "I am." He didn't bat an eyelid. "I
am." There was a man who had surrendered, he had given

up, and he still believed in victory. This little guy impressed me, with the spontaneity of his responses, and I've got no reason to doubt he was telling it as he felt it, right from the heart.'

Searching for enemy east of Coral, an Australian Army pilot saw what he believed were telephone cables strung through the trees, and followed them to what seemed to be a head-quarters area, later believed to be that of 7 NVA Div. Artil-lery was concentrated on the target, and airstrikes were called in. Bill Raggatt, A Company 1RAR, counted seven B52 strikes and eight jet-fighter attacks controlled by FAC.

The sheer weight of US Air Force power was demonstra-ted by the huge B52s, each delivering up to thirty tons of bombs, but flying so high they could not be heard. Attacking the reported positions of VC/NVA, they trailed their 750lb bombs across the areas of jungle. The first those on the ground knew was the unannounced flash and thunder of the long strings of explosions, and the shaking earth. Some of these were six kilometres away from Coral and Balmoral, close enough for concussion to be felt.

At Coral, Second Lieutenant Mal Meadows was enjoying 'a quiet period, with a brew on, and the ground just started to shake; the noise was awesome. Then on the horizon we could see the dust starting to rise. We did not see the aircraft, but after a long search in the sky, did find them, very high, leaving vapour trails.'

Further around the perimeter, Geoff Bowcock was in the 12 Platoon position, and 'heard the first couple of single explosions, which developed into an earth-shaking roar'.

In the quiet night, the invisible bombers overhead were sometimes announced by a strange rattling noise far up in the blackness, which listeners realised was made by bombs, sheer numbers of bombs, clanging off each other in their fall. Then would come the stupendous purple shockwaves and the quaking ground.

Even away in Saigon, buildings shook, windows rattled, doors rumbled in their fittings, glassware clinked, and in one house at least the occupants thought the VC were trying to break in, so seized their collection of guns to fight the battle of Cach Mang Boulevarde. After a short time, realisation dawned, and they went back to bed.

On 3 and 4 June platoon-sized patrols swept the areas around the base, with no contact. At 1130 on the 4th orders were issued for the abandonment of Coral.

Blue Keldie's APCs were deeply involved in escorting convoys back to Nui Dat, in all shepherding 300 vehicles along the dangerous roads.

Also on 3 June Colonel Dunstan's HQ issued a résumé of the enemy situation in AO Surfers. It recapitulated the actions since 29 May, pointing out that no major attacks had been made by the enemy since 27–28 May, though night-time reconnaissance of the fire support bases continued. 7 NVA Division was believed to be regaining its strength with manpower from infiltration groups, and not likely to attack Coral or Balmoral 'in the immediate future'.

Lieutenant Colonel Kelly, the artillery commander, decided that it would be better to expend the accumulated artillery ammunition rather than carry it all back to Nui Dat, so ordered it to be fired on likely targets. The sudden increase in gun activity, plus the noise, brought Colonel Dunstan into the artillery CP. When he found it was simply to get rid of ammunition, he put a quick end to the firing. The sudden sustained artillery fire had also caused concern among some in the rifle companies and in other units, who presumed heavy contact was in progress.

On the 4th all AFVs regrouped at Coral, then moved to Nui Dat via the US base Bearcat the next day. On 5 June platoon-sized patrols continued to operate around the base, covering the areas from the north-west around to the south-east. No contact was made.

The NVA/NLF leaders had abandoned the area to 1ATF, and either given up efforts to force a way through, or were diverting their groups around Coral and Balmoral.

On the move back from Coral, one of Peter Badman's tanks, described in uncomplimentary terms as 'a beast' had to be towed most of the way. For some reason, its engine would run for only four minutes, then stop for half an hour, and nothing would make it go for longer. The crew and RAEME staff were at their wits' end. From being a willing worker, the tank became a fifty-ton monster. It had to be towed up to each of the twenty or so bridges on Route 15, unhitched, the engine started, and driven across the structure with due care for the ageing steel and construction, within the four minutes.

Finally it was hauled into the US base at Bearcat, after a day-long journey of towing, unhitching, starting, creeping across a bridge, hitch up again, tow ... The RAEME mechanics climbed over it, determined to locate the fault. And half a worn-out tank suit, used as a rag, was found in the carburettor.

The last night at Coral was, for some, most nerve-wracking. They could not believe that the enemy had not noticed the withdrawal, and would not react strongly against the dwindling forces in the base. 'The last night was the worst' for Bob Carbury, who 'could not sleep at all. This is it; they've left us'.

Next day, the move back to Nui Dat began, and Carbs went in road convoy. 'I was glad to get out of Coral. It was good to get back to Nui Dat.'

Alan Floyd, gun number in 102, agreed it was 'good to be back at base. Clean clothes, clean bedding and mountains of good food'.

During the evacuation, the engineers were tasked with blowing up the various command posts which had been dug in the base, and went about their job placing explosives in the necessary places. The Arty CP required a certain amount of attention. However, when it was destroyed, no one was warned, and there were many convulsive moves towards the weapon pits nearby by those who reacted instinctively to what they thought was another attack.

Major John Kemp, commanding the engineers, went to Colonel Dunstan and asked if the big CP could be blown up, rather than filled in by his men working to replace the dirt. Dunstan wanted it to be collapsed, and agreed to the use of explosives, stipulating, 'but if anything comes out of it, I'll kill you'. When it did go, 'the biggest lump of timber I've ever seen flew up, to about thirty or forty feet. I didn't see anything of Kemp for some time!'

Similarly, when Tony Hammett blew up his company CP, resolved not to leave it for the enemy, consternation was caused around them, as his warning had not been passed on, or even recorded at battalion HQ.

The hapless artillery radars had a minor disaster on the flight out, when the machine itself was somehow dropped from beneath its Chinook, just outside the Fire Support Base, and did not survive the fall.

On the 6th the last elements of Keldie's A Sqn 3 Cav, with the Dusters and US tanks from 3/4 Cav, withdrew, moving away cross-country.

The rifle companies were flown out in Chinooks, and Colonel Dunstan, with a few staff, were still in the desolated base. Chinooks shuttled back and forth, and when there was only one company left, a certain feeling of tension began to creep in, as the flying activity was obvious to the enemy, and there was the chance that they might regain some of their former aggressiveness, making life difficult for the few Australians at Coral. Then the Chinooks stopped coming.

Time passed, but no helicopters came back. Nui Dat could not be contacted with the radios and aerials available, so Dunstan sent up a Sioux helicopter, to try to raise them from a few thousand feet above, where better radio conditions might be encountered. The Sioux returned, and the pilot said to Dunstan, 'You're not going to like this, sir. The G3 Air has held the Chinooks on the strip at Nui Dat, as there is a leave party which wants to do some shopping at the PX in Long Binh, and he is having trouble locating them!'

Dunstan was still breathing fire when he arrived at Nui Dat, and burst into Brigadier Hughes' office, demanding the sacking of the officer concerned for his interference in a tactical operation, which could have had serious repercussions. Hughes calmed him down and the officer survived.

In C Company 1RAR was a tall young soldier, so tall he was called 'Treeburst': Charley Godley. His tent was furthest from the showers, yet he somehow managed to be first there whenever the unit returned from operations. When he was asked how he succeeded in doing this, he merely smiled, and said, 'Cleanliness is next to Godley-ness.'

The last troops out of Coral were Bob Hennessy's B Company, escorting the artillery road convoy. He was looking forward to being on his own, independent of battalion direction, and with considerable firepower on call was anticipating enemy resistance along the road south to Tan Uyen. One of Keldie's APCs had been destroyed down that way earlier, in a clash with NVA. But, as it had throughout the entire operation, the limelight avoided B Company. There was no enemy reaction, and the Australians drove off, out of AO Surfers.

The Aussies left AO Surfers with a variety of feelings. Some wanted to stay, as they had obviously beaten the enemy, but others were glad to leave. Still others wondered why the bases were not leap-frogged over one another, all around the region, up to the Cambodian border, to continue the disruption caused the NVA and VC.

Bob Hennessy had been told by Lieutenant Colonel Bennett that the base was to move to the north, towards the Song Be, and more heavy fighting was anticipated. Hennessy was rather surprised to receive orders for a move to the south.

Lieutenant Colonel Shelton, CO 3RAR, wanted to stay. 'The longer we were in an area, the more we were able to do, because we became more conversant with the enemy and terrain. I wasn't keen to leave Coogee for Balmoral, and when told we were leaving Balmoral, felt cheated again.'

Stan Carbines, 102 Battery, thought 'we were all very pleased to leave Coral. It left us with memories to last a lifetime. The thing was that we had come under pressure and had done the things we were trained for. We felt pretty pleased with our efforts.'

Warrant Officer Wally Thompson, CSM C/1RAR, believed the operation should have been ended when it did. The units and men had been in the field for six weeks, under strain for all that time, even if not under fire. An aspect of the air-mobile and APC-borne operations which is not always taken

314

into consideration is that while helicopters and APCs make travel easier for the soldier, they also make him available for use to a far greater degree than was possible in wars up to 1965.

Wally Thompson makes the point that units in previous wars were 'in the line' for relatively short periods, of weeks or even days. The soldier in a forward unit in Vietnam was under the strain of exposure to the enemy for almost his entire time in the country. To cover the areas which 1ATF did in the six weeks to 8 June would have required something like two AIF Divisions; 1ATF did it with two battalions, two batteries of guns, two squadrons of armour. So Thompson believes that by 8 June, 1ATF was ready for a rest, out of the operational area. In fact, after a short time at Nui Dat, they were back in the neighbouring region.

Others, such as Paul 'Richo' Richardson, in D/1RAR, were somewhat annoyed by what they saw as a continuation of the hop, skip and jump methods from 1965, when the allies arrived in areas unknown to them, but beat the enemy into submission, then left, allowing him to recover. They believed that allied forces should have stayed longer, really grinding down the enemy structure, and achieving a satisfying result of bringing security and support for the Saigon Government—the reason for being there in the first place.

Lieutenant Colonel Bennett felt a 'certain kind of sadness on our part, in that having spent a lot of time there, the area was then given up, but I guess the writing might have been on the wall then.'

The men of the infantry, artillery and tanks, both as groups and as individuals, came out of the operation with a deeper appreciation of the realities of war. The soldiers now understood the reason for many of the lessons and the points the more experienced members had tried to make. For many, the fighting at Coral was seen as a turning-point or benchmark in the tour of duty. After it, there was much more professionalism, a more serious acceptance of the business of soldiering.

Lieutenant Colonel Bennett: 'It was very obvious to us all that we were a very untried battalion, but that was really throwing us into the deep end, and the battalion came out of it extremely competent, and confident in their own ability. I don't think the battalion looked back from there.'

'It made us aware,' as Garry Prendergast, B/1RAR put it, 'that it was no longer a game, no longer a fun thing. People could get killed.'

Captain Phil Davies, Assistant Operations Officer, 1RAR, saw it as 'our initiation to war, and from that point of view we were lucky that it went as it did, that we didn't get a bloody nose with a lot more casualties. It probably set the battalion off on to a very good footing.'

For Second Lieutenant Phil Busby, 'it certainly was the making of 12 Field Regiment, no doubt about that.'

Major Blue Keldie saw that there was 'no doubt the use of armoured HQ in Fire Support Bases was well proven; from then on ACVs were used as Task Force HQ in Fire Support Bases.'

The operation in AO Surfers had been going for three weeks; 1ATF had succeeded without doubt in disrupting the NVA approach and assembly of forces for the attacks on Saigon; and it was time to begin preparation for a further phase.

The Australian bulwark had held despite a numerically superior, brave and tenacious enemy advancing across terrain he considered his own.

14 In Retrospect

A fool learns by his own experiences;
a wise man learns by others.
Otto von Bismarck

AS THE AUSTRALIANS LEFT the Surfers AO, almost all of them felt confident in their units and personal ability to cope with whatever the enemy might do. They had gone into the area after a period of prolonged but unprofitable patrolling, and been subjected to determined attacks by a brave enemy. Literally overnight, they had to adjust from a war of seeking enemy over a wide area to one of defending positions against aggressive foe who did 'come looking for you'.

Many pondered why the operation was brought to an end, when the enemy obviously had been battered. Paul Richardson wonders why 'we didn't stay there, or somebody relieve us and continue and really annihilate them, I'm buggered if I know. We simply flew out and that was the end of the story.'

At battalion commander level, Lieutenant Colonel Jim Shelton echoed the views of front-line Diggers such as Richo. 'I always like getting into an area and staying there. The troops become more conversant with the terrain and the standard of the patrolling improves. I always used to get wild—we'd just begin to get an area under control, the contacts were going nicely, the ambushes were going on, and we'd be moved again. [At Coogee] we were in a very good position to do some good interception of the enemy who were pulling out of Saigon and trying to get out of the area.'

There was speculation tht the operation had been terminated so the Australians could be at Nui Dat to meet the Prime Minister, John Gorton, who arrived in Vietnam at this time. However, Major Keldie was later posted to Washington, and

317

was able to check this with the relevant US Army authorities. The visit of John Gorton had no effect on the operation in the NVA corridor, and it was coincidental that Coral and Balmoral were closed. In fact, the Australians could have been redeployed a few days earlier for IIFFV reasons.

As Brigadier Hughes pointed out, 'The overall defence of Saigon was in the hands of IIFFV, and the commander, General Fred Weyand, had 1st, 9th and 25th Divisions, 198 Light Brigade and ourselves, and there was a series of South Vietnamese divisions. It was their responsibility to manage the overall strategy of the defence of Saigon, and it was their decision we come home. It was nothing to do with us, and we were, in fact, out of our area of responsibility. Our area was back in Phuoc Tuy.'

In Brigadier Hughes' opinion, 'the operations at Coral and Balmoral were the most intense period which Task Force Headquarters had experienced. We were subjected to rocket and mortar fire, but my impression was that, apart from the lad who did not know if his rifle would fire, everybody was cool, calm and collected. They may well have been apprehensive, but everybody got on with the job and communications worked, support worked, normal reporting and resupply, all those things which you expect a headquarters to do, still functioned, despite noisy activities quite close outside. I was very pleased with the way the headquarters worked.'

Noel Sproles, a permanent Duty Officer at TFHQ, has a somewhat lower opinion, feeling that the Task Force staff, at some levels, was 'psychologically overwhelmed and should have gone out'. Sproles believes the Australian leadership was 'uninspired', and that while the TF HQ performed well later, it was unprepared to go into a situation such as it found in AO Surfers, despite the available information.

Another adverse opinion is held by Ian Ahearn. Both at Coral and since, he 'did not think we had an aim to the operation, apart from fight off attacks on the fire support base, after the first night, and patrol during the day to see what the enemy was up to. It certainly wasn't offensive, and certainly we only waited to see what the enemy would do to us. Overall, I don't believe the operation was a successful one. I don't believe we had any aim apart from maintaining the integrity of the fire support bases.

'It was my first experience of non-military decisions being made. I remember distinctly having to tell the soldiers of the battery that they would no longer be able to accompany the infantry on clearing patrols, standing patrols, since there weren't going to be any. For the period we were at Coral, only company-size patrols moved outside the wire, and they had to be back in before last light. In essence we gave up no-man's-land to the North Vietnamese. There were no SAS patrols operating, no standing patrols, no ambush patrols. We simply surrendered outside to the North Vietnamese. Rumour at the time had it that it was a decision made in Canberra. It could just as well have been a decision made in Vietnam, because of sensitivities of politicians and, I suppose, military, to casualties.

'Trying to explain the reason for not patrolling, when I had not been given a reason, is a bitter memory. I am still bitter about it to this day. It is difficult to lead soldiers when you are unable to explain apparently illogical decisions.'

But there was patrolling, as the numerous small combats in preceding pages show. The intensity of the fighting in the attacks on the fire support bases, and in the bunker complexes, testified to the aggressiveness of the enemy in the area. The ferocity of the action on 30 May, when Digger Campbell was in a situation which had potential for disaster, showed what the enemy could do, if given opportunity.

As long as 1ATF occupied the allocated area, and the ratio of casualties was so much in the Australians' favour, with the NVA coming to the bases, into the co-ordinated fire support, then the enemy was responding to 1ATF, and not the other way round.

There were barely enough men to protect Coral, as well as maintain some patrolling presence in the immediate area. It would not have taken much imagination for the enemy to persist with a contact such as those of Hammett and Campbell, engage the relief force, and probe or attack Coral, even with a force as small as a company, or battalion-minus. The commander at Coral would then have been presented with an unenviable choice of responses, compounded by a lack of invaluable rifle companies.

However, as the tired troops withdrew from an area where they had confronted the best the NVA could do, few felt that the operation had been of no use. Even in the relatively constricted world of the rifle platoons, it was obvious, as John Salter put it, that they 'had achieved something. If they were attacking us, they were not attacking someone else, so we had occupied their minds for a while.'

At Task Force level, Brigadier Hughes 'was very confident that we had done a good job, and were very pleased with ourselves. We had stopped a lot of North Vietnamese, killed a lot, taken a number of prisoners, and obviously disrupted what had been a regular line of communications. We got quite a good chit full on that point of view.'

From 1RAR, Lieutenant Colonel Phil Bennett thought that 'we were a very untried battalion, but that was throwing us in off the deep end. The battalion came out of it extremely confident, confident in their own ability, and I don't think they looked back. In the old familiar terms, the battalion had been well and truly blooded. They had a fairly unique experience, handled it very well, and they knew they were good.'

Lieutenant Colonel Jim Shelton, CO 3RAR, believes that 'the Task Force fought quite a good battle. It was different from what we were doing, and we gave better than we got. We were calling the tune, not the enemy.'

Commenting on his battalion, Jim Shelton noted that 'the companies took on the personality of the company commander. A Company, Hori Howard, would be our quickest company to move. He could move very quickly; he took risks but he could cover ground. B Company was Bert Irwin—that company could be given anything to do. They would take it as a challenge and would do it. If I gave Bert what he considered to be an easy job, he would sneer at me. C Company was under Ian Hands, a personality in his own right, a very happy company. Then D Company with Peter

Phillips, a very quiet man, but an extremely good company commander.

'The senior NCOs had a lot of service, good experience and set a high example for the rest of the NCOs. The soldiers were a happy smattering of Regulars with service in Malaya and Borneo, and extremely good National Servicemen, who were in the prime of life, 20 to 22. They never complained about being in Vietnam, just got on with the job, no problems at all. Everyone was in together and they got on with it.

'Dick Lippett was a very good doctor for 3RAR, very interested in soldiers. He used to get around a lot and talk to the soldiers. He had this great desire to close with the enemy, which is not a doctor's role. I'd already had to speak to Dick a couple of times because he wasn't where we wanted him to be, he was out looking for wounded. His heart was in the right place. We have a system where we bring the wounded to the doctor, because we've only got one doctor. I'd told him he wasn't to leave the RAP without me knowing, so I would always know where I could get hold of him quickly if we needed him.

'I was out in the Sioux [on the morning of the second attack]. He'd got the 3RAR wounded under control, and took it upon himself to go out [and subsequently was wounded]. I was angry, because I didn't want it to happen to him.'

The anger soon went; Lippett was too well liked, and, as stated earlier, 'had earned his Infantry Combat Badge the hard way'.

Lieutenant Colonel Kelly, CO 12 Field Regiment RAA, considered that 'we caused a reaction. It was obviously important to them, and we must have caused numerous casualties. I do not think the 7 NVA Division would have been a viable force for some time afterwards. It was one of the few places where the enemy was prepared, not just to stand and fight, but to come and seek us out, which made him very vulnerable. Once we got over that first night, and the shock of it, we were never in doubt about our own ability.'

At the bottom of the ladder, Bob Carbury, 102 Battery Q-store man, when asked about breaking up the NVA attacks on Saigon. 'didn't even know that's what they put us there for. I wondered for years why they put us there. I'd say we did a good job of it. Judging by the drag marks there the second morning [16 May], there were an awful lot of dead Vietnamese they'd taken with them, more than we buried.'

Armies being what they are, some of the participants in the actions around Coral and Balmoral were not sure what they were doing there, or if the units were intended to be in those locations, and what, if anything, was achieved. Many of the younger, junior ranks were not much interested in the information passed on at O Groups, as wherever they went, whoever the enemy was, their own jobs remained the same, their horizons limited to their immediate group of infantry section, gun crew or equivalent.

They soldiered on, wondering about the things that concern soldiers through the centuries: Would there be a water resupply? Mail? What would be in the rations? Can I get a pair of new socks out of the system? They presumed that the operation had been successful as there had been relatively few Australian casualties while many enemy had been seen to be killed, wounded and captured; apart from bombardments, the enemy had learned to keep away during the last week or so. And there were many more months of operations stretching ahead into the unseen future before they finished with this tour of duty; this operation was only the beginning.

The NVA Regiments and Infiltration Groups which dashed themselves against Coral and Balmoral would undoubtedly have moved into the attacks on Saigon, if they had not been consumed in the actions around the FSPBs. The individual NVA soldier, newly arrived in the south, and told that he would be taking part in the glorious final actions against the Saigon regime, had a rude awakening. On the other hand, the Australian soldier left the scene with improved morale and confidence in himself, his unit and formation.

Some people took the wider view, that since the military defeat of the Saigon Government in 1975 was a Communist victory, the operation was ultimately useless. Australian forces were sent to South Vietnam—whatever the underlying political moves and motives—to assist the Saigon Government, which, in the final analysis, was a democracy, though President Thieu did imprison particularly annoying political opponents and close down newspapers. Despite the repressive measures used by himself and his predecessors since 1954, democracy was bubbling and boiling in South Vietnam, with an ever-changing mass of dozens of opposition parties and coalitions, a lively newspaper world, and a population who did understand the Western concept of democracy. Whatever else the Communists may achieve, they cannot exterminate the concept of democracy; too many South Vietnamese have been exposed to it.

By late 1971 there was little to occupy 1ATF in their allocated area of Phuoc Tuy. Liberal Party Prime Minister William McMahon began the withdrawal of the Australian forces, and there were no combat units left by the time Gough Whitlam came to power to December 1972 (despite Labor Party mythology that 'Whitlam brought the troops home from Vietnam'.)

In April 1972 the South Vietnamese Armed Forces defeated an offensive by North Vietnamese troops who were heavily supported by tanks, artillery, antiaircraft and logistics elements. It seemed that at last they could defend themselves. The collapse of 1975 is one of the military phenomena of the twentieth century, and amazed even Hanoi.

However, allied operations around Saigon in 1968 were a success, and a defeat for Hanoi. The regime there gained no advantage for use in Paris; they threw away thousands of their own countrymen in the series of February, May and August attacks, the population of the South did not support them, and there was nothing remotely resembling a general uprising. This has not been forgotten, and very few Southerners are in positions of authority in the regime.

As for the enemy himself, Australian opinions vary, depending on their experience, outlook and proximity to the NVA/VC.

'I was a little surprised,' said Brigadier Hughes, 'at his determination to push us off his line of communication. I would have thought that he would have achieved his aim by just going around. He knew where we were; where our bases were; our patrols fanning out. He would have had to go a fair way around, into the American brigade next door if he went west; to the east, I don't think there was anybody. I don't think much of him.'

To Colonel Don Dunstan, 'he didn't compare in robustness with our people, but he had great dedication, or, the other option, he was doing as he was told or get a bullet between the eyes. I couldn't regard them as a high-calibre enemy at all; wouldn't compare them with the Japanese or Chinese.'

At battalion level, Lieutenant Colonel Bennett thinks the NVA were 'in some ways extremely proficient and professional, yet in others so repetitive. Not lacking in bravery or initiative. To have battle procedures in place that allowed them to try a battalion attack that night on a battalion group seen appearing into a landing zone towards last light, is pretty professional stuff. Mind you, they probably had the advantage of knowing the area well. They were determined, they pressed home their assaults, but they don't like artillery, mortar fire and aircraft. They melted them dramatically. I don't think they took too kindly to the flechette rounds that we whacked out of the Anti-armour Platoon; must have given them a hell of a surprise.'

Col Adamson, commanding A Company 1RAR at Coral, believes that the NVA 'was not the superman that people talk about. Fairly ordinary, in fact. Pretty determined, but not as well led as he could have been. Despite at least thirty-six hours reconnaissance, they did not discover the gap between myself and C Company, and they did not discover the lack of wire on our perimeter. Led by people who perhaps did not know as much about war as their leaders say they do; good on theoretical and political dogma, not too hot on winning a war. The real lie to come out of the Vietnam war is that it was guerrillas and freedom fighters who beat the South Vietnamese.'

324

However, Neil Weekes, commanding 3 Platoon in A Company, believes the enemy did know of the inter-company gap, but were prevented from moving through by the intense artillery fire placed across it. Weekes considers the NVA to have been 'a well-trained professional man; a courageous enemy'.

Mal Meadows, commanding 1 Platoon, rates the NVA leaders highly in one aspect; they were able to send battalions into the attack, into 'the sort of fire that we were putting out'.

Paul Richardson, Section Commander in D/1RAR, thought him 'a tenacious little bugger. He did a bloody good job for the conditions he lived under, and the distances he had to travel, and so forth.'

Peter Geil, 6 Section, 8 Platoon, C Company 3RAR, was very impressed with the quality of the NVA. He once watched a group of five moving towards an ambush, but unlike many VC, these fellows moved professionally, with weapons ready to fire, not talking, alert and using field signals. The leading NVA detected or suspected something, they halted outside the ambush, took cover and were gone. Peter found their display of expertise frightening to watch.

'Pretty game or doped to the eyeballs,' thought Bob Carbury, who weathered both attacks at Coral, and had much of his Q-store damaged by NVA mortars and rockets. 'The way they ran across that clearing—pretty game, dedicated, or mad.'

Another characteristic of the Vietnamese soldier noted by several people, including Barry Brown of C/1RAR, was his personal cleanliness in the field. Whereas the Aussie would keep all but a tiny amount of water for drinking, the Viet-namese washed themselves daily. They were also able to maintain cleaner uniforms and equipment as they often travelled from jungle base to base, rather than constantly living and sleeping closer to nature as did the Americans and Australians. A small difference, but significant.

However, the NVA and VC soldier was often let down by his leaders, who seemed unable to adapt to changing situations.

'Their tactics were peculiar,' said Colonel Dunstan. 'We

would never use them; expensive in manpower. They were mechanical in their timing. I used to get out of bed about ten minutes before their usual time, and walk over to the command post, and I knew I'd be just in time, before the first rocket came over. That was how precisely they would operate.'

'The NVA leadership was pathetic,' decided George Hulse. 'They did not respond to our threat the way they should have; they lost their advantage by sending in troops in penny packets. They wasted their soldiers' lives.'

Mick Bindley 'did get the impression that they tend to be somewhat inflexible. When they were told to do something, they did it, and they didn't seem to be able to change in the process. I think this was clearly indicated on the first night. Maybe a quick realisation of where they were going, and a flanking movement, may have achieved their aim much better than a straight frontal assault. But I don't think they thought they were doing a frontal assault. I think their reconnaissance was based on the original gun line, which would have been in quite a different direction.'

'A very capable enemy, but inflexible,' said Ian Ahearn, 102 Battery Gun Position Officer. 'What robbed him of success that first night was inflexibility. Without communications and the ability to react to a changing situation he was operating to a fixed timetable. I have no doubt they saw us turn the guns around, and knew they were assaulting into the muzzles, but because the operation had been set up on original reconnaissance information, it went ahead.'

It can be argued that later attempts at reconnaissance were frustrated by the presence of the rifle companies moving away from the gun position. While not patrols as such, but moves to allocated ambush positions from which to begin patrolling next day, they again prove the value of dominating the surrounding area.

Ahearn believes that the Australians 'were lucky, particularly at the gun position on the first night. Everything went wrong for the North Vietnamese commander. Up until he launched his attack, everything had been going right. He'd managed to approach and dig in. Though detected by the

1RAR mortar platoon, inexperience in our own commanders *and* experience in Phuoc Tuy Province led to wrong conclusions and wrong reactions. There is no doubt in my mind that if we had not readjusted for the fire task to the north, we would have been overwhelmed much the same way the mortar platoon was.'

The charge of inflexibility can also be levelled against the allied commanders, for their reliance on helicopters, and their reluctance to adopt irregular timings. As Lieutenant Colonel Jim Shelton pointed out, 'We do the same thing. All the time, we would fly in early in the morning into one of these areas. We wanted to change the pattern when we moved into Balmoral. The enemy got used to the way we operated, and we got used to the way he operated.'

None of the Australian senior officers managed to build up a picture, an image, of their counterparts. The enemy leaders remained a faceless presence. Their methods were identified and anticipated, but they never coalesced into a human figure. There were no known persons, such as a Rommel, on the other side of the clearings.

It was during Mr Gorton's visit to 1ATF that some disillusionment was felt by veterans of the battles. In conversation with him, they found that he did not seem to know, or have been told of, the actions north-east of Saigon in the previous four weeks. In addition, the soldiers were all cleanly and neatly dressed, but Gorton wore an unlaundered, baggy set of greens, shirt unbuttoned almost to the waist, scruffy boots and a generally untidy appearance. The Diggers expected their prime minister to be better dressed, no matter where he was visiting.

Actually, Mr Gorton had been informed of the recent battles during his visit to the USA, and on arrival in Vietnam, but his information was general in nature, lacking the detail engraved so vividly and lately in the Diggers' minds.

The PM had expressed a wish to meet the soldiers, so in 1RAR they were gathered in groups near the Battalion Intelligence Section, where the captured weapons were displayed. With Mr Gorton were the Australian commanders, and the

South Vietnamese Ambassador to Australia, accompanied by his wife, who was trim and charming in national dress.

Digger Campbell was on the edge of a group when the PM began talking to one of the corporals from his company, described as 'a Queensland hill-billy, a good NCO, with a little knowledge of military law'. The corporal knew that a person in the ranks could step out before an inspecting officer and voice a complaint. As Campbell recalls, the chat between PM and Corporal went as follows:

PM   How are you going?
Cpl   Good. How are you going?
PM   OK. Got any worries?
Cpl   Yes. How about some new machineguns?
PM   Haven't you got any machineguns?
Cpl   Yes, but they're no bloody good.
PM   What's wrong with them?
Cpl   Well, I think they're the same bloody ones I used on my first tour here two years ago. In my last contact, my gun had twenty-three stoppages.

At this stage Campbell decided discretion was called for, so he struck up a conversation with the attractive wife of the ambassador. But this 'proved to be less entertaining, as she quizzed me on the AK47 and SLR. But the corporal made his point.'

Next day, what Digger Campbell described as 'every armourer in Vietnam' descended on 1RAR and every single weapon in the battalion was overhauled.

Now the corporal had the taste of victory. A few weeks later, another visitor, a general from Australia, was to visit the battalion, and similar arrangements were made to allow him to mix with the Diggers. Campbell intercepted the corporal 'on his way to ambush the general,' and asked him, 'What's the question this time?'

'Well, I want to know why we're rationed to two cans of beer per man per day while in base.' This time he did not win.

Probably the single most important result within the family of the Australian Army was that the tank, after decades of denigration in an infantry-dominated Army, had proven itself to all arms. (It is worthy of note that, at time of writing some eighteen years after the events at Coral and Balmoral, there are again moves and recommendations by people, whose qualifications do not appear to include an understanding of the lessons of military operations, to reduce or abolish the tank component in the Army.)

It should be remembered that though Brigadier Hughes had Major Badman reconnoitre routes from Nui Dat to Coral, there were no further large attacks on Coral or Coogee to warrant calling tanks forward before he left on leave. In addition, tanks were known to require a large maintenance and resupply effort, but would be deployed into a remote area far distant from their base, with the wet season about to begin. It would have needed the collapse of only one of the decrepit bridges along the route to deposit a fifty-two-ton Centurion into the river below, halting the squadron approach, and adding further to the image of the tank as a white elephant.

But, for the tank crews of C Squadron, 1 Armoured Regiment, the operation was a vindication of their existence. Arriving half-way through the operations in AO Surfers, they proved their worth in every action thereafter.

The commander of C Squadron, Peter Badman, is of the opinion that 'when the tanks were put into the battle, it was the opportunity to go on with the offensive. The success of [Major Tony] Hammett was due to the tanks, and so was the half-troop of tanks in getting [Major Digger] Campbell out; we made all the difference at the infantry level. Thereafter, company commanders were only too eager to have a troop of tanks with them. They couldn't do enough for us and our fire power.'

This is echoed by Lieutenant Gerry McCormack, commanding Badman's 1 Troop, who recalls the 'acceptance the infantry then came to have for the tanks, and the way they would go out of the way to get tanks incorporated into

operations, and the decided interest they took in infantry—
tank co-operation.'

Lieutenant Mick Butler, 2 Troop, believed his men 'performed superbly, with excellent discipline and fire control.
The Centurion was magnificent'.

The dramatic successes of the tanks at Coral, and the subsequent acceptance of them by the other battlefield arms, may
have been the single greatest benefit to the Australian Army
of later years.

'It was great to see the tanks go into action and be successful,' said Captain Alan Vickers. 'A lot of the credit goes to
blokes like Mick Butler and Gerry McCormack, who were
very good troop leaders. Operating tanks in that country was
a terrible test of man and machine. If you told the Brits years
ago that the Centurion would be running around places like
Vietnam they'd have laughed at you, but they were very
successful.

'Why weren't people awarded decorations? We weren't
experienced in the ways of getting decorations or awarding
them, and in our view those fellows were doing the job
they'd been trained for. In retrospect, they should have been
put up for something.'

The question of awards and decorations is a sensitive one,
and outside the scope of this book, but several people commented, like Alan Vickers, on the paucity of such recognition.

Leigh Boneham, 1RAR mortars, 'could never understand
why Tony Jensen did not get something for his role at Coral.
He did a fantastic job, and led from the front. I always had a
feeling of confidence when he was around. He proved what
a strong person he was, never showed weakness; it amazed
me that he never was recognised for the job he did.'

Tony Hammett regrets not recommending Gerry Mc-
Cormack and some of his own infantry company leaders for
decorations.

Mick Bindley referred to the time-frame for recommending people, that the paperwork was due in June, but the battalion was actually in the field, and also referred to the quota
for decorations being almost filled at the time. The existence
of a quota had always been denied by the Department of

Defence, policy allegedly being that awards were made on merit. Yet the OC of a small specialist unit which had been quite successful told the author that when he enquired about the matter, was advised to forget it, as the unit totalled twenty-six all ranks, and the scale of awards began with the Mention in Dispatches, at the rate of one per 150 men per six months.

A decision which caused considerable comment at the time, and during interviews for this book, was that of Brigadier Hughes to go on leave during the operations in AO Surfers. Many expressed surprise that he did so, saying that a commander's place during a battle is with the troops.

However, as he explained, 'at the time I went on leave there was no guarantee that the rest of the battle was going to continue. We had given a fairly bloody nose on two occasions to the enemy; but, in any case, what is a Deputy Commander for? How do you think that the Task Force functions if you become a casualty? The difficulty about being Deputy is that you never get the opportunity to practise command because the Commander is always there. It has been my philosophy that the commander must not only command, but train everybody in his headquarters to do the job that they would have to do. The Deputy Commander has got to be able to command the Task Force.

'I felt it was an obvious opportunity. I had every confidence in him. I'm sorry if the Task Force felt I let them down, but I thought I left them in very good hands.'

A member of Hughes' staff felt that 'it was the right thing to do. It would show he had confidence in his Deputy. If he stayed it would have shown he felt the situation was out of hand, his deputy was incompetent, and that only he was the bloke that could do the job. It was the harder of the two decisions. It would have been easier to stay. I've always been amazed that people have not looked at it that way.'

Wally Thompson, at the time CSM C/1RAR, later Sergeant-Major of the Army, makes the following point about the Coral–Balmoral actions in particular and service in Vietnam in general. 'This was our third operation within an operation, and I think this is very important. Soldiers in World War II, say, New Guinea or other phases, had big contacts when they advanced, but it was such a long line of communication that only the first company or battalion would be engaged, and then they would go down to the end of the column.

'In Vietnam, because of helicopters and APCs, we had mobility. On this operation, I'd say what we did would have taken two World War II divisions to cover and operate. We started in the Hat Dich, moved up further into the Trang Bom area, then we moved up again [to Coral].

'Now if we were in World War II as foot soldiers and had to walk that distance, without helicopters or APCs, we'd have had time to recoup, to get ready for the next stoush, but you never had that in Vietnam. This operation really went on for two months.

'So, you know, you do get tired. I think that's a point that doesn't necessarily come out. Really, the helicopters and APCs were a godsend, but they made our mobility so much quicker that we were in action more often. If a trouble spot blew up, you were there.

'That's a point that is very important. Old soldiers from World War II say we had all these [modern] things, but they didn't have this constant going.'

Memories of the actions are as varied as the men who hold them, and do not necessarily reflect their rank and position at the time. Below are what are recalled by some of the participants, after many years, as the most vivid memory of the battles at Coral, Coogee and Balmoral. Many other memories of incidents and events have been included in the accounts of the battles and intervening days, but these are collected separately to illustrate the wide variety of 'most vivid memory'.

The initial lack of co-ordination of the local defence of Coral on 12 May is what remains with Colonel Dunstan. 'It taught me a lesson. You've always got to have a local defence commander.'

'The noise' remains to this day in Neil Weekes' memory.

'The absolute pandemonium. The difficulty in communicating with the forward troops, telling them what was going on. And a fear, of personal failure, of not doing the right thing, of letting the men down.'

For Weekes' company commander, Col Adamson, 'one thing strikes me as really vivid. Four o'clock on the morning of the 16th, three American gunships attacking a couple of NVA heavy machineguns located about 500 metres north of my location. The three gunships were racing down the fire of tracer put at them, without faltering, and at the same time the NVA were firing in the face of the rockets that were quite clearly seen coming out of the gunships. That is so vivid.'

John Salter, commanding 10 Platoon, D/1RAR, has three: the assault, 'in World War I and World War II fashion, across that open paddock [on the morning of 13 May]; the NVA on fire, lit up like a Christmas tree; and Richo [Richardson] coming along with a cigarette as I lay on my back in the too-short shell scrape [on the morning of 16 May].'

Ray Curtis, Salter's sergeant, also recalls 16 May, 'when the order came to fix bayonets ... Tony Hammett called to ask how many enemy were coming. A few minutes later, when the platoon were singing "Waltzing Matilda", Hammett calling again to ask why they were singing and not fighting.'

For Tony Jensen, 1RAR Mortar Platoon, it is the determination to hold their ground and call in artillery rather than leave it; the NVA officer who peered over the mound of spoil at him, then 'strolled away'; the accuracy of fire from Spooky, the armed DC3, from which the rain of machinegun fire would be placed to within twenty metres of friendly positions, at night, amid the lights, flashes and glares below the plane.

Enemy fire, of course, comprises many individual recollections of any combat.

Kim Patterson, Ops Officer 1RAR, will always remember 'the solid line of muzzle flashes as they began the attack'.

The sense of impotence under bombardment remains with Phil Busby, 'when there's nothing you can do to stop it, and the only protection is what's over your head'. And yet,

333

'unless it's happening to you in your area, it does not have the same significance. I can distinctly remember sitting there, above ground, with my soldiers, watching the flashes about a hundred metres away when the other side of the base was being hit.'

The same feeling of uselessness under bombardment springs to mind for Matt Cleland, 102 Field Battery, as he waited in his pit for the mortar barrage on the night of 15–16 May to cease, so he could go to the guns, and begin doing something.

The mortaring also stands out in the recollections of Wally Thompson, CSM C/1RAR at the time. 'You can hear them come in, but you've got to force yourself to get out and find out what happened.'

The sound of the rockets overhead, and the tank–infantry battle in the bunker system of 26 May will always remain with Paul Richardson. 'How we survived that one without getting hit, I don't know. I guess you do some silly things under fire. You sort of don't think about your own safety, but get in there and try and do the best you can, I guess.'

Food and living conditions were mentioned by many, including the shortage of water, and some vehement denials of receiving any beer in the field. Many references were made to the dry dusty conditions at the beginning, and the water and mud when the wet season broke.

'The bloody tuna we ate for three weeks,' was the spontaneous answer of Garry Prendergast and Jazza Smith, 6 Platoon, B/1RAR, to the question of 'the most vivid memory'.

For some young men, the clearest memory is connected with the realisation that war is a dangerous business; people are killed, friends and acquaintances will be no more, and their relatives have yet to know of their loss.

The sight of the row of Australian dead, boots protruding from the groundsheets, which greeted the arriving road convoy on the morning of 13 May, for John Goodwin, radio mechanic, is 'probably the most vivid memory of my life. It was a real shock; it was devastating'. Equally vivid is the memory of Harry White killed next to him in the mortar attack of 16 May.

Compassion surged in Neil Lloyd-Jones, battery surveyor in 102 Battery, on the morning after the first attack, as the casualties were being loaded into the helicopters. 'I really felt sorry for mothers that day. I never think much about those sort of things, but my immediate reaction was to think that some poor mother, at lunch-time today, or afternoon or something like that, is going to get some really bad news.'

Soldiers came to have compassion for their fellows, in other units, as when Stan Carbines, artillery, watched the infantry going out on patrol, towards the enemy.

From the point of view of a tank commander, Gerry McCormack remembers the faces of the infantry peering out of the foliage as his Centurion ground towards them, and the courage needed by the corporal who 'obviously had to decide which was the greatest danger, his men being squashed by the tank, or him being shot by this fellow three metres in front of him, who had just shot two mates, and he stood up and grabbed my attention, with a pretty ashen look on his face.'

'The satisfaction that one really could help the grunts in their dugouts with extra ammo,' is one of Gus Ballentine's deepest recollections. 'Maybe it sounds unimportant, but I won't forget it.'

The infantry may be interested in the most vivid memory of an Army Aviation pilot. Peter Spoor can still 'smell that peculiar smell of a body that has been in the jungle for two weeks without a shower, and climbs into the helicopter with you.'

The feelings included respect and admiration for those who served alongside, the familiar faces.

During the second attack on Balmoral, the sight of 'Corporal Mancer, standing out in the open, fully in view of everyone, hurling grenades into the pit', remains with Mark John, commander of 11 Platoon D/3RAR.

Alan Floyd, gun number in 102 Battery, has never forgotten the bravery of 'the 21-year-old gunners who stood by their guns in the face of the enemy, particularly the boys on No. 4 gun, who should have been recognised.'

Many of the commanders made the point that they were impressed, and remain so over the years, with the high quality of young soldiers who were National Servicemen. While they understandably were waiting for the end of their military commitment, they were fine young Australians and good soldiers.

The ability of the young officers employed as Forward Observers, who 'did a great job' around Coral, remains the most vivid memory for Major General Jack Kelly, then CO 12 Field Regiment RAA; of his gunners, 'living in the gun position like infantry. They would breed their own rats and run their own rat races, and all that sort of thing. Always something happening, always amusing themselves, and therefore always a joy to go and talk to them.'

In the course of the interviews and discussions with participants in the Coral–Balmoral operations, and in others, there were many references by people of all ranks to the value of the training received. The matter of training is outside the scope of this book, but numerous unprompted remarks were made, some of which are included in the accounts of the various actions. The general tenor of the comments was that people found themselves doing what they had been trained to do, reacting naturally to the situation.

12 Field Regiment and 102 Battery placed listening posts and machinegun teams forward of their position; gun crews fired over open sights and defended their weapons and pits; next morning, clearing patrols went out, and, as Greg Ayson recalled, put into practice what they had been taught; Mick Bindley noticed the way in which Les Tranter's platoon cleared and searched the bodies in the position; the rifle companies were able to adapt swiftly to the techniques of working with tanks, though only a few had actually done so—thorough training as infantrymen and common sense brought results; Gerry McCormack spoke of the surprise at the ease with which correct training came into play during the bunker fighting.

Many other instances were noted. There was no substitute for good training, which provided the basis for units and individuals to react to normal and unusual situations. Ossie Kleinig, 3RAR, made the point that it takes relatively little to bring a well-trained soldier to the standard of being able to cope with a difficult situation, but it is another matter entirely if the soldier is raw or poorly trained.

The solid foundation of the Australian successes in AO Surfers was the thorough training of all ranks involved in the actions. Without it, the North Vietnamese would have been the victors.

Appendix 1
Australians killed in AO Surfers

Pte	D.E. Abbott	1RAR	30 May 68
Pte	E.J. Bailey	1RAR	13 May 68
Pte	L.N. Brown	3RAR	26 May 68
Pte	A.J. Cooper	3RAR	26 May 68
Cpl	I.K. Dawson	1RAR	14 May 68
Pte	J.W. Desnoy	3RAR	26 May 68
Cpl	R.B. Hickey	1RAR	13 May 68
Sgt	P.E. Lewis	3RAR	13 May 68
Pte	R.L. McNab	1RAR	13 May 68
LCpl	W.H. Martin	1RAR	16 May 68
Pte	C.R. Nisbet	1RAR	14 May 68
Pte	J.A. O'Brien	1RAR	13 May 68
Cpl	J.G. Pearce	1RAR	14 May 68
Gnr	C.J. Sawtell	12 Fd Regt	13 May 68
Gnr	I.J. Scott	12 Fd Regt	13 May 68
Pte	L.R. Sheppard	1RAR	13 May 68
Pte	W.M. Thomas	3RAR	26 May 68
Pte	B.M. Trimble	1RAR	13 May 68
Pte	A.J. Wallis	1RAR	16 May 68
Pte	R.C. Watson	1RAR	13 May 68
Pte	H.W. White	1RAR	16 May 68
Cpl	J.H. Whitton	1RAR	13 May 68
Pte	J.T. Worle	3RAR	28 May 68
Sig	A.H. Young	104 Sig Sqn	16 May 68
Pte	B.T. Young	1RAR	16 May 68

Appendix 2
After-action Reports

The After-action Reports were quite long and have been condensed to the few paragraphs which follow.

The 1ATF after-action report concluded that the operation had been a success, as the Task force had interrupted a main infiltration route into Saigon, and inflicted heavy casualties on the enemy, as well as identifying seven infiltration groups —four for the first time. Three of the more significant points noted were the need for battalions to concentrate at night in view of the enemy's ability to launch regimental-size attacks, the effectiveness of armour–infantry teams against prepared positions, and 'the need for a local defence commander of field rank with a small headquarters to layout, co-ordinate and command the local defence of a large FSPB'.

Unit after-action reports listed the lessons learned, or re-learned. The effectiveness of armour in that type of country was noted; its mobility alone was responsible for many successes; use of ACVs in HQs was well proven; the Australians again showed their ability, and gained respect for the NVA; digging in well in those circumstances was relearned; the tendency to fire high with infantry weapons at night needed constant checking; and it was noted the enemy also had his problems, which affected his operations.

1RAR listed the lessons learned as the necessity to dig in properly before last light; to be able to indicate friendly positions accurately to air support by day and night; that artillery and mortar fire are better able to inflict enemy casualties than air support; fire control at section level was a must; that infantry–tank co-operation was relearned; that

339

communications nets were still easily overloaded; battalion-level control of the landing zone was necessary; Dustoff should be from a pad or clearing if possible, and winches used only in emergency; that good junior leadership was as necessary as ever, and that in general the training in Australia was of value.

Appendix 3
Patrol Actions around FSPB Coral

The 1ATF After-action Report includes patrol clashes in the area of FSPB Coral, while the 1RAR log includes references to the battalion patrolling effort around the base. These show that the battalion as a whole was active around Coral, and that the neighbourhood was not given up to the NVA.

12 May 68   Arrival; B and D Companies contact enemy while moving away from FSPB Coral.

13 May   First attack on Coral; B and D Companies make contact while moving back to Coral.

14 May   A platoon from each company patrols out to 1000 metres from perimeter; 2, 5, 7, 9 and 12 Platoons have contact. Eleven enemy KIA.

15 May   1, 2, 3 and 10 Platoons make contact or sightings.

16 May   Second attack on Coral.

17 May   A platoon from each company patrols out to 1000 metres from perimeter; 5 and 12 Platoons make contact or find materials, equipment, baseplate positions, etc, resulting in one NVA KIA.

18 May   Redeployment of defences at Coral; only standing patrols out during this activity.

19 May   Each company had platoon ambushes out; 1 Platoon engaged 3–5 enemy, 11 Platoon found one body.

20 May   Platoon ambushes, as for previous day; 12 Platoon engaged one enemy; 7 Platoon found one body.

21 May	C and D Companies patrol, finding weapon pits and a body; enemy sighted.
22 May	C Company patrol, finding mortar bombs, other items and a body; 5 Platoon finds enemy observation post. Mortar bombardment in early morning hours.
23 May	D Company patrol; enemy sighted and weapon pits found; C Squadron Centurion tanks arrive.
24 May	Platoon ambushes forward of perimeter during the day.
25 May	B Company escorts 3 Troop of Centurion tanks to FSPB Balmoral; contact with bunker system en route; 8 Platoon found enemy body.
26 May	Mortar and RPG bombardment during attack on FSPB Balmoral. D Company and 1 Troop of Centurion tanks move to area of contact on 25 May, engaging enemy in bunker system; platoons from other companies patrol, with 2 Platoon finding mortar and RCL items.
27 May	3 Platoon, 5 Platoon and C Company patrol, C Coy killing one NVA.
28 May	Mortar and RPG bombardment during attack on FSPB Balmoral. A Company with tanks patrolled, and platoons from other companies patrolled elsewhere; four bodies found, enemy sighted.
29 May	B Company with tanks, 3 Platoon, 9 Platoon and D Company (minus) patrolled; bunker systems found.
30 May	C Company engaged enemy in bunker system; twenty-four NVA KIA by body-count, with another twenty-one possibly KIA.
31 May	A and D Companies patrolled, finding base areas and killing one enemy.
1 Jun	B Company and tanks patrolled, while other companies sent out platoon patrols.
2 Jun	C Company, with tanks and APCs, returned to the area of their 30 May contact, finding five NVA bodies and three weapons; other companies sent out platoon patrols.

3 Jun	Platoon patrols from each company; no contact.
4 Jun	Platoon patrols; no contact.
5 Jun	Platoon patrols; no contact.
6 Jun	Evacuation of FSPB Coral.

Exclusive of the references to the major attacks on the base, and enemy contacted during clearing patrols subsequent to these actions, the 1RAR log contains at least seventy-one references to patrols, patrol actions, or results of patrols during the time spent at Coral. While no night ambushing and patrolling was done, the battalion was active during the day. Every company was tasked; every platoon was involved.

It must also be assumed that other enemy in the area would have seen our patrols, while remaining unseen or avoiding contact, and reported on return to their unit.

Appendix 4
VCINVA Units Identified in Actions in AO Surfers 12 May–6 June 1968; Casualties Inflicted.

141	NVA Regiment	
165	NVA Regiment	
85	Regiment	
32	Infiltration Group	
165	"	"
233	"	"
269	"	"
275	"	"
D 280	"	"
745	"	"
NAM HA	"	"

13 May
  269 and 275 Infiltration Groups
  K2 and K3 Battalions, 141 NVA Regiment
16 May
  269 and 275 Infiltration Groups
  K2 and K3 Battalions, 141 NVA Regiment
  C17 Recoilless Rifle Company
  C18 Anti-aircraft Company
26 May
  165 NVA Regiment
28 May
  233, D280, 745 and Nam Ha Infiltration Groups
  K2, K3 and possibly K5 Battalions, 165 NVA Regiment
30 May
  Probably 141 NVA Regiment

31 May
   C8 Company, D27 Battalion, 85 NVA Regiment

1ATF participation in Operation Toan Thang prior to 12 May 1968 had resulted in nine enemy KIA, two WIA and twelve weapons captured.

From 12 May to 6 June, the actions in AO Surfers resulted in 267 VC/NVA KIA, determined by body-count, plus at least another sixty possibly killed; seven wounded; and eleven prisoners, as well as three detainees and two Hoi Chanh (surrendered enemy).

Weapons captured were thirty-six crew-served and 112 small arms, plus 144 grenades; mines, mortar bombs, food and miscellaneous equipment.

The above figures are conservative. The full extent of the damage to the NVA formations will probably never be known, as the Infiltration Groups were thrown into the attacks on arrival, losses made up with yet another group and the process repeated; individuals counted for little.

Both prepared but empty and filled-in mass graves were found as the operation continued, but not investigated. Some of the Australians wondered at the mentality of their enemy, and what they thought while digging the large holes before the attacks, knowing their leaders anticipated enough casualties to require the graves. The Vietnamese themselves probably cannot compile accurate figures of their real losses.

Appendix 5
The Vietnamese Enemy

The forces opposing 1ATF were 7 NVA Division, and local VC units used for reconnaissance, guides, logistics, liaison and similar tasks. 7 NVA Division commanded two fighting regiments, 141 and 165, both referred to above as being in recent clashes with US forces. The Division was continually brought up to strength by Infiltration Groups, formed bodies of troops who had marched down the Ho Chi Minh Trail, or, as it was known to the NVA, the Truong Son Trail.

The North Vietnamese Army was born in the jungled mountains along the Vietnam–China border in 1944, when ex-history teacher Vo Nguyen Giap formed his first platoon. Less than ten years later, after defeats and victories against the French Union armies, Giap's divisions achieved their greatest success at Dien Bien Phu.

The French command selected a battlefield in a mountain valley, far from their bases around Hanoi, on the assumption that they would be able to resupply by air, and that the Vietnamese enemy would be able to concentrate only infantry against them. The infantry would obligingly come down into the valley and be smashed by superior French firepower.

Unfortunately for the elegant graduates of St Cyr, Giap's commanders brought their artillery with them, as well as anti-aircraft guns. Firing from covered positions, they destroyed the French guns, forced the French Air Force to halt transport aircraft use of the airfield, and then proceeded to overwhelm the French infantry positions in the valley.

Acts of great bravery and leadership by members of the French units in the valley were useless. The Vietnamese had the French where they wanted them, and were paying back the excesses of ninety years of French arrogance, assumed cultural superiority and use of police and military against the colonial subjects.

Peace talks had begun in Geneva, and the Vietnamese Communists were speaking from a position of strength, as Dien Bien Phu began to sink under the tides of Giap's infantry. The talks ended with France admitting defeat and agreeing to leave Indochina.

After the French departure, the Army in the Communist North was used in reconstruction projects and as the power behind the Party, enforcing the decisions to collectivise the land and crushing the peasants' revolt in Ho Chi Minh's home province of Nghe An.

Gradually the Army became more and more involved in the armed struggle in the South, as Hanoi used open military force to overthrow the Saigon regime. First individuals, then groups, and finally entire Regular units were sent south to join the fighting.

Hanoi denied any involvement in the southern war, insisting that it was a completely home-grown revolution. But prisoners, surrendered enemy, weapons, documents, uniforms and a multitude of other items and sources of information contradicted this obvious lie. After the victory in 1975, the southern exploits of the NVA were admitted and made subject of propaganda material, with the famous Ho Chi Minh Trail elevated almost to the status of a national shrine. The 'useful idiots' of the West, who supported Hanoi throughout the war, and parroted their statements, presumably swallowed their shame on realising they had been played for fools, and looked around for another cause.

But throughout all the years of battle, of peace talks, of political manoeuvring, it was the Vietnamese peasant, the *bo doi* of the infantry, who fought, bled and died where his masters sent him. He had no politicians and academics to support him if he did not wish to join the march south, no organised demonstrations against the war, no neighbouring country into which he could scuttle, no overseas travel or working holiday conveniently extended until he was beyond draft age. His life was controlled from morning to night by a totalitarian regime which told him what it wanted him to know, and told him when he was needed to help 'liberate the South'.

The horrendous losses on the southern battlefields meant a continual call for recruits and reinforcements. By late 1967, the Northern recruit received three to six months training before his departure along the Trail. Only about one day was devoted to close order drill and ceremony (the reader can imagine the horror in certain Western armies!) and the remainder to handling small arms, grenades, explosives, bayonet, first aid, camouflage and ambush, and anti-chemical training.

The daily programme included physical training and a small amount of hand-to-hand combat positions and movements. The conditioning for the arduous march south was done by carrying heavy loads during training marches.

A typical daily schedule would see the soldier rise at 0530, wash and breakfast, then begin training at 0630, continuing until 1130, when there would be a two- or three-hour break. Training would go on till about 1700, when another two-hour break would occur, then a final two hours of political lectures and review of the day's training lessons would be held, until about 2100.

Very little live firing was done, sometimes only as few as five rounds of rifle ammunition per man. In battle, this became evident by the large numbers of tracer bullets streaming skyward.

Equipment and clothing issued was the bare minimum, comprising two sets of clothing, weapon, equipment, pack, hammock, mosquito net, waterbottle and eating utensils. Personal items such as soap and toothpaste had to be purchased out of the monthly pay of five piastres.

Soldiers were organised into three-man cells, and on these were built the squads, platoons, companies and battalions. The three lived, worked, marched, fought and struggled together. The figure three reflects the political influence which permeated the Communist armies. Two men can become disaffected, or one can dominate the other; four can see a development into two pairs; three is the optimum number for maintenance of control when living in the close working environment of a Communist organisation.

The leader of the three-man cell was responsible to the squad leader for reporting on his two companions. The cell in many ways represented a continuation of family life for the soldier; the other two became his brothers. The place of parents was taken by the political and military commanders. The system allowed control over each man in all daily activities, including battle.

Selected soldiers received further training, such as signals, medical, artillery, anti-aircraft, truck-driving, and so on. As the expertise of the NVA and VC reconnaissance squads impressed their opponents, including the Australians, a brief description of that training is relevant.

Reconnaissance trainees were selected from young, fit members of the Communist Party or Youth Labour Group, with at least seven years of education. The subjects taught were techniques of movement through various types of terrain, camouflage, swimming, observation and penetration of fixed defences, mine detection and removal, map- and compass-reading, small arms handling and firing, infantry tactics, and the inevitable political indoctrination. However, owing to the insatiable demands of the combat formations, the training was often incomplete, too fast and poorly presented.

A special class of VC–NVA soldier was the sapper. This simple title described the VC–NVA equivalent of a type of assault demolitions commando. Sappers were organised into sub-units and units, and were employed as the spearhead of an assault on an enemy position. Their role was to penetrate the defence barriers and obstacles, and destroy HQs, defence posts, aircraft, petrol stores and similar, opening the way for the attack force and creating confusion in the enemy camp.

Often volunteers, but sometimes merely allotted to a sapper unit because of their high standard achieved in other training, sappers were encouraged to believe they belonged to an élite combat arm. In addition to the basic and reconnaissance training described above, the sapper received even more in the techniques of crossing all types of terrain and man-made obstacles, observing installations and detecting weaknesses in defences, assault and demolition, penetration and withdrawal, and reporting on their actions.

Complementing all the training a soldier received, whatever his arm of service, was political instruction and indoctrination. Just as the Japanese in the Pacific Islands knew little or nothing of what went on in other areas, as the flow of information was controlled by his superiors, so the NVA soldier was presented with the Party version of events, and that version only.

Political officers were selected after a careful examination of their personal background, experience and achievements, and received their own training in courses controlled from a high level in the military and political organisations.

By the time an NVA soldier arrived in the South, he was a highly disciplined and motivated member of a unit which was led by officers who had proven themselves at their profession, be it military or political command. Some doubts may have begun to grow during the privations of the trek, and after seeing the effect of the US air campaign coupled with the jungle illnesses in causing losses before the actual work of liberation had begun.

One of the major weaknesses of the VC–NVA was medical treatment and casualty evacuation. For wars in general since 1900 the ratio of deaths to wounded who survived was 1:4. A high proportion of VC–NVA casualties were deaths, either dying in action, soon after in the evacuation phase from the battlefield, or in the hospital system. Analysis of captured documents and statements by prisoners, over a period of years, resulted in the information that VC–NVA killed to wounded ratio was about 1:1.9. Here the three-man cell was used, in which if one was wounded, the other two were to carry him from the scene.

Far away in the North, the female members of their families were urged to live up to 'The Three Responsibilities': *for production* while husband or son are away; *for the family*, so husband or son can serve with a peaceful mind; and *for service in combat* when required.

350

Once the soldier left the North, he could look forward only to military service in the South until final victory, with a very small chance of returning to the North as a cadre or battle casualty. For the great majority, it was death by wounds or illness. Buoyed by propaganda, an entire generation of young men marched south, to destruction by allied firepower.

The young men who would face the young Australians in AO Surfers were generally keen to do so. Most of them had not yet experienced the deluge of high explosive which marked the defensive battles of the South.

The Western world has entire libraries of books by and about the participants in their modern wars, from the American Civil War through the World Wars to Vietnam. The Vietnamese *bo doi* himself is unsung, except by Party propagandists.

Sources

Information forming the basis of this book came primarily from interviews with the hundred people listed below. Organisations providing documentary material are listed after the individuals.

Lieutenant Colonel Colin Adamson, Colonel Ian Ahearn, Lieutenant Colonel Gavin Andrews, Mr Gordon Alexander, Mr Greg Ayson, Brigadier Peter Badman, Mr Gus Ballentine, General Sir Phillip Bennett, Colonel Mick Bindley, Mr Tony Bonavita, Mr Geoff Bowcock, Lieutenant Colonel David Brook, Mr David Brooks, Mr Barry Brown, Mr Ian Brown, Lieutenant Colonel Phillip Busby, Major Mick Butler, Lieutenant Colonel Ian 'Digger' Campbell, Lieutenant Colonel Geoff Cameron, Lieutenant Colonel Dave Candow, Mr Stan Carbines, Mr Bob Carbury, Mr Lorne 'Doc' Clarke, Mr Matt Cleland, Brigadier Geoff Cohen, Lieutenant Colonel John Crossman, Mr Alan Cunningham, Captain Ray Curtis, Mr Larry Darcy, Brigadier Phil Davies, Mr Graham Dawes, Mr Frank Dean, Mr John Dellaca, Mr Gary Dee, Colonel Peter Desmond, Lieutenant Colonel Glen Duus, Lieutenant General Sir Donald Dunstan, Mr Wally Fiedler, Mr John Flood, Mr Alan Floyd, Mr Andy Forsdike, Brigadier Alf Garland, Corporal Peter Geil, Mr John Goodwin, Mr Joe Griffin, Captain W.H. Grimes, Mr Geoff Grimish, Brigadier Tony Hammett, Mr Ron Hedges, Colonel Bob Hennessy, Major General Hori Howard, Major General Ron Hughes, Mr Mal Hundt, Lieutenant Colonel Tony Jensen, Lieutenant Colonel Mark John, Sergeant John Kearns, Brigadier John Keldie, Mr Edward 'Ned' Kelly,

Major General John Kelly, Lieutenant Colonel Ossie Kleinig, Mr Jack Langley, Major James Litchfield, Mr Neil Lloyd-Jones, Mr Terry Loftus, Mr Trevor Lowe, Lieutenant Colonel Bob Lowry, Colonel Gerry McCormack, Mr Ivan Maher, Mr Dave Mancer, Mr Wayne Meech, Major Mal Meadows, Mr Geoff Murray, Lieutenant Colonel Les Myers, Mr Perry Neil, Dr Neville O'Connor, Mr Rod Orford, Mr Alan Parr, Lieutenant Colonel Kim Patterson, Mr Arthur Penn, Major General Peter Phillips, Major Garry Prendergast, Mr Bill Raggatt, Warrant Officer 2 Paul Richardson, Lieutenant Colonel John Salter, Brigadier J.J. Shelton, Captain Brian Smith, Mr Peter Spoor, Mr Noel Sproles, Major Ross Stevens, Lieutenant Colonel Bill Studley, Colonel Bernard Sullivan, Warrant Officer 1 Wally Thompson, Father John Tinkler, Mr John Taylor, Major Les Tranter, Mr Richard Utting, Mr Alan Vickers, Mr Wally Wayne, Lieutenant Colonel Neil Weekes.

Material provided below is gratefully acknowledged:

Australian War Memorial (Coral Collection, curator W.L. Fogarty): 'Firesupport Base Coral' by Captain A.H. Jensen, *Infantry Magazine*, 1972, and article describing the D/1RAR–2 Tp C Sqn 1 Armd Regt battle in the bunker system on 26 May 1968, by Lieutenant Colonel Hammett, while at Australian Staff College, 1972, and sequence of events, 1RAR, 12 May–6 June 1968.

Lieutenant Colonel Adamson provided diagrams of unit and sub-unit locations at FSPB Coral, which form the basis for the relevant maps in this book, taken from vu-graphs prepared for a talk by General Dunstan to Australian Staff College, Queenscliff, 1969.

Lieutenant Colonel Cameron provided 1ATF Intelligence Summaries, May–June 1968. These had already been loaned to a student at ANU, at the direction of a serving general officer, and were considered to be in the public domain.

Major Fred Greenway donated the Vietcong artwork and sketches.

Brigadier Hammett loaned the Summary of the Enemy Situation, from IIFFV Opord 7/68, and 1ATF Opord 19/68 dated 22 April 1968; the 1ATF After-action Report Op Toan

Thang Phase 1; 1RAR After-action Report Op Toan Thang dated 30 June 1968; 1RAR War Diary Log Sheets 12–15 May 1968; correspondence Hammett–Badman 1978–79; Report by GPO 102 Battery, events 12–19 May 1968; 'Memories of Coral'—brief handwritten accounts by W.V. Raggatt, D.W. Cunningham, L. Tranter, E. Kelly, plus the 'War diary' of 2Lt C.H. Forde, 5 Pl B Coy 1RAR, May 1968, and 'Memory of Coral' for C.H. Forde by Bombardier A. Forsdike.

Major General Kelly provided draft of 'A Task Force Operation' (a double-spaced eight-page account).

A thoughtful person sent a copy of the Operation Order of 10 May 1968, but did not identify himself.

Many of the individuals listed above sent copies of newspaper clippings, and articles in military and civilian magazines, as well as notebooks and O groups from the time.

Documents made available in the War Memorial archives were: AWM 181: Vietnam records, 'Herbicide Series', the commander's diaries of 1ATF and 3RAR for May 1968. These are identified in the text as the example following:

1035 1RAR to TF: C Company wants airstrike.

The *Defence Force Journal* kindly allowed use of information in articles in the May and June 1969 issues of the former *Army Journal* by Major A.B. Garland, describing the first and second 'Viet Cong General Offensives'.

As usual, the staff of the Australian War Memorial did their best: Ian Affleck, John Bullen, Brian Butler, Steve Corvini, Helen Creagh, Bill Fogarty, Andrew Jack, Tony Rudnicki, Bronwyn Self, Beryl Strusz, John Trouten.

Photographic items are credited individually as they appear in the text, but this opportunity is taken to thank the following: Australian War Memorial; RAN Fleet Air Arm Museum; Mr Greg Ayson, Major M. Butler; Lieutenant Colonel Ian Campbell; Mr Bob Carbury; Mr Lorne Clark; Lieutenant Colonel John Crossman; Mr Peter De Jong; Mr John Dellaca; Mr Wally Fiedler; Mr Alan Floyd; Mr Kevin Fowler; Mr R. Gould; Captain W.H. 'Mick' Grimes; Warrant Officer 2 G. Johnson; Warrant Officer 1 Trevor

Lowe; Mr Perry Neil; 1RAR; Brigadier J.J. Shelton; Major Les Tranter.

Special thanks must go to the following: Dalton Neville, for his photographic assistance; Ray Payne, who voluntarily runs a C Company 1RAR newsletter and assists in arranging reunions, as well as keeping people in touch, for help in locating people; Terry Loftus, VVAA, for similar assistance; Kym Perry, of 'The Wordworks' in Canberra, for unfailing assistance and expertise in the demonology of word-processors, fishing back from some unknown corner of the disk chapters I thought were lost forever; and Brigadier Tony Hammett, who located people and then hounded and threatened them until they agreed to assist, and returned the tape cassettes sent to them, with questions of events long ago. Where applicable, AWM reference numbers are given.

My thanks to you all.

I have woven the threads of personal recollections and dry wordage of official reports to present a picture of the events at Coral–Coogee–Balmoral; any errors in the tapestry are mine.

Index

356

190-9, 203-9, 213-9, 221-7, 230,
234, 236, 241, 248, 252-60, 265,
267-8, 277, 285-8, 291, 301, 303,
306-7, 310-4, 318-20, 322, 325,
329-32, 336, 341-3
Manly AO 15, 18, 28, 31, 60, 104,
209, 213
Surfers AO 14-18, 20-2, 27, 29, 56,
302, 314, 316-18, 329, 337, 345

Personnel

Adamson, Colin Major 46, 49, 62, 88,
93, 95, 107, 111, 117-19, 132, 149,
154-8, 164, 168, 174-5, 178, 183,
228, 324, 333

Ahearn, Ian Lieutenant 25, 34-6, 41,
56-7, 67, 71, 77, 85-6, 88, 92, 96,
99, 123, 151-2, 255, 318, 326

Allen, Len Sergeant 219, 224, 234, 237

Alexander, Gordon Lieutenant 41-3,
51, 53-4, 111-2, 166, 174, 243, 246,
252-3

Altham, Brian Captain 41, 54, 68

Andrews, Gavin Major 23, 46, 51, 54,
57, 85, 95, 100, 102, 119, 184, 196,
202

Annesley, Laurie Warrant Officer 2
221

Auhl, Geoff Captain 168

Ayson, Greg Gunner 62, 73, 98, 336

Badman, Peter Major 26, 198-9, 203,
204, 221, 248, 268, 277, 292, 300,
303, 311, 329

Bailey, Errol Private 107, 338

Basford, John Gunner 110

Ballentine, Gus Sergeant 141, 143,
146, 148, 167-8, 181-2, 335

Barents, Private 157

Bedford, Maurie 'Barney Rubble'
Private 147, 159

Bennett, Phillip Lieutenant Colonel
19, 23, 46-9, 69, 75, 80, 91, 94, 96,
104-8, 121, 132, 139, 157, 162, 180,
184-5, 190, 225, 241, 252, 258-9,
291, 300, 314-5, 320, 324

Bindley, Mick Captain 22, 38-43, 47,
69, 76, 93-6, 101, 105-6, 146, 161,
241, 330, 336

Boneham, Leigh Private 106, 116,
167, 201, 330

Bowcock, Geoff Lieutenant 42, 52,
55, 89, 111, 114, 120, 122, 127-9,
171, 172-3, 178, 190, 244-56,
258-9, 310

Boyd, Corporal 64-5, 110

Briggs, 'Pablo' Gunner 110

Britten, Corporal 219, 234, 237, 271

Brook, David Captain 20, 24-5, 34-6,
57-8, 67, 73, 79, 85, 88, 104-5, 119

Brooks, David Sergeant 134, 212, 215,
231, 239, 269, 276, 305-6

Brown, Barry Private 325

Bryant, Trevor Gunner 143, 151

Bullen, John Captain 124, 137, 139,
142, 194-5, 200, 226-7

Burns, Bombardier 98

Burton, Bill Corporal 246, 254-6,
287, 292

Busby, Phillip Second Lieutenant 109,
189, 201, 316, 333-4

Bushby, Staff Sergeant 261

Butler, Mick Lieutenant 204, 217-19,
221, 233-4, 236-8, 269-85, 330

Campbell, Ian Major 46, 50, 89, 93,
108, 117-18, 121-2, 130, 149, 154,
157, 165, 242, 257, 261, 287,
289-300, 304, 319, 328-9

Cameron, Geoff Major 14, 19, 20,
28-9, 144, 180, 259, 263

Candow, David Major 60, 213, 232,
239, 279, 286

Callis, Nev Sergeant 250, 292

Carbines, Stan Gunner 45, 58, 67, 78,
106, 119, 143, 151, 207, 304, 306,
314, 335

Carbury, Bob Gunner 58, 74, 79, 88,
101, 261, 307, 312, 321, 325

Charlton, Brett Private 101

Chinn, George Warrant Officer 2,
109

Clarke, Lorne 'Doc' Corporal 89, 108,
182, 260-1, 290, 295

Cleland, Matt Lieutenant 22, 57, 67,
71-2, 86, 334

Cohen, Geoff Major 28-32

Collinson, John Lieutenant (NZ)
102-3, 119, 138-9, 147

Constable, George Major 204-6, 225

357